P9-CQW-902

ELECTION

Edited by Heather MacIvor

2010 ☐ Emond Montgomery Publications Limited ☐ Toronto, Canada

Copyright © 2010 Emond Montgomery Publications Limited. All rights reserved. No part of this publication may be reproduced, stored in a retrieval system, or transmitted, in any form or by any means, photocopying, electronic, mechanical, recording, or otherwise, without the prior written permission of the copyright holder.

Emond Montgomery Publications Limited
60 Shaftesbury Avenue
Toronto ON M4T 1A3
http://www.emp.ca/university

Printed in Canada on recyled paper.

We acknowledge the financial support of the Government of Canada through the Book Publishing Industry Development Program (BPIDP) for our publishing activities.

Acquisitions and development editor: Mike Thompson
Marketing manager: Christine Davidson
Director, sales and marketing, higher education: Kevin Smulan
Supervising editor: Jim Lyons
Copy editor: Claudia Forgas
Production editor: Debbie Gervais
Proofreader: Paula Pike
Text designer: Tara Wells
Cover designers: Stephen Cribbin & Simon Evers
Cover photo: GetStock.com/Steve Russell

Library and Archives Canada Cataloguing in Publication

Election / edited by Heather MacIvor.

Includes index.
ISBN 978-1-55239-321-5

1. Elections—Canada—Textbooks.   I. MacIvor, Heather, 1964–

JL193.E39 2010   324:60971   C2009-905997-5

Brief Contents

Contents

PART TWO   LEGAL AND INSTITUTIONAL FRAMEWORK

Preface

This book was conceived of as a resource that would cover all key elements of the course, usually offered at the intermediate undergraduate level, that typically goes by the name of "Electoral Politics," "Parties and Elections," or some variation on those terms. While a great many excellent books on elections are available—in fact, many have been written by the contributors to this volume—we saw a need for something that covered this topic more widely, and with an undergraduate reader very much in mind. We trust that people will find this book broad enough in its scope, and in the perspectives it offers, to appeal to almost any approach that an instructor teaching such a course may wish to take.

But as this project developed, it was clear that not only is the level of scholarship sufficiently high to make it very well suited as a complement to an upper-year or graduate-level course, but at the same time, the aspects of Canadian politics that enter into the discussion here—which include history, law, media, institutions, regional issues, voter behaviour, party politics, political strategies, and more—and the clear, concise presentation of these varied topics also serve to make this book a potentially valuable asset to other, more general undergraduate courses in Canadian politics. We hope some instructors will consider it for their lower-level Canadian politics courses, particularly when such courses are offered during one of Canada's increasingly frequent election seasons.

I wish to thank all of the authors for their excellent contributions. They have made the job of editor much easier than I had any right to expect. My biggest "thank you" goes to Mike Thompson at Emond Montgomery Publications, who put so much time and effort into this book that his name belongs on the cover. He should be recognized as the co-editor, not just the publisher. I'd also like to thank Emond Montgomery production manager Jim Lyons and copy editor Claudia Forgas for their efforts. As always, I am grateful to Kendal McKinney for his love and support.

The publisher wishes to thank the following people for their assistance during the conception and development of this project: Joanna Everitt (University of New Brunswick), Larry LeDuc (University of Toronto), Judith McKenzie (University of Guelph), and Tamara Small (Mount Allison University).

About the Author

Heather MacIvor is an Associate Professor of Political Science at the University of Windsor. She teaches political theory and Canadian public law. Her research interests include the Charter of Rights, election law, and electoral systems. She is the author, most recently, of *Parameters of Power: Canada's Political Institutions*, 5th edition (Nelson, 2009).

About the Authors

Sujit Choudhry holds the Scholl Chair at the Faculty of Law, University of Toronto. He is cross-appointed to the Department of Political Science and the School of Public Policy and Governance, and is a Senior Fellow at Massey College.

John C. Courtney is Professor Emeritus of Political Science and Senior Policy Fellow of the Johnson-Shoyama Graduate School of Public Policy, University of Saskatchewan.

Munroe Eagles is Director of the Canadian Studies Academic Program and Professor of Political Science at the State University of New York (SUNY), Buffalo.

Joanna Everitt is Professor of Politics and Dean of Arts at the University of New Brunswick—Saint John, and a member of the Canadian Election Study team.

Thomas Flanagan is Professor of Political Science at the University of Calgary and a former federal Conservative campaign manager.

Patrick Fournier is an Associate Professor in the Department of Political Science at the Université de Montréal, and a member of the Canadian Election Study team.

Elisabeth Gidengil is Hiram Mills Professor in the Department of Political Science at McGill University, and Director of the inter-university Centre for the Study of Democratic Citizenship.

Annika Hagley is a PhD candidate in the Department of Political Science at the State University of New York (SUNY), Buffalo.

Ailsa Henderson is a Senior Lecturer and Marie Curie International Incoming Fellow in the Department of Politics and International Relations at the University of Edinburgh.

Lawrence LeDuc is Professor of Political Science at the University of Toronto.

Neil Nevitte is Professor of Political Science at the University of Toronto and a member of the Canadian Election Study team.

Michael Pal is a graduate student at the New York University School of Law.

Jon H. Pammett is Professor of Political Science at Carleton University.

Steve Patten is an Associate Professor and Undergraduate Chair in the Department of Political Science at the University of Alberta.

Andrea Perrella is an Assistant Professor in the Department of Political Science at Wilfrid Laurier University, and a member of the Management Board of the Laurier Institute for the Study of Public Opinion and Policy.

Dennis Pilon is an Assistant Professor in the Department of Political Science at the University of Victoria.

Tamara A. Small is an Assistant Professor in the Department of Political Science at Mount Allison University.

André Turcotte is an Assistant Professor in Communication in the School of Journalism and Communication at Carleton University.

PART ONE
Overview

CHAPTER 1

Introduction

Heather MacIvor

As these words are written (in late 2009), Canada has experienced 40 federal general elections. It seems to be a good time to launch a collection of original essays on Canadian elections—and not just because 40 is a nice round number. The preceding decade has witnessed an unusually large number of elections. Between 2000 and 2008, the average period between general elections was a little over two years; the average since 1867 is roughly three and a half years. By late 2009 the country had experienced five years of minority government and recurring bouts of election speculation. It is a good moment to remind ourselves that elections are about more than political brinksmanship.

This rapid series of elections has been accompanied by a historic decline in voter turnout. There may be a short-term connection between the two phenomena: Canadians are increasingly turned off by their political leaders' unwillingness to work together. But as Lawrence LeDuc and Jon H. Pammett explain in Chapter 12, long-term factors are at work in the turnout decline. The most significant factor is diminishing public interest in elections—especially among people of university age. If a new book on elections can help to inform and engage young Canadians, then its appearance is timely indeed.

This brief introduction identifies three broad themes that unify the following chapters and explains why each theme—historical perspectives, the national–local axis of federal elections, and the significant debates that continue among scholars —can be considered a strength of the book. Of course, the book does not neglect to provide accessible coverage of the key elements of election study, such as the electoral system and its laws, the practices of parties, and the various forces that come into play during an intense national election campaign. But by laying these larger themes over a description of the workings of our electoral system, readers are provided with a vivid and nuanced picture of this most important aspect of Canadian political life.

The History of Canadian Elections

One strength of the present volume is its broad historical perspective. However timely it might be, this book is more than a summary of Canada's recent elections. It describes and explains the past several campaigns, not as isolated events, but in the context of a rich political and social history. In some respects, our elections have changed surprisingly little since the 19th century. As Canadians have done since 1878, we choose a member of Parliament from a list of candidates nominated by the parties' associations in our particular constituency. We mark an X on the ballot to indicate which candidate we prefer. To be sure, we have more opportunities to vote than Canadians did in the past (see Chapter 4); but in most essential respects, the process of casting and counting our votes has survived unchanged for decades. So has the purpose and significance of general elections: the party that elects more MPs than any other forms the next government, and its leader becomes the prime minister of Canada. These are very high stakes, just as they were when Sir John A. Macdonald's Conservatives and their Liberal antagonists contended for power in the 19th century.

In Chapter 2, John C. Courtney provides a succinct overview of the salient trends in national electoral politics from Confederation to the present. The chapters comprising Part Two (3, 4, and 5) tell the story of the laws and institutions within which electoral competition unfolds. By showing how institutions can shape (and sometimes distort) that competition, these chapters set the stage for the descriptions of campaigning in Part Three. Dennis Pilon (Chapter 3) describes a voting system that has changed remarkably little since 1867, despite vociferous calls for reform. Chapters 4 (Heather MacIvor) and 5 (Michael Pal and Sujit Choudhry) summarize the laws that regulate election campaigns and the crafting of constituency boundaries. They show that some improvements have recently been made, but more needs to be done to ensure fairness to all players in the electoral system, be they parties, candidates, or voters.

Chapters 10 and 11 describe, respectively, the evolution of opinion polling and the study of voting behaviour. André Turcotte explores the increasingly sophisticated techniques of sampling, questioning, and analysis, which have allowed pollsters and party strategists to identify and woo undecided voters. Andrea Perrella uncovers the long-term influences on Canadian voting, such as region and religion, which persist despite an increasingly diverse population and the fragmentation of the national party system. Like the other authors in Part Four, Perrella allows us to look beyond the isolated events of recent elections, and to read them as chapters in a continuing story. In Chapter 13, Joanna Everitt and the Canadian Election Study team—Elisabeth Gidengil, Patrick Fournier, and Neil Nevitte—argue that durable party attachments shape voting choice today, as they did in the days of Sir John A. Macdonald. Chapter 14 presents Ailsa Henderson's taxonomy of regional voting "clusters," some of which are rooted in the earliest European settlements in North America. So we cannot understand what happens in a particular campaign unless we situate that election in its proper historical context.

If election outcomes are strongly affected by persistent voting patterns, it is also true that every campaign is characterized by unique events and conditions (see the appendixes in Chapter 2). A voter with an attachment to a particular party may abandon her political "default setting" because of a pressing issue, or because she dislikes the current party leader (Chapter 10). Strategists for the other parties will try to find that voter and to win her over, as Thomas Flanagan describes in Chapter 8. Flanagan draws on his extensive experience as a national campaign manager to describe the techniques of geographic and demographic "triage." He suggests that recent Conservative innovations have rewritten the informal rules for all Canadian parties—or at least for those that can afford to mount a "permanent campaign." (The playing field has recently been skewed, in part, by amendments to the party finance laws described in Chapter 4.)

Chapter 9 describes another set of innovations: the ever-evolving technologies of information and communication. Tamara A. Small surveys the impact of the Internet and social networking sites on campaigns and concludes that our parties have been slower than those in the United States to realize their full potential. The next time you read a news story about the uniqueness of a particular political event, you might pause to ask whether the media's emphasis on novelty adds much to our understanding of elections.

National and Local Campaigns

A second strength of this book is its recognition that Canadian elections unfold locally as well as nationally. Because of our single-member voting system, Canadian elections have always been won or lost in the constituencies. Yet many accounts of general election campaigns ignore local "ground wars," focusing instead on the national "air war" and countrywide survey data. A "star" candidate might rate a mention in a news story; a constituency might feature as the backdrop for a visit from the party leader; but otherwise, one could mistake a Canadian general election for a nationwide referendum on which party leader should become prime minister. (Perhaps this misperception helps to partially explain the often-lamented fact that Canadians are not nearly as knowledgeable about the workings of their electoral system as one would hope.)

This book corrects that erroneous impression. Chapter 6 turns the spotlight on constituency electioneering. Munroe Eagles and Annika Hagley demonstrate that a strong local campaign can make the difference between winning and losing a seat, which in turn—given the closeness of recent federal elections—can determine which party forms the government. So it is no coincidence that, as Steve Patten explains in Chapter 7, national party officials are asserting an unprecedented degree of control over the process of nominating candidates.

Indeed, Flanagan argues in Chapter 8 that a national campaign can only achieve its objectives by controlling the campaigns in its targeted constituencies. The increasing sophistication of polling techniques, discussed in Chapter 10, allows analysts to measure the impact of national voting trends on local races. By highlighting the growing integration between the national and constituency campaigns, these chapters break new ground in the study of Canadian elections. But they do so without understating the importance of local issues and candidates in our national politics.

Debates Within the Discipline

The study of elections has always attracted many of the most able scholars in political science. It is no reflection on their skills that they often reach divergent conclusions on key points. This book acknowledges some of these unresolved issues. For example, Courtney and Pilon disagree over the advisability of electoral reform. Courtney (Chapter 2) argues that our current voting system encourages national parties to build political coalitions across regions, and that this fosters Canadian unity. Pilon (Chapter 3) counters that the system rewards parties that focus their efforts in a handful of locations, balkanizing our politics and hampering regional accommodation. This debate cannot be fully resolved unless Canada adopts a new voting system—which, as both authors agree, is very unlikely.

Another dispute concerns the relative importance of various factors on Canadian voting. We cannot be certain whether Canadians are more strongly influenced by their parents' partisan leanings, by their own religious beliefs, or by a momentary impulse in the voting booth. The frequency and intensity of party identification has been a particular bone of contention. As Everitt et al. explain in Chapter 13, basic methodological issues continue to divide scholars seeking to measure voters' attachment to specific parties (or their lack thereof). Chapters 10 to 14 describe the current state of the pollsters' art, and summarize the best available information about what motivates Canadian voters. They offer fascinating glimpses into the reasons why we vote the way we do—and, in the case of Chapter 12, why fewer of us choose to vote at all. Given that disappointing fact, one must hope that the Canadian election process—and the Canadian electorate itself—will continue to evolve, such that more and more citizens will wish to exercise their most basic democratic right.

CHAPTER 2

Forty and Counting

John C. Courtney*

Introduction

Two features of Canadian elections can be adduced from the 40 federal elections held between 1867 and 2008. First, that nearly century-and-a-half period has been marked by three relatively discrete phases of electoral and party development, and second, in spite of monumental changes that have been made to voter registration, the franchise, electoral districting, election finance, and electoral administration, the method of electing MPs (plurality voting) has remained as it was at the time of Confederation.

The three distinct periods of electoral and party development in Canada are, broadly, 1867–1917, 1921–1988, and 1993–2008. The boundaries of these periods have been set by a unique configuration of parties and a particular frequency of elections. For its part, the institutional framework within which elections have been held since Confederation has grown more expansive and inclusive (as with the franchise, which is now enjoyed by all Canadian citizens 18 years of age and over); democratic (as with constituency boundary reforms that have effectively transferred the boundary delimitation power from parliamentarians to independent commissions); and state-determined (as with election expense and party finance regulations). But the changes to Canada's electoral institutions have not included changes to the voting system. The country's elections continue to be held under the rules of simple plurality voting, or more commonly the "first-past-the-post" or single-member plurality (SMP) system. Intermittent moves to replace plurality voting with some form of proportional representation have so far been unsuccessful.

---

* I am grateful to Jade Buchanan for his research assistance.

Periods of Electoral and Party Development

A few simple statistics help explain how elections and the party system in Canada have changed over the years. Tables 2.1 and 2.2 present data on two important features of elections for each of the three periods of development: the share of the total popular vote of the two major parties, the Liberals and Conservatives (see Table 2.1), and the total number of candidates and the number of candidates per seat (see Table 2.2). Table 2.3 lists the number of elections and the average length of time between elections for each period. The data in those tables contribute to the narrative about parties and elections in Canada.

1867–1917

First, a word about the nascent parties that sought to control the House of Commons in the early post-Confederation elections. There was no doubt that Sir John A. Macdonald had established an unchallenged title to form the country's first government. It was a loose alliance of French-Canadian ultramontanists, English-speaking Montreal commercial and business interests, Upper Canadian Loyalists, and anti-Catholic Orangemen. Following the elections of 1867 and 1872, Macdonald's Liberal-Conservative Party (as the Conservatives then styled themselves) was larger than any other group, a fact made possible in no small part by the addition, through Macdonald's consummate skill, of those members derisively known as the "waiters on Providence" and "loose fish." These were men (it was to be 50 years before the first woman would be elected to Parliament) who saw themselves as elected less to support a party than a ministry, and any ministry would do if the right assurances could be provided.

What Macdonald crafted in those early years was a classic brokerage party, one that sought to accommodate regional, linguistic, and religious differences through the negotiating skills of a respected leader. The approach that Macdonald took to governing a socially diverse and sparsely populated country served as the model that later leaders, from Wilfrid Laurier to Stephen Harper, sought to emulate—some clearly with greater success than others. The country's first effectively brokered party remained in office for nearly 30 years (except for four years when Alexander Mackenzie's equally heterogeneous Liberal Party held office in the wake of Macdonald's resignation over the Pacific Scandal), but finally collapsed under the combined weight of Quebec's distress over the hanging of Louis Riel, the religious fallout from the Manitoba Schools controversy, and a succession of ineffectual leaders following Macdonald's death in 1891.

For the party and electoral systems, Macdonald's legacy was considerable. Canada's first prime minister established not only the accommodative, brokerage party, which became the model of choice for political leaders of the 20th century. He also demonstrated that it was possible given a plurality vote electoral system to "divide and conquer" political opponents and remain in office for extended periods of time. Laurier, King, St. Laurent, Trudeau, and Chrétien all profited from that lesson, and in the process turned the Liberal Party into, as it has often been characterized, the "natural governing party" of 20th-century Canada.

TABLE 2.1   Combined Popular Vote of the Liberals and Conservatives, 1867–2008 (% rounded)

	Number of elections	Lib./Cons. total (%)	Range (%)	Median (%)
1867–1917	13	97.7	91–99	98.0
1921–1988	21	75.3	68–91	75.6
1993–2008	6	62.1	57–66	63.5

TABLE 2.2   Number of Candidates per Federal Election and per Seat, 1867–2008

	Number of candidates per election (average)	Number of candidates per seat (average)
1867–1917	424	2.0
1921–1988	978	3.7
1993–2008	1,759	5.8

Together, the Conservatives and Liberals monopolized federal elections throughout Canada's first half century. In the 13 elections between 1867 and 1917, they captured 97.7 percent of the popular vote between them, a feat unthinkable by today's electoral standards, and a demonstration of the fact that third parties were simply not a factor in the electoral competition during the first period of party development (see Table 2.1). The same point is made differently in Table 2.2, where the average number of candidates per seat in Canada's first 13 elections is found to be exactly two.

Indeed, for Canada's first three elections it was clear that the "party system" was truly in its infancy stage: fully one-quarter of all federal constituencies in the elections of 1867, 1872, and 1874 had only a single candidate running in them. Election by acclamation has long since disappeared from the federal electoral scene. Of the 135 Commons' seats won by acclamation in general elections, all but five were between 1867 and 1917. The last "acclaimed" candidate to be chosen to sit in Parliament was elected in 1957.

According to the *Constitution Act, 1982* (section 4(2)), the maximum life of a Parliament is to be no more than five years, unless extended with the approval of two-thirds of the members of the House of Commons "in time of real or apprehended war, invasion or insurrection." For decades, conventional wisdom in Canada suggested that federal elections would be held more or less every four years. That was certainly true in the first period of electoral and party development when the 13 elections were held, on average, 3.8 years apart (see Table 2.3). Behind that figure lies a more profound point about parties and elections. All of the first 13 governments commanded a clear majority of seats in the Commons, which meant that the timing of elections was firmly in the hands of the government of the day.

Canada's first period of party development was tied to the electoral system in several important respects. Brokerage parties (first the Conservatives under Macdonald,

**TABLE 2.3   Time Between Elections, 1867–2008
(average number of years)**

	Number of elections	Years between elections (average)
1867–1917	13	3.8
1921–1988	21	3.1
1993–2008	6	2.5

then the Liberals under Laurier) used the first-past-the-post system to their advantage. Elections were held, on average, at regular intervals of nearly four years, and one-party dominance became the norm. These factors helped set the stage for Liberal hegemony through the 20th century. Had the question of electoral reform come up, which it did not in any serious way, the two major parties would have opposed it, for both felt the system worked to their advantage given the right conditions. Between them, the two major parties enjoyed all but complete monopoly over the total popular vote, and though a sizable number of Commons' seats went uncontested, the average number of candidates per seat was two—a figure unimaginable by today's standards. In 12 of the 13 elections held between 1867 and 1917, the winning party gained a clear majority of the votes cast. That remarkable run of majority governments has not been equalled since. (For the distribution of seats and votes in all federal elections, see Appendix 2.1 in this chapter.)

1921–1988

The 1921 election proved to be a major turning point in Canadian elections and the federal party system. The defeat of Arthur Meighen's Unionist government (composed of Conservative and breakaway Liberals during the First World War election in 1917), the meteoric rise of the largely agrarian protest party (the Progressives), and the selection of the consummate brokerage politician, William Lyon Mackenzie King, as Liberal leader following Laurier's death in 1919, combined to change the dynamics of elections and of Parliament. King's Liberals won the election, but for the first time in Canadian history a government party fell slightly short of a majority of Commons' seats. The Progressives won the second-largest number of seats, and the Conservatives fell to third place in the House. For the first and only time in the 1921–1988 period, a party other than the Liberals or Conservatives formed the Official Opposition.[1]

The electoral success of the Progressives in 1921 was short-lived. They nominated fewer candidates, elected fewer members, and received a smaller percentage of the vote in each of the three subsequent elections they contested—1925, 1926, and 1930. Having had several of their key policies implemented by a politically adroit government, and having lost MPs to other parties (primarily the Liberals), the Progressives found it increasingly difficult to maintain a distinct identity worthy of widespread electoral support. The outcome was the temporary restoration of the two-party system in the 1930 election—an election that brought about the defeat of King's government and its replacement by the Conservatives under R.B. Bennett.

The electoral success of the newly created Co-operative Commonwealth Federation (CCF) and Social Credit parties in the 1935 election brought four parties into the Commons—a first in Canada. But like the Progressives before them, the CCF (and its successor, the NDP) and Social Credit had to operate within a parliamentary and electoral context whose principal features had been fashioned by two parties during the earlier stages of political development. Both the CCF and Social Credit began more modestly than the Progressives. In the 1935 election, both parties fielded fewer candidates than had the Progressives in 1921, and, not surprisingly, they received a smaller percentage of the total vote, a smaller number of seats, and even more regionalized support than the Progressives.

However, in at least one respect an essential political lesson had been learned from the brief existence of the Progressives. If parties wished to survive (something that was far less certain for Social Credit with its "group government" heritage than the CCF), they had little choice but to accept the electoral, institutional, and parliamentary imperatives of Canadian politics. At a minimum this meant (1) endowing the parliamentary leadership with the authority to act; (2) forming a tightly knit parliamentary caucus; (3) accepting the authority of a whip; (4) insisting on party discipline and a reasonable degree of parliamentary cohesiveness; and (5) waging electoral battles within the confines of the single-member-district simple-plurality-vote system. The vagaries of plurality voting were demonstrated in spades by the different fates of the Social Credit and CCF.

As is so often the case with parties of strong regional but scarce national support, Social Credit's strength (principally in Alberta) was also its weakness. In the seven elections from 1935 to 1958, Social Credit never once gained as many votes as the CCF. Yet it twice won more seats than the CCF, and twice won nearly as many seats. At six of those elections the CCF won between two and three times the number of votes of Social Credit—in 1945 the spread between the two parties amounted to 12 percentage points—yet the CCF elected only 28 MPs to Social Credit's 13. These figures reflected the CCF's conscious attempt, at best matched by only modest success, to become a national political force composed of something more than a purely regional support base. For its part, Social Credit ran fewer than 100 candidates per election, and the great majority of those were in the four Western provinces. Its undoing in the West (and, by extension, in the whole of Canada) came with the massive swing to the Conservatives in 1958, when Social Credit garnered barely 3 percent of the national vote and failed to elect a single member. The CCF was better able to withstand the shock of that election, gaining 10 percent of the popular vote and electing eight MPs, largely because it had developed a more national/less regional constituency of support during the previous two decades.

The increase in the number of parties in the Commons meant that the timing of elections was no longer the exclusive prerogative of the government. Mackenzie King's 1921 election victory was followed by a second "minority" election in 1925. But they were not the only elections during the second period of electoral and party development in which no one party won a clear majority of seats. The elections of 1957, 1962, 1963,

1965, 1972, and 1979 all ended in minority Parliaments. Moreover, in 1926 following the resignation of the King government and the Commons' defeat of Meighen's short-lived Conservative government, and in the Parliaments of 1962–63, 1972–74, and 1979–80, the government was defeated by no-confidence votes that forced an election.

Cracks in the seemingly cemented two-party system of Canada's early elections had been introduced first by the Progressives in the 1920s and were then expanded a decade later with the electoral success of the CCF and Social Credit. The conversion of the CCF into the NDP in 1961 and the modest success of the Ralliement créditiste du Québec in the seven federal elections between 1962 and 1979 drove home the fact that Canada was no longer a two-party country. In the post-1993 election period, the House of Commons routinely was composed of four or five parties.

Many of these points are captured in the three tables in this chapter. In the period between 1921 and 1988 the combined Liberal and Conservative share of the popular vote slipped to an average of 75.3 percent, with a range of 68 to 91 percent over the 21 elections (see Table 2.1). The average number of candidates per general election more than doubled from what it had been during the earlier period, a fact that reflected the existence, at least at elections if not always in Parliament, of a multiparty electoral system. It went from 424 per election in the first period to 978 in the second, with an average of 3.7 candidates per constituency, up from 2.0 in the earlier period (see Table 2.2). Finally, a government's life expectancy was reduced by more than half a year, from an average of 3.8 to 3.1 years, a reflection of the fact that better than one-third of the elections held between 1921 and 1988 resulted in minority Parliaments and that nearly one-fifth resulted from defeats of the government by the combined opposition on the floor of the Commons (see Table 2.3).

The second period of electoral and party development demonstrated several important features, a number of which have also defined the third period. Regionally strong but nationally weak parties (Social Credit and Ralliement créditistes) could function well and win representation in Parliament out of proportion with their share of the national popular vote. The reverse was also the case. Third parties seeking national more than concentrated regional support (CCF/NDP) could expect to fare less well than parties with regional bastions of electoral strength. The fate of the Conservatives in 1921 showed that it was possible for one of the two major parties to forfeit its place as either government or major opposition party yet, with the passage of time, return to office.

As had been the case in the first period of electoral and party development, first with the Conservatives and then with the Liberals, one party could be dominant over an extended time. In the second period, that role fell exclusively to the Liberal Party, a fact Reg Whitaker captured in the title to his study of the Liberal Party, *The Government Party* (Whitaker 1977). Between 1921 and 1988, 21 federal elections were held. The Liberals won 14 of them and held office for 51 of the 67 years. That the Liberals won a clear majority of the popular vote in only two of those 14 elections is further evidence of how the number of parties and candidates competing in general elections had changed from the first period. It also stands as further testimony to the probability that plurality voting, given a multiparty system, will lead a party to victory with a majority of the seats but without a majority of the votes.

Lastly, with the increase in the number of parties competing for office and the growing regionalization of party electoral support, minority Parliaments emerged as a not uncommon outcome in Canadian elections. That, in turn, shifted a measure of control over the timing of elections from government to opposition hands.

1993–2008

The 1993 election brought an abrupt end to the earlier party system. The Conservative government of Kim Campbell (the successor to Brian Mulroney, who had held office since 1984) came crashing to an end. Reduced to two seats in the Commons and 16 percent of the popular vote, the Progressive Conservatives (the party's name since 1942) lost official party status in Parliament and became the smallest of five parties in a House with a majority Liberal government under Jean Chrétien. Along with the Conservatives, the NDP had been reduced for the first time since the party's formation in 1961 to single-digit representation—nine seats.

No less newsworthy to political analysts and the general public was the sudden emergence of the Bloc Québécois (BQ) and the Reform Party of Canada as major players in the new Parliament. At the time of the previous election in 1988, the BQ had not existed and the Reform Party (founded in 1987) had not elected a single candidate. The overnight electoral success of the two parties speaks to the potential that upstart parties have to enter Parliament under plurality voting if their support is limited geographically and their campaign is targeted at a narrow rather than a broader range of voters. Both Reform and the BQ had regional concentrations of support in 1993, unlike the Conservatives and NDP, whose support was more widely dispersed across the country. Reform won 52 seats, all but one in the Western provinces, and the BQ became the Official Opposition with 54 seats, all in Quebec—the sole province in which they ran candidates. The irony of a party seeking Quebec's separatism from Canada having become Her Majesty's Loyal Opposition escaped few Canadians. As it turned out, the 1993 election produced the first of three successive (in the term adopted by several media commentators) "Pizza Parliaments."

Plurality voting in single-member districts contributed to the stunning results of 1993. The Liberals won all but one of Ontario's 99 seats with 53 percent of that province's vote, and the 54 BQ seats in Quebec (out of 75 in the province) came from the party having won 49 percent of that province's vote. The Progressive Conservatives had been supported by 16 percent of the voters nationally, Reform by 18.7 percent. But Reform gained 52 seats, because of its regional strength, to the Progressive Conservatives' 2. With 7 percent of the vote the NDP won 9 seats, but with 13.5 percent (smaller than the Progressive Conservatives' support), the BQ won 54 seats. Predictably, the inequitable conversion of votes into seats led to calls for replacing plurality voting with some (undefined) form of proportional representation.

The vote/seat imbalances continued in the 1997 and 2000 elections, perhaps most notably when the Liberals were returned to office in 1997 with a slight majority of seats but only 38.5 percent of the popular vote. That level of support for a party winning a majority in the Commons was unprecedented in the history of Canadian elections. Once again, Ontario ensured that the Liberals stayed in office. All but 2 of Ontario's 103 seats returned a Liberal. Regional concentrations of votes also helped the BQ and the Reform Party (which took over in 1997 as the Official Opposition), but once again dispersion of votes continued to hurt the NDP and the Progressive Conservatives. The Progressive Conservatives won nearly as many votes as the Reform Party (18.8 percent versus 19.4 percent) but only one-third the number of seats (20 versus 60), whereas the NDP captured more votes than the BQ (11.0 percent versus 10.7 percent) but less than half the number of seats (21 versus 44). The details varied somewhat in the 2000 election, by which time the Reform Party had been refashioned as the Canadian Reform Conservative Alliance, but the picture remained essentially the same.

The dynamics of party competition changed from the first three elections of the third period of electoral and party development to the final three. The elections of 2004, 2006, and 2008 all produced minority governments, the first Liberal under Paul Martin and the last two Conservative under Stephen Harper. In 2003, the Progressive Conservative–Alliance merger (which created today's Conservative Party of Canada) reduced the number of parties in serious electoral competition from five to four. However, in spite of the change of government in 2006, the last three elections produced something approximating a stalemate in levels of party support and numbers of seats in Parliament. For the first time in Canadian elections, the Green Party ran a complete or nearly complete slate of candidates in 2004, 2006, and 2008. In 2008 the Greens gained 6.8 percent of the popular vote—a record for the party.

The 1993–2008 period charted new waters for the Canadian party and electoral systems. Minority Parliaments became as common as majority ones, with the unsurprising consequence that elections became more frequent than they had been in the two earlier periods of development. Over the course of the third period, a general election has been held on average every two and a half years (see Table 2.3). The growth in the number of parties in Parliament and competing in elections brought a sharp increase in the number of candidates. An average of 1,759 candidates per election (compared with 424 in the first period and 978 in the second) were nominated in the elections between 1993 and 2008. This works out to nearly three times (5.8 versus 2.0) the average number of candidates per constituency in the first period of development (see Table 2.2). Finally, the combined Liberal and Conservative share of the total popular vote slipped even further from what it had been previously. Barely 62 percent (range 57 percent to 66 percent) of voters cast their ballots for these parties in the six elections of the third period. The other 38 percent gave their support to regionally strong parties (BQ and Reform/Alliance), a national party with a small and dispersed support base (the NDP), a smattering of Independent or fringe party candidates, or a relatively new entry on the party roster (the Greens).

Change and Continuity

As noted at the outset of this chapter, many fundamental reforms have been made to electoral institutions in Canada from the time of the early post-Confederation elections. The franchise, originally limited to a select group of property-owning males, is now universal. In fact Canada enjoys one of the most inclusive franchises in the world. Electoral boundary readjustments, once the exclusive purview of those most directly affected by the geographically defined borders of constituencies, the elected members, are now redrawn every ten years by committees that serve at arm's length from Parliament and whose decisions are final. In the past 40 years election expenses and candidate and party fundraising and expenditure rules have become increasingly strict, with a healthy measure of state financial support. And electoral administration, through the Office of the Chief Electoral Officer, is internationally recognized as one of the finest non-partisan electoral administrations in the world.

What has not changed since Confederation is the plurality voting system. It might seem that the logic of the changes in the party system between 1867 and 2008 would lead, inexorably, to a replacement of plurality voting with some variant of proportional representation. As noted, the number of candidates has increased along with the increase in the number of parties. The likelihood that an election would produce a minority Parliament has increased with the growth in the number of parties and candidate. In turn, the time between elections has fallen. (As an aside, it should be noted that the increased frequency of elections may be a contributing factor to "voter fatigue" and help explain the lower voter turnouts of recent elections.) Moreover, when vote/seat conversions are made, regional parties have benefited from plurality voting while smaller national parties have been penalized. And as the share of the total popular vote won by the two historically dominant parties in Canada has slipped from one period to the next to its most recent average of 62.1 percent, the chance of an election producing a "double majority" government (a clear majority of both seats and votes) has become extremely slim. Together, these developments would seem to offer sufficient reason to change the method of voting.

However, as compelling as the case may seem for adopting proportional representation, it is clear that certain practical obstacles have stood in the way of changing the voting system to some non-plurality method of voting. Those obstacles remain very much in play today. The support of governing elites and the agreement on a single alternative to the current system are clearly the most pressing hurdles to be overcome. So far these have not come to pass. The record shows that regardless of what they may say while in opposition, neither of the two major parties has shown any serious interest in electoral reform when in office. A compounding difficulty is that among those who support proportional representation, there is no overwhelming preference for one non-plurality vote system. Mixed member? Party-list proportional representation? Single transferable vote? Runoff? Some other proportional option? Preferences vary among proportional representation advocates.

Media commentators and editorialists are also divided on the issue of replacing plurality voting—some are in favour, others are opposed. And there is division over electoral reform among academics and interested opinion leaders who have entered the electoral reform debate. At the provincial level it is important to note that five provinces, including the largest three, have considered over the course of the past decade changing to non-plurality voting, but none has made the change. Two (New Brunswick and Quebec) declined to follow through on recommended changes, and three (Ontario, British Columbia, and Prince Edward Island) saw proposed proportional electoral schemes defeated in province-wide referendums. That is significant, for without the "provincial test tubes" of electoral change having adopted non-plurality voting (provinces were, after all, first out of the gate in adopting female suffrage laws, independent electoral commissions, election expense legislation, party leadership conventions, and permanent voters' lists), the federal level has no examples of successful change to "point to" and be able to emulate. And the bottom line is that the electorate has shown little sustained interest in the issue of electoral reform. Responding favourably to the occasional poll on the possibility of replacing plurality voting with proportional representation is one thing. But the translation of that interest at the grassroots level into civic action groups or voter advocacy groups pressing for electoral change has simply not happened.[2]

Regardless of the practical hurdles to introducing proportional representation in Canada, there may be good reason to urge caution about replacing plurality voting. The call for careful forethought should not be taken, as it sometimes is by those who dismiss such calls about electoral change, as a case *against* a more proportional electoral system. It is nothing of the sort. Rather, it should be seen for what it is intended to be: an appeal for a balanced consideration of the known strengths and weaknesses of plurality voting and the presumed benefits of some (unspecified) form of proportional voting for Canadian government, representation, and parties. Simply put, what is often overlooked in the debate over electoral systems is the impact that a change in the method of voting would have on party and voter strategies.[3]

If it is true, as Dennis Pilon suggests in Chapter 3, that critics of proportional representation paint "a gloomy picture" of minority or coalition governments, they are mistaken. Minority governments (forget coalition governments, of which Canada has had only one at the federal level, the 1917–1921 Unionist government of Conservatives and some dissident Liberals) can be every bit as productive as, and in some cases more productive than, majority governments. What it takes is the right alignment of such critical elements as responsible (and responsive) government leadership, political will, an ineffective or divided opposition, and generally popular public policies. Not all minority governments (and for that matter, not all majority governments) have the same capacity to deliver sound government. A comparison of, for example, the policy output of the Pearson minority governments of 1963–1968 and the Harper minority government of 2006–2008 with the Mackenzie King minority government of 1925–26 and the Diefenbaker minority Conservative government of 1962–63 makes the point about how effective some minority administrations can be in implementing a defined agenda and how ineffective and unstable others can be.

It is an indisputable fact that plurality voting in a highly regionalized, federal, bilingual, and multicultural country such as Canada offers *incentives* to those parties seriously intent on gaining office. It is in their interest to construct reasonably centrist, accommodative, brokerage, or, if you will, "big tent" parties that attempt to breach the various social and geographic cleavages. This is what Macdonald, Laurier, King, and St. Laurent succeeded in doing. It is what Diefenbaker, Pearson, Trudeau, and Mulroney tried, but with varying degrees of success and, in some cases, disastrous outcomes. The "big tent" approach is what Thomas Flanagan in Chapter 8 refers to as "broadcasting" under single-member plurality (SMP) as opposed to "narrowcasting" under proportional representation.

Parties' electoral strategies are shaped by the method of voting. In Flanagan's words, this means that with narrowcasting under proportional representation a party's "winning strategy is to cultivate [its] electoral base and keep lines of communication open with selected other parties in order to participate in a government coalition after the election." Under SMP a party "cannot limit itself to delivering clear messages to stable groups of core supporters; it must reach out in an attempt to persuade the undecided, which often leads to taking vague or fuzzy positions" (see page 157). One of the concerns about replacing SMP with proportional representation stems from this difference in electoral incentives and party strategies. In a country with regional, linguistic, federal, and social cleavages, Canadians interested in exploring the pros and cons of different voting methods should not overlook one important question: Would it be worth sacrificing the incentive to accommodate regional and social cleavages through intra-party, *pre-election* negotiation that SMP encourages in a country as diverse as Canada?

Why did the Alliance and Progressive Conservative parties merge in 2003? Why did Stephen Harper reach out to include Quebeckers and erstwhile Alberta Reform/Alliance supporters in the "big tent" he was determined to create in the Conservative Party before the 2006 election? Why did Brian Mulroney embark on a similar strategy in the lead-up to the 1984 election by bringing into the same tent known Quebec nationalists and Western Canadians opposed to "any more giveaways" to Quebec? They were intent on "broadcasting" their party. That the Mulroney big tent collapsed in the early 1990s, with the consequence that the BQ and the Reform Party ascended quickly on the political map, is an object lesson on how fragile brokered parties can be, given the right combination of issues. In this particular case the refitting of the military's CF-18 jets in 1987 and the failure of the Meech Lake Accord in 1990 proved to be the principal catalysts for the party's implosion.

What makes "broadcasting" so problematic in the post-1993 political environment for both of the two major parties and, for that matter, the NDP, if it chooses to become a more centrist party, is that the BQ continues to corner the Quebec election market. So long as the BQ remains the dominant factor in Quebec's federal political arena, it is difficult to see a successful return to a true "big tent" party that gains office with electoral strength and elected members in every region. For that matter, it is unlikely that majority governments are in the offing unless, as with the Chrétien Liberals from 1993 to 2000, Ontario delivers its entire province-wide delegation to a single party.

The 1980 federal election (in which the Trudeau-led Liberals won two seats in the four Western provinces combined) is often cited as proof of Alan Cairns's point that

SMP in Canada exacerbates regionalism and regional tensions under winner-take-all rules. (Cairns 1968).[4] But the fact is that no election occurs in isolation. Earlier election results, policies thwarted or abandoned in Parliament, leadership manoeuvres, inter-party deal making, and voter expectations (which, in turn, contribute to "retrospective voting" [Fiorina 1981]) precede any election. Perhaps the best example of a centrist party that brokered its transnational coalition into an electoral majority is the Trudeau Liberals who swept into office in 1968. It is now often forgotten that in that election Liberals won more seats and more votes in the four Western provinces combined than any other party. More than one-third of the MPs from Western Canada were Liberal.

In 1968 the Liberal cohort sent to Ottawa was large enough to make its presence felt in caucus and Cabinet. Judging by contemporary accounts, Western Liberal MPs did exactly that. Yet on the issues that were most critical to the resource and agricultural sectors of the West, issues such as rail transportation, freight rates, grain stabilization, resource taxation, and oil pricing, the Trudeau government was seen to have failed the West. Trudeau's rhetorical taunt, "Why should I sell your wheat?" only aggravated the Liberal cause in the West. By the elections of 1979 and 1980, a fundamental shift in party preferences had taken place among voters in the four Western provinces, and the Liberal pre-eminence of a decade earlier had been forfeited. This example serves as a reminder that no election should be examined in isolation from those that preceded it.[5]

Conclusion

This chapter has set forth the three periods of electoral and party development in Canada. It has argued in the preceding section that on the level of practical politics, several serious obstacles have yet to be overcome to see proportional representation introduced. Moreover, as tempting as "electoral reform" might be, given the shifts in party and candidate numbers, major two-party support, and frequency of elections, the consequences for parties, voters, representation, and political systems must first be fully understood.

The fact is, no electoral system is neutral. How it distributes votes into seats ultimately affects the composition of governing institutions and the content of public policy. Accordingly, the links between the constitutional principles (in this case, those of Canada), party incentives, representative practices, and such vital institutions as Parliament, Cabinet, and the Prime Minister's Office (the key instruments within which political decisions are made) deserve full consideration before the plurality electoral system is changed.

NOTES

1. The Progressives were never comfortable in their role as Official Opposition. The parliamentary "group" (a revealing label most of the Progressives preferred over "party") effectively chose not to play the role of the Official Opposition in Parliament, leaving that role to the third-place Conservatives.

2. For more on the obstacles that would need to be overcome to replace the plurality voting system with proportional representation, see Courtney (2005, 155–158).
3. The cases for and against proportional representation and the claims that voter turnout and female representation would increase under proportional voting are examined in Courtney (2004, chap. 6.)
4. For a powerful empirical critique of Cairns, see Lovink (1970).
5. For a fuller explication of this point, see Courtney (1980, 442–447).

DISCUSSION QUESTIONS

1. Which are "better" for Canada and Canadians—majority or minority governments?
2. Parties adapt their electoral strategies to the method of voting. How would the parties now in Parliament, as well as the Green Party, change their electoral strategies under proportional representation?
3. It is often argued that "big tent" parties are well suited to Canada's diverse and regionalized society. Select three examples of big tent parties from Canadian history and account for their electoral success.

FURTHER READING

Blais, André, ed. 2008. *To keep or to change first past the post? The politics of electoral reform.* Oxford: Oxford University Press.
Carty, Ken, William Cross, and Lisa Young. 2000. *Rebuilding Canadian party politics.* Vancouver: UBC Press.
Courtney, John C. 2004. *Elections.* Vancouver: UBC Press.
Courtney, John C. 2007. Canada's electoral system. In *Canadian parties in transition*, ed. Alain-G. Gagnon and A. Brian Tanguay, 279–301. Peterborough, ON: Broadview Press.
Howe, Paul, Richard Johnston, and André Blais, eds. 2005. *Strengthening Canadian democracy.* Montreal: Institute for Research on Public Policy.
Pilon, Dennis. 2007. *The politics of voting: Reforming Canada's electoral system.* Toronto: Emond Montgomery.

REFERENCES

Cairns, Alan. 1968. The electoral system and the party system in Canada, 1921–1965. *Canadian Journal of Political Science* 1 (1): 55–80.
Constitution Act, 1982. 1982. Schedule B to the *Canada Act 1982* (UK), 1982, c. 11.
Courtney, John C. 1980. Reflections on reforming the Canadian electoral system. *Canadian Public Administration* 23 (3): 427–457.
Courtney, John C. 2004. *Elections.* Vancouver: UBC Press.
Courtney, John C. 2005. Is talk of electoral system just whistling in the wind? In *Strengthening Canadian democracy*, ed. Paul Howe, Richard Johnston, and André Blais, 149–158. Montreal: Institute for Research on Public Policy.
Fiorina, Morris. 1981. *Retrospective voting in American elections.* New Haven, CT: Yale University Press.
Lovink, J.A.A. 1970. On analyzing the impact of the electoral system on the party system in Canada. *Canadian Journal of Political Science* 3 (4): 497–516.
Whitaker, Reg. 1977. *The government party.* Toronto: University of Toronto Press.

Appendix 2.1: Canadian Federal Election Results, 1867–2008

Note: Under the party-by-party totals, the first number in each cell is that party's percentage of the national vote. The number in parentheses is the percentage of seats won.

Election #	Year	PM(s) following election	Majority or minority	Total seats in HoC	Seats won by PM's party	Lib.	Cons.	CCF/NDP	SC	BQ	Prog/RPC/CA	Other
1	1867	Macdonald (Cons.)	Majority	181	108	49 (40)	50 (60)	—	—	—	—	1 (0)
2	1872	Macdonald (Cons.)	Majority	200	104	49 (48)	50 (52)	—	—	—	—	1 (0)
3	1874	Mackenzie (Lib.)	Majority	206	138	54 (67)	45 (33)	—	—	—	—	1 (0.5)
4	1878	Macdonald (Cons.)	Majority	206	142	46 (31)	53 (69)	—	—	—	—	1.2 (0)
5	1882	Macdonald (Cons.)	Majority	211	139	47 (34)	50 (66)	—	—	—	—	2.5 (0.5)
6	1887	Macdonald (Cons.)	Majority	215	126	49 (41)	50 (59)	—	—	—	—	1 (0)
7	1891	Macdonald/Abbott/Thompson/Bowell/Tupper (Cons.)	Majority	215	121	47 (44)	51 (56)	—	—	—	—	2 (0)
8	1896	Laurier (Lib.)	Majority	213	118	45 (55)	46 (41)	—	—	—	—	9 (3)
9	1900	Laurier (Lib.)	Majority	213	133	51 (62)	47 (38)	—	—	—	—	1 (0)
10	1904	Laurier (Lib.)	Majority	214	138	52 (65)	46 (35)	—	—	—	—	1.5 (0.5)
11	1908	Laurier (Lib.)	Majority	221	135	50 (61)	47 (39)	—	—	—	—	2.7 (0.4)
12	1911	Borden (Cons.)	Majority	221	134	48 (39)	51 (61)	—	—	—	—	1.4 (0)
13	1917*	Borden/Meighen (Unionist)	Coalition	235	153	40 (35)	57 (65)	—	—	—	—	3 (0)
14	1921	King (Lib.)	Minority	235	116	41 (49)	30 (21)	—	—	—	23 (27)	6 (2)
15	1925†	King (Lib.)/Meighen (Cons.)	Minority	245	99	40 (40)	47 (47)	—	—	—	9 (10)	5 (2)
16	1926	King (Lib.)	Majority‡	245	116	46 (52)	45 (37)	—	—	—	5 (8)	3 (2)
17	1930	Bennett (Cons.)	Majority	245	137	45 (37)	49 (56)	—	—	—	3 (5)	3 (2)
18	1935	King (Lib.)	Majority	245	173	45 (71)	30 (16)	9 (3)	4 (7)	—	—	13 (3)
19	1940	King (Lib.)	Majority	245	181	52 (74)	31 (16)	9 (4)	3 (4)	—	—	7 (2)
20	1945	King/St. Laurent (Lib.)	Majority	245	125	41 (51)	27 (27)	16 (11)	4 (5)	—	—	12 (5)
21	1949	St. Laurent (Lib.)	Majority	262	193	50 (74)	30 (16)	13 (5)	2 (4)	—	—	5 (2)
22	1953	St. Laurent (Lib.)	Majority	265	171	49 (65)	31 (19)	22 (9)	5 (6)	—	—	4 (2)
23	1957	Diefenbaker (Cons.)	Minority	265	105	41 (40)	39 (42)	11 (9)	7 (7)	—	—	3 (1.5)
24	1958	Diefenbaker (Cons.)	Majority	265	208	34 (19)	54 (79)	10 (3)	3 (0)	—	—	1 (0)

(Continued)

Appendix 2.1   Continued

Election #	Year	PM(s) following election	Majority or minority	Total seats in HoC	Seats won by PM's party	Lib.	Cons.	CCF/ NDP	SC	BQ	Prog/ RPC/CA	Other
25	1962	Diefenbaker (Cons.)	Minority	265	116	37 (38)	37 (44)	14 (7)	12 (11)	—	—	0.4 (0)
26	1963	Pearson (Lib.)	Minority	265	129	42 (49)	33 (36)	13 (6)	12 (9)	—	—	0.4 (0)
27	1965	Pearson/Trudeau (Lib.)	Minority	265	131	40 (49)	32 (37)	18 (8)	8 (5)	—	—	1 (1)
28	1968	Trudeau (Lib.)	Majority	264	155	45 (59)	31 (27)	17 (8)	5 (5)	—	—	1 (0.4)
29	1972	Trudeau (Lib.)	Minority	264	109	39 (41)	35 (41)	18 (12)	8 (6)	—	—	1 (1)
30	1974	Trudeau (Lib.)	Majority	264	141	43 (53)	35 (36)	15 (6)	5 (4)	—	—	2 (0.4)
31	1979	Clark (Cons.)	Minority	282	136	40 (40)	36 (48)	18 (9)	5 (2)	—	—	1 (0)
32	1980	Trudeau/Turner (Lib.)	Majority	282	147	44 (52)	33 (37)	20 (11)	2 (0)	—	—	1 (0)
33	1984	Mulroney (Cons.)	Majority	282	211	28 (14)	50 (75)	18 (11)	1 (0)	—	—	3 (0.3)
34	1988	Mulroney/Campbell (Cons.)	Majority	295	169	32 (28)	43 (57)	20 (15)	—	—	2 (0)	3 (0)
35	1993	Chrétien (Lib.)	Majority	295	177	41 (60)	16 (1)	7 (3)	—	14 (18)	19 (18)	4 (0.3)
36	1997	Chrétien (Lib.)	Majority	301	155	38 (52)	19 (7)	11 (7)	—	11 (15)	19 (20)	2 (0.3)
37	2000	Chrétien/Martin (Lib.)	Majority	301	172	41 (57)	12 (4)	9 (4)	—	11 (13)	26 (22)	2 (0)
38	2004	Martin (Lib.)	Minority	308	135	37 (44)	30 (32)	16 (6)	—	12 (18)	—	6 (0.3)§
39	2006	Harper (Cons.)	Minority	308	124	30 (33)	36 (40)	17 (9)	—	10 (17)	—	6 (0.3)§
40	2008	Harper (Cons.)	Minority	308	143	26 (25)	38 (46)	18 (12)	—	10 (16)	—	8 (0.6)§

Key to parties:

- Lib.: Liberal Party of Canada
- Cons.: Includes Progressive Conservative Party of Canada (1942–2003) and Conservative Party of Canada (2003–).
- CCF/NDP: Co-operative Commonwealth Federation (1933–1961) and New Democratic Party of Canada (1961–).
- SC: Social Credit (includes the Ralliement créditiste du Québec).
- BQ: Bloc Québécois (1993–).
- Prog/RPC/CA: Progressives (1921–1935); Reform Party of Canada (1987–2000); Canadian Alliance (2000–2003).

* The 1917 election was highly unusual. See Appendix 2.2 in this chapter, Election #13.

† For an account of the King–Byng Affair, see Appendix 2.2 in this chapter, Election #15.

‡ The 1926 election is generally considered a majority, though by some strict, technical definitions, it was a minority.

§ The one seat assigned to "Other" in both the 2004 and 2006 elections was won by an Independent, as were the two seats assigned to "Other" in 2008. None of the smaller parties won seats in either election. In 2008, however, the Green Party gained a considerable 6.8 percent of the popular vote.

Appendix 2.2: A Brief History of Canadian Elections

Heather MacIvor

The following summaries of 20 notable federal elections provide further detail on the broader historical themes, issues, and trends discussed previously in the main body of this chapter. These are the stories behind the elections that have helped define Canadian politics, and served as critical turning points in Canada's evolution.

Election #1, 1867: The First National Election
Because both parties had supported Confederation, the opposition Liberals had difficulty distinguishing themselves in the public mind from the Conservatives. Their campaign called for free trade with the Americans, which was very popular in southern Ontario and Quebec but not in areas with a strong residual attachment to the British Empire. The Conservatives took 108 of the 181 seats in the House of Commons. Almost three-quarters of eligible electors—a relatively small minority of the population (see Chapter 4)—turned out to vote.

Election #2, 1872: Growing Pains
In Sir John A. Macdonald's first administration, regional tensions emerged. Macdonald participated in British negotiations with the Americans over trade and other outstanding issues. The British government granted fishing rights in Canadian waters to American fishermen, without compensating Canada for the loss of fish stocks. This provoked outrage in the Maritime provinces of New Brunswick and Nova Scotia, most of whose inhabitants were already opposed to Confederation. To make matters worse, the British–US agreement did not guarantee access to American markets for Canadian goods. Ontario manufacturers wanted reciprocity (now called *free trade*). So the Liberal provincial government became even more opposed to the Macdonald Conservatives. Finally, the new Western provinces of Manitoba and British Columbia accused Macdonald of failing to keep his promise to link Canada by rail from sea to sea.

In 1872, unlike 1867, the federal Liberals were sufficiently united to present themselves as an alternative government. Macdonald knew that he had a fight on his hands. He solicited large sums of money from Montreal financier Sir Hugh Allan in exchange for the right to build the Canadian Pacific Railway (CPR). The Conservatives managed to win the election, once again forming a majority government. However, when the "Pacific Scandal" became public in 1873, Macdonald and his Conservatives were forced from office.

Election #3, 1874: The Emergence of a Two-Party System
After governing as caretakers for several months, the Liberals under Alexander Mackenzie sought their own mandate from the electors. Despite his lack of charisma,

Mackenzie's promises to end political corruption resonated with Canadians in the wake of the "Pacific Scandal." The Liberals captured 138 of the 206 seats in the House of Commons.

Election #4, 1878: Macdonald's Return and the "National Policy"

The 1878 federal election was the first to be dominated by economic issues. A severe recession in the United States was hurting the Canadian economy. While the Conservatives offered the "National Policy," the Liberals were firmly (and wrongly) convinced that Canadians would prefer free trade over protectionism. The nail in their coffin was Mackenzie's *Canada Temperance Act*, which restricted the sale of liquor. The law was very popular in some parts of Canada, but it infuriated thousands of hotel and tavern keepers (and their customers).

By 1878, Macdonald had become a masterful speaker and political organizer. While out of office, the Conservatives had begun to hold political picnics during the summer months. As many as 20,000 people would attend to eat, mingle, and listen to a fiery speech by Sir John A. In the era before mass media, oratory was an essential skill in Canadian electoral politics. In the end, Macdonald and his party won a majority of the seats in every province except New Brunswick. They would form three more majority governments before the Conservative dynasty ended in 1896.

This campaign poster from 1891—the year of Macdonald's death, shortly after his final victory—harkened back to his earlier electoral glories, but by the time of the next election in 1896, a new era of Liberal dominance had begun.

Election #8, 1896: The Dawn of Liberal Dominance

The 1896 general election is considered a landmark in Canadian political history. It ushered in what would become a sustained period of Liberal dominance under Liberal prime ministers Wilfrid Laurier, Mackenzie King, and Louis St. Laurent. For the first time, the Liberals were perceived as the party best able to deal with economic problems. The Liberals were also seen as the party best positioned to reconcile linguistic and religious conflict. Laurier had remodelled his party in his own image: moderate, bilingual, and optimistic about Canada's future.

Election #12, 1911: The First Free Trade Election

After spending 15 years in opposition to the Laurier-led Liberals, the Conservatives finally returned to power under Robert Borden, who had led them for a decade and two election losses before this win. The Conservatives managed to reverse the results of the 1908 election, winning 61 percent of the seats, and garnering just over 50 percent of the popular vote.

Borden ran against the Liberal government's controversial free trade agreement with the United States (also known as *reciprocity*), and was supported by powerful business interests in Toronto and Montreal, who regarded any such agreement as a threat to the protections they enjoyed. This change in allegiance to the Conservatives was counterbalanced somewhat by a shift in allegiance by many Western Canadians toward the Liberals. The expanding agricultural industry on the Prairies saw the opportunity to reach the large US market, and thus supported reciprocity.

Another controversial issue at the time concerned the Canadian Navy, which had recently been established by the Laurier government. Conservatives preferred instead to provide financial support to the British Navy.

The 1911 election is frequently compared with that of 1988, in which Brian Mulroney and John Turner sparred over the free trade issue once again, but with the ironic twist that in 1988, Mulroney's victorious Conservatives were pro-free trade.

Election #13, 1917: A Wartime Election and the Conscription Crisis

There should have been a national vote in 1916: the previous election had been held in 1911, and the 1867 Constitution imposed a five-year limit on the length of a Parliament (see Chapter 4). The Liberals had agreed to extend Parliament for an extra year so that the government could concentrate on the war effort, resulting in Canada's longest Parliament. But by late 1917, in the darkest days of the First World War, Laurier refused to grant a further extension. He wanted a national referendum on Borden's proposal to introduce conscription, but the prime minister refused. It was obvious to everyone that this issue would dominate the campaign, and perhaps tear the country apart.

The Conservative/Unionists insisted that conscription was "a military necessity." To make it more palatable, Borden promised that returning soldiers would be given job training and other benefits after the return of peace. But he could not prevent the opposition from portraying the conscription bill as an attack on Quebec, given the low levels of volunteer enlistment in that province. The divisions in the country were exacerbated by Unionist campaign rhetoric, which portrayed Quebec nationalist leader Henri Bourassa (and, by implication, Wilfrid Laurier) as a traitor to the King and a covert supporter of the enemy.

For their part, the remaining Liberals argued for lower prices and a crackdown on war profiteering. Instead of imposing conscription through a parliamentary statute, Laurier proposed a renewed appeal for voluntary enlistment and a referendum on forced recruitment. The Liberals tried to reframe conscription as a class issue rather than a matter of patriotism, by attempting to appeal to those whom conscription would affect most: farm families and urban working families who could not afford the loss of a son's labour or a husband's wage.

To boost its chances, the Union government made two changes to the voting rules. First, as described in Chapter 4, it enfranchised the close female relatives of servicemen. Second, it passed the *Military Voters Act*, which allowed servicemen to vote in any riding in the country. The government may have won as many as 14 additional seats by redistributing the military vote to ridings where Liberal candidates held a slight lead. The Unionists won 90 percent of the seats in Ontario with a voter turnout rate of 79 percent. Other anglophone provinces had similar results, leaving Quebec as the only place where Laurier and the Liberals enjoyed support.

As anticipated, this election was one of the most divisive in Canadian history. Twenty-two Labour candidates ran and Western discontent was on the horizon. In the short term, Borden's Unionist government captured 153 of 235 seats. Over the long term, the rifts between regions, classes, and language groups would continue to shape Canadian electoral politics.

Election #14, 1921: Canada's First Minority Government

This election, in which the Liberals replaced the Unionist government formed during "the Great War," marked the debut of William Lyon Mackenzie King, who would become the longest-serving prime minister in Canadian history. It is also a notable election in that it saw ten MPs elected from outside the three largest parties, among them J.S. Woodsworth of the Independent Labour Party. Woodsworth, who had been a central figure in the 1919 Winnipeg General Strike, went on to be the first leader of the social democrat Co-operative Commonwealth Federation (CCF, later the NDP).

Another sign of the changing times was the introduction of the vote for the majority of women. Along with that breakthrough, Agnes MacPhail of the Progressive Party became the first woman to be elected to federal Parliament.

King's Liberals dominated in Eastern Canada, making a clean sweep of Quebec. The aftermath of the Conscription Crisis a few years before had resulted in Liberal dominance at the polls in that province that would last for decades.

The Liberal minority briefly became a majority when two Progressive MPs crossed the floor in 1922, but with two by-election losses in 1923, they were returned just as quickly to minority status.

Election #15, 1925: King's Tenuous Grip on Power and the King–Byng Affair

King's struggles in the election of 1925 culminated in the famous King–Byng Affair of June 1926. The Conservatives actually won the plurality of seats (115, to the Liberals' 99), but Liberal Prime Minister Mackenzie King managed, with the support of the Progressives, and despite losing his own seat, to remain in office. Shortly afterward, however, a bribery scandal erupted that threatened to bring the Liberals down. Facing certain defeat in the House, King went to Governor General Lord Byng on June 26 and requested a dissolution of Parliament, which was refused. Instead, Lord Byng called on Conservative leader Arthur Meighen to form a government, but it was also short-lived. After Meighen lost the confidence of the Commons, Lord Byng granted a dissolution. This conflict between the Liberal prime minister and the Governor General has gone down in Canadian history as the "King–Byng Affair."

Election #17, 1930: The First "Air War" and the Great Depression

Two features of the political landscape changed between 1926 and 1930. The first was the transformation of election campaigning by the introduction of radio broadcasting. For the first time, party leaders and other senior party figures were able to make instant contact with national audiences. Second, the Great Depression had begun in October 1929, when the New York stock market crashed. Given the state of the Canadian economy in the 1930s, some observers marvelled at Mackenzie King's luck in losing the 1930 election.

One reason for the loss was the popularity of the new Conservative leader, Calgary lawyer and businessman R.B. Bennett. He promised to fix the broken economy and put Canadians back to work. He had already put his party's electoral machinery to work, setting up a national office and hiring an experienced staff (whom he paid with his own money). Bennett's skillful campaign, combined with King's growing unpopularity, produced a Conservative majority including 24 seats in Quebec. But after five years, the Depression was still wracking the country—along with a severe Prairie drought that wrecked the region's agricultural sector.

Election #18, 1935: "King or Chaos"

The Liberals had an easy task in this campaign: most voters were already convinced that they could not trust the Conservatives to manage the economy for another five years. However, this sentiment did not necessarily translate into support for the Liberals. In response to Bennett's perceived lack of concern for the victims of the Depression and the "dust bowl," former Conservative Cabinet minister H.H. Stevens founded the Reconstruction Party. The 1935 election also marked the emergence of the CCF and Social Credit. All three of the protest parties siphoned Western votes from the Liberals and especially from the Conservatives. The CCF had been founded in Regina in 1933, and was made up of farm and labour groups, former Progressives, and socialists. It elected seven candidates in 1935; Social Credit won 17 seats on the Prairies, and Stevens won his own seat. The Conservatives were reduced to 40 seats, mostly in Ontario.

As Appendix 2.1 demonstrates, the Liberals received the same percentage of votes in 1935 as in 1930. The difference between victory and defeat lay in the distribution of the non-Liberal (or anti-Liberal) vote. In 1930 the Conservatives managed to collect almost half of the vote, because they were the only credible alternative. But by 1935 the non-Liberal vote was split among several parties, and the Tories could only manage 30 percent of the total. (See Chapter 3 for an explanation of Canada's electoral system and the impact of varying vote distributions.)

Election #23, 1957: The Unthinkable Happens— The Liberals Lose an Election

Although it may be difficult to imagine an election campaign without wall-to-wall television ads, the 1957 election was the first in which television played a significant role. Although the Liberals retained a television coach, only one Cabinet minister seized the opportunity to learn proper TV technique. Meanwhile, John Diefenbaker had a highly skilled campaign and public relations team. Diefenbaker's voice and speaking style were well suited to the new medium. St. Laurent loathed television, dismissing it as a tool to deceive the public.

These differences were more than cosmetic. The 1957 election campaign was unusually strongly focused on the party leaders. The Liberals, under 76-year-old St. Laurent, ran a dull campaign devoid of new ideas. Their image of arrogance, after 22 uninterrupted years in power, was particularly unflattering next to Diefenbaker's novelty and charisma. The Progressive Conservatives promised that a Diefenbaker government would be inclusive, modern, and above all *different*. Even though the Liberals captured 41 percent of the popular vote to the Progressive Conservatives' 39 percent, the Tories won more seats (112/265, compared with 105 for the Liberals and 45 for third parties). The election result shocked everyone, including most PC supporters; up to the very end of the campaign, polls suggested that the Liberals would win their sixth consecutive mandate.

Election #24, 1958: Diefenbaker Wins Big in a Snap

Only nine months after Diefenbaker's surprise 1957 victory, the Progressive Conservatives all but swept every province except Newfoundland. Diefenbaker's campaign emphasized a grand vision for the country including the rapid development of Canada's north. In a short time, Diefenbaker had transformed the Progressive Conservatives from an Ontario-based rump to a truly national party. Quebeckers did not warm up to new Liberal leader Lester Pearson, so they were open to their provincial government's exhortations to elect a strong contingent in the Diefenbaker government. The CCF was also badly hurt, falling from 25 seats in 1957 to only 8 in 1958. By the 1962 election, it would be defunct, replaced by the NDP of Tommy Douglas.

Election #25, 1962: The Beginning of the End for Diefenbaker

Diefenbaker encountered numerous problems in government, some of his own making. His PC Cabinet was at loggerheads with the public service, especially over defence and foreign policy. Diefenbaker believed that previous Liberal governments had been too cozy with the Americans, and he was reluctant to involve Canada too deeply in the Cold War with the Soviet Union. One flashpoint was his refusal to allow the Americans to arm their cruise missiles on Canadian

With a Diefenbaker win looking likely in 1958, this poster from the Quebec campaign advised people to vote for the Progressive Conservatives to ensure that the province would not be isolated entirely from the levers of power within the next government.

soil with nuclear warheads. Another was his poor personal relationship with US President Kennedy, who was a popular figure in Canada.

The perennial issue of Canadian–American relations was only one reason why the Progressive Conservatives could not repeat their 1958 landslide. Their weak Quebec MPs, most of whom were affiliated with the provincial Union Nationale rather than the PC Party, had not served their constituents well. The Union Nationale itself had nearly collapsed after the death of Premier Maurice Duplessis in 1959, and had been replaced in power by the Quebec Liberal Party. The Quiet Revolution was under way. As the provincial government pursued a vigorous program of economic and social modernization, Québécois nationalism grew. These factors, coupled with a widespread feeling that Diefenbaker had failed to deliver on his promises, cost the PC Party 36 of its 50 Quebec seats.

In the short term, the Liberals could not capitalize. The Ralliement créditiste du Québec came from nowhere to win 26 seats. The Liberals won only three more percentage points of the vote in 1962 than in 1958; but they managed to double their seats from 48 to 99. However, they only gained 10 seats in Quebec. For its part, the PC Party fell from 54 to 37 percent of the vote and from 208 to 116 Commons seats (out of 265). The new PC government would be the first of three consecutive minorities. Both of the main parties had lost support to "third" parties: the NDP and two Social Credit parties (Alberta and Quebec).

Election #26, 1963: The Return of the Liberals

After his party's poor showing in the 1962 election, Diefenbaker would have been well advised to keep his Cabinet united in order to avoid another dissolution. But in early 1963 his defence minister resigned over the nuclear missile issue, and the PC government collapsed. Diefenbaker's exhausted, divided troops faced a modern, vigorous Liberal Party—although Pearson himself belonged to the same generation as the discredited prime minister.

Partly because of slick advertising techniques borrowed from the Kennedy Democrats in the United States, the Liberals managed to win a plurality of the seats. They were helped by a dip in the Créditiste vote—the Liberals won 12 additional seats in Quebec—and by PC losses in Ontario and the Atlantic provinces. The Progressive Conservatives fell to 33 percent of the vote (to the Liberals' 42 percent). They would not form another government for 16 years.

Election #28, 1968: Trudeaumania

Trudeaumania was not just a response to the political and personal style of the new Liberal leader. Trudeau's political ideas also generated enthusiasm, particularly his call for a "Just Society" in Canada. His implacable opposition to Quebec nationalism also appealed to many Canadians who were alarmed by the Quiet Revolution.

Although the Liberals' popular vote rose by only 5 percentage points compared with 1965, they gained 24 seats and formed a majority government. They would remain in power for another 16 years, with one brief PC interregnum.

Election #31, 1979: The Clark Interlude

By the late 1970s, the Trudeau government was badly affected by political and personal scandals. Liberal strategists hoped to capitalize on Joe Clark's youthfulness and lack of experience, adopting the slogan "A Leader Must Be a Leader." The Progressive Conservatives stuck to their game plan, attacking the Liberals' poor management of the economy. In May 1979 the Progressive Conservatives won a minority government with 136 seats to the Liberals' 114. The NDP captured 26 seats and Social Credit managed to hold onto 6 seats. The Progressive Conservatives did well in Ontario (57 out of 95 seats) and in Alberta (21 out of 21 seats), but won only 2 seats in Quebec.

Balance of Power   February 3/79

This political cartoon by Duncan Macpherson from early 1979 depicts Pierre Trudeau and Joe Clark wooing NDP leader Ed Broadbent in the run-up to the election. The question of NDP support for one of the two main parties—particularly during a minority Parliament—has long been an important dynamic in Canadian politics.

Source: Copyright, Estate of Duncan Macpherson. Reprinted by permission of Torstar Syndication Services.

Election #33, 1984: The Mulroney Landslide

Almost immediately after the Liberals' 1980 election victory, the economy hit an iceberg. Inflation soared, the gross domestic product shrank, and the Liberals took the blame. The party, which had long been weak in the four Western provinces, provoked deep and lasting anger in Alberta with its National Energy Program (NEP). By fall 1980, when he introduced the NEP, Trudeau was also pursuing his cherished constitutional reform agenda. After two years of political and legal turmoil, the *Constitution Act, 1982* was proclaimed into law. Although Trudeau is fondly remembered today as the father of the *Canadian Charter of Rights and Freedoms*, his package of constitutional amendments had been adopted without the consent of the separatist Quebec government. So his greatest achievement was, and remains, widely unpopular in Quebec; the Liberal Party has never fully recovered.

Brian Mulroney crafted a shrewd appeal to disaffected Quebeckers, angry Western voters, and Canadians who just wanted a change from the Liberals. His Progressive Conservatives won 211 of 282 seats, the third-largest landslide in Canadian history. The Liberals suffered their worst defeat ever. They were reduced to 40 seats—only 10 more than the NDP. A large chunk of the electorate switched from the Liberals to the Progressive Conservatives in 1984; the most pressing goal of the new governing party was to hold on to them.

Election #35, 1993: The Electoral Earthquake

The 1993 election brought about one of the greatest political upheavals in Canadian history. The Progressive Conservatives under Brian Mulroney's successor, Kim Campbell, were reduced to 2 seats, while the NDP dropped to 9 seats. Their place in the Commons was taken by two new political parties: the Reform Party and the Bloc Québécois (BQ). While the Reform Party had a national base of support and ran candidates in all ridings (after 1988), its major appeal was in Western Canada. Ironically, the separatist BQ became Her Majesty's Loyal Opposition by winning the second-largest number of seats.

Election #40, 2008: Where Do We Go from Here?

Perhaps no election has ever left Canadians feeling so uninspired about the state of national politics as that of 2008. Stephen Harper had no sooner initiated fixed election dates than Canadians found themselves voting for the third time in only four-and-a-half years. Perhaps unsurprisingly, voter turnout was the lowest on record, and the day after, virtually nothing had changed; Harper's Conservatives had another minority.

While some Canadians implored Parliament to roll up their sleeves and make minority governments work, others lamented that a new fifth player (the Green Party) made it that much less likely that anyone could ever achieve a majority.

Indeed, the rancorous tone of the election season was set early with the controversy over whether Green leader Elizabeth May should be allowed to take part in the leaders' debates, while the low-brow nature of some election ads also put many Canadians off. It did not help that Canadians were simultaneously watching the historic and inspiring US campaign, which resulted in Barack Obama winning election to the White House.

Meanwhile, as noted previously in the main body of this chapter, electoral reform initiatives that might potentially undo certain problems afflicting Canada's electoral system have stumbled at the provincial level in recent years, with referendums being defeated in Ontario, Prince Edward Island, and twice in British Columbia.

It is often noted that shifts in party systems are marked by periods of uncertainty. Given the widespread sense among Canadians that recent elections and the resulting Parliaments have been found wanting, it is entirely possible that we may be experiencing the end of our current party system, and are on the cusp of yet another significant shift.

PART TWO
Legal and Institutional Framework

CHAPTER 3

Understanding Electoral Systems

Dennis Pilon

Introduction

Elections are complex events that involve competing interests and demands. To accommodate and sometimes moderate the potential for conflict that can emerge from any encounter between differing, strongly held, political views, elections are governed by a myriad of explicit and often highly technical rules that apply to both politicians and voters. Altogether, these rules comprise the electoral system of a given jurisdiction. At its best, an electoral system helps assure access, fairness, transparency, and equity in the political competition that occurs during an election campaign as well as the accuracy of election results. Not every electoral system necessarily accomplishes these normative objectives. Societies differ, times change, and needs change, all of which means that there can be no one perfect set of electoral rules that will suit everyone at all times. For these reasons, electoral systems must always remain essentially unfinished in their design, open to being "reformed" in one way or another. In addition, the rules of the political game are not free of politics either. Just how to "do" elections can itself be the subject of political dispute and struggle.

An electoral system is essentially the how-to manual for a modern democracy. Yet its rules are poorly understood by the public, despite their centrality to modern elections. Even political actors—politicians, party elites, media commentators—tend to be familiar only with those aspects of an electoral system that they engage with directly. This limited familiarity undoubtedly reflects the scope and complexity of modern electoral systems. The most recent *Canada Elections Act* runs to more than 340 pages, which means that clearly there are a lot of rules to be familiar with. And while some of these rules are simple and straightforward, others seem arcane and hopelessly complex. It may be helpful to think of an electoral system as similar to the code that runs in the background of a computer program. For example, when we open a word-processing program, we see a page and a toolbar, but behind the fancy graphics are complex mathematical codes that create the interface we see and shape the options we can choose from. In a similar way, elections appear to be all about the politicians, political parties, controversial issues, and media coverage—the stuff we see when we turn on the television or radio, or open a newspaper. But running in the background of every election is an electoral system, a complex body of rules and practices that gives shape to how elections are conducted and sets parameters that both politicians and voters must observe.

Electoral systems consist of rules on candidacy, party registration, enfranchisement, voting, vote counting, campaign spending, and more. Other chapters in this book take up a number of these areas. This chapter will focus on one key area—for some, *the* key area—of electoral systems: the voting system, or the rules governing how votes cast in an election are converted into representation in legislatures. To this end, the chapter will set out the component parts of a voting system, the basic structure of a range of voting systems, the diverse views on voting system effects, where voting systems come from, and recent initiatives in Canada toward voting system reform.[1]

Voting Systems

A voting system is the subset of electoral rules that determines how votes cast in an election will be translated into representation. The rules of a voting system guide the actions of both voters and those responsible for counting the ballots. The voting system sets out how voters should mark their ballots, how those votes should be aggregated before they are counted, and how winners will be determined. These three broad areas of concern are referred to as ballot design, districting, and voting formula (Rae 1971). Every voting system comprises these three distinct component parts (see Table 3.1).

The Component Parts of a Voting System

Ballot design involves how voters are to mark their ballots. Some ballots call for voters to mark their choice nominally, with either a check or an "X" next to their choice. Others ask voters to mark their choice ordinally, ranking the candidates in terms of preference (first, second, third, and so on).

Districting refers to the geographical area within which the votes will be gathered and counted as well as to the number of candidates to be elected. Sometimes the district is the whole country (as is the case in Israel), but typically districts are smaller, representing particular defined areas. Such districts may elect only one member, or two, or ten, or thirty, or more.

Voting formula refers to how the aggregated votes will be added up to determine a winner or winners. In some cases, a winner just needs to get a plurality of the votes, or more votes than any other individual candidate. In others, the winner must gain a majority of the votes cast. Finally, in still other cases, the formula allots representation in proportion to the votes cast for different competitors.

TABLE 3.1   Voting System Components

	Plurality	Majority	Proportional
Ballot design	Nominal	Nominal/ordinal	Nominal/ordinal
Districting	Single/multi-member	Single/multi-member	Multi-member/mixed
Formula	Plurality	Majority	Proportional

As can be seen, choices must be made with each component part of the voting system. When the factors of ballot design, districting, and formula are combined in different ways, they produce different voting systems. However, it should be noted that certain design elements are incompatible with others. For example, a plurality formula cannot be combined with a preference ballot structure, nor can a party list proportional representation (PR) system be instituted in a single-member district. This is where the "system" part comes in. The component parts of a voting system do not work in isolation; they have their effect through their systemic interaction.

Types of Voting Systems

There are essentially three major types of voting systems: plurality, majority, and proportional, with a smaller category of semi-proportional systems that do not fit neatly into the typology (see Table 3.2).

Plurality Voting Systems

Plurality voting systems combine single- or multi-member districts with the plurality voting formula and a ballot structure calling for a nominal "X" to indicate the voter's choice or choices. To gain election under this system, the winning candidate need only have more votes than any other individual candidate. If just two candidates are running, the winner will have more than 50 percent of the vote. But if three candidates are running, the winner could succeed with as little as 34 percent of the vote. Such results are not merely a statistical possibility. In the 2004 federal election, one candidate won his riding with just 27 percent of the total (Saskatoon/Humbolt). Canada and the United States use single-member plurality (SMP) for most elections, although both have used multi-member plurality for national and subnational elections in the past. Although multi-member plurality has fallen out of favour in recent years, it is still used in a few municipal contexts, such as Vancouver's ten-member city council. In a multi-member plurality election, voters have as many votes as there are candidates to be elected, and winners are the top vote-getters. For example, in Vancouver voters have ten votes and the election winners are the candidates with the top ten vote totals. The United Kingdom used plurality exclusively until recently, but now uses it only for national elections and local elections in England and Wales.

TABLE 3.2   Major Voting Systems

Voting system family	Voting system variants	Voting system use by country
Plurality	Single-member plurality	Canada, United States, United Kingdom
	Multi-member plurality	Canada, United States (some local elections)
Majority	Majority runoff	France
	Alternative vote	Australia (lower house)
Proportional	Party list	Norway, Sweden, Finland, Denmark, Belgium, Netherlands, Italy
	Mixed-member proportional	Germany, New Zealand
	Single transferable vote	Ireland, Malta, Australia (Senate)
Semi-proportional	Limited vote	United States (some municipal elections)
	Cumulative vote	United States (some school board elections)
	Single non-transferable vote	Japan (1947–1993)
	Mixed-member majority/ parallel	Japan, Italy (1994–2004)

Majority Voting Systems

Majority voting systems combine single- or multi-member districts with a majority voting formula and a ballot structure calling for either a nominal or an ordinal marking. There are basically two approaches to majority voting: the majority runoff system and the alternative vote system.

Majority Runoff

The majority runoff system requires voters to mark an "X" on their ballot; and if one candidate gains a majority in the first round of voting, that person wins the seat. But if no candidate gains a majority of the vote, a second round—literally a "run off"—of voting is held a few weeks later, usually involving just the two most popular candidates from the first ballot. In this way, by narrowing the field of candidates, usually one of the remaining candidates will gain a majority of the vote in the second round. In practice, majority runoff rules may vary: some countries require low vote-getters to drop off the ballot while others do not. Canadian political parties use a variation of the majority runoff system when they elect their leaders, although in these cases the rounds of balloting may continue beyond just two if a candidate has not secured a majority.

Alternative Vote

The other approach to majority voting is the alternative vote (AV) system. Here, voters are required to mark a numeric preference for the candidates on their ballot. At the end of balloting, the first preference choices for the candidates are added up; if a candidate has secured a majority of the ballots cast, she can be declared the winner. However, if no candidate has gained a majority of the votes cast, then the lowest vote-getter is eliminated and her ballots are redistributed on the basis of the second preferences indicated on the ballot. If a candidate now has a majority, a winner can be declared; if not, the process is repeated until someone does gain a majority.

Countries using these systems include France (majority runoff) and Australia (alternative vote). Both of these approaches to majority voting are typically conducted in single-member ridings, although multi-member ridings have been used in the past.

Proportional Voting Systems

Proportional voting systems are varied and flexible. They can combine single- and multi-member districting, or simply use one or a number of multi-member districts combined with a proportional voting formula and a ballot structure allowing for nominal or ordinal choices. There are three basic forms of PR: party list, mixed-member proportional, and the single transferable vote.

Party List

The party list form of PR uses multi-member districts in which voters typically indicate support for different lists of candidates representing different parties. After balloting, the votes are totalled and parties receive representation in proportion to the votes cast for them. Thus, if Party A gained 30 percent of the total vote, then the top 30 percent of the names on that party's list would be declared elected. In some cases, party list systems allow voters to give preference to particular names on a party list, and if enough voters alter the order of the list, it can alter the order of who gets taken off the party's list, although in practice such individual preferences usually have little impact on the results. Party list PR was commonly adopted in Western countries that changed their voting system in the early 20th century, and today is associated with the Scandinavian and Benelux countries.

Mixed-Member Proportional

The mixed-member proportional (MMP) form of PR uses both single-member and multi-member districts in which voters usually mark two ballots, one for an individual running in the local single-member riding, and one for their party preference from a national party list. After balloting, the results of the local contests are added up according to plurality voting rules, and then the party ballot results are totalled. The party ballot results are used to establish what the overall proportional results of the election should be. If a party gains 30 percent of the party vote, then it is entitled to 30 percent of the total seats when the election is completed. To determine which members of Party A will gain election, a number of steps must be taken. First, any members of Party A who have won the local single-member plurality contests are declared elected. Second, these winners are subtracted from the total percentage of seats to be accorded to Party A. Finally, the rest of Party A's representatives are drawn from the party list. Let's say that Party A's victories in the local ridings amount to 15 percent of the total seats up for election. Because Party A won 30 percent of the party vote, it is still entitled to another 15 percent of the total representation available, which would then be drawn from its list in the order established by the party. In a sense, MMP looks like two elections: one in which parties win local ridings and another in which the party list process compensates parties whose popular vote exceeds the percentage of seats won in the local contests. This system was invented in postwar Germany and was most recently introduced in New Zealand.

Single Transferable Vote

The single transferable vote (STV) form of PR uses multi-member districts that typically range in size from three to five members. Here, voters mark their choices preferentially (first, second, third, etc.) across the range of individual candidates contesting the election. To win a seat, a candidate must win a quota or proportion of the overall vote. For instance, in a five-member riding, a winner would require roughly 20 percent of the total votes to secure election. After balloting, the votes are totalled on the basis of the first preferences marked. If a candidate has achieved the quota, that person is declared elected. If no candidate has achieved the quota, then the lowest vote-getter is dropped and his or her ballots are redistributed on the basis of the second preferences marked. This process is repeated until someone gains a quota and is thus elected. When someone achieves the quota, the votes gained in excess of the quota are also redistributed, although only for a portion of their original value. Let's say that Candidate A has achieved twice the quota. What this means is that she really only requires half of each vote cast for her to secure election—the other half of each vote can go to help someone else gain election. This is how STV produces proportional results. Of course, not all examples are so mathematically simple, and today computer counting is popular for STV elections. This process of elimination goes on until all the positions in the multi-member riding have been filled. STV is currently used in Ireland, Malta, and at various levels of government in Australia. Historically, STV was widely used in Canada, with provincial applications in urban ridings in Alberta and Manitoba and municipal applications in Winnipeg, Calgary, Vancouver, and 16 other local governments (Pilon 2006).

Semi-Proportional Voting Systems

Systems in the last subcategory of voting systems are often referred to as "semi-proportional" because they produce results that are not fully proportional but tend to offer better minority representation than either plurality or majority voting systems. Three of these systems are actually variants of multi-member plurality voting: the limited vote, including the single non-transferable vote; the cumulative vote; and the mixed-member majority system.

Limited Vote

With the limited vote, electors in a multi-member constituency have fewer votes than the positions to be filled. For example, in a three-member riding with limited voting, voters would have two votes. What this means is that a minority that votes strategically will have a good chance of gaining representation because the "limit" on the votes prevents the largest group of voters from winning everything. The single non-transferable vote (SNTV) is a more extreme form of the limited vote because it limits the number of votes that voters may cast to one. This has the effect of forcing both major and minor competitors to be very strategic in assessing their voting support and how many candidates they should run.

The limited vote was used historically in the United Kingdom and Ontario, and is currently used for a host of local elections in the United States. SNTV was long used in Japan, Taiwan, and South Korea, although recently some of these countries have adopted different systems.

Cumulative Vote

The cumulative vote operates in an opposite fashion to the limited vote. Instead of limiting the number of votes an elector can cast, the cumulative vote allows him or her to cast multiple votes for the same candidate. For example, voters in a three-member riding would get three votes, which they could cast in any combination for a single candidate or multiple candidates. They could give one vote to one candidate and two votes to another, one vote to three different candidates, or all three votes to one candidate.

The cumulative vote was used historically for school board elections in the United Kingdom and has been mandated by the US courts for use in a number of school board elections, particularly across the American South. It was also used for a hundred years in Illinois for state elections.

Mixed-Member Majority System

The most recent semi-proportional voting system to emerge has been the mixed-member majority system (MMM), which is also known as a *non-compensatory mixed system* or the *parallel system*. Basically, this system looks like the MMP system, with legislative representation split between single-member riding MPs and party list MPs. The key difference between this system and MMP is that there is no compensatory relationship between the two levels of representation. What this means is that the two arenas—the local choice and the party list choice—run "parallel" to each other as self-contained elections, leading to results that may depart substantially from proportionality. For example, let's say that there are 100 seats to be elected, half in single-member ridings and half from a party list pool. When the votes are counted, Party A has won 40 local riding seats and 40 percent of the party list votes. Under MMP rules, Party A would be awarded no more seats because the 40 local riding victories already equal 40 percent of the party list total. However, under the parallel system, Party A would win the local 40 seats and be awarded 40 percent of the party list pool as well, adding 20 more seats to the party's total seats.

The parallel system offers something to smaller parties in that it has a party list pool of seats. However, in its larger workings this system tends to inflate support for larger parties, leading to less-than-proportional results overall. The parallel system has been recently introduced in Japan, Russia, and a host of other countries.

Voting System Effects

Any debate over voting systems is really a debate over voting system *effects*. In Canada, proponents of change assume that the adoption of a different voting system would allow voters and parties to act differently. Thus, it is not merely that different voting systems count votes differently, it is that different voting system arrangements alter the incentives that voters and parties have to do certain things, either to vote for one party over another, or to try to appeal to one group of voters over another, et cetera. Defenders of our plurality voting system highlight the potential effects of change, painting a gloomy picture of minority or coalition government, a proliferation of parties, and a general increase in political instability. Yet before the substance of these claims can be explored, we must address a more elementary question, one that the pro and con sides may overlook, which is whether we can say that voting rules have any real impact at all. Academics fall across the range of debate: some argue that voting systems have a strong impact, others suggest that the effects of voting systems are mild, and still others claim that voting systems have no discernible effects at all.

Academic Debates Over the Importance of Voting Systems

Academics have long debated the importance of voting systems. On one side, some believed that voting systems were largely a result of or response to other social and political forces. Lipset and Rokkan argued that different voting systems, following party systems, resulted from differing patterns of social and political cleavages in modern societies. Thus, societies with few social cleavages used plurality or majority voting systems, while societies divided by multiple social cleavages opted for proportional voting systems. In this model, then, the voting system is an effect or result of other political forces (Lipset and Rokkan 1967; Rokkan 1970). On the other side, some argued that voting systems conditioned or created the party systems. Duverger argued that the voting system was the key causal factor in determining the nature of the party system in a given locale. Thus, the use of plurality or majority voting contributed to the existence of a two-party system, while the use of proportional voting allowed the multiparty system to emerge. In this model, the voting system is the cause of the political results, such as the kind of party system that is produced (Duverger 1954). Although a great deal of debate has ensued over these points, they are not in fact mutually exclusive. It is possible both that social factors contribute to the adoption of a particular voting system and that, once adopted, the voting system conditions the nature of political competition.

Few serious scholars today hold to either extreme view—that is, that voting systems have no effect on political results or that voting systems are the key factor affecting political results. Instead, the real debate is about the relative weight of voting system effects and whether the trade-offs produced by any given system are worthwhile. Some academics admit that Canada's use of the single-member plurality system does exert some influence on the results of our elections, but they would add that it is just one factor among many and as such not terribly important. Others argue that the use of our SMP system has not prevented new parties or ideas from emerging in Canada when these became sufficiently popular (Courtney 1999). Still others suggest that SMP clearly affects who and what is represented in our legislatures, but in the end this is not very important because it has little impact on how our executive-Cabinet form of government operates in Parliament (Aucoin and Smith 1997). Some point to the high degree of turnover in the membership of the House of Commons, suggesting that this proves that our current system is already quite responsive to what voters want (Lortie 1997). Others argue pragmatically that changing political structures will be very difficult and only take resources away from more important challenges to the substance of politics (Jenson 1997). In all of these defences, there is a bias that political organizing, mobilization, or the countervailing influence of other institutions can and will ultimately trump any of the admitted effects of the voting system.

The Mechanical and Psychological Effects of Voting Systems

Such defences ignore the ways in which voting system effects are dynamic, shaping not just static results but the very process of contestation from which results emerge. Duverger (1954) characterized it as a combination of mechanical and psychological effects. *Mechanical effects* refer to the observable qualities of a voting system. Plurality, for instance, will reward voting support that is concentrated geographically over voting support that is more dispersed and spread out. In Canada this has meant that regionally concentrated parties like Social Credit and the Bloc Québécois tend to be overrepresented, while more regionally dispersed national parties like the NDP are consistently underrepresented. A PR system, by contrast, would probably respond to voting support more equally regardless of where the votes are cast. Such effects are easy to track and quantify.

Voting systems also have *psychological effects*. For example, because plurality systems tend to discriminate against voting support that is dispersed, some voters may decide not to support political options that they fear are not popular in their geographic area. Of course, the end result is a self-fulfilling prophecy. Because people fear that their choice may be unpopular in their area, they vote for something else, thus helping to make their fear a reality. These sorts of psychological effects, although more difficult to track and prove than mechanical effects, are nonetheless real. Thus, the fact that new parties emerge in Canada from time to time or a great many MPs fail to get re-elected does not necessarily vindicate our present electoral arrangements. Neither tell us very much about the impact of our current system.

An appreciation of these mechanical and psychological effects leads to a shift in emphasis about the relative weight of the voting system in affecting political results in Canada. All the stuff of politics—culture, organization, issues, mobilization—matters, but gauging how they interact in the context of the voting system is also crucial to understanding Canada's political system and its results. The importance of this interaction can be seen in a couple of areas. First, the voting system affects the incentive structure for both parties and voters. Both make decisions about how to act based on how effectively they think they can get their message across and achieve results through the existing institutional arrangements. Second, the voting system affects the kind and degree of diversity that is represented in our legislatures, from the diversity of party viewpoints to the social diversity embodied in the elected members. How accurately the election results reflect what the public wants, or whether parties make an effort to represent everyone in society, is crucially influenced by the choice of voting system.

The effects of voting systems, then, are less about the production of specific results and more about affecting the nature of political competition. This conclusion cuts across both the strong and weak "effects" positions in the academic debates. The strong position held that PR would lead to a multiparty system and plurality would lead to a two-party system, while the weak position argued that demands from society would overcome institutional constraints. The evidence over the last 50 years shows that a number of PR-using countries have had small party systems (Germany, Austria), and a number of plurality-using countries have had multiparty systems (Canada, India). This evidence would seem to support the weak effects position. On the other hand, we can point to recent changes in voting systems that appear to have allowed for an expansion of the party system, particularly in the conversion from plurality to PR, and some dynamic changes in the social diversity of the representatives (New Zealand). This evidence would seem to support the strong effects position. In fact, neither position captures what is going on. Instead, we need a model that combines social and institutional factors, recognizing that a change in institutions may affect how politics works, but that it does not produce any specific results on its own. As Peter Mair notes, voting systems "provide at best 'facilitating conditions,' the impact of which will also be mediated by a variety of other institutional cultural factors" (1992, 85). In a nutshell, voting systems are like the aperture through which politics tries to flow—they are basically more or less permissive, more or less competitive. The dam affects the flow of water, but not if there isn't any water flowing.

Assessing Voting System Effects

Voting system effects are not automatic or unaffected by social context, but researchers have highlighted some broad generalizations about their workings nonetheless. Here, we will briefly review some of the typical effects attributed to plurality voting systems and various forms of PR, and the academic debates as they pertain to the Canadian context.

Researchers who study the effects of plurality voting have identified a number of general tendencies associated with the system. First, plurality voting systems typically produce single-party legislative majority governments because of the system's tendency to overrepresent the leading vote-getter. Thus, parties that gain between 40 percent and 50 percent of the popular vote may expect to gain 60 percent to 75 percent of the seats, depending on how the opposition vote is divided. Second, plurality voting systems tend to discourage the formation of new parties and hinder the success of third parties because to gain access to the system, such competitors must be able to come first in a riding against the existing major parties. Third, plurality voting systems tend to reward parties with geographically concentrated support over parties with more dispersed levels of support (Blais 1991, 240–243; Norris 2004, 84–98). What these tendencies amount to is a voting system regularly associated with single-party majority government and a fairly small, stable two-party system—one in which each competitor regularly alternates as the government and opposition, with perhaps one more party emerging from time to time that focuses on regional demands (Powell 2000).

On the whole, plurality's defenders tend to approve of its general tendencies as a necessary set of limits that help democracies function. Thus, for them, plurality's tendency to create majority governments out of minority voting support for the leading party is a good thing because it contributes to government stability and clarifies just who is responsible for policy outcomes. This means that a government can effectively introduce policies, and voters know whom to hold accountable for them. If voters are unhappy with the government, plurality's tendency to overrepresent can work for the opposition as voters shift their support and "throw the rascals out." Plurality's defenders also applaud the system's tendency to restrict party competition as they see this as an effective check on extremism and an incentive to political co-operation. As new parties face serious obstacles to break into the system, political interests are instead encouraged to work within existing "big tent" parties that can broker an effective consensus among different views (Powell 2000). John Courtney (1999) claims that Canada's plurality system has led to the creation of "pan-Canadian" political parties capable of brokering the difficult compromises necessary to keep the country together. The geographic bias of plurality is also defended as a key element of local representation and accountability in the larger political system.

Needless to say, such assessments of plurality have fuelled much debate. For example, the facts in the Canadian context seem at odds with these generalizations. In 27 federal elections since 1921 (which signalled the end of the traditional two-party system), the country has produced only a slight tendency for majority government, with 16 legislative majority governments elected versus 11 minority governments. And far from the two-party ideal, the Canadian Parliament has been a three-, four-, and five-party system at different times in this period. Alternation in government has also been uncommon, with the federal Liberals winning 19 of the 27 elections and governing for 65 of 88 years since 1921. Despite claims by Courtney and others that plurality would encourage big tent parties to reach out across the country, the election results demonstrate a regular failure of parties to do so. A decade before Courtney's observations, Alan Cairns (1968) had already pointed out that exaggerated regionalism was a much more typical result of our voting system than pan-Canadianism. Since then, the regionalizing tendencies of our voting system have been only too apparent, particularly in the 1980 election that witnessed a majority Liberal government gain no seats in the West despite considerable voting support, and the 1993 federal election, which translated what were diverse views across the country into regionalized blocs of support for one party or another (Swayze 1996). Since 2004, this exaggerated regional representation, particularly in Quebec and Alberta, has contributed to a succession of minority governments at the federal level.

Of course, where governments are elected with a majority of the legislative seats under plurality, they can act decisively, just as the voting system studies suggest. Thus Mulroney's Conservative majority in 1988 was widely interpreted as an endorsement of his policy to pursue a free trade agreement with the United States, one his government quickly acted on. However, recently critics have wondered if such "efficiency" itself is desirable, especially considering that such legislative majority governments seldom enjoy a majority of the popular vote. Mulroney's free trade "majority" really only represented 42 percent of the electorate (Law Commission of Canada 2004). Indeed, since 1921, only two single-party governments (1940, 1958) have been elected with a clear majority—51 percent or more—of the popular vote. Other concerns about Canada's experience with plurality involve questions of representation, specifically the underrepresentation of women compared with other Western industrialized countries, and the undue strategic calculations that the system requires of voters to assure that they do not "waste" their vote on an uncompetitive local candidate. Still, in comparative studies of voter attitudes to democratic institutions, Canadians rank theirs highly, even though they give poor marks to the political system as a whole (Nevitte 2002). Whether out of ignorance, self-interest, or enlightened approval, it would appear that the recent populist ire of Canadian voters against politicians does not extend to the voting system.

Researchers studying the long-term effects of PR have underlined a number of general tendencies with these systems. First, PR systems tend to produce either a minority or a coalition government. This occurs because the systems tend to produce legislative results that roughly mirror the popular vote for parties and, because no one party typically gains a majority of the votes, no one party gets a majority of the seats. Second, PR systems are more open to multiparty competition because the threshold for election is lower and the district from which votes are drawn is bigger. Thus, in PR systems, a new political competitor need only gain a quota of the total votes in a fairly large district rather than secure more votes than all others in a much smaller riding, as is the case in plurality systems. Third, PR systems tend to be more broadly representative, in terms of both the diversity of parties that are included in the legislature and governing ranks as well as the diversity of individual legislators (Blais 1991, 243–246; Norris 2004, 88–93, 187). What these tendencies amount to in Western countries is a voting system regularly associated with multiparty coalition government and a fairly stable multiparty system—one in which new competitors have access to the system, coalitions of parties (typically comprising a dominant party and a smaller ally or allies) alternate in government, and representatives better reflect the social diversity of the polity (Powell 2000).

Critics of PR paint a different picture of its general tendencies, claiming it can contribute to government instability, a fragmented party system, legislative sclerosis, domineering parties, and a lack of clear accountability between government actions and the politicians responsible. Many of these claims often appear overstated and/or poorly supported. In terms of governing stability or policy implementation, for example, there is much evidence that PR systems in postwar Western European countries have managed both effectively (Lijphart 1999). Moreover, party dominance is a fact of life in all Western political systems, regardless of voting system. However, in three areas—policy efficiency, government formation, and voters' control over specific politicians—there is something to the concerns raised about PR systems. It is fair to suggest that decision making in PR systems is less decisive and efficient, largely as a result of coalition politics. As no one party will probably have the votes to implement its policies alone, a lengthy process of policy brokering may take place. It is also true that the connection between voting and government formation is less direct in PR systems than in plurality systems because governments in PR are usually a coalition of different parties. Sometimes these coalitions are put together after the election, although in many cases voters do know ahead of the election date which parties plan to work with each other. Finally, voters' ability to discipline particular politicians is less likely in PR systems because local representation is typically weak (Germany) or non-existent (party list PR systems). However, the latter is not true for the STV form of PR, used in Ireland, where local accountability is considered to be very high (Marsh 2007).

Of course, the seriousness of the complaints made against PR depend on the value one places on these particular attributes. Some suggest that a long-term brokering of a policy consensus is preferable to an efficient introduction of policy, precisely because the former will have stronger elite and public support behind it, and thus said policies stand a greater chance of succeeding (Lijphart 1999). Others might see the weaker direct public influence over government formation as an acceptable trade-off for more representative results in terms of party and social diversity, and, by extension, greater pluralism in the voices heard in the deliberations (Pilon 2007). Finally, the concern that PR systems lack local representation assumes that this feature accomplishes a great deal in other voting systems—and there is no consensus on this point (Curtice and Shively 2000; Morgenstern and Swindle 2006).

Where Do Voting Systems Come From?

Canada remains one of just three major Western countries that use the plurality voting system. The United States and the United Kingdom also use it, although British loyalty to the system may be waning—over the last decade, the UK introduced a host of proportional voting systems for regional and local elections. Everywhere else, people vote using other methods. A few Western countries use majority voting (France, Australia) but, on the whole, most Western democracies use some form of proportional representation. In fact, they have been using proportional methods of voting for nearly a century. Tellingly, none of the newly democratizing countries in the former Soviet bloc or the Global South have opted for first-past-the-post either.

So why does Canada use the plurality system? Why do most other Western countries use something else? Some say that institutions like voting systems mirror the broad cultures in which they are used, that the Anglo-American democracies are "adversarial" and thus favour the all-or-nothing approach of plurality while European countries are allegedly more consensual and thus favour the more inclusive, cooperative style of PR. Others suggest that these institutions emerged and remain in place somehow through the consent of the governed. But such explanations quickly falter when confronted with the actual historical record of the origins of Western voting systems and their reform. In Canada, as elsewhere, voting systems emerged from struggles over power, not principle, while their reform was often fuelled by considerations of partisan advantage.

The History of Voting System Reform in Canada

There has been considerably more debate over, and change to, Canadian voting systems than most contemporary political analysts realize (this section draws from Pilon 2006). Political self-interest fuelled early calls for proportional voting at the federal level from some Ontario Liberals in the 1870s and Quebec Conservatives in the first decade of the 20th century. Provincial Liberals in Ontario were responsible for the country's first voting system reform in 1885, introducing the limited vote in Toronto to break the Tory stranglehold on the city's MPPs. From the First World War to the 1950s, the voting system and its reform was a regular topic of debate and struggle at all levels of government and in most areas of the country.

At the federal level, proposals for voting system reform were discussed every decade from the First World War to the late 1940s. Parliamentary committees produced reports on the subject in the 1920s and 1930s, and a vote to experiment with proportional voting in a few urban ridings held in 1923 gained considerable support, although not enough to pass. Indeed, the failure of PR to be introduced in the 1920s was, on the surface, somewhat surprising in that two of the three parties elected to the 1921 Parliament, together comprising a majority of voting members, had committed themselves in the election campaign to the introduction of proportional voting. But, here too, examining party interests is informative. What had changed between 1921 and 1923 was the federal Liberal Party's sense of confidence about its political future. Before the 1921 election, the Liberals appeared to be unravelling under the pressure of the wartime split in the party that divided English and French members, and the move by farmers and labour—usually key constituencies in the Liberal coalition—to run under their own party banners after the war. After the election, however, despite the breakthrough for the farmers' Progressive Party and the minority governing status of the Liberals, the party felt more confident about eventually recouping its losses. But the Liberals would continue to dangle voting reform before voters and other parties over the next decade whenever conditions appeared to be disadvantageous to their party.

Although voting reform stalled federally, it occurred at the municipal and provincial levels. Over the interwar period, 19 towns across Western Canada adopted proportional voting systems for civic elections, while Alberta and Manitoba both adopted mixed majority/PR voting systems for provincial elections. Elite and party self-interest did not motivate all of these changes, although it was key for the ones that remained in place for any length of time. During and after the First World War, idealistic civic reformers were successful at getting PR adopted either by referendum or by a vote of city council in a number of smaller Canadian towns. But they could not keep these new voting systems on the basis of civic reform arguments. In most locales, voters quickly grew tired of the complicated counting procedures required for proportional voting, the delays in getting the results, and the fact that the system did not seem to produce markedly different results that might have been achieved under a plurality voting system. Small towns like Nelson, New Westminster, and Mission, British Columbia, used PR once and then sought repeal almost immediately.

But where politics was sharply divided, particularly along class lines, voting system reforms tended to be motivated by the self-interest of traditional parties, and these changes proved more long-lasting. Manitoba's Liberal government rushed through changes to municipal and provincial voting systems in 1920, fearing that political support for organized labour was rising precipitously. Around the same time in Alberta, the newly elected United Farmers government introduced similar changes to benefit itself and divide its opponents in the traditional parties. In each case, values took a back seat to political expediency. Both provinces gained extensive experience with these majority and proportional voting systems, using them from the 1920s to the 1950s.

After the Second World War, interest in voting system reform again rose in the face of political uncertainty. At the federal level, some Liberal and Conservative MPs worried about rising support for the socialist Co-operative Commonwealth Federation (CCF), especially in the wake of the CCF's election to provincial government in Saskatchewan in 1944 and the party's surprisingly strong showing in Ontario in 1943. Many MPs and influential business groups thought some kind of majority voting was required at the federal level to keep the CCF out of power nationally. Interest was particularly strong in the run-up to the 1945 and 1949 federal elections. But the CCF breakthrough never came, and interest in the issue died out.

At the provincial level, voting system reform remained a hot topic in certain locales. In British Columbia, a coalition of Liberals and Conservatives had ruled the province for most of the 1940s. After the 1941 election, in which the CCF emerged with the most votes, the two traditional parties decided to work together rather than let the left "go up the middle" between them and win on a vote split. Although the coalition was successful and popular as a governing body through two elections, there was constant pressure within the different parties for the coalition to end. When the arrangement finally broke down in 1951, the government introduced a majority voting system to prevent the CCF from benefiting from vote splits between Liberal and Conservative voters. The plan worked, but the former coalition partners were outflanked by a new centre-right populist party called Social Credit.

The repeal of the majority and PR systems in Canada's Western provinces was also motivated by party interests rather than principle or values. In British Columbia, the new governing Social Credit Party turned its minority government of 1952 into a majority government in 1953. Although majority voting had helped secure its surprise victory, the party decided that it didn't need majority voting anymore and returned to plurality voting instead. In 1955 and 1956, Alberta and Manitoba also abandoned their voting systems in favour of a return to plurality voting. Although all sorts of public-spirited rationales were offered for the decisions, the evidence is fairly clear that party self-interest was paramount in motivating the changes.

The Modern Period of Voting System Reform

Another discussion of voting system reform began in Canada just as the last remnants of the former period were extinguished. Winnipeg was nominally still using a proportional voting system for city elections when the Manitoba provincial government amalgamated it into its surrounding suburbs in 1972, an occasion that allowed a complete government restructuring and return to traditional plurality voting. A year later, Calgary also removed the last remnants of its half-century of municipal voting reform when it repealed the majoritarian alternative vote in favour of plurality as well (reforms in the early 1960s had converted the city's STV system to an AV system). Yet just four years later, interest in proportional voting systems on the national scene was resurrected in response to the separatist threat embodied in the election of the Parti Québécois as a provincial government in 1976. Three years later, the Pépin-Robarts Task Force on Canadian Unity called for a very modest and only mildly proportional reform to Canada's voting system.

In the same year, Canadian political scientist William Irvine published the first serious political monograph on the question, entitled *Does Canada Need a New Electoral System?* His answer was yes, and he was not alone—a number of other respected political analysts also thought some kind of mild reform was in order (Irvine 1979). The NDP's Ed Broadbent attempted to get the issue moving politically during debates over redistricting in 1978, and was offered a chance to put a proposal on the issue to the House by Pierre Trudeau in 1981 (whose Liberals were still smarting over being shut out of the West despite considerable voting support in the 1980 election). However, provincial NDP forces vetoed his efforts. In various proposals, PR or a limited form of PR was touted as a potential salve for resurgent regional woes, the crisis of Canadian unity, and the call to balance the representation of the major parties in all parts of the country (Seidle 1996). But nothing ultimately happened. Regionalism, Canadian unity, the balkanization of party support in successive elections—these issues did not prove serious enough to motivate any governing party in Canada to consider voting system reform. Even the sop to PR in the 1992 Charlottetown Accord, where the to-be-elected Senate would use STV, was quickly traded away by political elites before the deal came to a public vote.

Although Canadian voting system reform initiatives appeared stalled, there were surprising and unexpected changes effected in other Western countries (for various treatments, see Shugart and Wattenberg 2001; Colomer 2004; Gallagher and Mitchell 2005; Blais 2008). Political scientists had long characterized voting systems as nearly impossible to change, given the political self-interest of politicians in maintaining the rules that benefited them. Nonetheless, by the 1990s, France, New Zealand, Italy, Japan, and the United Kingdom had all reformed aspects of their voting systems. Some were short lived (France), or directed at lower-level jurisdictions (United Kingdom), but all involved political struggles that had deep economic implications. In the UK and France, voting system reform was part of a political initiative by the left to move to the centre of the political spectrum. In Italy and Japan, political elites latched on to voting system reform as a means of breaking up traditional political allegiances, particularly those defining the country's economic trajectory. Meanwhile, in New Zealand voting system reform emerged as a reaction to the Labour Party's move to the right and embrace of neo-liberal economic policy.

In Canada, the voting system also came back to prominence by the end of the century. The breakup of Canada's traditional party system in the 1990s brought renewed attention to the distortions of the SMP system, highlighting its regional over-representation and often extreme distortions between party votes and party seats. The three-party system of the 1980s gave way to a five-party system in the 1990s, and then a four-party system after 2003. Yet there was no return to politics as usual. Instead, the four-party system contributed to the election of minority governments in 2004, 2006, and 2008. At the same time, concerns over declining voter turnout and the apparently rising public hostility to conventional politics moved some elites to reconsider voting system change as a potential solution (Seidle 2002; Tanguay 2009). Pushing elite interest was the rise of new public advocacy groups (for example, Democracy Watch, Fair Vote Canada) focusing on democratic reform, specifically the voting system, as well as increased academic interest. By 2003, PR was consistently making the agenda of proposed solutions to Canada's "democratic deficit." For example, in 2004 the Law Commission of Canada released a report calling for the introduction of a mixed-member proportional voting system for federal elections. But despite the persistence of a federal multiparty system, some discussion in Parliament, and an increase in media interest in the issue, the traditional national parties have shown little desire for voting system reform. Instead, most of the debate on the question has remained at the provincial level, with discussions in Prince Edward Island, New Brunswick, Quebec, Ontario, and British Columbia.

Provincial Initiatives

Provincial interest in voting system reform emerged for a host of reasons, some similar to the federal level, some entirely different (see various chapters in Milner 2004; Massicotte 2008). Similar to federal experience, public opinion about government and politicians at the provincial level had been sinking for some time along with voter turnout. A number of provincial politicians thought a consideration of voting system reform might reverse these trends. But in a departure from federal experience, provincial election results delivered a series of seemingly perverse results throughout the 1990s. In the Maritimes, opposition parties were often reduced to a handful of seats despite considerable support, thus limiting how effective they could be as the opposition and calling the legitimacy of the system into question. Governments in Prince

Edward Island and New Brunswick began studying voting system reform as a means of correcting this problem. In Quebec and British Columbia, elections took place in which the party with the most votes did not "win" the election. Such counter-intuitive results moved the parties affected to promise a review of the voting system if they gained power. Meanwhile, in Ontario the Liberal Party made consideration of voting system reform one of its democratic reform planks in the run-up to the 2003 provincial election. When these governments came to power, they did follow through on their promises to consider reform, although all dragged their feet on the issue for most of their first mandate. Again, the rise of public advocacy groups focusing on voting systems—Fair Voting BC, Mouvement pour une démocratie nouvelle in Quebec, and Fair Vote Canada—made a difference in keeping the issue on the agenda.

Events started rolling when Quebec and British Columbia struck their reform bodies. Quebec used a combination of legislative committees and public consultations to consider changes to the voting system. As all three legislative parties had committed to voting system reform in the election campaign of 2003, a consensus for change appeared highly likely, and indeed early on a proposal for a non-proportional mixed voting system emerged. Over the next few years the government continued to pledge support for the change, although specific details about when the system would be introduced or take effect kept changing.

In late 2003, British Columbia's Liberal government made good on its promise to create a public body to study the provincial voting system and perhaps make recommendations for change that would be subject to a referendum. The BC Citizens' Assembly on Electoral Reform (BC-CA) comprised 161 people chosen randomly to represent each riding across the province. After a year of learning about voting systems, hearing from other citizens and experts, and deliberating among themselves, the BC-CA recommended that BC adopt an STV form of PR. Despite indifference from the media and a lack of adequate funds from government to promote the vote, nearly 58 percent of voters in the 2005 referendum were prepared to try out the new system, even though few really understood how it worked. However, as the government had established a super-majority rule for the referendum to pass, 58 percent was declared a defeat. Although it was pressured to introduce the change anyway, the government refused and instead offered another vote on the question in the 2009 election as a compromise. In the Maritimes, Prince Edward Island moved quickly from a report recommending a vote on a mixed-member proportional system to a vote in November 2005. In the same year, the New Brunswick government agreed to abide by the direction of an expert panel on voting systems about how to consider reform, and Ontario's Liberal government established the terms for their Citizens' Assembly, modelled roughly on the BC process.

But despite all this activity, the commitment of provincial politicians to the issue has proven to be largely superficial. In each case, the governments have acted to either stall the decision-making process or rig the process against the likelihood of change. Thus, the Quebec government kept consulting on the question and putting off the decision about when the new system would be introduced or take effect (Cliche and

Charbonneau 2006; Massicotte 2008). The election of a majority Liberal government in the province in 2008 appeared to signal an end to the discussion for the time being. In British Columbia, the government lumbered the referendum process with a super-majority rule, a decision with no precedent in either voting system reform or Canada's use of referendums, and starved the public education budget of funds in 2005 (Pilon 2007). In the rerun of the referendum in 2009, the government did provide $500,000 to both the Yes and No campaigns, but it appeared to have little impact on helping the public become informed on the issue. On election day 2009, the 2005 results were basically reversed: the STV received just 39 percent of the vote, while the first-past-the-post system received 61 percent. Yet many voters complained that they were unaware of the referendum or the rationale for it. In Prince Edward Island, the government kept changing the rules of the process in the weeks before the vote, including what would be considered a winning threshold, while refusing to fund public education or open enough polling stations on the voting day (McKenna 2006). Not surprisingly, 64 percent of PEI voters stuck with traditional voting methods. New Brunswick's Conservative premier committed to a referendum vote on a PR system for 2008, but then called a snap provincial election in 2006 before allowing voters to decide on the issue. His successor promptly declined to follow through with the previous government's commitment. In Ontario, the government waited until late in its first term to finally act on its commitment to create a Citizens' Assembly, thus limiting public exposure to the process and reform ideas before a vote might be taken. It also followed British Columbia's cynical lead of imposing a super-majority requirement on the result. The Ontario media attacked both the Citizens' Assembly and its voting reform proposal, and failed to provide either substantive or balanced coverage on the issue. Again, most voters pleaded ignorance about both the referendum and its substance and opted to endorse the status quo by a whopping margin—63 percent (Leduc, Bastedo, and Baquero 2008; Cutler and Fournier 2008). The result of all this effort has been no voting system change at all.

It is telling to compare the successful voting system reforms in other countries recently or those in Canada's past with the consistent pattern of failure of efforts to reform Canada's voting system over the past four decades. Attempts to dislodge plurality based on regional issues, Canadian unity, distorted party standings, and—most recently—concerns about declining public confidence in the political system have all proven insufficient motivators for change. Without some party—specifically, a potentially governing party—seeing change as being in its electoral self-interest, the chances of reform appear to diminish considerably. Internationally, changes occurred as part of a process of shifting the left toward the centre of the political spectrum and a struggle over the national or international orientation of the economy, depending on how that affected the larger party system. In some cases, PR was part of a struggle to prevent that shift (New Zealand), while in others it was part of helping it come to pass (Italy, Japan, and the United Kingdom). But Canadian circumstances are different, and the electoral left and the national/international aspects of the economy do not play the same signal role in our party system as they do in other Western systems. This may prove a crucial stumbling block to change. Or it may mean that wholly new factors might come into play, such as the mobilization of the electorate for a referendum or a court challenge to the existing system based on Charter guarantees of equality.

Conclusion

Electoral systems are complex bodies of rules that guide modern democratic practices, although they operate largely unnoticed by most of the public. Primarily, this is because of their complexity and, frankly, their yawn-inducing dryness. Complex or not, most rules seem deadly dull. Many electoral system rules are administrative and uncontroversial—but not all. Some rules, such as the voting system, are intensely political and are carefully guarded by political elites who tend to resist changes that they fear may threaten their interests. While academics still debate voting system effects, the actions of political elites on the question of voting system reform clearly demonstrate that voting systems do matter. In this chapter, we have reviewed the basic component parts of voting systems and the typical voting systems constructed from them, the debates over voting system effects, and the history of voting system reform in Canada. Despite considerable contemporary interest in voting system reform, it is unlikely that Canadian voting systems will change any time soon, given the failure of all recent voting system reform initiatives.

NOTE

1. This chapter is an excerpt from my book *The Politics of Voting* that has been revised, updated, and reconfigured for this collection.

DISCUSSION QUESTIONS

1. Why do political scientists disagree about the pros and cons of different voting systems?
2. Which voting system do you think is best for Canada and why?
3. Why might politicians in particular be unwilling to change the voting system?

FURTHER READING

Blais, André, ed. 2008. *To keep or to change first past the post?* Oxford: Oxford University Press.
Cairns, Alan C. 1968. The electoral system and the party system in Canada, 1921–1965. *Canadian Journal of Political Science* 1 (1): 55–80.
Courtney, John. 2004. *Elections.* Vancouver: UBC Press.
Pilon, Dennis. 2007. *The politics of voting: Reforming Canada's electoral system.* Toronto: Emond Montgomery.

REFERENCES

Aucoin, Peter, and Jennifer Smith. 1997. Proportional representation: Misrepresenting equality. *Policy Options* 18 (9): 30–33.
Blais, André. 1991. The debate over electoral systems. *International Political Science Review* 12 (3): 239–260.
Blais, André, ed. 2008. *To keep or to change first past the post?* Oxford: Oxford University Press.

Cairns, Alan C. 1968. The electoral system and the party system in Canada, 1921–1965. *Canadian Journal of Political Science* 1 (1): 55–80.

Canada Elections Act. 2000. SC 2000, c. 9.

Cliche, Paul, and Jean-Pierre Charbonneau. 2006. Reform of the voting system: How to put an end to this saga. *Le Devoir*, December 19.

Colomer, Joseph. 2004. *The handbook of electoral system choice.* Houndsmill, UK: Palgrave Macmillan.

Courtney, John. 1999. Electoral reform and Canada's parties. In *Making every vote count: Reasssessing Canada's electoral system*, ed. H. Milner, 91–100. Peterborough, ON: Broadview Press.

Curtice, John, and Phil Shively. 2000. Who represents us best? One member or many? CREST Working Paper 79, National Centre for Social Research and the Department of Sociology, University of Oxford.

Cutler, Fred, and Patrick Fournier. 2008. Did the Citizens' Assemblies affect voting in BC and Ontario? Paper prepared for When Citizens Decide: The Challenge of Large Scale Public Engagement. Centre for the Study of Democratic Institutions at the University of British Columbia, May 1–2.

Duverger, Maurice. 1954. *Political parties.* Repr.; New York: John Wiley, 1963.

Gallagher, Michael, and Paul Mitchell, eds. 2005. *The politics of electoral systems.* Oxford: Oxford University Press.

Irvine, William. 1979. *Does Canada need a new electoral system?* Kingston: Institute of Intergovernmental Relations, Queen's University.

Jenson, Jane. 1997. Out of proportion. *Canadian Forum* 75 (857): 27–29.

Law Commission of Canada. 2004. *Voting counts: Electoral reform for Canada.* Ottawa: Law Commission of Canada.

Leduc, Lawrence, Heather Bastedo, and Catherine Baquero. 2008. The quiet referendum: Why electoral reform failed in Ontario. Paper prepared for the annual meeting of the Canadian Political Science Association. University of British Columbia, June 4–6.

Lijphart, Arend. 1999. *Patterns of democracy.* New Haven, CT: Yale University Press.

Lipset, S.M., and S. Rokkan. 1967. Cleavage structures, party systems and voter alignments: An introduction. In *Party systems and voter alignments*, ed. S.M. Lipset and S. Rokkan, 1–64. New York: Free Press.

Lortie, Pierre. 1997. A minimalist electoral reform agenda. *Policy Options* 18 (9): 22–25.

Mair, Peter. 1992. The question of electoral reform. *New Left Review* 194 (July/August): 75–97.

Marsh, Michael. 2007. Candidates or parties? Objects of electoral choice in Ireland. *Party Politics* 13: 4.

Massicotte, Louis. 2008. Electoral reform in Canada. In *To keep or to change first past the post?* ed. A. Blais, 112–139. Oxford: Oxford University Press.

McKenna, Peter. 2006. Opting out of electoral reform: Why PEI chose the status quo. *Policy Options* 27 (5): 58–61.

Milner, Henry. 2004. *Steps toward making every vote count: Electoral system reform in Canada and its provinces.* Peterborough, ON: Broadview Press.

Morgenstern, Scott, and Stephen Swindle. 2006. Are politics local? An analysis of voting patterns in 23 democracies. *Comparative Political Studies* 38 (2): 143–170.

Nevitte, Neil, ed. 2002. *Value change and governance in Canada.* Toronto: University of Toronto Press.

Norris, Pippa. 2004. *Electoral engineering: Voting rules and political behavior.* Cambridge: Cambridge University Press.

Pilon, Dennis. 2006. Explaining voting system reform in Canada: 1874 to 1960. *Journal of Canadian Studies* 40 (3): 135–161.

Pilon, Dennis. 2007. *The politics of voting: Reforming Canada's electoral system.* Toronto: Emond Montgomery.

Powell, G. Bingham, Jr. 2000. *Elections as instruments of democracy: Majoritarian and proportional visions.* New Haven, CT: Yale University Press.

Rae, Douglas. 1971. *The political consequences of electoral laws.* New Haven, CT: Yale University Press.

Rokkan, Stein. 1970. *Citizens, elections, parties: Approaches to the comparative study of the processes of development.* New York: David McKay.

Seidle, Leslie. 1996. The Canadian electoral system and proposals for reform. In *Canadian parties in transition,* 2nd ed., ed. A. Brian Tanguay and Alain-G. Gagnon, 282–306. Toronto: Nelson Canada.

Seidle, Leslie. 2002. Electoral system reform in Canada: Objectives, advocacy and implications for governance. Discussion Paper F/28, Canadian Policy Research Networks.

Shugart, Matthew, and Martin Wattenberg. 2001. *Mixed-member electoral systems: The best of both worlds?* Oxford: Oxford University Press.

Swayze, Mikael Antony. 1996. Continuity and change in the 1993 Canadian general election. *Canadian Journal of Political Science* 29 (3): 555–566.

Tanguay, Brian. 2009. Reforming representative democracy: Taming the democratic deficit. In *Canadian politics,* 5th ed., ed. J. Bickerton and A. Gagnon, 221–248. Toronto: University of Toronto Press.

CHAPTER 4

Canada's Election Law: Less Than Meets the Eye?

Heather MacIvor

Introduction

In recent years, the seemingly obscure topic of Canada's election law has attracted more attention than usual. One reason is the sheer frequency of voting. Fifty-five months elapsed between the 1988 and 1993 federal elections, whereas three federal elections were held in the 53 months from June 2004 to October 2008. Another reason is the Liberal "sponsorship scandal,"[1] which helped to drive that party from power in the 2006 election. During that very campaign, it was later alleged, the Conservative Party deliberately circumvented the spending limits set by the *Canada Elections Act*.[2] Election law became a hot topic, for all the wrong reasons.

On one hand, Canada is a world leader in election law and administration. New and developing democracies often ask Elections Canada, the national agency that runs our elections and referendums, for assistance with electoral administration. Transparency International, a global non-governmental organization (NGO) that tracks political corruption, ranks Canada first in the Americas and ninth in the world for clean politics and government (Transparency International 2009, 2). Another NGO, the International Institute for Democracy and Electoral Assistance (IDEA), recently reported that "Among the established democracies Canada stands out for its highly successful effort (the *Canada Elections Act* 1974) to rid itself of the spectres of corruption and scandal usually connected with the funding of politics by means of an effective political finance regime" (Nassmacher 2003, 33).[3]

On the other hand, Canadians are as skeptical about corruption in our national politics as anyone in the world (Transparency International 2007, Table 4.2). A third NGO, Global Integrity (2008), gave Canada only a "moderate" rating in its 2008 worldwide report on political corruption, partly because of a "very weak" score on the enforcement of national political finance laws. As I will argue in this chapter, Canada has a comprehensive election law and excellent electoral administration. What we lack is the political will to enforce the law, especially the provisions that supposedly prevent political parties and candidates from raising and spending money in inappropriate ways. Our elected politicians like to pass laws that appear tough and effective, but it is not always clear that they intend to live by them.

For our purposes, "election law" is the body of formal rules that governs the choice of democratic governments and the conduct of political campaigns. It includes three distinct sets of rules:

- constitutional law (both entrenched text and court rulings);
- statutes passed by Parliament, and open to amendment by a majority vote; and
- regulations and administrative guidelines issued either by the Cabinet or by the agency that oversees elections.

This chapter describes Canada's federal election laws. (For the sake of clarity, it focuses on constitutional and statute law and omits most of the detailed regulations and guidelines.) This chapter will also go beyond the strict definition of *election law* to consider the laws that pertain to parties and other "political entities" between campaigns. Some of the laws that affect our elections are discussed elsewhere in this book (see Chapter 5 by Michael Pal and Sujit Choudhry, and Chapter 6 by Munroe Eagles and Annika Hagley). Here, we will focus on the laws that apply directly to the main participants in the electoral process: officials, voters, political parties, and candidates. We begin with a look at the sources of Canada's election law. Then we explore two key categories of election law: the "rules of electoral organization" and the "rules of electoral competition" (Mozaffar and Schedler 2002). We conclude with a discussion of the paradox of the Canadian electoral system: strong election law and administration combined with weak enforcement.

The Sources of Canada's Election Law

The Constitutional Foundation

Canada's principal constitutional documents, the *Constitution Acts* of 1867 and 1982, provide few rules for electing members of the House of Commons (or the provincial legislatures). The Fathers of Confederation assumed that the new Dominion of Canada would conduct its elections as Britain had done, and that all British citizens would be entitled to vote in Canada. Until 1874, the founding provinces applied their own laws to federal elections. The 1867 Constitution did provide for the creation of electoral districts; it also required that a federal general election be held at least once every five years. But it did not identify those who were entitled to vote, or the rules and procedures by which they could do so.[4]

The *Constitution Act, 1982* contains the *Canadian Charter of Rights and Freedoms*. The guarantees of fundamental freedoms and democratic rights, sections 2 to 5, are reproduced in the Appendix to this chapter. Section 2 protects political speech and collective action for lawful purposes. Section 3 guarantees the right to vote and to run as a candidate in federal and provincial elections. Section 4 extends the time limit in section 50 of the 1867 Constitution to the provincial legislatures, while providing for exceptions in extreme circumstances. Section 4(1) has been effectively modified by statutes in several provinces, and by a 2007 amendment to the *Canada Elections Act* (discussed below), which set "flexible fixed" election dates at four-year intervals. Section 5 replaces section 20 in the 1867 Constitution, which required Parliament to meet once a year, and extends that requirement to the provinces.

Sections 4 and 5 of the Charter have attracted little attention from the public or the courts. In contrast, sections 2 and 3 have generated a considerable volume of commentary and judicial interpretation. Before the Charter, the courts' only role in the electoral process was to resolve disputed elections. Individual judges also conducted recounts in especially close races. Otherwise, the judicial branch of government had very little to do with the electoral process.[5] Back in 1982, entrenching freedom of political expression and the right to participate in politics seemed perfectly straightforward. Section 3 attracted almost no attention during the intergovernmental negotiations that ultimately produced the Charter (MacIvor 2006, chap. 9). But the past quarter-century has witnessed numerous disputes over the meaning and application of sections 2(b) and 3, some of which produced significant changes to the *Canada Elections Act*.

To understand why section 3 has had this unexpected effect, we must first understand the way in which judges interpret the Charter. Before a court can decide whether or not an impugned (challenged) law violates a particular section of the Charter, it must identify the purpose of the specific right or freedom at issue. In the first place, judges must interpret the wording of the specific Charter guarantee in the context of the entire Constitution. Unlike most of the entrenched rights, section 3 cannot be overridden by federal or provincial legislators.[6] Section 1 of the Charter guarantees the entrenched rights and freedoms "subject only to such reasonable limits prescribed by law as can be demonstrably justified in a *free and democratic society*" (emphasis added). Given that standard, it is difficult to justify laws that restrict the right to vote or the expression of political views.

Second, judges must examine the history and evolution of that right or freedom in Canada and comparable countries. In the 19th century, the right to vote and to run in federal elections was confined to white male British subjects at least 21 years of age who owned or occupied sufficient property (Elections Canada 1997a, 49). The franchise (the right to vote) was associated with wealth, not with citizenship. In the 20th century, the vote was recognized as a civil and human right, and the franchise expanded. Today all Canadian citizens are entitled to vote, regardless of personal

BOX 4.1
Disenfranchising Young Canadians

In 1970, the statutory voting age was lowered from 21 to 18 years (Elections Canada 1997a). Few Western democracies allow persons younger than 18 to vote, although the reasons for denying the franchise to younger persons are rarely explained. There is nothing in the text of section 3 of the Charter to explain the age barrier, unless the word "citizen" is interpreted to exclude persons under 18. But that interpretation is not consistent with current practice. Young workers pay income taxes; young offenders accused of serious criminal offences may be tried as adults; and most of Canada's political parties allow people as young as 14 to become members.[7] When the governing party holds a leadership contest, any number of 14- to 17-year-olds can participate directly in the choice of prime minister; but they cannot vote for a local MP in their own constituencies.

A recent Charter challenge to the voting age was rejected by an Alberta judge. Although he found that denying the franchise to young people violated section 3, he considered the law to be justified under section 1. The law's objective was to ensure a rational and informed electorate, an important goal in a free and democratic society. To meet that goal, a legislature must somehow distinguish between children and adults. The judge concluded that the 18th birthday is no more arbitrary than any alternative cut-off date; therefore, the age restriction does not offend the Charter.[8]

characteristics. The only exceptions are people under the age of 18, the chief electoral officer (CEO), and returning officers (except in the case of a tie between two candidates). Therefore, any law that restricts voting rights must meet stringent criteria for justification. Chief Justice McLachlin made this abundantly clear in the 2002 *Sauvé* ruling, which struck down a section of the *Canada Elections Act* denying the vote to federal prisoners. She wrote: "The right to vote is fundamental to our democracy and the rule of law and cannot be lightly set aside. Limits on it require not deference, but careful examination" (*Sauvé v. Canada (Chief Electoral Officer)* 2002, para. 9, per McLachlin CJ).

To date, the Supreme Court of Canada has identified two purposes of the right to vote.

The first purpose is to entitle every Canadian citizen to "effective representation" in the House of Commons and provincial legislatures. In the words of then-Justice McLachlin, "Each citizen is entitled to be *represented* in government. Representation comprehends the idea of having a voice in the deliberations of government as well as the idea of the right to bring one's grievances and concerns to the attention of one's government representative" (*Reference re Prov. Electoral Boundaries (Sask.)* 1991, para. 32, per McLachlin J).[9] In practical terms, this means that every Canadian's vote need not count for exactly as much as another's: "deviations from absolute voter parity may be justified on the grounds of practical impossibility or the provision of more effective representation." Otherwise, "dilution of one citizen's vote as compared with another's should not be countenanced" (para. 34).

The second purpose, as per section 3 of the Charter, is to give "every citizen of this country the right to play a meaningful role in the selection of elected representatives who, in turn, will be responsible for making decisions embodied in legislation for which they will be accountable to their electorate" (*Haig v. Canada; Haig v. Canada (Chief Electoral Officer)* 1993, para. 61, per L'Heureux-Dubé J). This interpretation of section 3 emphasizes the electoral *process*, whereas "effective representation" targets the *outcome* of an election. Note that the Charter does not guarantee the right to vote in municipal elections or in referendums; the wording restricts the guarantee to federal and provincial elections.

In practice, the right to play a "meaningful role" in the electoral process means at least two things. First, it means that each citizen is entitled to cast an *informed* vote in an election (*Harper v. Canada (Attorney General)* 2004, para. 71, per Bastarache J). This interpretation of section 3 reinforces the protection of political expression under section 2(b). The Supreme Court distinguishes between expression that is central to a free and democratic society, which includes election campaigning, and "peripheral" expression whose restriction by law requires little justification (for example, child pornography) (MacIvor 2006, 259–265). The Court has consistently held that the law may not be used to restrict debate, advertising, or other expressions of political opinion, except where such restrictions are necessary to prevent the wealthy from monopolizing the airwaves and other media (*Libman v. Quebec (Attorney General)* 1997, para. 47, *per curiam*; *Harper v. Canada (Attorney General)* 2004, para. 72, per Bastarache J).

Second, it means that Canadians can only play a "meaningful role" in elections if they have a variety of political parties and candidates from which to choose. As the Supreme Court stated in 2003, "political parties act as both a vehicle and outlet for the meaningful participation of individual citizens in the electoral process" (*Figueroa v. Canada (Attorney General)* 2003, para. 39, per Iacobucci J). Any party that runs candidates and offers a unique policy perspective enables its supporters to play a meaningful role in the electoral process, regardless of its size or wealth. It follows that the law should not worsen the disadvantages that smaller, poorer, or newer parties suffer in comparison to their bigger, richer, and long-established rivals.

The right to run for public office has received considerably less attention than the right to vote. In the only major ruling to date, the Supreme Court of Canada upheld a New Brunswick law that prohibited anyone convicted of violating the province's election law from seeking election for five years. The Court held that the law infringed section 3, but the infringement was justified under section 1. In effect, the importance of maintaining the integrity of the electoral process outweighed the relatively short period of disqualification (*Harvey v. New Brunswick (Attorney General)* 1996, per La Forest J).

The democratic rights guaranteed in the Charter are uniquely important, but not unlimited. A federal or provincial legislature can restrict the exercise of the franchise, as long as the restriction meets stringent tests of justification. Laws that impair the ability of political parties or candidates to communicate with voters, or that impede the free transmission of information to the electorate, are not always subject to the same strict scrutiny. In summary, the adoption of the Charter has reshaped the *Canada Elections Act* in ways that no one could have anticipated in 1982.

Statute Law

The word *statute* refers to an ordinary written law that can be adopted, amended, or repealed by a simple majority in both Houses of Parliament. The *Canada Elections Act* sets out the rules for everyone directly involved in choosing the members of the House of Commons. In the 2008 federal general election, 14 million voters cast ballots for 1,601 candidates. Most did so at 65,000 polling stations staffed by over 200,000 workers in 308 constituencies. Canadians overseas voted by special postal ballots, including soldiers serving in Afghanistan, as did prisoners held in federal and provincial jails.[10] The sheer complexity of the process requires comprehensive legal regulation. The Act is a massive statute with over 550 sections. At the same time, the central purpose of all democratic elections—to produce results that are perceived to be fair and accurate, even by the losers—demands a high degree of impartiality and transparency.

Among other things, the *Canada Elections Act*

- defines the powers of the CEO, the official who is ultimately responsible for the conduct of national elections in Canada, and sets out the structure of Elections Canada, the agency that administers federal elections and referendums;
- defines the variety of roles and tasks to be performed by deputy returning officers (DROs) and other temporary staff before and during election day;
- establishes the permanent voters' list, formally known as the Register of Electors, and empowers the CEO to collect the information needed to keep it up-to-date;
- sets out detailed rules for casting and counting ballots;
- prescribes criteria for candidacy to the House of Commons;
- regulates political finance; and
- lists the penalties for anyone who is proven to have violated any of the rules.

Since the adoption of the first *Dominion Elections Act* in 1874, the statute has undergone dozens of amendments.[11] For our purposes, the following are the most important:

- The 1920 *Dominion Elections Act* established a non-partisan electoral agency (Elections Canada is discussed below) and created the position of chief electoral officer.
- The 1970 *Canada Elections Act* recognized the existence of political parties and allowed them to identify candidates on the ballot.

- The 1973 *Election Expenses Act* (which took effect after the 1974 general election) imposed a new political-finance regime on political parties and candidates.
- The 2000 *Canada Elections Act* reorganized a confusing patchwork of amendments into a coherent statute.
- Bill C-24, which took effect at the start of 2004, extended the political-finance regime to new political entities and restricted contributions.
- Most recently, the 2006 *Federal Accountability Act* tightened political-finance rules even further.

As we go through this chapter, the central trend in the Act's evolution will become apparent: many, if not most, amendments were adopted to benefit the party in power at the time. Some amendments were intended to give the governing party a political advantage; for example, the Borden government enfranchised the wives and mothers of Canadian soldiers during the First World War because it expected them to vote in favour of its military policy (Elections Canada 1997a, 57–58, 67–68). Other amendments were intended to capitalize on their opponents' perceived corruption, to fend off new competitors, or to shield their own party against real or potential scandal. The cumulative result is an election statute that looks tough and effective but is actually riddled with loopholes—especially in the provisions on political finance, which we will examine in "The Six Political Entities" further below.

The Rules of Electoral Organization

Elections Canada

Elections Canada is "autonomous from the executive branch of government" (Wall et al. 2006, 7), both organizationally and financially. The CEO, who heads the agency, reports directly to the House of Commons. The agency's funding comes directly from the legislative branch, instead of being controlled by a minister or department. This strict independence from the executive branch is relatively common among newer democracies, but surprisingly rare among established ones. For example, the United States and the United Kingdom allow the executive branch of government (at the local or regional level) to play a role in election administration, even though the political executive is controlled by one of the parties contending for power.

Although the CEO is nominated by the prime minister of the day, his or her appointment must be ratified by all of the parties represented in the House of Commons at the time. The CEO serves until the age of 65, unless he or she chooses to resign earlier; the CEO cannot be fired without the agreement of a majority in both Houses of the federal Parliament.[12]

The agency's independence from political interference is reinforced by the procedure for filling two particularly sensitive positions: the commissioner of Canada elections (CCE) and the broadcasting arbitrator. The CCE is in charge of investigating alleged violations of the *Canada Elections Act* by voters, election officials, parties, candidates, or other participants in an election or referendum. Before the *Federal*

Accountability Act took effect in late 2006, the CCE was also responsible for deciding whether or not to prosecute an alleged offence under the *Canada Elections Act*; today that power rests with the director of public prosecutions (MacIvor 2008, 138). The broadcasting arbitrator is tasked with allocating paid and free broadcasting time among the registered political parties during an election campaign. Both officials are appointed by the CEO and report to him or her, thus insulating them from pressure by elected politicians.

Under normal conditions, Elections Canada employs roughly 330 people at its Ottawa headquarters. By the end of an election campaign, which can last anywhere from 36 to 54 days,[13] it must provide more than 200,000 trained staff to 15,000 polling stations in 308 separate constituencies (Elections Canada 2009b, 7). This extraordinary effort is assigned to 308 returning officers (ROs), one for each constituency.[14] Until recently, the ROs were appointed by the Governor-in-Council—in practice, by the party in power at a given time. This often gave rise to perceptions of political bias against candidates from other parties. To make matters worse, the quality of the patronage appointees was uneven; incompetent ROs could not be removed and replaced by Elections Canada. Nor could the agency count on a full slate of ROs if an unexpected election occurred.[15] The hiring process was finally reformed by the 2006 *Federal Accountability Act*, which empowered the CEO to appoint ROs on the basis of merit. A majority of the 308 ROs who served during the 2008 general election were experienced election workers who had been re-appointed by the CEO after consultation with the major political parties in their constituencies; the rest were chosen in a competitive hiring process (Elections Canada 2009b, 9). ROs work part-time until a campaign begins, and full-time throughout the campaign period until a week or two after voting day.

Preparing for Election Day

The campaign period officially begins as soon as the Governor General dissolves Parliament for a general election. The process is called "dropping the writ," because the official proclamation of dissolution authorizes the CEO "to issue a writ [of election] to the returning officer for each electoral district" (*Canada Elections Act* 2000, section 57(1.2)). Until recently, the power to call an election—hence, the power to determine the timing of the vote—rested exclusively with the prime minister. Although the Governor General issues the proclamation, he or she only does so at the request of the PM. If he or she so chose, a prime minister could call a snap election to capitalize on favourable political circumstances (as former Liberal prime minister Jean Chrétien did in 2000), or delay the call to give his own party more time to prepare for a campaign. As we will see later in this chapter, the spending limits only apply during the campaign period. A party with a lot of cash can spend millions on advertising and other expenses before the writ drops. Critics have argued that the governing party has an unfair advantage over its rivals: only it knows when the campaign would officially begin, thus drawing the attention of voters who ignore political messages between elections. Some have also suggested that the unpredictable timing makes the job of preparing for elections more costly and difficult than it needs to be, and increases the difficulty of recruiting candidates and election workers (Milner 2005, 21–22).

In 2007 the Harper government passed Bill C-16, which amended the *Canada Elections Act* to establish "fixed" dates for future federal general elections. The new section 56.1 reads as follows:

> (1) Nothing in this section affects the powers of the Governor General, including the power to dissolve Parliament at the Governor General's discretion.
>
> (2) Subject to subsection (1), each general election must be held on the third Monday of October in the fourth calendar year following polling day for the last general election, with the first general election after this section comes into force being held on Monday, October 19, 2009.

As previously noted, the law modifies the effect of section 4(1) of the Charter. Whereas the Charter sets a maximum of five years between general elections, except in times of war, section 56.1 of the *Canada Elections Act* reduces that period to four years.

Despite the adoption of fixed dates, Canadians went to the polls a year early (on October 14, 2008). Prime Minister Harper violated the spirit of his own law by asking the Governor General to dissolve Parliament less than three years after the 2006 election. He did so because the political conditions for the Conservative Party were more favourable in October 2008 (at the start of an anticipated recession) than they seemed likely to be in October 2009 (Clarke, Kornberg, and Scotto 2009, 257). In other words, he was motivated by the same political self-interest that had guided his predecessors. At the time of writing, the long-term impact of the fixed-date law was impossible to predict.[16] If and when Canadians begin to elect majority governments again, the statutory four-year limit between elections could become significant. In the past, some majority governments have hung on for the full five years in hopes of a miraculous political resurrection (usually in vain). However, most prime ministers with majorities have gone to the polls after roughly four years. In that sense, Bill C-16 will have little effect on the timing of elections.[17]

Whenever the writ drops, the RO has to set up an office and put the electoral machinery in motion immediately. The RO has roughly five weeks to recruit and train hundreds of temporary staff, oversee the nomination of candidates, explain the complex rules in the *Canada Elections Act*, and ensure that the election proceeds smoothly in her constituency. Each constituency is divided into roughly 200 polling divisions, or "polls." Each station serves the residents of several polls, each of which requires its own polling clerk to manage voting and assist in counting the ballots.

The RO receives a preliminary list of electors from Elections Canada shortly after the campaign period begins. Until recently, she would have been responsible for compiling the voters' list from scratch. Voters used to be enumerated (that is, counted) at the start of each general election campaign. Two-person teams went door-to-door, recording and registering all of the eligible voters at each residential address. The enumerators were chosen by the incumbent MP and the second-place party in the previous election. Enumeration consumed considerable time and money, although it did have advantages. It was a useful reward for loyal campaign workers, thus helping to maintain strong party organizations in the constituencies. More important, it let voters know that an election campaign was under way and reminded them that their votes mattered (Black 2003, 3–5).

In 1996 the *Canada Elections Act* was amended to provide for the creation of the National Register of Electors. A final door-to-door enumeration took place in April 1997 to lay the foundation for a permanent list, which would be updated continuously. New voters would be added when they turned 18 or received Canadian citizenship; voters who died or left the country permanently would be deleted; changes of address would be obtained from the Canada Revenue Agency and provincial motor licensing bureaus. The change was touted as a way to save money, shorten the campaign period, and provide better service to all election participants (Elections Canada 1996, Part I).

In practice, the Register has not been as up-to-date and accurate as it was supposed to be. The coverage of the eligible population is less comprehensive than under the old enumeration system, which raises questions about the Register's contribution to falling voter turnout (Black 2003, 19–23). The sheer volume of updates needed— 760,000 additions, 302,000 deletions, and nearly 5 million address changes between the 2004 and 2006 elections alone (Elections Canada 2006, 16–17)—seems to have overwhelmed Elections Canada. Just over 6 percent of the electorate, some 730,000 people in all, registered to vote at the polling booth in October 2008 (Elections Canada 2009b, 24). These were Canadian citizens whose names had been left off the Register. Given the low overall turnout rate in the 2008 election (just under 60 percent[18]), one wonders how many voters are still unregistered because they did not bother to show up.

As the campaign progresses, the RO and staff are busy adding voters to the list, securing accessible polling places, and sharing information with Elections Canada. The names of candidates must be confirmed, ballots printed, election-day workers recruited and trained, and ballot boxes distributed. To complicate matters still further, the growing popularity of postal and advance voting forces election officials to prepare even earlier than in the past.

Casting and Counting the Ballots

Until recently, most Canadians had to vote in person. Today, thanks to post-Charter amendments to the *Canada Elections Act*, a Canadian studying overseas or spending the winter in Florida can vote by special postal ballot. Mailed ballots are separated by constituency and counted at Elections Canada headquarters; the results are transmitted to the ROs to be added to the candidates' totals. For those Canadians who are at home but unable to vote on election day, there are now three full days of advance voting. In 2008, more than 1.5 million voters chose to cast their ballots in advance. Their ballots were counted at the same time and in the same place as those cast on election day.

BOX 4.2
Veils and Votes

In October 2006, the Harper government introduced a package of amendments to the *Canada Elections Act*, many of which had originally been proposed by the CEO. One section of Bill C-31 introduced new identification rules at polling places. For the first time, a voter would have to present documents containing a photograph and a current address before being allowed to cast a ballot. If she did not have the proper identification, she would still be allowed to vote if she swore an oath declaring her name and address, or if another voter with the correct documentation formally vouched for her identity. The stated purpose of the amendments was to deter voter fraud, such as voting more than once in a given election by impersonating another elector (House of Commons 2006a, 25–27).

In summer 2007, the question of how to identify female voters who covered their faces—mostly Muslim women wearing the *niqab* or the *burka*—suddenly became a hot issue. Three federal by-elections were scheduled to take place on September 17 in Quebec, following months of controversy in that province over "reasonable accommodation" for members of ethnic and religious minorities. Newly appointed CEO Marc Mayrand announced on September 10 that the Act contained no provision to require veiled voters to expose their faces before they could cast ballots (Elections Canada 2007a). Mayrand told angry MPs that he had to balance the risk of voter fraud against the religious rights of veiled women, and that if Parliament wanted to strike a different balance it should amend the law (House of Commons 2007).

Despite the media hysteria, the CEO subsequently reported that the three Quebec by-elections went smoothly (Elections Canada 2008c, 16). Nonetheless, the Harper government insisted that the CEO's decision had made a mockery of the democratic process. According to the minister then responsible for the Act, "In several places in the ridings in Quebec where the by-elections were occurring, people voted while purposefully concealing their faces for no justifiable reason. I think we recall seeing on television one even wearing a pumpkin on their head" (van Loan 2007, 2).

In October 2007 the Harper government introduced Bill C-6. It would have amended the *Canada Elections Act* to require a veiled voter to uncover her face so that election workers could verify her photo ID. Because the Bill did not ensure the presence of female election workers at every polling station, it could have prevented some Muslim women from exercising their democratic rights. The government allowed the Bill to languish on the Order Paper, likely because public concern died down quickly. It lapsed when Parliament was dissolved for the 2008 federal election.[19] At the time of writing, it had not been reintroduced.[20]

Counting begins after all of the polls in a riding have closed. The DRO in charge of each polling station is the only person authorized to open the sealed ballot boxes after the end of voting. The DRO counts the ballots "in the presence of the poll clerk and any candidates or their representatives who are present or, if no candidates or representatives are present, in the presence of at least two electors" (*Canada Elections Act* 2000, section 283(1)). The observers are there to make sure that the count is conducted fairly and accurately, and that all participants can have faith in the integrity of the result.

The DRO begins by tallying the number of voters who have cast ballots at that particular polling station, and accounting for all of the ballots supplied to it. Then he opens the ballot box and dumps the ballots onto a table. He picks up each ballot in turn, checks the validity of the vote, and shows it to the observers. If the voter has not marked the ballot, or has voted for two or more candidates, the ballot may be rejected by the DRO. Rejected ballots are set aside, pending a possible judicial recount. Candidates and their representatives should refrain from objecting to the validity of a ballot on partisan grounds; for example, a stray pencil mark should not be used to disqualify a vote for one's opponent as long as the elector's intention is clear. At every stage, the ballots must be handled with great care to ensure that the result can be verified by the RO. The total number of votes for each candidate is certified by the RO once he or she has all of the results from the DROs and the special ballot team in Ottawa.

Tying Up Loose Ends

Once a winner has been declared in each constituency, the RO completes the writ of election and returns it to the CEO. When a race is decided by a narrow margin, the ballots are recounted under judicial supervision.[21] There were six such recounts following the 2008 general election. Of the five that were completed, four confirmed the election-night result.[22]

Once the business of the election has been wrapped up, the CEO is required to submit a formal report to the Speaker of the House of Commons within 90 days. In addition to the official voting results, the report describes the work undertaken to prepare for and administer the election, along with any problems that cropped up and recommendations for solving them. As the weeks pass, candidates' and parties' official agents face the deadlines for disclosing their election contributions and expenses (discussed below); reimbursements are paid out following the receipt of the reports.

Meanwhile, the CCE deals with hundreds of complaints and reports about alleged infractions of the *Canada Elections Act* (Elections Canada 2009b, 34–35). Although a majority are trivial, others require more extensive investigation. Most are settled by means of compliance agreements, in which the offender acknowledges breaking the law and undertakes to refrain from doing so in the future. Although compliance agreements are described on the Elections Canada website, the names of the offenders are usually concealed. In rare cases, a violation of the Act triggers a criminal penalty. Such penalties always fall at the low end of the spectrum, notwithstanding the availability of stiffer sanctions under the Act.

To demonstrate the lax enforcement of our election laws, consider three offences committed in a suburban Toronto constituency during the 2004 election campaign. In February 2008 the successful Liberal candidate, Wajid Khan, pleaded guilty to overspending his legal limit by more than $30,000. He could have been fined $1,000 and sentenced to three months in jail; instead, he was assessed a $500 fine. A local car dealership that directly paid almost $90,000 worth of campaign expenses for Mr. Khan paid a $2,000 fine.[23] It could have been fined up to $5,000, and one or more of its principals could have been jailed for as long as five years. Finally, the head of the Liberal constituency association pled guilty to paying over $40,000 of campaign expenses from the association's bank account, thus violating the legal barrier between the candidate's campaign finances and the constituency organization (discussed below). He could have faced the same penalty as the car dealership; instead, he only had to pay a $400 fine.[24] The relative mildness of the punishment is compounded by the fact that it took almost four years for the offences to be uncovered and prosecuted. Khan was re-elected as a Liberal MP in 2006, although he subsequently crossed to the Conservative Party and lost his seat in the 2008 election. We will return to the problem of enforcing the election laws in the conclusion to this chapter.

The Rules of Electoral Competition

The Six Political Entities

Currently, the *Canada Elections Act* regulates six "political entities":

- registered political parties;
- candidates for the House of Commons;
- electoral district associations (EDAs), which are the local constituency associations of the registered parties;
- candidates for the leadership of a registered party;
- contestants for a party's nomination in a particular constituency; and
- "third parties": groups and individuals who participate in election campaigns by trying to persuade other voters, but who do not seek office for themselves.[25]

The regulation of candidates began with the 1874 *Dominion Elections Act*, which required candidates—more accurately, their official agents—to submit spending reports after election day. The only sanction for failing to report was to forbid an elected MP from taking his or her seat in the Commons. Consequently, few of the unsuccessful candidates complied (Royal Commission on Electoral Reform and Party Financing 1991, 422). There was no regulation of parties until 1970; as far as the law was concerned, candidates ran as isolated individuals rather than partisan teams.[26]

Even after a wide-ranging election finance law was adopted in 1974, big loopholes remained. The local constituency associations of the registered parties were completely unregulated, as were leadership contests and local nomination battles. The Royal Commission on Electoral Reform and Party Financing recommended that the existing

regulatory regime for parties and candidates be extended to these three political entities, which play crucial roles in Canadian politics and government (Royal Commission
on Electoral Reform and Party Financing 1991, chaps. 5 and 7). A leadership contest
in a governing party chooses a prime minister for the entire country. Of Canada's 22
prime ministers since Confederation, ten were initially sworn in between elections.
Nomination battles in "safe" seats can determine the identity of the next MP before
the election even happens (Cross 2006, 173). In 2004, more than a decade after the
royal commission's report, Bill C-24 broadened the reach of the election law. Today,
most of the key party activities—including candidate nomination and leadership
selection—are subject to state regulation.

Registration

Before a political entity can be regulated, it must be registered. The process of registration requires the submission of crucial information (names, addresses, financial
data) along with proof of validity—for example, the names and addresses of 250
people who are members of a party, or a signed declaration from the leader attesting
that a particular constituency association is affiliated with his party. Candidates are
the exception: nomination papers contain all the necessary information. Political
parties have been required to register with the CEO since 1970, when party labels
were first added to the ballots. Registration was extended to constituency associations,
leadership races, and nomination contests by Bill C-24. For political parties, registration is crucial: registered parties are entitled to identify their candidates on the ballot,
to issue tax receipts for contributions, and to receive a share of the free and paid
broadcast time provided during election campaigns.

Between 1970 and 2003, parties seeking to register or to stay registered had to
nominate at least 50 candidates in a federal general election. That requirement was
struck down in the *Figueroa* ruling by the Supreme Court of Canada. The majority
held that the 50-candidate threshold infringed section 3 of the Charter because it
deprived smaller parties of the benefits of registration. The infringement was not
justified under section 1, partly because there was no rational connection between
the objective attributed to the threshold—protecting the integrity of the political financing regime, specifically parties' power to issue tax receipts—and the number of candidates which it could field in a given election (*Figueroa v. Canada (Attorney General)*
2003; MacIvor 2004).

The Court gave Parliament 12 months to enact a new party-registration law. The result
was Bill C-3, which was adopted in 2004. The Bill was an attempt to balance the imperatives imposed by *Figueroa* against the need to deter anyone who might seek to register
a fraudulent "party." In particular, the government wished to prevent abuse of the political tax credit (see "Public Subsidies: Direct and Indirect" below) by groups that were
not genuine political parties. It was also concerned that "third parties" would register
as political parties solely "to take advantage of the higher spending limits without
fielding candidates" (Mayrand 2008). (See the discussion of "third-party" regulation
in Chapter 6 by Munroe Eagles and Annika Hagley.) Bill C-3 added a new definition

of "political party" to the Act: "'political party' means an organization one of whose fundamental purposes is to participate in public affairs by endorsing one or more of its members as candidates and supporting their election" (*Canada Elections Act* 2000, section 2(1)). Nearly four years after the Bill was adopted, CEO Marc Mayrand told a Senate committee that the measures were working well; no changes were needed to ensure the integrity of the financing regime. Some of the registered parties themselves were more skeptical, but they did not persuade the committee to call for amendments (Standing Senate Committee on Legal and Constitutional Affairs 2008).

As of April 2009, there were 19 registered parties in Canada—almost double the number of registered parties in 1997.[27] Despite the dramatic increase, the lower threshold for registration has had relatively little impact on elections. In 2008, the five largest parties collectively received more than two-thirds of the broadcast time, ran four-fifths of the candidates, spent the vast majority of reported election expenses, won 99 percent of the votes, and qualified for almost every penny of subsidies from the public purse.

Agency

The principle of agency has been part of Canada's national election law since candidates were first regulated in 1874. Registered parties have been required to appoint agents since 1974, and the remaining political entities since 2004. The major parties have entire organizations for the purpose (for example, the Federal Liberal Agency). The concept of agency distinguishes between a political entity and the person or group who manages its financial affairs. Every political entity must appoint an official agent before it can register with the CEO (or, in the case of candidates, before they can be officially nominated). Once appointed, the agent is solely responsible for receiving and recording donations, monitoring expenditures, and disclosing all financial transactions to Elections Canada.

If a candidate's or party's post-election fiscal report is incomplete or deceptive, the agent risks punishment under the *Canada Elections Act*. In 2008, for example, the CCE negotiated a compliance agreement with an official agent who submitted an incomplete report after the 2006 general election. In some instances, both the agent and the entity are held liable; after the 2004 election, a New Democratic candidate and her agent were each fined $50 for failing to submit the required documents to Elections Canada before the deadline.[28]

Disclosure

In theory, requiring political entities to publicly disclose their financial transactions promotes integrity and transparency. It also provides citizens with important information about candidates and parties: who supports whom financially, and which interests a particular government might feel obliged to advance (Elections Canada 2005, 83). In practice, the fact that disclosure rules are made by political entities themselves tends to undercut their effectiveness.[29] Ideally, "the information disclosed should be accurate, publicly available, understandable to potential users and timely" (Nassmacher

2003, 45). Although the disclosure provisions in the *Canada Elections Act* are among the most comprehensive in the world, they do not meet this standard.

As previously noted, the 1874 *Dominion Elections Act* required the agents for successful candidates to report their election expenses. The law was amended in 1908 to require the disclosure of contributions and other campaign revenues (Royal Commission on Electoral Reform and Party Financing 1991, 422). Parties were first subjected to disclosure in 1974, and the remaining political entities in 2004. The official agents for constituency associations and registered parties have to file annual reports with the CEO, detailing the amount and the source of all contributions larger than $200. Each registered party also has to file an election expenses return no later than six months after each general election. Candidates' agents have four months to file their campaign returns. Nomination contestants who received and/or spent more than $1,000 in pursuit of their party's endorsement for a seat in the Commons must file returns within four months of the nomination meeting.

There is nothing "timely" about these disclosure rules. If a successful candidate accepted an illegal or morally questionable contribution, and included it in his election return to the CEO, none of the people who voted for him would find out about it until well after election day. Similarly, a corrupt practice by a nomination contestant or a registered party would only come out, if at all, too late to permit an informed choice. The only exception involves party leadership contestants. Their agents are required to disclose all contributions, including the name and address of each contributor, at the time of registering to compete in a leadership race. Three weeks before the date of the leadership vote, they must file a list of contributors from the date of registration to the date four weeks prior to the vote; that is followed by weekly reports up until the end of the contest. In this respect, the only Canadians who are entitled to cast a fully informed vote are the tiny minority who choose party leaders.[30]

If timeliness is lacking, so is the assurance of accuracy. The CEO has no power to verify the disclosures submitted by political entities. He or she cannot conduct an independent audit, nor can he or she seize records that may have been withheld. Among the regulated political entities, only candidates are required to attach bank records to their election expense returns. This requirement does not deter untraceable cash transactions, but it may help Elections Canada to detect suspicious transfers of cash between registered parties and their candidates.[31] Most financial reports have to be accompanied by a statement from a professional auditor, attesting to their accuracy. But this means little or nothing, because the auditor can simply say that the return accurately reflects the financial records that he or she was allowed to examine—which may or may not represent the sum total of all transactions.[32]

Spending Limits

Campaign spending limits for parties and candidates were introduced in 1974. The limit for each party depends on the number of constituencies in which it nominates a candidate. The basic formula allows a party to spend 70 cents, adjusted for inflation, for every voter registered on the permanent voters' list. The 2008 spending limit for a party that ran a full slate of 308 candidates was just over $20 million. The same formula is used to calculate the limits for individual candidates, subject to adjustments for exceptionally large and/or thinly populated constituencies. The spending limits for candidates in the 2008 general election ranged from $67,176 (the PEI riding of Malpeque) to $120,646 (the suburban Toronto riding of Oak Ridges-Markham) (Elections Canada 2008a); the average was just over $88,000 (Elections Canada 2009b, 18). There are no legislated limits for leadership contestants; instead, the parties set their own caps. Nomination contestants may spend up to 20 percent of the candidate spending limit in that constituency in the preceding general election.

Imposing separate limits on registered parties and their candidates may seem illogical. Candidates run on behalf of parties, so why shouldn't they be treated as one cohesive entity? The answer is that failing to distinguish between party and candidate spending would make the regulatory regime all but useless. Consider the Conservative Party, which ran 307 candidates in 2008 and was therefore entitled to spend nearly $20 million. The party declared election expenses totalling $19,418,580.[33] Had each of its candidates spent the average amount permitted by law, they would have collectively spent roughly $27 million. If there were no separation between party and candidate limits, the Conservative Party as a whole would have laid out at least $50 million during the 2008 election campaign. The Conservatives' financial advantage over the other parties would have been crushing, instead of merely overwhelming.[34]

The spending limits for political entities only apply during the campaign period. In other words, they take effect when the writ drops and expire on election day. The Conservatives have taken advantage of this timing by spending millions of dollars on advertising between elections—the first Canadian party with the means to mount a "permanent campaign." (See Chapter 8 by Thomas Flanagan.) They used their overflowing bank account to run advertisements ridiculing Liberal leader Stéphane Dion starting shortly after the December 2006 leadership convention (Flanagan and Jansen 2009, 210–212). Partly in consequence, Dion never really caught on with voters; he was widely blamed for the party's poor showing in the 2008 election (Jeffrey 2009, 63–97; Clarke, Kornberg, and Scotto 2009, 268–270).

In 2009 a Liberal senator introduced an amendment to the *Canada Elections Act* that would have pushed back the application of the spending limits to three months before election day.[35] This change seems to follow logically from the adoption of fixed election dates. However, a British Columbia law that limited the amount of campaign advertising which a "third party" could purchase in the 60 days before the start of a campaign was struck down by the British Columbia Supreme Court in March 2009; the judge found that the infringement of section 2(b) of the Charter could not be justified under section 1 (*British Columbia Teachers' Federation v. British Columbia (Attorney General)* 2009). Because the proposed amendment to the *Canada Elections Act* would cover a period half as long as the BC law, its constitutionality is questionable.

Public Subsidies: Direct and Indirect

For nearly a century after Confederation, Canada's political parties received little financial support from the public purse. The parliamentary wings (also called *caucuses*) of the governing party and the Official Opposition were entitled to extra sums to cover their leaders' office expenses. The stipends were extended to all official parties—those represented by at least a dozen MPs—in 1963 (Courtney 1978, 37). The caucus stipends were increased in 1969, to cover the cost of permanent research offices (54–55). Individual MPs were also entitled to send letters and other material to their constituents, which were often of an explicitly partisan nature. The creation of the Canadian Broadcasting Corporation in 1936 provided parties with an indirect subsidy of a different kind: free airtime on the national radio network for campaign broadcasts (41–43).[36] Today, registered parties are still entitled to free airtime on Canada's main television and radio networks during election campaigns.

The most important indirect subsidy provided by the 1974 legislation was the tax credit for political donations. When an individual or a corporation gave more than $100 to a registered party, the official agent was required to issue a tax credit to the donor. The amount of the credit could then be deducted from the donor's income or corporate tax for that year. Although the credit is always smaller than the donation, it is subtracted directly from tax owing (as opposed to taxable income). This makes the political tax credit considerably more valuable than a charitable credit.[37] There are no reliable recent estimates of the annual cost of the political credit, or of its impact on the generosity of potential donors.[38] Some experts on political finance consider the tax credit to be a model for other countries to emulate because it encourages individuals to become involved in the political process and reduces the influence of corporations in Canadian democracy (Nassmacher 2003, 36). But given that fewer than 1 percent of Canadians[39] gave money to registered parties in 2007, the effectiveness of the credits is open to question.

Direct subsidies to Canada's extra-parliamentary parties were introduced in 1974, as part of the attempt to lessen the influence of corporate funding in national politics. Each registered party was entitled to a reimbursement amounting to 22.5 percent of its declared campaign expenses, as long as it filed the post-election financial report on time.[40] In 1996, a threshold was inserted to prevent frivolous parties from claiming public funds. A party had to win at least 2 percent of the national vote, or 5 percent of the total vote in the constituencies where it ran candidates, in order to qualify for the reimbursement. The 1974 legislation also provided for reimbursements to candidates: 50 percent of declared campaign expenses would be paid from public funds to any candidate who won at least 15 percent of the vote in his or her constituency. Bill C-24 lowered the candidate threshold to 10 percent of the vote.

Bill C-24 introduced a new direct subsidy. Since January 1, 2004, a registered party that meets the vote threshold for reimbursement is also entitled to an annual allowance from the federal treasury. The amount of the subsidy is determined by the number of votes that a party won in the preceding election. Each vote was originally worth $1.75 per year; after indexing for inflation, the per-vote subsidy had grown to almost $2.00 by 2009. The allowance is paid quarterly to the headquarters of each recipient party. To date, only five parties have qualified for the allowance: the four currently represented in the House of Commons—Conservatives, Liberals, Bloc Québécois, and New Democrats—plus the Greens, who surmounted the 5 percent threshold in 2006 and 2008.[41]

Shortly after the 2008 election, the Harper government delivered a statement to the Commons on Canada's deteriorating fiscal situation. Finance Minister Jim Flaherty announced that "our Government is eliminating the $1.95-per-vote taxpayer subsidy for politicians and their parties, effective April 1, 2009" (Department of Finance 2008, 9). The annual cost of the allowances is a little over $25 million per year, a minuscule fraction of the federal government's total spending (see Table 4.1). Most observers saw the promise, not as an indication of sound fiscal management, but as "an avowedly partisan declaration of renewed war" (Dornan 2008, 8). Had Flaherty carried it out, the Conservatives would have been the only party capable of repaying its campaign debts in a timely fashion. The other parties, especially the Liberals, would have been plunged into crisis and perhaps even bankruptcy. The three opposition parties banded together, agreeing to form a coalition and topple the Conservatives. The Harper government quickly withdrew the threat to eliminate the allowances; Harper persuaded the Governor General to suspend Parliament until after Christmas, and the coalition eventually fizzled. At the height of the political showdown, 61 percent of respondents to a national survey said that they were opposed to the "taxpayer-funded subsidy" (although this result might have been coloured by the less-than-neutral language of the question) (IPSOS-Reid Public Affairs 2008, 9).

Contributions

Before Bill C-24 took effect, there were no limits on political contributions in Canada. Any individual, corporation, or association could give as much money as they wished to a party or candidate, as long as the source was Canadian. That changed at the start of 2004: corporations and unions were prohibited from donating money to registered parties (and leadership contestants). They could give a total of $1,000 annually to any

TABLE 4.1   Donations and Allowances, Canada's Major Political Parties, 2003–2007

Year	Total donations from individuals	Total donations from corporations and unions	Annual allowances	Totals
2003	$20,349,772.00	$18,865,058.00	n/a	$39,214,830.00
2005	$32,935,230.79	n/a	$24,425,091.00	$57,360,321.79
2007	$27,557,768.10	n/a	$27,874,826.00	$55,432,594.10

n/a = not available.

Source: Financial data posted on the website of Elections Canada. http://www.elections.ca.

of the other regulated entities. Individual citizens and permanent residents were allowed to donate a maximum of $5,000 to all political entities in a given calendar year. Subsequently, the *Federal Accountability Act* banned all corporate and union donations to political entities, and lowered the ceiling on individual contributions. At the time of writing, a Canadian citizen could legally donate $1,000 (adjusted for inflation) to a registered party and an additional $1,000 (in total) to its constituency associations, candidates, and/or nomination contestants during a given calendar year. Finally, he or she could donate up to $1,000 to one or more party leadership contestants during any given leadership race.

The new contribution limits created immediate problems. Party members who attended a national policy or leadership convention, and paid several hundred dollars in registration fees, could only make small donations to the party for the rest of that year in order to avoid exceeding the cap. (The parties themselves had to keep a lid on convention costs so that their members would not break the law just by registering.) Instead of asking large corporations for a few big donations, parties were forced to ask hundreds of individuals for small donations. The Conservatives had the direct-mail, telephone, and computer technology to do this very successfully. For their part, the Liberals were forced to prop up the first Harper minority government (2006–2008) because they could not afford to contest an election campaign (Jeffrey 2009, 78–81).

The annual party allowances (discussed in the previous section) were intended to compensate the major parties for the loss of revenue resulting from the contribution limits. As Table 4.1 shows, that compensation has been more than adequate.

However, the very generosity of the allowances may have created a serious imbalance within party structures. The contribution limits make it harder for the parties' constituency associations to raise money, whereas the allowances are paid to their national headquarters. This feast-and-famine situation could further erode the parties' constituency associations, which are the foundation of our electoral politics.

The strict contribution limits also raise the prospect that donors will circumvent the law, either by splitting large donations among several people[42] or by securing large loans from people who would previously have donated the money (and who, presumably, would be willing to "forgive the loan" if they could get away with it).[43] Finally, the contribution limits have been lowered but the spending limits remain intact. If the legal supply of campaign funds cannot keep up with the demand, the law will actually increase the potential for corruption instead of reducing it.

Conclusion

We have seen that Canada's election law is among the best in the world, as is the agency that administers that law. On the other hand, its enforcement by our executive and judicial branches of government is less than adequate. In part, this arises from the loopholes in the law approved by the legislative branch, whose members (apart from senators) are directly elected under the rules in the *Canada Elections Act*. The conflict of interest is obvious. No matter how arm's-length the electoral agency may be, it can only work with the laws that are passed by Parliament. Elected politicians are always keen to capitalize on the issue of the moment—whether that be veiled voters or a scandal involving their opponents. But they are much less keen to bear the brunt of tough laws themselves. When the political will to enforce the law is lacking, neither the law itself nor its enforcement will be as strong as it should be. As a former deputy CEO put it, "without enforcement, laws—no matter how well intentioned—have little value" (Davidson 2004, 537). In a nutshell, Canada has too much election law and too little enforcement.

At the same time, the Charter and Bill C-24 have dragged the courts into purely political disputes. Between 2003 and 2008, judges in Ontario and Alberta were asked to settle disputes between the Conservative Party and two of its candidates (*Riddell v. Conservative Party of Canada* 2007; *Knox v. Conservative Party of Canada* 2007). The Ontario Court of Appeal and the Federal Court of Canada resolved two lawsuits arising from the merger of two registered parties to create the Conservative Party (*Ahenakew v. MacKay* 2004; *Stevens v. Conservative Party of Canada* 2005). The Federal Court also ruled on the appropriateness of the Liberal Party's decision to refund campaign deposits to leadership candidates (*Rae v. Canada (Chief Electoral Officer)* 2008). Although judges are understandably reluctant to determine the outcome of a political contest, they have little choice but to answer questions arising from the application of statute law to previously unregulated activities. The de facto treatment of Canada's registered political parties as "public utilities" has subjected them to greater judicial scrutiny, for better or for worse (van Biezen 2004).

Although the future is unclear, we can safely predict that Canada's election laws will continue to be shaped by political self-interest. It also seems clear that the courts will be called on to settle disputes among political entities that, until recently, would have been dealt with privately. The public airing of such disputes is unlikely to enhance Canadians' faith in their politicians or to encourage them to vote (see Chapter 12 by Lawrence LeDuc and Jon H. Pammett). Neither would a more aggressive approach to enforcement by the CCE, at least in the short term. If party members or officials were tried and convicted of violating the financial provisions in the *Canada Elections Act*, public confidence in the integrity of politics would fall even further. In the long term, however, Canadians might be reassured to see their political leaders actually obeying the laws that they impose on everyone else.

Better yet, the writing of Canada's election laws could be assigned to a non-partisan body that has no conflict of interest. Although this would be a radical step, it would greatly reduce "the risk that self-serving legislation poses to the democratic process" (Feasby 2007, 565). Paradoxically, it may be necessary to modify a core democratic principle—that the laws should be made by elected legislators—in order to strengthen Canadian democracy as a whole.

APPENDIX: RELEVANT SECTIONS OF THE
CANADIAN CHARTER OF RIGHTS AND FREEDOMS

2. Everyone has the following fundamental freedoms:

(a) freedom of conscience and religion;

(b) freedom of thought, belief, opinion and expression, including freedom of the press and other media of communication;

(c) freedom of peaceful assembly; and

(d) freedom of association.

3. Every citizen of Canada has the right to vote in an election of members of the House of Commons or of a legislative assembly and to be qualified for membership therein.

4. (1) No House of Commons and no legislative assembly shall continue for longer than five years from the date fixed for the return of the writs of a general election of its members.

(2) In time of real or apprehended war, invasion or insurrection, a House of Commons may be continued by Parliament and a legislative assembly may be continued by the legislature beyond five years if such continuation is not opposed by the votes of more than one-third of the members of the House of Commons or the legislative assembly, as the case may be.

5. There shall be a sitting of Parliament and of each legislature at least once every twelve months.[44]

NOTES

1. In 2002, the federal Auditor General found that several contracts under the federal Sponsorship Program had been issued to Montreal-based advertising firms, which did little or nothing for the money. Subsequent investigations revealed that the firms in question had close ties to the Quebec wing of the Liberal Party of Canada (the LPCQ). When he appeared before a federal Commission of Inquiry into the Sponsorship Program and Advertising Activities (the Gomery commission), former advertising executive Jean Brault testified that his firm, Groupaction, had been given contracts on the understanding that he would kick back part of the sponsorship money to the LPCQ in concealed donations. He gave the party at least one envelope stuffed with untraceable cash, and paid the salaries of three people who were working full-time for the LPCQ. See Commission of Inquiry into the Sponsorship Program and Advertising Activities (2005, chap. 9). At the time of writing, no one involved had been charged with violating the party finance rules in the *Canada Elections Act*. The statute of limitations had elapsed for most of the alleged offences, so there seemed to be no prospect of any prosecutions.

2. In April 2008, the Ottawa headquarters of the Conservative Party of Canada (CPC) was searched by investigators and members of the RCMP. They were looking for evidence pertaining to an alleged violation of election finance rules during the 2006 campaign. In the affidavit attached to the search warrant, an assistant chief investigator in the office of the Commissioner of Canada Elections laid out the details of a suspected "in–out" scheme. A person or persons at Conservative campaign headquarters had contacted the campaigns of several dozen CPC candidates, asking them if they planned to spend the maximum

amount prescribed by law. If the campaign manager said no, the CPC promised to wire a sum of money (usually in the thousands of dollars) into the campaign's bank account after the candidate's official agent had pre-arranged with the bank to wire exactly the same amount of money back to the CPC. The party would then purchase television advertising worth the same amount as the transferred sum, and claim that the candidate had paid for it. In so doing, the CPC allegedly hoped to conceal over a million dollars' worth of advertising expenditures—which pushed it well over its legal spending limit in the 2006 campaign—while allowing 67 of its candidates to claim extra election expenses. Because half of candidates' declared election expenses are reimbursed by the federal treasury, artificially inflating those expenses would result in overpayment to the candidates (and, ultimately, to their local Conservative constituency associations). Elections Canada discovered the alleged scheme, likely by comparing the campaigns' bank records to the claims on their disclosure forms. In April 2007 the chief electoral officer informed the candidates involved that they would not be reimbursed for their share of the questionable advertising expenses. On May 11, several of the candidates launched a lawsuit against the chief electoral officer in the Federal Court of Canada; less than a week later, Elections Canada referred the matter to the commissioner of Canada Elections for investigation and possible prosecution. At the time of writing, the civil proceeding had not been resolved and no charges had been laid. See *L.G. Callaghan et al. v. Chief Electoral Officer* (n.d.) and Elections Canada (2008b).

3. Shortly after Nassmacher's report was published, Canada's political finance laws were overhauled; it could be argued that they are no longer "highly successful" in deterring corruption, if they ever were.

4. There was no national franchise until 1920 (Elections Canada 1997a, 40). The exception was a federal law in effect from 1885 to 1898; it was repealed by the Laurier Liberals, reflecting their provincialist leanings.

5. A few court rulings dealt with the "political rights" of Canadians in fairly broad terms, but without immediately affecting the election laws. For example, the Supreme Court of Canada struck down an Alberta censorship law in 1938, partly on the ground that it conflicted with the sections of the 1867 Constitution that established a parliamentary system of government in the new Dominion. See *Reference Re Alberta Statutes—The Bank Taxation Act; The Credit of Alberta Regulation Act; and the Accurate News and Information Act* (1938, 132–133).

6. Section 33 of the Charter, better known as the "notwithstanding clause," allows federal and provincial legislatures to pass a law that violates one or more of the fundamental freedoms (section 2), legal rights (sections 7 to 14), and equality rights (section 15). Any such law must explicitly state that it operates "notwithstanding" the Charter guarantee in question, and it automatically expires at the end of five years unless it is re-enacted in the same form. The democratic rights are expressly exempted from the application of the override clause. Because of its unpopularity, section 33 is rarely invoked; see MacIvor (2006, 379–383).

7. I am indebted to my MA student Chuck Andary for this argument. See Andary (2009).

8. See *Fitzgerald v. Alberta* (2002). The judge also found that the age restriction violated the guarantee of equality in section 15(1) of the Charter, but that violation was justified as well.

9. See the discussion of this case in Chapter 5 by Michael Pal and Sujit Choudhry.

10. See Elections Canada (2009b, 25–30) for voting statistics and Appendix I, Tables 1 and 2 for numbers of staff and candidates, respectively.

11. Elections Canada has prepared a "Table of Amendments," listing changes to the election statute since 1873. It can be accessed in the "Election Law, Policy and Research" section of the Elections Canada website: http://www.elections.ca.

12. The terms of the CEO's tenure are set out in section 13 of the *Canada Elections Act*.

13. By law, the campaign cannot be shorter than 36 days. There is no statutory maximum length. The longest campaign in recent memory began in late November 2005, with the fall of the Liberal minority government led by Paul Martin, and ended on January 23, 2006. The exceptionally long campaign (55 days) was made necessary by the Christmas holidays.

14. A new type of official was added in 2003, when Elections Canada created the position of field liaison officer as a kind of intermediary between the Ottawa headquarters and the individual ROs. Twenty-four (now 28) field liaison officers were hired, mostly from the ranks of able and experienced returning officers. Each was assigned to assist a specific group of constituencies by providing crucial information and ensuring that deadlines were met (Elections Canada 2006, 35).

15. These complaints were repeated numerous times in the CEO's statutory reports to Parliament. For a concise summary, see Elections Canada (2005, 14–17).

16. In January 2009, Progressive Conservative Senator Lowell Murray introduced a bill in the Senate to repeal the fixed election dates. At the time of writing, Bill S-202 had not been voted on.

17. This is not to suggest that fixed dates have no benefit. Former CEO Jean-Pierre Kingsley described the administrative advantages to the House of Commons Committee studying the Bill:

> [A]t the issue of the writ, returning offices could be up and running with communications technology installed and staff hired and trained. … This would allow for better service to electors, and a fixed date would also allow my office a greater advance opportunity to identify and secure locations for polling stations. This would include firm commitments for access to sites that are accessible, thus resulting in improved locations and greater convenience for electors.
>
> Knowing the date of the election in advance would also permit targeted updates of the National Register of Electors … This would result in a more up-to-date preliminary list of electors for candidates at the start of the election and fewer revisions to the list during the electoral period.
>
> Holding elections at a fixed date would also be beneficial for our outreach and education programs, as well as for our advertising, which could be implemented more effectively before and during general elections. (House of Commons 2006b, 12)

18. The official figure is 58.8 percent (Elections Canada 2009b, 30).

19. Interestingly, another change to the new regime in Bill C-31 did make it through the legislative process. Bill C-18, introduced a few weeks after Bill C-6, made it easier for electors living in rural constituencies to confirm their addresses at the polling booth. The Conservative Party does very well in rural ridings.

20. Elections Canada commissioned surveys of voters and election officials shortly after the 2008 vote. Neither reported any significant problems with the new voter identification rules, apart from the need to provide proof of address (which posed difficulties for some young, poor, and Aboriginal voters). The results of the surveys are available at http://www.elections .ca/content.asp?section=loi&dir=res/40eval&document=index&lang=e&textonly=false (see Elections Canada 2009c).

21. Where the first- and second-place candidates are separated by less than 1/10 of 1 percent of the number of valid votes cast in that constituency, section 300 of the *Canada Elections Act* requires an automatic judicial recount. In other close races, a voter may request a judicial investigation of the results; if there are reasonable grounds to suspect that an error has occurred in the original count, a judge will order that the ballots in that constituency be

counted a second time (section 301). The process is explained in detail in a December 2008 ruling by the Ontario judge who supervised the recount in *Kitchener-Waterloo: Kitchener-Waterloo (Electoral District) (Re)* (2008).

22. One of the six recounts was terminated after a sample of the ballots was recounted, showing that the initial result was correct. The overturned result occurred in the Quebec riding of Brossard-La Prairie, where the Bloc Québécois candidate had been declared the winner on election night but the Liberal candidate was awarded the seat following the recount. See Elections Canada (2009b, 31, Table 7).

23. Only the candidate's official agent is permitted to spend money for campaign purposes.

24. The description of the offences associated with the 2004 Liberal campaign in Mississauga-Streetsville is taken from Elections Canada (2004). The information about maximum penalties under the *Canada Elections Act* is taken from Elections Canada (2007b).

25. The laws regulating "third parties" are discussed in Chapter 6 by Munroe Eagles and Annika Hagley.

26. On the legal status of Canadian parties before 1974, see Courtney (1978).

27. Source for the number of registered parties in 2009: Elections Canada (2009a). Source for the number of registered parties in 1997: Elections Canada (1997b, 100).

28. The illustrative examples are taken from the "Commissioner of Canada Elections" section of the Elections Canada website (www.elections.ca), which was accessed in May 2009.

29. The author of a recent global survey of political finance law put it more bluntly: "scholars of political funding have almost exhausted the vocabulary of contempt in describing the ineffectiveness of these [disclosure] rules" (Pinto-Duschinsky 2002, 80).

30. The value of this timely disclosure became evident during the 2006 Liberal leadership contest. The registration report of one contestant revealed an apparent attempt to circumvent the contribution limits by splitting large donations among several members of at least four different families—including young children, who could not possibly have donated more than $5,000 each. The appearance of impropriety was heightened by the fact that several of the adults worked for the same large corporation. See MacIvor (2008, 109).

31. See the discussion of the alleged Conservative "in–out" scheme in note 2, above.

32. The auditor's report attached to the New Democratic Party's 2008 election expenses return is fairly typical in this regard. It states: "The Act ... does not require me to report, nor was it practicable for me to determine, that the accounting records include all transactions relating to the election expenses incurred by the Party" (Lyon 2009).

33. This information appears on page 3 of the 2008 post-election campaign return filed by Conservative Fund Canada (the party's official agent) with the chief electoral officer. It was accessed at www.elections.ca in April 2009.

34. On the might of the Conservative fundraising machine, see Flanagan and Jansen (2009). Indeed, the party is accused of having violated the limits in the 2006 campaign (see note 2, above).

35. Bill S-236, *An Act to Amend the Canada Elections Act (Election Expenses)*, was tabled by Senator Dennis Dawson on May 26, 2009. At the time of writing, the bill had not become law.

36. The formula for allocating the time among the various parties clearly favoured the larger and more established parties (as, indeed, does the current formula).

37. The royal commission pointed out that charitable donations greater than $1,150 produced bigger tax savings than political contributions. See the Royal Commission on Electoral Reform and Party Financing (1991, 312). However, such generous donations to political entities are now illegal.

38. The Royal Commission on Electoral Reform and Party Financing found that an average of 90,000 individuals per year had claimed an average of nearly $7 million annually from 1974 to 1989. That works out to about $77 per year per donor. It also reported that "the value of tax credits claimed was equal to 29 per cent of the parties' total revenue during the 1985–88 cycle and 30.7 per cent of their total revenue during the 1981–84 cycle" (Royal Commission on Electoral Reform and Party Financing 1991, 312–313).

39. The actual number is 172,843. It was calculated by adding up the number of individual contributors disclosed to Elections Canada for the 2007 fiscal year by all 14 registered parties at the time.

40. Originally, each party was entitled to repayment of 50 percent of its reported expenditures on advertising. The formula was changed to 22.5 percent of total election spending in 1983 (Royal Commission on Electoral Reform and Party Financing 1991, 363).

41. Shortly after Bill C-24 took effect, several of the smaller parties went to court to have the vote threshold struck down. They argued that restricting the annual allowances to the larger parties contravened the Supreme Court ruling in *Figueroa* (2003). In 2006, a judge of the Ontario Superior Court ruled that the threshold infringed section 3 of the Charter and could not be saved under section 1. Judge Matlow nullified the threshold and retroactively awarded the smaller parties the allowances to which they would have been entitled since the law took effect on January 1, 2004. The federal government appealed the ruling to the Ontario Court of Appeal, which reversed Matlow's finding on justification and upheld the threshold. The Supreme Court of Canada refused to hear the smaller parties' appeal (*Longley v. Canada (Attorney General)* 2007).

42. See note 30, above.

43. The problems arising from the use of loans by the 2006 Liberal leadership contestants are described in MacIvor (2008, 119–123).

44. The consolidated texts of the *Constitution Act, 1867* and the *Constitution Act, 1982* can be downloaded from the website of the federal Department of Justice: http://laws.justice.gc.ca/en/Const/ConstDoc.html.

DISCUSSION QUESTIONS

1. Do you believe that political parties play a vital role in Canadian elections? If so, should their internal activities be regulated by the government, either between or during election campaigns? If not, why not?

2. In your opinion, should political parties and candidates be subjected to campaign spending limits? Why or why not?

3. Should political parties receive annual allowances from the public purse just for soliciting votes—which is, after all, their raison d'être? Should they be required to do something else to qualify for allowances, and if so, what? Or should they be denied public funds altogether?

4. Some political observers argue that the Bloc Québécois should not receive direct or indirect subsidies from the federal treasury, on the ground that its principal goal is to take Quebec out of Canada. Do you agree? Why or why not?

FURTHER READING

Websites

The website of Elections Canada is a gold mine of information about election law and political finance: http://www.elections.ca.

The International Institute for Democracy and Electoral Assistance (IDEA) publishes outstanding handbooks on election law and administration, most of which are available for free download from its website: http://www.idea.int.

Books and Articles

Austin, Reginald, and Maja Tjernström, eds. 2003. *Handbook: Funding of political parties and election campaigns.* Stockholm: International Institute for Democracy and Electoral Assistance.

Canada. Royal Commission on Electoral Reform and Party Financing. 1991. *Final report: Reforming electoral democracy*, vol. 1. Ottawa: Supply and Services Canada.

Pinto-Duschinsky, Michael. 2002. Financing politics: A global view. *Journal of Democracy* 13 (4): 69–86.

van Biezen, Ingrid. 2004. Political parties as public utilities. *Party Politics* 10 (6): 701–722.

REFERENCES

Ahenakew v. MacKay. 2004. 71 OR (3d) 130, 2004 CanLII 12397 (CA).

Andary, Charbel. 2009. The constitutionality of the voting age in Canada. MA major paper, University of Windsor, Department of Political Science.

Black, Jerome H. 2003. From enumeration to the national register of electors: An account and an evaluation. *IRPP Choices* 9 (7): 3–36. http://www.irpp.org.

British Columbia Teachers' Federation v. British Columbia (Attorney General). 2009. 2009 BCSC 436.

Canada. Department of Finance. 2008. Protecting Canada's future: Economic and fiscal statement, November 27. http://www.fin.gc.ca/ec2008/pdf/ecspeech-eng.pdf.

Canada. House of Commons. 2006a. *Improving the integrity of the electoral process: Recommendations for legislative change—Report of the Standing Committee on Procedure and House Affairs.* June 2006. http://www.parl.gc.ca.

Canada. House of Commons. 2006b. *Minutes of proceedings and evidence of the Standing Committee on Procedure and House Affairs.* September 26. http://www.parl.gc.ca.

Canada. House of Commons. 2007. *Minutes of proceedings and evidence of the Standing Committee on Procedure and House Affairs.* September 13. http://www.parl.gc.ca.

Canada. House of Commons. 2008. *Minutes of proceedings and evidence.* March 13. http://www.parl.gc.ca.

Canada. Royal Commission on Electoral Reform and Party Financing. 1991. *Final report: Reforming electoral democracy*, vol. 1. Ottawa: Minister of Supply and Services Canada.

Canada. Standing Senate Committee on Legal and Constitutional Affairs. 2008. *Eleventh report.* http://www.parl.gc.ca/39/2/parlbus/commbus/senate/com-e/lega-e/rep-e/rep11may08-e.htm.

Canada Elections Act. 2000. SC 2000, c. 9.

Clarke, Harold D., Allan Kornberg, and Thomas J. Scotto. 2009. None of the above: Voters in the 2008 federal election. In *The Canadian federal election of 2008*, ed. Jon H. Pammett and Christopher Dornan, 257–289. Toronto: Dundurn Press.

Commission of Inquiry into the Sponsorship Program and Advertising Activities. 2005. *Who is responsible? Fact finding report*. Ottawa: Minister of Public Works and Government Services.

Courtney, John C. 1978. Recognition of Canadian political parties in Parliament and in law. *Canadian Journal of Political Science* 11 (1): 33–60.

Cross, William. 2006. Candidate nomination in Canada's political parties. In *The Canadian federal election of 2006*, ed. Jon H. Pammett and Christopher Dornan, 171–195. Toronto: Dundurn Press.

Davidson, Diane R. 2004. Enforcing campaign finance laws: What others can learn from Canada. *Election Law Journal* 3 (3): 537–544.

Dornan, Christopher. 2009. The outcome in retrospect. In *The Canadian federal election of 2008*, ed. Jon H. Pammett and Christopher Dornan, 7–15. Toronto: Dundurn Press.

Elections Canada. 1996. *Canada's electoral system: Strengthening the foundation (annex to the report of the chief electoral officer of Canada on the 35th general election, part I)*. Ottawa: Chief Electoral Officer of Canada.

Elections Canada. 1997a. *A history of the vote in Canada*. Ottawa: Minister of Public Works and Government Services Canada.

Elections Canada. 1997b. *Report of the chief electoral officer of Canada on the 36th general election*. Ottawa: Chief Electoral Officer of Canada.

Elections Canada. 2004. Sentencing digest—2004 general election. http://www.elections.ca/content.asp?section=loi&document=2004ge&dir=sen&lang=e&textonly=false.

Elections Canada. 2005. *Completing the cycle of electoral reforms: Recommendations from the chief electoral officer of Canada following the 38th general election*. Ottawa: Chief Electoral Officer of Canada. http://www.elections.ca.

Elections Canada. 2006. *Report of the chief electoral officer of Canada on the 39th general election of January 23, 2006*. Ottawa: Chief Electoral Officer of Canada. http://www.elections.ca.

Elections Canada. 2007a. The chief electoral officer of Canada, Marc Mayrand, clarifies application of the new voter identification provisions of the Canada Elections Act. Speech presented at National Press Theatre, Ottawa, September 10. http://www.elections.ca/content.asp?section=med&document=sep1007&dir=spe&lang=e&textonly=false.

Elections Canada. 2007b. Table of offences—Canada Elections Act. http://www.elections.ca/content.asp?section=loi&document=index&dir=leg/fel/oth&lang=e&textonly=false.

Elections Canada. 2008a. *Final election expenses limits for registered political parties: 40th general election—October 14*. http://www.elections.ca/content.asp?section=pas&document=index&dir=40ge/limpol&lang=e&textonly=false.

Elections Canada. 2008b. Information to obtain a search warrant—April 16, 2008. Ottawa: Commissioner of Canada Elections. http://www.cbc.ca/news/background/parliament39/pdf/Search-warrant-1.pdf.

Elections Canada. 2008c. *Report of the chief electoral officer of Canada following the September 17, 2007, by-elections held in Outremont, Roberval–Lac-Saint-Jean and Saint-Hyacinthe–Bagot*. Ottawa: Chief Electoral Officer of Canada. http://www.elections.ca.

Elections Canada. 2009a. Registered political parties and parties eligible for registration (April 30). http://www.elections.ca/content.asp?section=pol&dir=par&document=index&lang=e&textonly=false.

Elections Canada. 2009b. *Report of the chief electoral officer of Canada on the 40th general election of October 14, 2008*. Ottawa: Chief Electoral Officer of Canada. http://www.elections.ca.

Elections Canada. 2009c. Research documents: 40th general election evaluations. http://www.elections.ca/content.asp?section=loi&dir=res/ 40eval&document=index&lang=e&textonly=false.

Feasby, Colin. 2007. Constitutional questions about Canada's new political finance regime. *Osgoode Hall Law Journal* 45 (3): 514–568.

Federal Accountability Act. 2006. SC 2006, c. 9.

Figueroa v. Canada (Attorney General). 2003. [2003] 1 SCR 912, 2003 SCC 37.

Fitzgerald v. Alberta. 2002. 2002 ABQB 1086.

Flanagan, Tom, and Harold J. Jansen. 2009. Election campaigns under Canada's party finance laws. In *The Canadian federal election of 2008*, ed. Jon H. Pammett and Christopher Dornan, 194–216. Toronto: Dundurn Press.

Global Integrity. 2008. *Global Integrity scorecard: Canada 2008.* http://report.globalintegrity .org/Canada/2008/scorecard.

Haig v. Canada; Haig v. Canada (Chief Electoral Officer). 1993. [1993] 2 SCR 995.

Harper v. Canada (Attorney General). 2004. [2004] 1 SCR 827, 2004 SCC 33.

Harvey v. New Brunswick (Attorney General). 1996. [1996] 2 SCR 876.

IPSOS-Reid Public Affairs. 2008. Media government coalition: Detailed tables—December 2–3. http://www.globaltv.com/globaltv/national/documents/Crisis_Tables2.doc.

Jeffrey, Brooke. 2009. Missed opportunity: The invisible Liberals. In *The Canadian federal election of 2008*, ed. Jon H. Pammett and Christopher Dornan, 63–97. Toronto: Dundurn Press.

Kitchener-Waterloo: Kitchener-Waterloo (Electoral District) (Re). 2008. 93 OR (3d) 751, 2008 CanLII 64382 (SC).

Knox v. Conservative Party of Canada. 2007. 2007 ABQB 180; 2007 ABCA 295, 143, 141.

L.G. Callaghan et al. v. Chief Electoral Officer. n.d. FCC. http://cas-ncr-nter03.cas-satj.gc.ca/ IndexingQueries/infp_moreInfo_e.php?T-838-07.

Libman v. Quebec (Attorney General). 1997. [1997] 3 SCR 569.

Longley v. Canada (Attorney General). 2007. 2007 ONCA 149.

Lyon, William. 2009. Auditors' report. April 8. http://www.elections.ca/pol/exp2008/ndp.pdf.

MacIvor, Heather. 2004. The Charter of Rights and party politics: The impact of the Supreme Court ruling in *Figueroa v. Canada (Attorney General).* *IRPP Choices* 10 (4): 1–26. http://www.irpp.org/choices/archive/vol10no4.pdf.

MacIvor, Heather. 2006. *Canadian politics and government in the Charter era.* Toronto: Thomson Nelson.

MacIvor, Heather. 2008. A missed opportunity: Political finance and the Federal Accountability Act. *Journal of Parliamentary and Political Law* 1: 138.

Mayrand, Marc. 2008. Testimony before the Standing Senate Committee on Legal and Constitutional Affairs. In *The proceedings of the Standing Senate Committee on Legal and Constitutional Affairs—Evidence for March 13, 2008.* 12 (9). http://www.parl.gc.ca.

Milner, Henry. 2005. Fixing Canada's unfixed election dates: A political season to reduce the democratic deficit. *IRPP Policy Matters* 6 (6): 21–22.

Mozaffar, Shaheen, and Andreas Schedler. 2002. The comparative study of electoral governance—introduction. *International Political Science Review* 23 (1): 7.

Nassmacher, Karl-Heinz. 2003. The funding of political parties in the Anglo-Saxon orbit. In *Handbook: Funding of political parties and election campaigns*, ed. Reginald Austin and Maja Tjernström, 33–52. Stockholm: International Institute for Democracy and Electoral Assistance. http://www.idea.int/publications/funding_parties/upload/ chapter_3.pdf.

Pinto-Duschinsky, Michael. 2002. Financing politics: A global view. *Journal of Democracy* 13 (4): 69–86.

Rae v. Canada (Chief Electoral Officer). 2008. 2008 FC 246.

Reference Re Alberta Statutes—The Bank Taxation Act; The Credit of Alberta Regulation Act; and the Accurate News and Information Act. 1938. [1938] SCR 100.

Reference re Prov. Electoral Boundaries (Sask.). 1991. [1991] 2 SCR 158.

Riddell v. Conservative Party of Canada. 2007. 2007 CanLII 414 (ON SC).

Sauvé v. Canada (Chief Electoral Officer). 2002. [2002] 3 SCR 519, 2002 SCC 68.

Stevens v. Conservative Party of Canada. 2005. 2005 FCA 383.

Transparency International. 2007. *Global corruption barometer 2007—report.* http://www.epac.at/download/GCB_2007.pdf.

Transparency International. 2008. *Transparency International corruption perceptions index 2008.* http://www.transparency.org/policy_research/surveys_indices/cpi/2008.

van Biezen, Ingrid. 2004. Political parties as public utilities. *Party Politics* 10 (6): 701–722.

van Loan, Hon. Peter. 2007. *Minutes of proceedings and evidence of the House of Commons Standing Committee on Procedure and House Affairs.* November 27. http://www.parl.gc.ca.

Wall, Alan, et al. 2006. *Electoral management design: The international IDEA handbook.* Stockholm: International Institute for Democracy and Electoral Assistance. http://www.idea.int.

CHAPTER 5

Constituency Boundaries in Canada

Michael Pal and Sujit Choudhry

Introduction

In Canadian federal elections, political candidates fight over electoral constituencies (which the *Canada Elections Act* calls *electoral districts*, and which are popularly known as *ridings* or *seats*) created by independent electoral boundary commissions. The relative lack of political and legal debate surrounding the process of boundary delimitation is belied by the importance of ridings to our democracy. Indeed, ridings are the basic institutional building block of democracy in Canada (Courtney 2001, 4). They enable local representation and citizen engagement. Votes are not aggregated across Canada as a whole, but at the riding level, and it is the seat count—not the share of the popular vote—that is the principal basis on which a party is entitled to form a government that enjoys the confidence of the House of Commons. Ridings are central to ensuring that our system of electing members of Parliament (MPs) to govern on our behalf in the House of Commons meets the set of values that are embodied in the term *representative democracy*.

In Canada, independent, non-partisan bodies known as *electoral boundary commissions* delimit electoral boundaries for federal ridings. They have been lauded for admirably breaking with earlier, discredited practices for drawing electoral districts (Courtney 2001, 11, 35–56). Based on the Australian model, their introduction in 1964 was an improvement over the partisan excesses and blatant self-interest that characterized the earlier era in which electoral boundaries were drawn by elected politicians themselves. Elected politicians grouped voters into ridings not for the benefit of the people or to further any goal of democratic fairness, but to maximize the governing party's chances of re-election—a practice known as "gerrymandering" (Carty 1985; Courtney 2001, 11; Burke 1999).

A quick comparison with the United States, where boundaries are still drawn by legislatures, reveals the benefits of the Canadian/Australian model. In a recent infamous episode, the Democratic Party's state legislators in Texas fled across the border to prevent the Republican majority in the state legislature from conducting a vote that would see riding boundaries redrawn to enhance the Republican's electoral performance in congressional elections. The American approach is characterized by a high degree of partisan rancour and controversy.

While a marked improvement over the nakedly partisan process of the past, the current Canadian system for drawing electoral boundaries remains a work-in-progress. It has drawn significant criticism in recent years. As the basic building block of representative democracy in Canada, the criteria that should be used to design electoral districts—and the effects those districts have on voters and on the actual performance of government—raise fundamental issues that strike at the heart of democratic government. Should the number of persons living in each federal riding (the standard measure of riding size) be uniform across Canada, or vary by province or region? Should legislation constrain the power of electoral boundary commissions to tailor riding boundaries to local circumstances, or should they be given broad discretion? What values should be applied in determining where boundaries should be drawn? Does the relative number and size of urban or rural ridings matter? Should electoral districts be drawn to maximize the voting power of minority groups? We will touch on all of these questions in the course of this chapter.

Boundary Drawing in Canada

The History of Boundary Drawing in Canada

Prior to 1964, boundary drawing in Canada was subject to few rules and was handled by legislatures, and was therefore vulnerable to self-dealing and naked partisanship. While legislators occasionally made bargains across party lines, in general the approach of the governing party was to draw districts strictly in its self-interest.

Canada's federal electoral districts were redrawn nine times between 1872 and 1952. As John Courtney writes, "Without exception each was carefully managed by the government of the day" (Courtney 2001, 20). The defining practice associated with these years was the "gerrymander"—a term with a colourful provenance. The governor of Massachusetts in 1812 was named Eldbridge Gerry. He approved into law legislation that redesigned the state's electoral map to his own partisan advantage. One of the most shocking creations of that legislation was a district in a shape that resembled a salamander, which appeared to have been drawn with regard neither for the affinities of the people of the district nor for the communities in which they lived. Rather, the district simply put voters together who were likely to vote for the candidate favoured by the governor. In recognition of Governor Gerry's blatant partisanship and the strange shape of the district, the practice of drawing boundaries to deliberately manipulate electoral results by placing voters with a tendency to vote for a particular party in one district is now known as "gerrymandering."

Some Canadian politicians, including our first prime minister, John A. Macdonald, were noted gerrymanderers. Prime Minister Macdonald's Conservative Party practised gerrymandering with increasing relish during its years in power (Ward 1963, 27). Gerrymandering, however, was a regrettable practice by governments of all political stripes until 1964 (Carty 1985; Ward 1963). These early years of Canadian redistricting also introduced and foreshadowed some of the perennial debates in Canadian representative democracy.

In 1964, Parliament passed legislation that made a clean break from the practices of the past. Based on the Australian model, Canada moved away decisively from legislative districting, shifting that power to newly created, non-partisan electoral boundary commissions, which operated independently and at arm's length from political control (Carty 1985; Courtney 2001, 57–66). The so-called Australian model remains, in essence, the approach that we have today.

The Senate Floor Rule and the Grandfather Clause: Deviation from Representation by Population

Pursuant to a piece of federal legislation, the *Electoral Boundaries Readjustment Act* (the EBRA; discussed at length in "Boundary Drawing Today: The *Electoral Boundaries Readjustment Act*" below), these non-partisan, independent electoral boundary commissions now decide where to place the boundaries between ridings in a particular province, subject to the consultation mechanisms outlined in the legislation. The EBRA relates to the readjustment of electoral boundaries *within* a province. A distinct set of constitutional rules, however, governs the prior issue of the number of seats assigned to each province. The redistribution of ridings *across* provinces occurs after every decennial census.

Section 51 of the *Constitution Act, 1867* contains the current basic formula for redistribution, which is relatively simple and has been in place since 1985. Parliament has a base number of 282 ridings. One is assigned to each territory—Yukon, the Northwest Territories, and Nunavut. The remaining 279 ridings are distributed on the basis of the population of each province as calculated in the decennial census. The total population of the ten provinces is divided by 279 to arrive at the electoral quotient, which is used to determine how many seats each province will receive. The national electoral quotient is currently 107,200. What this means is that, on the basis of population alone, British Columbia, with a population of 3.9 million, is entitled to 36 seats. If this were the only step in calculating the number of ridings assigned to each province, electoral boundary redistribution would be straightforward.

However, two additional rules make redistribution more complex and controversial. First, the "Senate floor" rule (section 51A of the *Constitution Act, 1867*) prevents any province from having fewer MPs than it has senators. It was adopted by Parliament in the *Constitution Act, 1915*. The Senate floor rule freezes representation by province in the House of Commons at a "floor" below which the less-populous provinces cannot fall. For instance, Prince Edward Island would be entitled to one seat under representation by population, since it has a total population close to the national quotient of 107,200. Because PEI had four senators in 1915, however, it may never have fewer than four MPs. The Senate floor rule can only be altered in accordance with the amending formula in section 41(b) of the *Constitution Act, 1982*. Pursuant to section 41(b), any change to the Senate floor rule requires provincial unanimity, which is unlikely to occur on a heated political issue such as representation in the House of Commons. This rule benefits the Atlantic provinces, which have more senators than they would MPs under representation by population.

Second, the "grandfather clause" (section 51(1) of the *Constitution Act, 1982*) ensures that no province has fewer MPs than it had in 1986. This provision was added by the *Representation Act, 1985*, which was introduced by the Progressive Conservative government of Brian Mulroney. The grandfather clause provides another "floor" below which representation in a province cannot fall. This clause benefits the provinces of Saskatchewan, Manitoba, Quebec, Nova Scotia, and Newfoundland and Labrador. All five had a higher proportionate share of the national population in 1986 than they do now.

All provinces benefit from the special rules that govern the distribution of seats except for Ontario, Alberta, and British Columbia. The seven provinces that do benefit receive more seats in the House of Commons than their populations would otherwise dictate, as a deliberate decision of public policy. The result is that the ridings in those provinces have much smaller average populations than the ridings in the faster growing provinces of Ontario, Alberta, and British Columbia. The implication is that the votes cast by individual voters in these three provinces have less weight than those cast in the other seven provinces. The Senate floor rule and the grandfather clause reflect political compromises that were made at particular times in Canadian political history. One could argue that they are anachronistic and that they unduly dilute the principle of representation by population in the House of Commons. The other side of the argument is that they ensure regional representation. The Senate was originally designed to represent the regions in the federal legislative process. However, the Senate has lacked political legitimacy, both because its members are appointed rather than elected, and because it dramatically underrepresents the Western provinces. Therefore, the pressure for regional representation in Parliament has been directed at the rules governing the composition of the House of Commons. Are the Senate floor rule and the grandfather clause still appropriate or desirable? Should representation in the House be shaped in part by the need for regional representation? Should the reform of the rules governing representation in the House necessarily be linked to reforms that would inject democratic legitimacy into, and improve the regional representativeness of, the Senate? These remain live issues that Canada will need to confront in the next few decades.

Canadian Charter of Rights and Freedoms

The *Canadian Charter of Rights and Freedoms* sets out the additional constitutional rules that apply to drawing electoral boundaries. Once the number of seats has been assigned to each province (through the redistribution process outlined above), the electoral boundary commissions are empowered to design the electoral map.

At the federal level, the EBRA and decisions taken by electoral boundary commissions acting under the EBRA are subject to the Charter. In other words, the distribution of ridings within provinces must comply with the Charter. By contrast, the question of whether the allocation of ridings across provinces is subject to the Charter is much more complex. While the grandfather clause is likely subject to the Charter, the Senate floor rule is not. At the provincial level, the allocation of ridings must comply with the Charter as well.

The two relevant provisions of the Charter are section 3, which guarantees the right to vote, and section 15, which enshrines equality rights. Section 3 of the Charter states:

> Every citizen of Canada has the right to vote in an election of members of the House of Commons or of a legislative assembly and to be qualified for membership therein.

The relatively simple guarantees in section 3—that everyone has the right to vote and to serve in the House of Commons and provincial legislatures—belie their potential complexity. In particular, the Supreme Court has held that the "right to vote" guarantees much more than the simple right to cast a ballot in a federal or provincial election. The Supreme Court has interpreted the "right to vote" as guaranteeing federal prisoners the right to vote (*Sauvé v. Canada (Chief Electoral Officer)* 2002) and also the right of small political parties to access state subsidies proportionate to those received by large or established parties (*Figueroa v. Canada (Attorney General)* 2003). The case law on section 3 is covered in depth in Chapter 4 of this book by Heather MacIvor (see also Manfredi and Rush 2007).

The Supreme Court of Canada decision of most relevance to this chapter is *Reference re Prov. Electoral Boundaries (Sask.)* (1991), also known as the *Carter* decision. In *Carter*, the Court upheld a disputed provincial electoral map in Saskatchewan that deviated from the principle of representation by population quite dramatically in order to overrepresent rural ridings. A majority of the Court, in a decision written by now-Chief Justice Beverly McLachlin, upheld the electoral map as constitutional. Though *Carter* involved riding boundaries set for a provincial legislative assembly, it has been interpreted as being equally applicable to federal boundaries. The majority decision stated that population equality is the guiding principle in determining boundaries, but that deviations are permissible under section 3 of the Charter if they are made to ensure more "effective representation" for a particular group, such as rural voters. Indeed, a recent decision of the Federal Court of Canada has even gone so far as to conclude that a commission's decision to adhere to voter equality was unreasonable because the effective representation for a linguistic minority group was not adequately reflected in the electoral map (*Raîche v. Canada (Attorney General)* 2004).

However, by deeming the wide variance from population equality in the Saskatchewan electoral map to be constitutional, the Supreme Court severely weakened the principle of population equality. Though the *Carter* decision was issued in 1991, it remains the leading case for determining what electoral maps are permissible under section 3 of the Charter. Population equality is a principle more honoured in the breach than the observance in Canada. At the federal level, the courts, Parliament, and the Constitution all operate together to depart from the principle of population equality in the following ways: (1) the wide variance from population equality permitted by the *Carter* decision; (2) the statutory discretion for electoral boundary commissions to deviate by up to 25 percent above or below population equality in a province, and beyond that in special circumstances; and (3) the special rules governing the distribution of ridings across provinces that result in some provinces having a much larger average riding population.

The equality rights guarantee in section 15 of the Charter is the second provision of the Charter, along with section 3, that limits the decisions of electoral boundary commissions. Section 15(1) states:

> Every individual is equal before and under the law and has the right to the equal protection and equal benefit of the law without discrimination and, in particular, without discrimination based on race, national or ethnic origin, colour, religion, sex, age or mental or physical disability.

This provision prohibits discrimination on the basis of one of the grounds "enumerated" in section 15 (race, national or ethnic origin, etc.) or grounds "analogous" to the enumerated grounds, such as sexual orientation. For example, if the government were to refuse to hire an individual on the basis of her religion, that would violate section 15.

In voting rights cases, individuals or groups alleging that section 3 has been violated will often also argue that the same government conduct violates section 15. For instance, in *Carter* it was claimed that the overrepresentation of rural voters in the province discriminated against urban voters who were correspondingly underrepresented. The Court's majority did not accept this argument. However, section 15 will continue to be relevant in electoral boundary cases where there is a plausible argument that differences in riding size have the effect of disadvantaging one group of voters identified by one or more enumerated or analogous grounds in section 15, and that this disadvantage amounts to discrimination. Racial or religious minority voters, for example, who are often geographically concentrated within particular ridings, may be able to argue that the electoral map violates section 15 if those ridings tend to be larger than average.

Boundary Drawing Today: The Electoral Boundaries Readjustment Act

Within these constitutional constraints, the current federal electoral boundary process is governed primarily by the *Electoral Boundaries Readjustment Act* (EBRA). The EBRA creates electoral boundary commissions that are independent and non-partisan to draw the electoral maps for federal elections. The legislation provides for detailed rules on the times when electoral boundary commissions are constituted, the membership of the commissions, and the consultations that commissions must engage in. These are obviously important issues, but the EBRA's specificity on these issues contrasts with the very broad and often undefined language that it uses to actually describe the purposes and role of the commissions, including the factors that govern the manner in which commissions draw specific riding boundaries. The result is that commissions have enormous flexibility and are subject to minimal statutory constraints (see Levy 2008).

The EBRA creates one electoral boundary commission per province, which means that there are ten in total. Since each territory has only one riding whose boundaries coincide with the territorial boundaries, no commission is required in any of the territories. The commissions are constituted after each decennial census conducted by Statistics Canada. With each census, the commissions have the most up-to-date statistics on how many people live in each riding and, most important, the change in population from the previous boundary readjustment. Ridings in a fast-growing city, such as Mississauga, Ontario, can grow dramatically from one census to the next. In 1996, the riding of Mississauga West had a population of just over 99,000. According to the 2001 Census, the riding's population was over 150,000.

Each electoral boundary commission is composed of three members. The chair is selected by the chief justice of the province from among the judges of the provincial Court of Appeal or from another level of court within the province. The other two members are selected by the Speaker of the House of Commons; the only caveats are that these two members must be residents of the province and may not be MPs, senators, or members of a provincial legislative assembly.

The mechanisms for appointing members to an electoral boundary commission are potentially controversial. First, the role of the chief justice of a province in appointing a judge to serve as chair of the commission deviates in two respects from the general constitutional separation of powers between the executive and legislative branches of government and the judiciary. The chief justice's power of appointment inserts the senior-most members of the judiciary into a process that previously lay at the heart of Parliament's prerogatives. Moreover, judges chair the electoral boundary commissions. Presumably, both features were designed to insulate the process of electoral redistricting from partisanship by shifting important decisions to the judiciary, the most non-partisan and independent branch of government. Further, having a judge serve as chair was likely designed to bring a degree of impartiality to the deliberations of the commissions. However, given the inherently political nature of boundary delimitation, the judiciary has been thrust into a "political thicket" (*Colegrove v. Green* 1946, at 556, per Frankfurter J).

Second, the role of the Speaker of the House of Commons in appointing the two other members is a potential source of controversy. Though the Speaker occupies a non-partisan role within the House, she remains an elected MP with a party affiliation, a particular constituency to represent, and a self-interest in having the boundary commission in her province establish the boundaries of her riding in a way that is most favourable to her re-election. By having the Speaker appoint the majority of the members of each commission, some vestiges of political control over electoral boundaries potentially remain from the earlier system of partisan gerrymandering and could conceivably be abused.

Third, the EBRA does not set any criteria for the qualifications of the two commission members other than the chair, beyond the residency requirement and the prohibition on federal and provincial politicians. This absence of any statutory criteria raises issues about the commissioners and the criteria used by the Speaker to appoint them. For example, should the commission be as representative as possible of the population of the province? Should there be minority representation along the lines of race, religion, ethnicity, or other demographic criteria? Should the commissioners be chosen solely on the basis of expertise? If so, who possesses the greatest expertise? Is it lawyers, geographers, academics, or informed citizens? (Courtney 2001, 94–121). These potential sources of controversy are present whenever an electoral boundary commission is constituted under the EBRA.

Once the individual commissioners have been appointed in each province, the commissions must then begin the task of redrawing the electoral map. The commissions draw boundaries on the basis of total population, not simply the number of eligible voters. In other words, people who are not eligible to vote because they are below the age of 18 and/or non-citizens are counted for the purposes of drawing electoral boundaries. The idea behind using total population rather than voters is that an MP represents all who reside within his or her district, not simply those of voting age. Many urban MPs spend a great deal of their time helping individuals who are ineligible to vote, such as permanent residents who must wait three years before they can apply for citizenship with its attendant voting rights.

Sections 15(1) and 15(2) of the EBRA dictate what commissions can do. Section 15 imposes few constraints and confers enormous discretion on commissions to make decisions within the purposes of the Act. The guiding principle for commissions is that the "population of each electoral district in the province … shall … as close as reasonably possible, correspond to the electoral quota for the province" (section 15(1)(a)). What this means is that boundary commissions are obliged to place considerable emphasis on making sure that ridings in a province must, as much as is "reasonably possible," have the same population. This is the principle of voter equality or representation by population. The idea is that an individual voter in a riding with 25,000 people has far greater influence or voting power to affect an election than a voter in a riding with 100,000 people. On the basis of the principle of voter equality, each voter should have approximately the same voting power, and thus each riding should have approximately the same overall population.

This principle of voter equality contained in section 15(1)(a), however, is not the only principle that the Act stipulates should guide the drawing of electoral boundaries. Section 15(1)(b) tempers the principle of voter equality by obliging commissions to consider "community of interest," "community of identity," or the "historical pattern of an electoral district in the province." Therefore, individual equality is limited by community concerns.

Section 15(2) makes even more explicit the potential grounds for commissions to depart from individual voter equality. Commissions are enabled to depart from the principle of voter equality in order to respect "community of interest," "community of identity," or "the historical pattern" of a riding. The section then provides for a further exception. In departing from voter equality, commissions should strive not to exceed a deviation of 25 percent above or 25 percent below the average population of a riding in the province, except in "extraordinary circumstances." What qualifies as an "extraordinary circumstance" is not defined in the Act and has never been defined by the courts with any precision. As a result, boundary commissions operate essentially with minimal statutory constraints.

The EBRA obliges electoral boundary commissions to engage in extensive consultations with the public and with Parliament. Any MP is entitled to make representations to the commission. The commissions file their preliminary reports with the Speaker, who directs them to the House of Commons Standing Committee that deals with electoral boundaries. If an objection is filed to a preliminary report, MPs on the Standing Committee may question the map-makers and may propose alternative maps, which usually favour the political interests of the MPs who are involved. Along with appointment of the majority of members by the Speaker, this is the other remnant of parliamentarians' traditional role of drawing electoral boundaries themselves.

It is also worth noting that although the activities of electoral boundary commissions are theoretically independent once their members have been appointed, the federal government retains significant control over the process as a whole. The commissions are creatures of federal statute. Parliament always retains the ability to pass new legislation that can cease, suspend, or delay an ongoing electoral boundary readjustment. Parliament has done so many times in the past when MPs fretted over the political impact of a proposed or likely boundary readjustment (Jenkins 1998).

Federal Versus Provincial Processes

While this chapter focuses on federal electoral boundaries, it is worth noting that the processes for setting provincial electoral boundaries vary from province to province. Some provinces apply direct political control over the boundary process (for example, Prince Edward Island). Others apply the model of independent commissions (Courtney 2001, 183–195). Still others piggyback on the federal process of seat redistribution and readjustment; they structure provincial legislative assemblies with the same number of seats as the province has in the federal House of Commons, and rely on the same boundaries (for example, Ontario has done this recently, though with some amendments).

The sheer variety of approaches that are taken by governments across Canada to the issue of drawing electoral maps underscores that federalism is a significant feature of boundary drawing. Not only is there a commission for each province for federal electoral maps, with all commissions operating independent of one another within the minimal constraints of the EBRA, but for provincial electoral maps there is an even greater range. How Prince Edward Island chooses to design its provincial boundaries has no bearing at all on how British Columbia chooses to do so, or on how the federal ridings are designed for any province. Federalism in Canada permits this broad range of approaches.

Electoral Boundaries in Practice

The 2004 Redistribution

The most recent electoral boundary redistribution occurred in 2004, and was based on the 2001 Census. It increased the size of the House of Commons from 301 to 308 MPs. The seven additional seats were redistributed to the three fastest-growing provinces—Alberta, British Columbia, and Ontario. Alberta and British Columbia received two additional seats each, while Ontario gained three. At present, the total number of seats is 28 for Alberta, 36 for British Columbia, and 106 for Ontario.

The number of ridings assigned to the other seven provinces remained the same. However, the other seven provinces all benefit from one of the special clauses—the Senate floor rule and the grandfather clause. Newfoundland and Labrador has seven seats instead of the five that its population size warrants. Prince Edward Island has four seats instead of one. Nova Scotia and New Brunswick each has an additional three seats, bringing their totals to 11 and 10, respectively. Manitoba has an extra four seats (for a total of 14 seats) and Saskatchewan an extra five (for a total of 14 seats) over what representation by population would entitle them to have. The largest beneficiary of the grandfather clause is the province of Quebec. On the basis of population alone, it would be entitled to 68 seats. Because of the grandfather clause, Quebec has an additional seven seats for a total of 75, the second-largest number of seats of any province after Ontario.

Although Alberta, British Columbia, and Ontario all gained additional seats in the 2004 redistribution, voters in those provinces continue to be disadvantaged when the interprovincial distribution of House of Commons ridings is evaluated in terms of the principle of representation by population. According to the redistribution formula, prior to the application of the Senate floor rule and the grandfather clause, a House of Commons with 279 seats for the provinces had a national quotient of 107,220 people per riding. This figure, however, is not the actual average population of a riding in Canada. The seats resulting from the special clauses must be added to the calculation. With a total population of 30,007,094 according to the 2001 Census, and 308 ridings after the special clauses are applied, the average population of a riding in Canada is 97,426. In comparison, the average population of a riding in British Columbia is 108,548. Meanwhile, the average population of a riding in Alberta is 106,243, which is larger than all provinces except for British Columbia and Ontario. By contrast, the average population of a riding in Saskatchewan and Manitoba is only 69,924 and 79,970, respectively, well below the national average. In Prince Edward Island, there are only 33,824 people per riding on average. See Table 5.1.

To be sure, voters in Alberta, British Columbia, and Ontario do benefit from their provinces' relative size and consequent political influence. Moreover, by increasing the

TABLE 5.1   Population and Riding Distribution by Province and Territory

Province or territory	Minimum number of seats in accordance with the *Constitution Act, 1867*[a]	Calculations					Electoral quotient
		Population 2001	National quotient[b]	Rounded result	Special clauses[c]	Total	
Newfoundland and Labrador[d]	7	512,930	107,220	5	2	7	73,276
Prince Edward Island	4	135,294	107,220	1	3	4	33,824
Nova Scotia	11	908,007	107,220	8	3	11	82,546
New Brunswick	10	729,498	107,220	7	3	10	72,950
Quebec	75	7,237,479	107,220	68	7	75	96,500
Ontario	95	11,410,046	107,220	106	0	106	107,642
Manitoba	14	1,119,583	107,220	10	4	14	79,970
Saskatchewan	14	978,933	107,220	9	5	14	69,924
Alberta	21	2,974,807	107,220	28	0	28	106,243
British Columbia	28	3,907,738	107,220	36	0	36	108,548
Nunavut	1	26,745	—	—	—	1	—
Northwest Territories	1	37,360	—	—	—	1	—
Yukon Territory	1	28,674	—	—	—	1	—
Total	282	30,007,094				308	

[a] Assigns one seat each to Nunavut, the Northwest Territories, and the Yukon Territory (three seats).

[b] Uses 279 seats and population of provinces to establish national quotient (29,914,315 ÷ 279 = 107,220).

[c] Add seats to provinces pursuant to "senatorial clause" guarantee in the Constitution and "grandfather clause" (based on 33rd Parliament).

[d] On December 6, 2001, the name of the province of Newfoundland was changed to Newfoundland and Labrador.

Source: Elections Canada. n.d. *Representation formula using the 2001 Census figures.* http://www.elections.ca/scripts/fedrep/federal_e/red/appendices_e.htm.

number of seats in the fastest-growing provinces in the country, the 2004 redistribution helped alleviate inequality between voters. However, individual voters in all three provinces still suffer from vote dilution as regional considerations and representation for less-populous provinces continue to undermine the principle of representation by population.

The Urban–Rural Divide

As detailed in the numbers above, the 2004 redistribution tells the story of the relative weight of the right to vote *across* provinces. It does not illuminate relative voting power *within* each province, which is a product of the electoral boundary readjustment. After the 2004 redistribution assigned the number of seats to each province, electoral boundary commissions were forced to make difficult decisions about how to assign seats to different areas within a province, where to place particular boundaries, and whether or not to combine different population groups within a single riding.

Each commission produced a final report with its reasoning on the placement of the boundary lines. All of the provinces continued a trend identified in earlier readjustments (Pal and Choudhry 2007)—they overrepresented rural areas at the expense of urban areas. Some of this rural overrepresentation is legitimate. Ridings in the far north of Ontario and Quebec, for example, are larger than many European countries. Those ridings have smaller populations than a riding in Toronto or Montreal, because requiring them to meet the provincial average riding population would produce a riding much too large geographically for practical purposes. There are very few ridings, however, where deviations from population equality are appropriate.

Consider Ontario. The riding of Kenora in northern Ontario had a population of 60,500, 43 percent below the provincial average of 107,000 that was established by the 2004 redistribution (2001 Census data). Given its massive geographic size, it could be argued that making the riding any larger to encompass more people would harm the ability of an MP to represent his or her constituents. The riding of Stormont-Dundas-South Glengarry, however, is certainly not a remote, northern riding; it is situated close to the metropolitan reaches of Ottawa. It has a population of 99,000 (8.5 percent less than the provincial average) despite being adjacent to the now largely suburban riding of Nepean-Carleton, which has a population of 133,000 (2006 Census). The trend in every province is to overrepresent rural areas and to accept the corresponding urban underrepresentation as an acceptable cost. The result is a set of ridings in fast-growing urban areas with very large populations, such as ridings outside of Ottawa or Toronto.

Though the full data from the 2004 redistribution are not yet available, an analysis of the previous redistribution in 1996 on the basis of the 2001 Census demonstrates that the cost to urban voters of urban underrepresentation is high. The worth of one average vote under perfect population equality is 1. However, according to 2001 Census data, the worth of an average urban vote in Canada was only 0.96. In comparison, the average rural vote was worth 1.22. Urban voters in Ontario and Alberta were particularly disadvantaged: in Ontario, the worth of an average urban vote was only 0.91, while in Alberta, the worth of an average urban vote was 0.87 (Pal and Choudhry 2007).

Even in the seven provinces that benefit from the Senate floor rule and/or the grandfather clause, urban voters were still disadvantaged. In Quebec, for example, which gained seven seats due to the grandfather clause, urban votes were worth only 0.97 and rural votes 1.08.

It is likely that the 2004 redistribution alleviated urban vote dilution to some extent by increasing the size of the House of Commons overall, although research remains to be done. New seats were added to the fastest-growing provinces and then assigned by electoral boundary commissions within those provinces to the fastest-growing areas, typically suburban locales ringing the major cities in those provinces—Toronto, Vancouver, and the Calgary–Edmonton corridor. The redistribution only added seven seats, however, out of 301, or just over 2 percent of the total number of seats in the House of Commons. Urban vote dilution very likely continues to exist and to pose a significant challenge to the notion of voter equality.

Visible Minorities and Immigration

The underrepresentation of urban voters leads to a related phenomenon with troubling implications—the underrepresentation of visible minority voters. That the one leads to the other is a matter of long-standing demographic trends and settlement patterns.

First, Canada's population is increasingly concentrated in Ontario, British Columbia, Alberta, and Quebec, and in its major urban areas. Over 62 percent of Canadians live in British Columbia, Alberta, and Ontario. Over 80 percent of Canadians live in urban areas as defined by Statistics Canada. The two trends overlap—most persons in British Columbia, Alberta, and Ontario are concentrated in the largest metropolitan areas in those provinces—Vancouver, Calgary, Edmonton, and Greater Toronto. Overall, 64 percent of Canadians live in census metropolitan areas (CMAs). Fully 33 percent of the population lives in Toronto, Montreal, or Vancouver (Pal and Choudhry 2007; Reitz and Banerjee 2007; Statistics Canada 2001, 2003a, 2003c, 2005a, 2005b).

Second, increasing urbanization has been fuelled by immigration to Canada's largest cities. Between 1991 and 2001, Canada took in approximately 1.8 million immigrants. Over 94 percent of immigrants to Canada in the 1990s settled in CMAs. Immigration is driving population growth principally in urban areas. According to Statistics Canada projections, all population growth in Canada will be due to immigration by 2030 (Statistics Canada 2005b).

Third, these new urban immigrants are increasingly changing the face of Canadian society. Starting with the reforms to Canada's immigration laws from the 1960s onward, immigrants to Canada are now overwhelmingly visible minorities. Nearly 75 percent of immigrants between 1991 and 2000 were visible minorities. Fully 98 percent of these visible minority immigrants settled in CMAs. The vast majority of these immigrants hail from Asia and Africa rather than Europe. This settlement pattern is expected to continue into the future. Barring a dramatic decrease in the number of immigrants allowed to enter the country, or a move away from immigrants from source countries in Asia, Africa, and also Latin America, immigration will continue to transform Canadian cities.

If nearly all immigrants, the vast majority of whom are visible minorities, settle in our largest urban areas and urban voters are underrepresented in Canada, then urban underrepresentation necessarily will lead to the underrepresentation of visible minority voters.

According to the 2001 Census, the average urban visible minority vote in Canada was worth only 0.91, while the average rural vote was worth 1.22. Even within urban areas, visible minority voters were worse off than non-visible minority voters. The average urban visible minority vote (0.91) was still less than the 0.97 for non-visible minority urban voters. When the worth of an urban visible minority vote is compared with the worth of a rural vote and a non-visible minority urban vote, the numbers demonstrate that visible minority voters are not only concentrated in Canada's largest metropolitan areas but also concentrated electorally in the most populous and, hence, most underrepresented urban ridings in the country.

Why does visible minority vote dilution matter? There are three main reasons.

First, visible minority vote dilution raises serious constitutional questions. Since the right to vote is guaranteed equally to all citizens under section 3 of the Charter, legislation and electoral maps that give rise to visible minority vote dilution may run afoul of the Charter. Differential treatment of voters may be regarded by courts as constitutionally suspect. This unequal treatment raises the prospect of a court challenge by disadvantaged voters against an electoral map or the laws that have been interpreted by boundary commissions as permitting visible minority underrepresentation. For example, *Raîche* was launched to aid francophone voters, a minority in the province of New Brunswick as a whole, who wanted to ensure that a riding in the north of the province that traditionally had a francophone majority would still have one after the 2004 readjustment.

Second, visible minority immigrants are facing greater hurdles than before to become integrated into Canadian society. It now takes longer for immigrants to catch up to Canadian average income levels than it did for earlier generations of immigrants to Canada (Reitz and Banerjee 2007; Statistics Canada 2003b). On the assumption underlying our democratic system that politicians respond to the concerns voters express at the ballot box, one could conclude that the problems facing visible minorities are less likely to receive the policy attention that they would otherwise if their votes were worth the same on average as the votes of other Canadians.

Third, visible minority vote dilution challenges the basic legitimacy of Canada's democratic institutions. When an identifiable minority group of citizens is systematically underrepresented by the electoral process, there are potentially damaging consequences for the ability of Parliament to govern on behalf of all Canadians. The proper balance between immigration, multiculturalism, and integration is a topic of heated debate in Canada at the moment (Courchene 2006). Concerns about the impact of visible minority vote dilution are all the more salient given this background.

Put another way, if Canada is to integrate its new visible minority immigrants, it should do so on terms that are scrupulously fair, and our democratic institutions must be perceived as serving all citizens. These institutions must represent the interests of the newest members of our political community on a basis of equality.

Reform

A Constitutional Challenge?

We have detailed how the electoral boundary system works in Canada and outlined some of its major flaws. The natural question to ask is, How can these flaws, notably urban and visible minority vote dilution and regional inequities, be addressed?

One potential approach to reform is constitutional amendment. Constitutional amendments could enhance voter equality by modifying the rules that govern the distribution of seats across provinces. However, they are an extremely remote possibility considering the failure of governments to achieve constitutional amendments during negotiations over the Meech Lake and Charlottetown Accords. It is unlikely that any government will want to wade back into the morass of a constitutional debate with all of its competing interest groups, provincial demands, and political pitfalls. A change to the Senate floor rule, in particular, would require unanimous consent among the provinces. The four provinces that benefit from the clause would be disinclined to provide their consent. Reform driven by constitutional negotiations between the federal government and the provinces, therefore, is unlikely in the near term. By contrast, a change to the grandfather clause could occur through ordinary legislation—the process that was used to adopt the *Representation Act, 1985* in the first place. We address the likelihood of this possibility in the next section, "Political Reform?"

However, constitutional reform can be driven in ways other than constitutional amendments. The courts have the ability to strike down legislation, such as the *Representation Act, 1985* and the EBRA, or decisions of government institutions, such as electoral boundary commissions, that do not conform with the Charter or other parts of the Constitution. Litigation could be initiated by citizens who would argue that the *Representation Act, 1985*, the EBRA, or an electoral map in a province does not pass constitutional muster. The most likely provisions on which to base a constitutional challenge would be section 3 of the Charter, which guarantees the right to vote, and section 15 of the Charter, which guarantees equality rights.

The court process is lengthy, and any result would be uncertain. Courts are also bound by precedent—they must follow earlier case law. Given that the *Carter* decision was written by now-Chief Justice McLachlin, it is not clear that a McLachlin-led Supreme Court would overrule one of her earlier, seminal decisions if presented with an electoral boundaries case today. In *Carter*, the Chief Justice wrote for the majority that large variations from voter equality were justifiable under the Charter. A successful constitutional argument would likely have to rely on new evidence that rural overrepresentation comes at an unacceptably high cost for visible minority voters and is, therefore, unconstitutional. In other words, the Supreme Court might conceivably be open to revisiting *Carter* if presented with convincing evidence of changed factual circumstances.

Political Reform?

Although constitutional reform other than through the courts is a fleeting prospect, political reform of the rules governing electoral boundaries and the distribution of seats across provinces appears possible, through the legislative process. Prime Minister

Stephen Harper's government proposed Bill C-22 on November 14, 2007, which would have added seats to Alberta, British Columbia, and Ontario in the next redistribution to alleviate the underrepresentation of voters in those provinces. Bill C-22 was similar to an earlier version, Bill C-56, which was introduced in May 2007 but never passed. The newest version of the legislation would have increased the size of the House of Commons, keeping the number of seats assigned to the less-populous provinces constant, while increasing the number of seats assigned to the most-populous provinces.

There was one fatal flaw in this legislation—while voters in British Columbia and Alberta would effectively reach voter parity, Ontario's voters alone would have remained underrepresented. Bill C-22 would have added seven seats to British Columbia and five to Alberta, but only ten to Ontario, far short of the 21 that would be required to reach voter equality in the province. Predictably, once the ramifications of the Conservative legislation were understood, there was a political backlash. Premier Dalton McGuinty protested at what he saw as discrimination against Ontario. Suspicions were raised given the Conservatives' attempt to increase the number of ridings in areas of the country where they had relative strength—British Columbia and Alberta—while denying added representation to equally underrepresented voters in Ontario, where they had less prospect of winning seats at the time.

In December 2008, Prime Minister Harper and Premier McGuinty appeared to reach an agreement on the need to add more seats to Ontario as well. At the time of writing, no new legislation to this effect has yet been proposed or passed. Room for political compromise on additional seats for British Columbia, Alberta, and Ontario does appear to exist. Legislative change remains a viable option for reform.

It is worth noting that Bill C-22 would have only reformed the distribution of ridings *across* provinces, and would not have addressed the drawing of riding boundaries *within* provinces and, hence, the distribution of ridings between rural and urban areas. Thus, Bill C-22 would have left the problem of voter inequality between ridings within provinces unaddressed, as electoral boundary commissions would retain the ability to deviate from voter parity by 25 percent or potentially by an unlimited amount in undefined special circumstances. Amendments to the EBRA would be required to reform boundary readjustment.

A New Electoral System?

Another option for reform that has received great consideration at the provincial level is a change in electoral systems. Different electoral systems could alleviate some of the problems that we have identified. Referendums on electoral reform were recently held in British Columbia (2005 and 2009) and Ontario (2007). The proposals stemmed from recommendations of bodies known as Citizens' Assemblies. The Citizens' Assemblies consisted of randomly selected citizens, representing ridings in the province, who were chosen to be educated about and to deliberate on their preferred electoral system for the province over the course of several months. As democratic experiments go, the Citizens' Assemblies were innovative models designed to consider the status quo and reform options. It was presumed that randomly selected citizens have less self-interest in choosing an electoral system than politicians. It was also presumed that the general population of voters in a referendum on the electoral system would recognize the greater legitimacy of the choice of system recommended by the assembly.

In British Columbia, the Citizens' Assembly recommended a voting system called the single transferable vote (STV). STV would have done away with our traditional conception of one MP per riding, by introducing much larger ridings that would have multiple MPs to represent their constituents. In Ontario, the Citizens' Assembly recommended a mixed-member proportional (MMP) voting system, which was a hybrid between the first-past-the-post system used in Canada and more proportional systems such as those used in Italy or Israel. The Ontario Citizens' Assembly would have maintained the current system, but then added seats to be assigned proportionally based on the number of votes received by each political party. Such an approach is used in Germany and New Zealand.

Both STV and MMP would have retained geographic-based ridings to some extent. Boundaries would then have to be drawn between them, raising the issue of voter equality. Under STV, voter parity is much more likely. Under MMP, however, the seats elected on the first-past-the-post system would potentially lead to voter inequality. Given the small number of additional proportionally assigned seats that would be grafted onto the current system, voter inequality would remain potentially problematic in the absence of other reforms to ensure boundaries are drawn fairly.

Whatever the technical merits of STV or MMP, voters in British Columbia and Ontario rejected these options. In British Columbia, the referendum held in conjunction with the provincial election in May 2009 was actually the second referendum proposing electoral reform. In the first in 2005, a majority of voters opted for reform, but not in sufficient numbers to meet the super-majority threshold of 60 percent plus a majority in a certain number of ridings set by the British Columbia government. In 2007, in Ontario's first referendum in 83 years, voters were asked to choose between the MMP option and the first-past-the-post system already in use. The super-majority threshold set by the provincial government required 60 percent of the popular vote with a majority favouring change in at least 64 ridings for MMP to be passed. In the end, the debate regarding whether a super-majority requirement was appropriate was moot, as over 63 percent of voters opted for the status quo. Majority support for change existed in only a small number of ridings in Toronto. The lack of success by electoral reform advocates at the provincial level does not foreclose the possibility of a referendum at the federal level on a new electoral system.

Conclusion

While electoral boundaries have traditionally been only intermittently prominent in Canadian political discourse, the redistribution and readjustment of electoral boundaries should increasingly become a key issue of political, academic, and legal debate given their substantial impact on Canadian democracy. Although the history of drawing electoral boundaries in Canada has been at times ignominious, the process of drawing boundaries has never been peripheral to the effective performance of democratic institutions. The Canadian approach, which uses independent, non-partisan electoral boundary commissions in each province, has professionalized the process and largely taken partisanship out of the equation, although some remnants of the old system remain in place. Electoral maps have a profound impact on who wins elections, whose votes count for how much, and how Canadian democracy is built. Electoral boundaries are a fundamental building block of Canada's democratic architecture.

In the future, the increasing urbanization and diversity of Canada will pose a serious challenge to the legitimacy of these institutions, in the absence of some kind of reform. The underrepresentation of urban and visible minority votes is likely to lead to constitutional challenges in the courts or legislative reform in the political arena.

DISCUSSION QUESTIONS

1. What is the proper balance between representation by population and regional representation in the House of Commons? Consider the role of the Senate and the role of provincial governments.
2. Are the courts the preferred forum to achieve constitutional change, or is it better for democratically elected MPs to make changes to legislation?
3. What are the consequences for Canada of urban underrepresentation and visible minority underrepresentation?
4. Do elected representatives have too much or too little influence in the drawing of electoral boundaries?
5. Why have there been so few court challenges to electoral maps in Canada in comparison with the United States?

FURTHER READING

Carty, Ken. 1985. The electoral boundary revolution in Canada. *American Review of Canadian Studies* 15 (3): 273–287.

Courtney, John C. 2001. *Commissioned ridings: Designing Canada's electoral districts.* Montreal: McGill-Queen's University Press.

Pal, Michael, and Sujit Choudhry. 2007. Is every ballot equal? Visible-minority vote dilution in Canada. *IRPP Choices* 13 (1).

REFERENCES

Burke, Christopher M. 1999. *The appearance of equality: Racial gerrymandering, redistricting, and the Supreme Court.* Westport, CT: Greenwood Press.

Canada Elections Act. 2000. SC 2000, c. 9.

Canadian Charter of Rights and Freedoms. 1982. Part I of the *Constitution Act, 1982,* being Schedule B to the *Canada Act 1982* (UK), 1982, c. 11.

Carty, Ken. 1985. The electoral boundary revolution in Canada. *American Review of Canadian Studies* 15 (3): 273–287.

Colegrove v. Green. 1946. 328 US 549 (Supreme Court).

Constitution Act, 1867. 30 & 31 Victoria, c. 3 (UK).

Constitution Act, 1982. 1982. Schedule B to the *Canada Act 1982* (UK), 1982, c. 11.

Courchene, Thomas J., Keith Banting, and Leslie Seidle, eds. 2006. *Belonging? Diversity, recognition and shared citizenship in Canada.* Montreal: Institute for Research on Public Policy.

Courtney, John C. 2001. *Commissioned ridings: Designing Canada's electoral districts.* Montreal: McGill-Queen's University Press.

Electoral Boundaries Readjustment Act. 1985. RSC 1985, c. E-3.

Figueroa v. Canada (Attorney General). 2003. 2003 SCC 37.

Jenkins, Richard. 1998. Untangling the politics of electoral boundaries in Canada, 1993–1997. *American Review of Canadian Studies* 28 (4): 517–538.

Levy, Ron. 2008. Regulating impartiality: Electoral-boundary politics in the administrative arena. *McGill Law Review* 53 (1): 1–57.

Manfredi, Christopher, and Mark Rush. 2007. Electoral jurisprudence in the Canadian and U.S. Supreme courts: Evolution and convergence. *McGill Law Journal* 52 (3): 457–494.

Pal, Michael, and Sujit Choudhry. 2007. Is every ballot equal? Visible-minority vote dilution in Canada. *IRPP Choices* 13 (1).

Raîche v. Canada (Attorney General). 2004. 2004 FC 679.

Reference re Prov. Electoral Boundaries (Sask.). 1991. [1991] 2 SCR 158.

Reitz, Jeffrey G., and Rupa Banerjee. 2007. Racial cohesion, social cohesion and policy issues in Canada. In *Belonging? Diversity, recognition and shared citizenship in Canada,* ed. Thomas J. Courchene, Keith Banting, and Leslie Seidle, 489–545. Montreal: Institute for Research on Public Policy.

Representation Act, 1985. 1986. SC 1986, c. 8.

Sauvé v. Canada (Chief Electoral Officer). 2002. 2002 SCC 68.

Statistics Canada. 2001. *Visible minority groups 2001 counts, for census metropolitan areas and census agglomerations.* Ottawa: Statistics Canada.

Statistics Canada. 2003a. *Canada's ethnocultural portrait: The changing mosaic.* Ottawa: Statistics Canada.

Statistics Canada. 2003b. *Earnings of Canadians: Making a living in the new economy. 2001 Census analysis series.* Catalogue no. 96F0030XIE2001013. Ottawa: Statistics Canada.

Statistics Canada. 2003c. *Ethnic diversity survey: Portrait of a multicultural society.* Ottawa: Statistics Canada.

Statistics Canada. 2005a. *Population projections for Canada, provinces and territories, 2005–2031.* Catalogue no. 91-520-XIE. Ottawa: Statistics Canada.

Statistics Canada. 2005b. *Population projections of visible minority groups, Canada, provinces and regions, 2001–2017.* Catalogue no. 91-541-XI. Ottawa: Statistics Canada.

Ward, Norman. 1963. *The Canadian House of Commons: Representation.* 2nd ed. Toronto: University of Toronto Press.

PART THREE
Election Campaigning

CHAPTER 6

Constituency Campaigning in Canada

Munroe Eagles and Annika Hagley

Introduction

After more than two decades of majority governments, Canadian federal elections have once again become intensely competitive. On October 14, 2008, Canadians elected their third successive minority government—only the second time in Canadian history in which a string of close, consecutive election results has been returned. The relative weakness of partisan sentiments in Canada compels political parties to campaign aggressively in pursuit of floating voters (LeDuc 2007, 166–168). That pursuit plays out in two arenas that collectively constitute an election campaign. National party campaign organizations conduct an "air war," dominated by leaders' tours, opinion polling, and issue advocacy. Meanwhile, local campaign teams conduct a "ground war" organized around the 308 districts defined by the country's single-member plurality electoral system (see Chapter 3 by Dennis Pilon). Election night results reflect a combination of both dimensions of electoral campaigning and, as we will see, untangling the relative contribution of campaign efforts in each of the two arenas and their potentially unique or combined impact on election night returns is a challenging empirical task.

The difficulty of unpacking causality and making distinctions between the air war and the ground war have impeded our understanding of the importance of each campaign, both in its own right and relative to the other. It has also pro- longed the debate among researchers, practitioners, and journalists over the electoral impact of local campaigns. Despite skepticism from some quarters, recent scholarly literature and the empirical analysis within this chapter strongly support the idea that local campaigns are an important aspect of national campaigns. We conclude that constituency campaigns really can make a significant difference both locally and nationally, especially during periods of intense electoral competition.

Drawing on comparative research on local campaigning in Anglo-American democracies, we begin by identifying the main components of electioneering in the constituency trenches and introduce a general model of the transformation of local campaigning. We then touch on the regulatory regime that governs the conduct of the ground wars (and, in the process, identify the key sources of some of our data). Finally, we turn to a discussion of the general pattern of constituency campaigning in the 2008 federal election, with particular attention paid to the "marginals"—those districts where the 2006 result was particularly close. These highly competitive local races may have produced a seat change from party to party, based upon a relatively small shift in the behaviour of the local electorate. The culmination of our research leads to a simple multivariate analysis that we use to provide evidence of the effectiveness of local campaigning (net of other influences) and to give an indication of how important the myriad of local influences on election results—including the local campaign—appear to have been in the 2008 federal election.

Local Campaigns in Westminster-Style Single-Member Plurality Systems

Along with a parliamentary system "similar in principle" to that of Britain, Canada (and other former British colonies such as the United States and New Zealand) inherited the British single-member plurality (SMP) electoral system. In SMP systems, as explained in Chapter 3, all candidates for office must gain their seat by winning a plurality of votes within their district. In turn, governments are formed by the party winning the most seats. Millions of dollars and many thousands of person hours are expended by local candidates and their activist supporters in the constituency trenches during an election campaign. Lawn signs, billboards, local all-candidate debates and meetings, door-to-door canvassing and leafleting, advertisements on local radio and in local print media, Get Out the Vote (GOTV) campaigns on election day, and other labour-intensive efforts are the stock-in-trade of the traditional local campaign.

Table 6.1 summarizes some of the key dimensions of a local campaign that potentially interact with national (and regional/provincial) campaigns to produce a local electoral result. The table begins by noting features associated with the nomination process that in some cases create divisions within the local party association that may carry over into the ensuing electoral campaign. These divisions may be the result of a "star" candidate chosen to run in the district by the party leader and displacing the candidate favoured by local party officials and activists. Alternatively, rivals for a party's nomination may engage in costly or negative campaigning that may detract from the eventual candidate's competitiveness during the election campaign itself.

**TABLE 6.1   Key Dimensions of Local Campaigns That Affect
the Local Electoral Result**

Nomination process

Level of conflict within the local association

Contested/non-contested nomination

Mobilization of minority communities

"Star candidate" appointed by central party leadership

Special deals among parties (e.g., Liberals/Greens leaders were not opposed by the other
party in their respective ridings in 2008)

The local candidate

Incumbency

Local roots

Personal qualities and campaigning competency

Prior political experience (including controversies, party switches, etc.)

implications (?)

The local campaign context and effort

Level of campaign spending

Activities and availability of campaign volunteers

Professionalization of campaign staff

Application of computer technologies

 • voter identification and tracking

 • local polling

GOTV activities

Competitiveness (marginality) of seat

Strategic voting

Involvement of extra-local actors

Training offered by central party to local campaign managers/officials

Central party supply of party advertising materials

Visit to riding by party leader

Channelling of non-local funds to local candidate's team

Sending of volunteers to campaign in riding from other area ridings

Targeting by party phone call centres

Involvement of local third-party organizations (e.g., right-to-life groups, etc.)

In the same way that party leaders exert important influence on voting behaviour, so too do the experience, personality, or other qualities of the local candidate—articulateness, knowledge, media savvy, et cetera—also contribute to the nature of the local campaign and its eventual outcome on election day. In particular, incumbents have been shown to enjoy significant advantages when they re-offer for a seat. The extent to which a candidate can claim local roots may also affect his or her appeal to the electorate in the district. These and other qualities of local candidates have been shown to be decisive factors in the vote decision for a minority of Canadian voters. Estimates differ as to the percentage of the electorate who cast a ballot primarily on the basis of the local candidates' characteristics, ranging from approximately 27 percent of the electorate in 1988 (Bell and Fletcher 1991, 5) to 5 percent in 2000 (Blais et al. 2003, 657–664).

The level of local campaign effort expended by a candidate's team during the lead-up to the campaign and the campaign period also influences the local result. The strength of the local party organization on the ground plays a role in determining how many volunteers will be attracted to the campaign, and how effectively and efficiently they will be deployed. Technologies such as local polls and voter identification software assist in ensuring that volunteer and other campaign resources are directed to where they will be most efficacious. Finally, the strength of the local campaign organization is critical in delivering the party's support at the polls on election day. Kenneth Carty and Munroe Eagles (2005) have shown that various measures of campaign effort (whether measured by door-to-door canvassing, local campaign-related spending, or other factors) are related to the share of the local vote won by a party's candidates.

In the closest races, grassroots efforts tend to be the most intense and are likely to attract the attention—and resources—from the national campaign team. Of course, there is a natural tension between the local and national aspects of an election campaign. At the grassroots, a party candidate focuses on maximizing his or her vote. From the perspective of the national campaign, however, the objective is to maximize seats (and only secondarily votes). Visits by prominent party leaders and the channelling of extra-riding money or other resources into the local race has the potential to alter the local political landscape on election day. Research has also demonstrated that the relative balance of power among parties in a constituency creates incentives for a minority of Canadian voters to place "strategic" votes. Such strategizing occurs when supporters of a party that enjoys only minor popularity locally opts not to vote sincerely for their first choice and instead cast strategic ballots for a more locally competitive but less-preferred second choice. According to Blais (2002), in the 1988 Canadian federal election, those voters whose favoured party actually finished third in the riding cast a ballot for their second-preferred party at a ratio of 1 to 8. Polling in the 2008 campaign by Ekos Research Associates suggested that about 20 percent of voters would reconsider their current vote intention if they "knew the Conservatives were about to win a majority election in this election" (Winsor and Soroka 2008). Liberal and NDP candidates were expected to benefit most from strategic voting, with the polling firm Strategic Counsel regularly releasing tracking polls (on CTV and in the *Globe and Mail*) focused on the 45 closest riding races throughout the campaign, thereby providing voters who were inclined to vote strategically in competitive settings an unprecedented amount of information to assist them in the process.

In recent elections, the Internet has opened up another avenue for Canadians to cast a "strategic" ballot by coordinating their behaviour with voters in other ridings where the competitive position of political parties differs. When Voter A prefers a party that is locally unviable, she can register online (at Votepair.ca or the "Anti-Harper Vote Swap" Facebook site) and offer to exchange her vote with Voter B in a riding where her preferred party stands a stronger prospect of winning. Other voters registered on the site are able to swap their vote with Voter A if they see that their preferred party is more viable in Voter A's riding than their own. Pairing their votes enables both voters to support a viable candidate for their party. According to Votepair.ca, roughly 6,000 voters registered to swap their votes with others in the 2008 federal election, and two close races in the election were influenced by vote pairing (Votepair.ca 2008). Clearly, strategic voting of either type is an activity engaged in by a small minority of the Canadian electorate, but it seems plausible to expect that such efforts will grow in popularity as citizens seek to cast a meaningful and consequential ballot.

The Persistence of Constituency Campaigning

For some decades, most students of elections have been convinced that local constituency-level campaigns do not matter. According to these individuals the canvassing, sign-posting, and GOTV efforts of local campaigns are quaint and ineffectual vestiges of an earlier—pre-modern—phase of political development. With the demise of traditional campaign techniques, they argue that national party campaigns, which are driven by sophisticated polling and television messaging, and focused around the appeals of leadership, that determine election outcomes.

The view that the national campaign was dominant found its earliest incarnation within the context of British elections. With its class-based two-party system dominating most constituencies in the decades following the Second World War, Britain was thought to epitomize the nationalization of political forces in the modern world. In that context, David Butler and Dennis Kavanagh (1974, 201) argued that in Britain "party leaders are now able to communicate directly with voters via the mass media … elections now turn on national events and issues, and voters choose between competing national parties rather than rival local candidates." The idea that campaigns had modernized and nationalized became the conventional understanding of how electioneering was evolving in most countries. Such a view continues to influence pundits and scholars of elections, as evidenced by the comments of senior *Maclean's* political columnist Andrew Coyne, who wrote dismissively of the importance of local campaigning in Canada: "Of course, as anyone who's ever followed an election will know, local campaigns are largely a fiction. Probably 80 per cent or more of a voter's choice has nothing to do with his riding or the candidates in it. The leader, the party, the platform—these are what matter (probably in that order) and the parties know it, which is why most local ads are more or less indistinguishable from the national ones" (Coyne 2008). Even if Coyne is correct and local factors account for only 20 percent of voter choice, in today's competitive political context this percentage is more than enough to make or break governments.

In an era of declining voter turnout (at 59 percent, the 2008 turnout rate was the lowest yet recorded in Canadian history), identifying supporters and getting them to the polls is perhaps the most critical component of the local campaign. Therefore, traditional methods associated with the ground war in SMP electoral systems have remained constant. In recent years, traditional local campaign methods have been augmented by the application of more sophisticated voter identification and mobilization techniques and technologies. Indeed, the development and growing deployment of sophisticated voter management databases built around powerful geographical information systems (GISs) speaks to the continued relevance of local campaigning and have likely increased its effectiveness. Even with the availability of new technology, however, experimental research undertaken in New Haven, Connecticut by several researchers at Yale University suggests that traditional methods may remain more effective in enhancing turnout. They found that whereas phone calls and leaflets had relatively little effect on turnout, face-to-face contact by means of a door-to-door canvass had a strong effect in encouraging voting (Gerber and Green 2000).

In the face of mounting evidence, scholars have begun to rethink conventional accounts of the irrelevance of the local campaign. Ironically, the re-examination of the impact and significance of local party campaign activity in Anglo-American systems began in Britain, which has long been regarded as having among the simplest and most nationalized of party systems (Stokes 1975). Using evidence from surveys of party officials, election agents, and party members, as well as the financial records of local party activity, scholars such as Justin Fisher, David Denver, and Gordon Hands (2006), Paul Whiteley and Patrick Seyd (2003), Charles Pattie and Ronald Johnston (2003), and most recently Edward Fieldhouse and David Cutts (2009) have demonstrated that local party activity does matter to election outcomes. Their work has measured the shifting place of constituency organization and activity over several electoral cycles as the contesting parties moved in and out of government.

One of the key findings of comparative research in the area of campaigning is the growing tendency for local races in particularly competitive settings to attract the attention of national party strategists. The rationale for this is simple: where seats were narrowly won in the preceding election, relatively small shifts in the local vote are needed to deliver the seat to a different party. The strategy of "targeting the marginals" for particularly intensive and aggressive campaigning—both by parties wishing to defend their narrowly won seats and by rivals wishing to unseat them—has become a central feature of campaigns in SMP electoral systems (Johnston and Pattie 2006, 204–212; Ward 2003). As such, because of the transfer of campaign resources into marginal seats, these settings have become a key point at which the air and ground campaigns intersect (see Chapter 8 by Thomas Flanagan for a discussion of the Conservative party's targeting strategy). Other points of intersection involve party leaders' tours, in which key politicians for each party visit particular districts. These districts are selected either to provide a suitable backdrop for a major policy announcement (a farm district for an announcement dealing with agriculture, for example, or a fishing village for a proposed initiative dealing with marine resources) or because the local race is expected to be close and a visit from a party dignitary is predicted to shore up the local candidate's campaign (see Carty and Eagles 2005, chap. 7).

Clearly, the diversity of electoral districts and the varied competitive positions of the parties across them create a complex environment—one comprising a myriad of opportunities and constraints—for partisan mobilization. While the relatively large number of constituencies comprising Canada's electoral system has encouraged quantitative researchers to look for general patterns, more qualitative efforts have also been forthcoming. For example, Bell and Fletcher (1991) present case studies of constituency campaigning in five pairs of ridings in different parts of the country. A more ambitious attempt to develop a theoretical typological framework for understanding constituency campaigns has been offered by Anthony Sayers. An ethnographic analysis of local campaigning by the (then) three major parties in seven federal electoral districts in British Columbia in the 1988 contest led Sayers to identify four major types of local campaigns based on the party's local competitiveness, its organizational openness to challenges in the nomination of candidates, and the level of competition of the candidate's nomination process (Sayers 1999). According to Sayers, Canada's cadre-style (Liberals and Conservatives) local party associations located in competitive districts in which there was a contested nomination process typically saw the eventual nomination of *local notables.* The notable candidates went on to mount highly personalized *parochial campaigns* that were weakly integrated with that of the wider party strategy. Those same parties' less electorally appealing districts typically produce uncontested nominations, giving rise to *stopgap candidates* who run token campaigns that *parallel* those of their national party. Contested nominations in mass-style parties (like the NDP) produce *party insiders* who conduct *subsidiary campaigns* that are well integrated into the party's national campaign. Finally, incumbents (in all parties) and non-contested cadre party nominations in very competitive districts have *high-profile* candidates whose election campaigns constitute significant *components* of their national parties' overall election campaigns. (See Chapter 7 by Steve Patten for an explanation of the candidate nomination process.)

Parties may differ from one another in the nature of their local campaigning, and within parties the nature of grassroots electioneering will likely evolve over time. Two political scientists who have been very active in studying the local dimension of campaigning in Britain over time have developed a three-stage model to capture what they argue are the key aspects of modernization in constituency electioneering (Fisher and Denver 2008). In Table 6.2, we have adapted their model for the purposes of understanding Canadian constituency campaigns. Drawing on their work, we identify three features of the local campaign that are dynamic over time, in keeping with larger changes in mass communications technology and larger social transformations: duration and techniques, resources, and integration and targeting.

Following Fisher and Denver, we distinguish three stages of development, referred to as the *traditional, modern,* and *postmodern.* First, we look at the relative shifts in the mix of technology, the time frame of campaigning, and the application of labour-intensive activities (*duration and techniques*). The dimension of *resources* refers primarily to the availability and sources of money, labour, and expertise, with specific reference to the adaptability of the local campaign during the election period. Finally,

TABLE 6.2   A Developmental Model of Local Campaigning in Canada

[handwritten: everyone else]   *[handwritten: Conservatives in this stage]*

	Traditional stage	Modern stage	Postmodern stage
Duration and techniques	Little inter-election activity	Longer-term preparation	Permanent campaigning
	Primarily volunteer campaigners—labour-intensive	Specialist campaign committee appointed within local association	Specialist campaign committee directs campaign
	Low technology	Application of technology along with traditional methods	Technology replaces traditional labour-intensive methods
Resources	Autonomous constituency campaigns	Centralized and standardized party messaging	Decentralized campaign under strict central scrutiny
	No flow of money or other resources from outside riding	Volunteer workers directed by trained party professionals	Professional staff
	Adaptations during campaign the result of local canvassing	Multiple sources of information for modifying campaign strategy	Greater range of local polling and information gathering during campaign
Integration and targeting	"Whistle-stop" tours of party leaders	Leaders' tours target marginal seats	Party leaders only visit marginal seats
	Minimal efforts at "branding" and consistency of party message	"Star" candidates appointed by party leader	District campaigns more important than national campaign
	Little targeting of marginal ridings	Resource flows from national campaign to marginal seats	Targeting of individual voters by coordinated national and local campaigns

Source: Adapted from Fisher and Denver (2008, fig. 1, 799).

we look at the integration and relative importance of local campaigns within the larger party campaign effort (*integration and targeting*). We trace a general trend in which local campaigns gain in significance vis-à-vis the national campaign while simultaneously becoming more professionalized, more technology-dependent, and more continuous. Although the developmental nature of the model suggests that Canadian constituency campaigns should be moving over time from traditional to postmodern, the movement across stages is neither predetermined nor invariable.

Certainly, not all parties in Canada move through these stages simultaneously and, for a variety of reasons, some parties may lag considerably behind others. Moreover, changes in the priorities of different party leaders and shifts in the competitiveness (either national or local) of the party may both influence the techniques, resources, and level of integration of local campaigns, and there may be slippage back to earlier stages experienced by a party from time to time. Although we do not have sufficient information to fully test the suitability of this model, we present evidence in later sections of this chapter that touch on several dimensions of this account of the evolution of local campaigning.

Regulating Constituency Parties and Campaigns

In early 2000, the House of Commons introduced legislation limiting campaign-related expenditures by "third parties"—interest groups seeking to participate in the campaign—to $150,000 nationwide and to $3,000 in any particular constituency (adjusted for inflation annually). Groups spending less than $500 do not have to register with and report to Elections Canada, but all others must. In 2004, the new regulations were upheld by the Supreme Court of Canada, and they remain in place today. These constraints have not eliminated third-party involvement in federal elections—indeed, in the 2006 election, third parties collectively spent more than $1 million. As Chapter 4 by Heather MacIvor details, Canadian parties have become increasingly dependent on the state for funding and other resources. In return, all political entities are required to disclose their finances to the public. One welcome consequence of the new disclosure rules is a veritable goldmine of data provided by local and national party organizations and third parties, that can be used for research purposes. In the account of the ground war waged in the fall of 2008, we draw heavily upon these data.[1] (For a more comprehensive discussion of political finance, see Chapter 4. We have only touched on those developments in campaign finance regulation that are directly relevant to our data.)

The Ground War in the 2008 Federal Election

At the grassroots, party politics in Canada is extremely competitive. In the decade 1984–1994, for example, 80 percent of the constituencies were represented by members of at least two different parties. More recently, in 2006, the average margin of victory separating the winner from the runner-up was 20.7 percent; but nearly one-sixth of the seats (49 ridings) were decided by a margin of 5 percent or less. Only 21 seats separated the victorious Harper Conservatives from the Liberal runners-up, so small shifts in voter support in many ridings may well have resulted in a different outcome in terms of the government formed after the election. Similarly, in the 2008 contest, 42 districts were decided by similar victory margins, and 13 seats were decided by a 1 percent or smaller margin. The closest race in the country in 2008 was in the riding of Kitchener-Waterloo, where Conservative MP Peter Braid was re-elected by a mere 17 votes over his Liberal rival. The second-closest race was in the riding of Vancouver South, where Liberal Ujjal Dosanjh was able to retain his seat by a margin of only 20 votes. One important consequence of the closeness of riding races is high turnover rates in the House of Commons. For example, the 2008 election returned 74 rookie MPs (almost a quarter of all MPs) to the legislature, and after the election 208 MPs (53.4 percent of the total) had served less than five years (Public Policy Forum 2009). Canada's politicians, therefore, tend to be political amateurs (Atkinson and Docherty 1992).

In such a competitive environment, even relatively small shifts in voter support can be decisive. "Every riding is important. The closer ones, you need to watch a little tighter and I personally think the local Member of Parliament or the local people running can draw two, three, four or five per cent of the vote and that could make the difference between winning and losing," said Mike Wallace, Conservative MP for Burlington, Ontario, who won in 2004 by a margin of 4 percent (Rana 2008a). Others have rated the efficacy of a strong local campaign in attracting votes more highly. For example, Tom Flanagan, the former campaign director of the Conservative Party, describes what he refers to as the "Rule of Ten": "Canadian experience suggests that a strong local campaign backed up by a vigorous Direct Voter Contact (DVC) program can increase a party's vote share by as much as 10 percentage points over the results of the last election" (see page 158).

Local campaigning, then, is ignored at a candidate's peril. Parties and their candidates are well aware of this fact, as the relative amounts spent on the air and ground wars attest. In the 1988 general election, for example, the three principal parties spent about 30 percent more on their candidates' local campaigns than on their national party campaigns ($29 million versus $22 million; Stanbury 1991, tables 3.4 and 12.1). The same preoccupation with local campaigns can also be seen in the mobilization of large numbers of party activists engaged in voter contact on behalf of local candidates. About three-quarters of all local party associations rate the local canvass as "important" or "very important" to their campaign activity (Carty 1991, 185). The national election surveys have discovered that candidates and local party workers contact large numbers of Canadians during the campaign period, and it seems unlikely that they would sustain this level of effort and expenditure if there were no return in terms of votes.

Elections in Canada are expensive, but not prohibitively so by comparative standards (and particularly when the comparison is with the United States). As described in Chapter 4, political parties offering candidates in all 308 ridings were legally able to spend approximately $20 million on the air war during the 2008 campaign based on an allocation of 70 cents per elector in those ridings where the party fielded a candidate. In addition, local candidates were permitted to spend an approximate average of $85,000 in their ground wars. Candidates' precise spending limits are also determined by the number of electors on the rolls in the candidate's district, with an allowance of $2.07 for each of the first 15,000 electors in the constituency; $1.04 for each of the next 10,000 electors; and $0.52 for each additional elector. This allowance is increased when the number of electors per square kilometre in a constituency is less than ten (such constituencies are likely to be geographically larger than those with higher population densities). This means that a party fielding a full slate of 308 candidates could legally spend approximately $26 million in the constituency trenches in 2008. Of course, the amount spent locally depends on a variety of factors, including the candidate and local association's capacity to raise money, the competitiveness of the race, the presence of an incumbent, and a host of other factors. Although final expenditure reports for a handful of candidates for the 2008 federal campaign are not yet available from Elections Canada, it is possible to use the financial reports that have been filed to date (May 2009) to derive a general depiction of the local campaigns that were waged in the last election. The available data suggest that local campaigning was intense in the 2008 contest. In 2008, Conservative candidates spent an average of about 74 percent of the locally allowable limit ($N = 288$), while Liberal candidates ($N = 270$) spent on average only 53 percent of the legal limit, and NDP candidates ($N = 261$) spent only 28 percent. Bloc Québécois candidates ($N = 68$) spent on average 61 percent of the allowed limit.[2] By contrast, the Conservatives' "air campaign" spent almost $19.5 million, or 97.1 percent of its legal limit. The Liberals spent only 72.6 percent of their allowable national limit, whereas the NDP and BQ reported spending 83.8 percent and 96.3 percent of their respective legal limits.

Third parties were able to spend a maximum of approximately $183,000 in attempting to influence the election outcome. Sixty-four such organizations registered with Elections Canada, but most spent a small fraction of their allowable limit and a good deal of this expenditure was general in nature, not aimed at influencing any particular riding result. Table 6.3 provides a general indication of the distribution of the 2008 spending. In only one case—that of the ABC (Anything But Conservative) campaign led by popular Newfoundland Conservative premier Danny Williams in that province alone—was this type of campaigning likely to have produced much electoral impact. In that province, there were three Conservative seats going into the 2008 campaign, however, for the first time since the province joined Canada, all Conservative candidates went down to defeat on election night. After the election, defeated Conservative incumbent Fabian Manning (Avalon) told reporters: "When you're dealing with the popularity of the premier here in Newfoundland and Labrador and you have several of his ministers travelling around the riding, campaigning for the ABC campaign, I think it would be naive to think that it didn't play a part in tonight's results" (Canadian Press 2008).

As noted above, in their ground wars, candidates and local parties respond to a variety of features of the local constituency environment. A major determinant of their campaign effort is likely to be the probability of winning (or, for incumbents, losing) the race, something that can be gauged roughly from the previous result in the riding. When the last race was closely decided, candidates gear up their local effort in an attempt to gain the additional number of votes necessary to either protect their lead or swing the seat. In Figure 6.1, which shows the average amount spent by candidates from the four major parties in their local races as a function of the margin of victory in the 2006 election, it is clear that the intensity of local competition was much higher in the ridings that were won by the smallest margins in the preceding election.

TABLE 6.3   Selected Third-Party Interventions, 2008

Group	Amount spent	How spent?
ABC (Anything But Conservative) Campaign (NF)	$81,370	Newspaper ads; billboards; website in Newfoundland only
Alliance of Canadian Cinema, Television, and Radio Artists	$9,300	Newspaper ads in local papers in approximately 20 selected markets, esp. NB, ON, and BC
Canadian Labour Congress	$179,936	Newspaper ads coast to coast
Canadian Shooting Sports Association	$2,923	Posters to businesses and clubs; ad in "Canadian Access to Firearms"
Canadian Union of Public Employees	$174,687	Contributions to other third parties; ads in Halifax and Winnipeg; partnership with Smartvote
Citizens Against High Taxes	$2,240	Signs (Richmond, BC)
Common Sense Advocacy of Victoria	$3,518	Newspaper ad (Victoria, BC)
Dogwood Initiative	$3,287	Voice-mail messages and newspaper ad (Victoria, BC)
Le Sans-Chemise	$41,503	Variety of ads (French language)
Make Poverty History	$44,775	Media experts (CTV); print and electronic ads
National Citizens Coalition	$86,516	Ads taken out in AB and ON, and cities such as Ottawa and Regina
Saanich Peninsula Citizens Council	$3,155	Radio and newspaper ads (local)
Simon Fraser Student Society	$1,239	Three ads in student newspaper (the *Peak*)
Tourism Industry Association of Canada	$167,068	Print and online ads in the *Globe and Mail*, *La Presse*, *Vancouver Sun*, *Province* (Vancouver), and Cyberpresse

Source: Data taken from Elections Canada website. http://www.elections.ca.

According to this simple test, slightly more than a third of the total variation in mean spending by candidates is attributable to the narrowness of the 2006 local result.

Roughly the same conclusion emerges from an inspection of Table 6.4, which shows the level of spending (overall and by party) in the "target races" (defined either by the media or by a margin of victory in 2006 of 5 percent or less). Overall, candidates in races regarded as "targets" or close spent between 12 percent and 13 percent more than their counterparts in other ridings. Liberal candidates appeared to be the most responsive to the competitive context, spending on average about 22 percent to 25

FIGURE 6.1   Mean Percent of Limit Spent by the Major Parties and the 2006 Victory Margin

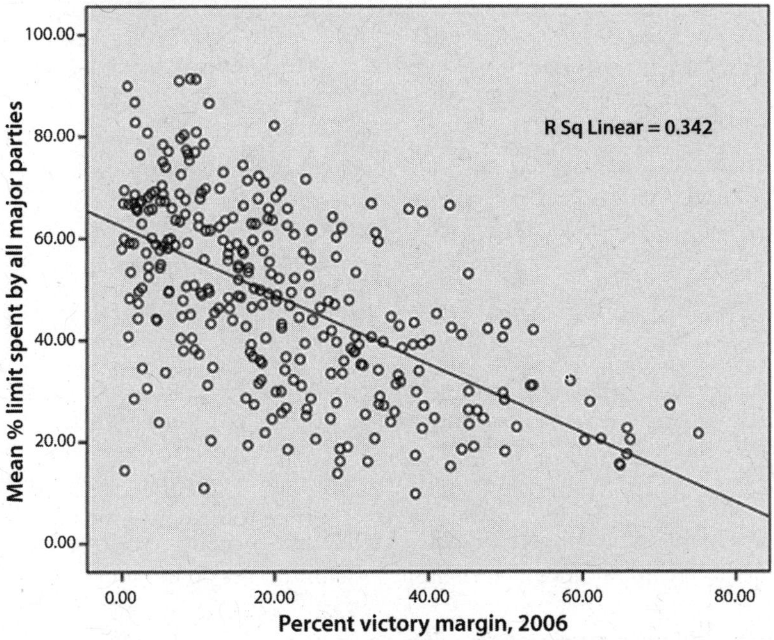

Source: Calculated using data from Elections Canada. http://www.elections.ca.

percent more in the closest races. Reflecting the party's greater financial resources, Conservative candidates spent more heavily in the non-targeted ridings than others. However, their spending was slightly higher in targeted races (and the difference in means was statistically significant). The relative financial weakness of most NDP candidates is clear in this table—even in targeted races their candidates could manage to spend on average less than a third of the legally allowable limit (and barely over a fifth of the limit in non-target seats). The BQ stands out as an anomaly in this respect, with candidates spending seemingly regardless of the closeness of the race (the difference in means between targets and non-targets was not statistically significant and, in any event, the party's candidates in non-target seats appeared to spend more heavily than in the closer races). However, notwithstanding this exception, it is clear that local parties and candidates respond to the opportunity that a marginal seat provides by raising and spending more campaign money. In the next section, we explore this pattern within each party more fully when we look at patterns of election spending and their effectiveness. We also briefly explore some of the races that produced results that deviated most strongly from general patterns of party support across the country predicted using a statistical model that controls for a variety of socioeconomic, political, campaign, and geographic factors that have been shown in previous research to be associated with patterns of party support (after provincial variations are statistically controlled). Although we cannot precisely determine why these ridings departed from

**TABLE 6.4   Percent of Allowable Limit Spent by Parties:
Target Versus Non-Target Seats**

	Conservatives		Liberals		NDP		BQ		Mean % limit spent by all major parties	
	Target	**Non-target**	**Target**	**Non-target**	**Target**	**Non-target**	**Target**	**Non-target**	**Target**	**Non-target**
Target (media)	76.1 (56)	68.4 (249)	65.8 (56)	43.3 (248)	31.2 (56)	22.1 (248)	59.3 (15)	59.1 (60)	59.1 (56)	46.1 (247)
Target (≤ 5% margin in 2006)	73.7 (44)	69.2 (261)	68.9 (44)	43.8 (260)	30.0 (44)	22.7 (260)	47.1 (9)	56.0 (66)	58.2 (44)	46.8 (259)

Note: Target seats were won in 2006 by a margin of 5% or less, as identified by Rana (2008a). Difference of means tests suggest that differences in spending between target and non-target seats was statistically significant at the 0.05 level or better for all except the BQ.

Source: Calculated using data from Elections Canada. http://www.elections.ca. Media targets are taken from Rana (2008b).

general patterns in the support for each party, in these deviating results we find strong evidence of the importance of specifically local influences on the vote.

The Local Campaigns of the Major Parties in the 2008 Federal Election

The Conservatives campaigned as the incumbent governing party in 2008, and hoped to swing enough seats their way to enable them to form a majority government. They entered the campaign in by far the strongest financial position, the result of a carefully planned strategy of fundraising that, in addition to the party's publically funded quarterly allowances, attracts some 175,000 donations (average value $115) to the party annually. According to one strategist commenting after the election: "We have created complex, leading-edge fundraising techniques such as data-mining, segmentation, targeted marketing and relationship management—all in an effort to move our pool of identified supporters up the support pyramid from supporters to members to donors" (Chase 2008). In this respect, in terms of the developmental model of local campaigns discussed earlier, Conservative campaigns appear to have entered the "postmodern" stage. By contrast, the Liberals remained handicapped by financial problems. One commentator noted after the election that whereas the Conservatives attracted 159,000 donations in 2007, the NDP received 53,000 but the Liberals could attract only 36,000 (Axworthy 2008). Not surprisingly, one of new leader Michael Ignatieff's announced priorities in rebuilding the Liberals after the 2008 defeat has been to adopt a stronger, more centralized, and more sophisticated information system to track Liberal support and assist in the conduct of local campaigns (Valpy 2009, A4).

As we saw earlier, differences in the ability to raise money are particularly strongly reflected in the spending behaviour of local candidates. Affluent parties tend to spend with less regard to local conditions, perhaps realizing that every vote earned on election day translates into a revenue stream to the party for the life of the Parliament. Less well-off parties are more constrained to focus on seat maximization and therefore tend to concentrate campaign efforts on the marginal seats where the probability of a victory seems more likely. Figure 6.2 illustrates the spending behaviour of candidates for each of the four major parties as a function of the closeness of the 2006 result. The patterns in these scatter plots show that the targeting behaviour of local parties goes beyond the concentration of campaign resources on the closest races. In general, all party candidates spend a lower proportion of the legal limit as the victory margin (separating the top two finishers) in 2006 grows. This is particularly true for the cash-strapped Liberals in 2008. The steep downward sloping line on the Liberal chart shows that Liberal candidates spent considerably less as the 2006 victory margin increased. The NDP's chart also shows a sensitivity to riding competitiveness, but the lack of viable campaigns in many competitive districts shows that this party remains weak in many parts of the country (especially in the province of Quebec). Both the Conservatives and the BQ candidates seemed less responsive than either the Liberals or the NDP to the local competitive context.

Therefore, local campaigns vary in their intensity, both among and within parties. How much impact does this spending have, net of other factors that influence patterns of party support? Table 6.5 extracts the results from a multivariate analysis (see the appendix) illustrating the impact of incumbency and campaign spending (the percentage of the allowable limit spent by candidates for a party) on the share of the vote going to a party's candidates in 2008. Incumbents typically enjoy a number of advantages when running for re-election, prominent among them being a stronger local party organization (Carty and Eagles 2005, 20–25). Our results confirm earlier research: incumbents for all major parties attract significantly greater electoral support than challengers for their party. Conservative incumbents won 16.1 percent more than non-incumbents, after controlling for other factors included in the statistical model. The average vote percentage for NDP incumbents was more than 15 percent greater than for NDP challengers, while Liberal incumbents were 12.7 percent more successful than Liberal challengers. While smaller, the incumbency advantage for BQ candidates in 2008 was still a substantial 11.7 percent.

Similarly, the results in the second row of Table 6.5 confirm earlier research in suggesting that campaign spending is an important determinant of constituency electoral outcomes. The impact is greatest for NDP candidates, where spending an additional 1 percent of the allowable constituency expense limit generates almost a quarter of a percent (0.24) increase in the share of the local vote going to NDP candidates. Spending an additional 1 percent of the limit by Liberal candidates was associated with a 0.14 percent increase in electoral support for their candidates, while the comparable figure for Conservative spending was 0.10 percent. Only in the case of the BQ was campaign spending found not to be a significant determinant of that party's share of the vote in Quebec constituencies. Since there are many complications in untangling the independent effect of local spending on votes, these estimates should

Conservatives strategy
spending most $ in
areas they
are least
likely to
win.

FIGURE 6.2   Targeting Strategies of Major Parties, 2008

Conservative targeting

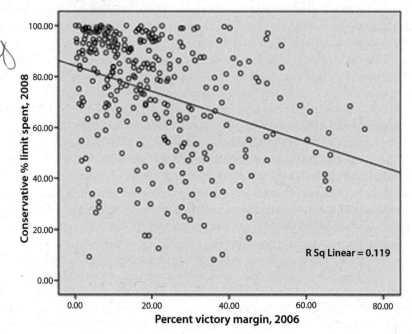

Liberal targeting

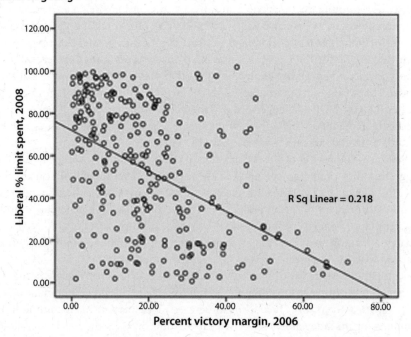

FIGURE 6.2   Continued

NDP targeting

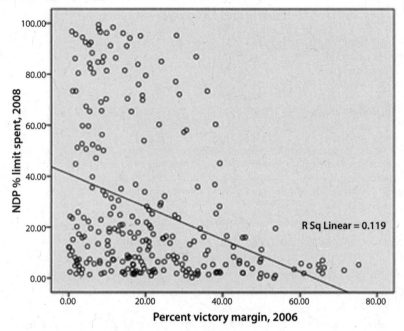

BQ targeting

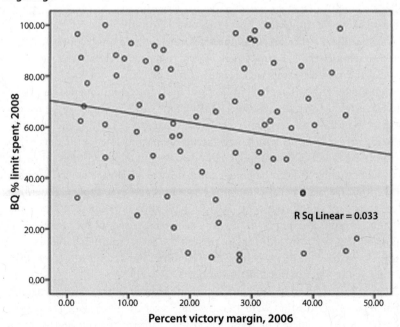

Source: Calculated using data from Elections Canada. http://www.elections.ca.

TABLE 6.5   Estimates* of the Impact of Local Spending and Incumbency on the Vote for Major Parties, 2008

	Conservative	Liberal	NDP	BQ
% of incumbent advantage over non-incumbent candidates for the party	16.1	12.7	15.3	11.7
% of legal allowable limit spent	0.097	0.14	0.24	n.s.

* Estimates are unstandardized OLS regression coefficients taken from regressions using the percentage of vote for each party as the dependent variable, and controlling for a range of other constituency and geographic characteristics. For those interested, the general results of the full models can be seen in the appendix to this chapter—full details are available from the authors.

n.s. = not significant.

be regarded as only general indications of the nature of this relationship (see Carty and Eagles 2005, 131–134). However, taken with evidence from other Canadian (and comparative) research, they do provide compelling evidence that the efforts of local campaign teams were successful in shaping riding-level electoral outcomes in 2008.

As a final indication of the impact of local factors on the 2008 outcome, we examine five instances for each party in which the statistical model we employ to estimate the importance of a variety of socioeconomic, ethnolinguistic, political, and provincial-level determinants of party support generates a predicted level of party support that is significantly different (either higher or lower) from the observed level of support that was recorded for the party after the votes were counted on election night. In other words, we identify the five constituencies where the general patterns we observe in the social and political bases were least useful in explaining the local outcome for a party/candidate and where, by implication, local factors intervened to distort the party's level of support. Because we lack direct measures of many of the factors that we expect to influence a party's performance in particular constituencies, we are not able to identify specifically which local factors are responsible for the deviation from the party's expected level of support. However, the model incorporates the local factors of incumbency and campaign spending in its general parameters, so the effects of these local factors have already been taken into account. Table 6.6 identifies the five most deviant riding results by party in 2008, showing in percentage terms how far the local result deviated from the expected result based on the general model of support for that party. In addition, we present the actual result in 2008 for the party, identify the party of the incumbent (if any) running, and describe the level of election spending by the party in the constituency.

Looking first at the most deviant Conservative results, three ridings virtually tied for having local results that were 16.6 percent lower than the level of Conservative support that was predicted by the relationships captured by our general model of

TABLE 6.6   Five Most Deviant Riding Results, 2008, by Party

	Riding	% Deviation from predicted vote	% Vote (2008)	Incumbent	% of legal spending limit
Conservatives	Acadie-Bathurst (NB)	−16.6	18.6	NDP	83.2
	Haldimand-Norfolk (ON)	−16.6	40.8	Cons	79.2
	Edmonton-Strathcona (AB)	−16.6	41.6	Cons	98.9
	Beauce (QC)	+16.3	62.4	Cons	79.5
	Trinity-Spadina (ON)	−15.9	13.8	NDP	57.1
Liberals	Saanich-Gulf Islands (BC)	+20	39.4	Cons	90.1
	Bonavista-Gander-Grand Falls-Windsor (NF)	+18.1	70.3	Lib	25.5
	York West (ON)	+13.7	59.4	Lib	45.9
	Labrador (NF)	+13.6	70.5	Lib	32.9
	Etobicoke North (ON)	+12.8	48.9	Open	69.4
NDP	St. John's East (NF)	+24	74.6	Open	98.4
	Avalon (NF)	−17.2	17.4	Cons	30.5
	Nickel Belt (ON)	+14.8	46.5	Open	67.4
	Sackville-Eastern Shore (NS)	+14.7	61.4	NDP	57.3
	Don Valley West (ON)	−13.4	10.2	Open	79.5
BQ	Gatineau	−17	29.2	BQ	88.2
	Longueuil–Pierre-Boucher	+14	46.1	Open	59.7
	Rimouski-Temiscouata-Les Basques	+12.9	44.7	Open	31.5
	La Pointe-de-l'Île	+11.5	56.1	BQ	64.7
	Repentigny	+11	53.1	Open	98.7

Source: Residuals derived from the regression analysis presented in the appendix to this chapter.

voting for the party in 2008. Acadie-Bathurst (NB) is the most francophone riding outside Quebec, and has been represented since 1997 by NDP incumbent Yves Godin. It was inhospitable ground for the Tory candidate, a businessman with no prior political experience. In the rural riding of Haldimand-Norfolk (ON), incumbent Conservative Cabinet minister Diane Finley's re-election campaign was probably hurt by the independent candidacy of Gary McHale. McHale, a libertarian who appealed to the riding's more conservative voters, probably took most of his 10.1 percent of the constituency vote from Finley. In Edmonton-Strathcona (AB), Conservative MP Rahim Jaffer narrowly held the seat in 2006 (having been first elected as a Reform MP in 1997) and lost it in 2008 to the NDP's Linda Duncan by a mere 442 votes. In the southern Quebec riding of Beauce, incumbent candidate Maxime Bernier had been much in the news earlier in the year for his careless handling of confidential files and his relationship with Ms. Julie Couillard. He had been forced to resign as Minister of Foreign Affairs some months before the election. None of this seemed to detract from his popularity, and he won almost two of every three votes cast. Businesswoman Conservative candidate Christine McGirr was unable to get much traction running against NDP incumbent Olivia Chow or Liberal candidate Christine Innes, a lawyer who is married to former Liberal MP Tony Ianno (who represented Trinity-Spadina (ON) for 13 years, between 1993 and 2006).

In the context of the party's worst electoral showing since Confederation, a number of Liberal campaigns met with unusual success in 2008. All five of the most deviant results for the party came in ridings where the local candidate attracted between 12.8 and 20 percent more of the vote than the general model of Liberal support predicted. In Saanich-Gulf Islands (BC), for example, Liberal candidate Briony Penn benefited from the withdrawal from active campaigning of the NDP candidate (Julian West) following revelations that he had behaved inappropriately at an environmental camp he had run. Since he withdrew after the deadline established by Elections Canada, his name remained on the ballot but the NDP won only 5.7 percent of the vote, while the Liberal vote share swelled by about 13 percent over their 2006 result. The party's better than expected finishes in York West (ON) and Etobicoke North (ON) came in heavily "ethnic" ridings where the party has established a dominant presence. The strongly positive results in Bonavista-Gander-Grand Falls-Windsor (NF) probably reflect the third-party ABC campaign mentioned above reinforcing the incumbency advantage of the two sitting Liberal MPs (Scott Simms and Todd Russell, respectively).

For the NDP, the 2008 election was a relative success, with the party winning 37 seats, up from 8 in its 2006 showing. Three of their most anomalous finishes in 2008 were in ridings where their candidate did much better than expected, based on the general patterns of NDP electoral support as captured by our general model. In St. John's East (NF), the retirement of Conservative incumbent Norm Doyle, coupled with the ABC campaign, opened up a three-way contest. Winning the seat for the NDP was former MP and provincial party leader Jack Harris, who had held the seat for nine months between winning a 1987 by-election and losing in the 1988 general election. In the neighbouring riding of Avalon (NF), however, NDP candidate Randy Dawe won about 17 percent less of the local vote than expected based on the relationships measured in the general model and the riding's characteristics. It is possible that Dawe's previous attempts to get elected in the region as a Progressive Conservative (1997) and a member of the Canadian Alliance (2000) made it difficult for him to gain traction in the two-way race between incumbent Conservative Fabian Manning and his Liberal challenger Scott Andrews. The latter won the riding with a margin of victory of about 10 percent. In Nickel Belt (ON), the resignation of the Liberal incumbent gave the NDP's Claude Gravelle an opportunity to regain some ground for the party. He had run unsuccessfully for the party in 2004 and 2006. In the riding of Sackville-Eastern Shore (NS), veteran NDP MP Peter Stoffer further consolidated his hold on the riding he first won in 1997, taking almost 15 percent more of the local vote than the model predicted.

The riding of Gatineau represents the BQ's most deviant local result in 2008. The incumbent Bloc MP Richard Nadeau faced Françoise Boivin for a second time in this election. Ms. Boivin won the seat in 2004 for the Liberals before losing to Nadeau in 2006. She ran in 2008 for the NDP and managed to reduce Nadeau's share of the vote by about 10 percent over the 2006 result. The remaining four most deviant ridings experienced higher levels of support than was predicted by the general model—all of them are traditional BQ strongholds, having returned MPs from this party since 1993 (the first general election contested by the party).

Conclusion

Federal elections are complex events. Ground campaigns are especially complex, since there are a myriad of factors that come to bear upon a constituency electorate and help shape the election outcome locally. In this chapter, we have shown that the local dimension of election campaigning is alive and well in Canada. Most of the local impact arises from the activities of political parties and their candidates, but third parties sometimes intervene in particular local races in an effort to influence the outcome. Supplementing the air campaigns waged by national party campaign organizations, each local party candidate raises and spends considerable sums of money in an effort to win a seat in the House of Commons. This spending is concentrated, as we would expect, on the most competitive ridings. We have shown that such spending is efficacious in attracting votes (for all parties except the BQ). Even when party strategies and information systems are increasingly centralizing information and strengthening the hand of the central party campaign apparatus in some cases (especially the Conservatives), votes are harvested riding by riding in the constituency trenches. As voter turnout declines, developing local party organizations capable of turning out the vote on election day are going to grow—not diminish—in importance.

Although we lack sufficient evidence to make a definitive judgment regarding the evolution of local campaigning according to the general developmental model discussed earlier, our data seem to suggest that most of Canada's local campaigns can be classified as "modern" under our developmental model. Only the Conservatives appear to have entered the postmodern phase in terms of their local campaigns. Our brief survey of the character of local riding-level campaigns suggests that a host of factors beyond party strategy and outside party involvement, however, combine to influence constituency electoral contests. The magnitude of these local deviations from more general patterns and relationships suggests that idiosyncratic factors can and do intervene to shape local outcomes in federal elections, and that national (and provincial) factors themselves do not account for constituency-level election outcomes. For all these reasons, a full understanding of the complexity of Canadian federal elections necessarily includes a local perspective.

APPENDIX

We used a statistical technique called regression analysis to estimate the direction, strength, and statistical significance of relationships among a wide variety of possible causes of constituency-level variation in party support (representing geographic, socioeconomic, cultural, and political variables) and the level of actual party support obtained in the 2008 federal election. Regression analysis is popular in social science because it allows investigators to assess the independent contribution of each hypothesized causal factor while statistically controlling the influence of all other causal variables included in the model. In most cases, the purpose of regression analysis is to identify and understand underlying relationships—in this case, to identify and understand the underlying causes of the variation in support for political parties. However, our goal for the purposes of this chapter is unusual in that we sought primarily to identify ridings in which the model we developed performed *least well* in explaining the local result. To do this, we looked at the level of party support that the model predicted for a given riding if the variables included in the model alone perfectly accounted for the party's local vote share (that is, no other unmeasured influences affected the outcome) and compared this predicted result with the actual result we observed on election day. Obviously, our model is a simplified version of reality, and, in particular, it does not include many direct measures of the kind of local influences that we have discussed (and that appear in Table 6.1). Thus, it is not surprising that the model's *predicted* values for a party's local electoral result are different from the *actual* vote observed on election day. In the language of regression analysis, the difference between the predicted and actual level of electoral support is known as a "residual." Constituencies with large residuals are ones that deviated most from the expectations of the general model, and we argue that those ridings are ones in which the local influences had the greatest impact in 2008.

Constituency-Level Models of Party Support, 2008*

	Variable	Conservative	Liberal	NDP	BQ
Constant		+	+	+	
Geography	NF	−	+	+	
	PEI		+		
	NS	−		+	
	NB				
	QC	−		−	
	MB	+	−	+	
	SK		−	+	
	AB	+	−		
	BC		−	+	
	North				
Socioeconomic	managers	+	+	−	
	university degrees	−		−	
	unemployed	−			
	agriculture	+		−	−
	French speaking				+
	immigrants	+	+		−
	total population		−		
Political	% incumbent advantage over non-incumbent candidates for the party	16.1	12.7	15.3	11.7
	% of legal allowable limit spent	0.097	0.14	0.24	n.s.
Adjusted *R*-squared		0.85	0.83	0.84	0.71
N		286	268	260	66

* OLS regression; direction of impact of statistically significant variables indicated (+ positive; − negative).
n.s. = not significant.

NOTES

1. Researchers in other settings have also relied heavily upon campaign spending data (captured by the regulatory regime in place to limit spending) as a proxy measure for the strength of the local campaign. In the British context, for example, Charles Pattie et al. (1994, 472–474) have argued that "local campaign spending is an acceptable measure of campaign effort." Unfortunately, this is less true in Canada. Earlier research suggests that there is little relationship between volunteers available for campaigning and the amount of money spent (see Carty and Eagles 2005, 124–125). Lacking any systematic information on campaign teams or local party organizations during the 2008 campaign, however, we are forced to rely on the financial data alone.

2. We do not examine Green Party campaigns in this chapter. This is because of the party's weakness in most settings. Although the party fielded 303 candidates in the 2008 election, most of these were token efforts launched by the party to harvest any votes that might be available to claim their "allowance" from the public purse (see Curry 2008). One of the candidates, Danielle Moreau in Longueuil–Pierre-Boucher, withdrew from campaigning on October 9 and supported the Liberal candidate not to fragment the "environmental vote." From this, and in light of the "whistle-stop" (non-targeted) nature of Elizabeth May's leader's tour, it seems likely to infer that Green campaigning at the grassroots is still at the traditional stage in the developmental model discussed earlier.

DISCUSSION QUESTIONS

1. Why did many scholars expect local election campaigns to diminish in significance over time relative to the national election campaigns organized by political parties?
2. Which of the local factors that influence electoral outcomes mentioned in this chapter seem to be the most important? Why?
3. What does it mean for parties to "target the marginals" in their campaigning? Why might they want to do this?
4. The legislation limiting campaign-related spending by third parties continues to be controversial in Canada. What do you think about this legislation? Should third parties be allowed to spend freely in support of particular parties and/or candidates during an election? Consider arguments for and against regulating third-party campaign-related activities.

FURTHER READING

Bell, David V.J., and Frederick J. Fletcher, eds. 1991. *Reaching the voter: Constituency campaigning in Canada.* Toronto: Dundurn Press.

Carty, R. Kenneth, and Munroe Eagles. 2005. *Politics is local: National politics at the grassroots.* Toronto: Oxford University Press.

CBC. 2008. Canada votes 2008. Riding-by-riding blog. http://www.cbc.ca/news/canadavotes/ridingtalk/.

Elections Canada. Voter information service. http://www.elections.ca/scripts/pss/FindED.aspx?L=e. (Information on parliamentary constituencies.)

Globe and Mail. 2008. Federal election 2008. http://v1.theglobeandmail.com/v5/content/election2008/hub-snapshot.html. (Website includes a link to the survey results of the 45 closest races in British Columbia, Ontario, and Quebec.)

Sayers, Anthony. 1999. *Parties, candidates, and constituency campaigns in Canada.* Vancouver: UBC Press.

REFERENCES

Atkinson, Michael, and David Docherty. 1992. Moving right along: The roots of amateurism in the Canadian House of Commons. *Canadian Journal of Political Science* 25 (2): 295–318.

Axworthy, Thomas. 2008. Only re-energized crew can bail out sinking Liberal ship. *Toronto Star*, October 18. http://www.thestar.com/printArticle/519696.

Bell, David V.J., and Frederick J. Fletcher. 1991. Electoral communication at the constituency level: A framework for analysis. In *Reaching the voter: Constituency campaigning in Canada*, ed. David V.J. Bell and Frederick J. Fletcher, 3–14. Toronto: Dundurn Press.

Blais, André. 2002. Why is there so little strategic voting in Canadian plurality elections? *Political Studies* 50 (3): 445–454.

Blais, André, Elizabeth Gidengil, Agnieszka Dobrrzynska, Neil Nevitte, and Richard Nadeau. 2003. Does the local candidate matter? Candidate effects in the Canadian election of 2000. *Canadian Journal of Political Science* 36 (3): 657–664.

Butler, David, and Dennis Kavanagh. 1974. *The British general election of February 1974.* London: Macmillan.

Canadian Press. 2008. ABC campaign successful in N.L. as Tories wiped out. *CTV.ca*, October 14. http://www.ctv.ca/servlet/ArticleNews/story/CTVNews/20081014/election2008_newfoundland_081014/20081014?s_name=election2008&no_ads= accessed 5/7/09.

Carty, R. Kenneth. 1991. *Canadian political parties in the constituencies.* Toronto: Dundurn Press.

Carty, R. Kenneth, and Munroe Eagles. 2005. *Politics is local: National politics at the grassroots.* Toronto: Oxford University Press.

Chase, Steven. 2008. Tories toe Harper government's line. *Globe and Mail*, November 16. http://www.theglobeandmail.com/news/national/article722581.ece.

Coyne, Andrew. 2008. Local campaigns are largely a fiction anyway. *Maclean's*, April 23. http://www.macleans.ca/columnists/article.jsp?content=20080423_16408_16408&id=8.

Curry, Bill. 2008. Greens scrambled to find candidates, e-mail suggests. *Globe and Mail*, September 18.

Fieldhouse, Edward, and David Cutts. 2009. The effectiveness of local party campaigns in 2005: Combining evidence from campaign spending and agent survey data. *British Journal of Political Science* 39 (2): 367–388.

Fisher, Justin, and David Denver. 2008. From foot-slogging to call centres and direct mail: A framework for analysing the development of district-level campaigning. *European Journal of Political Research* 47 (6): 794–826.

Fisher, Justin, David Denver, and Gordon Hands. 2006. The relative electoral impact of central party co-ordination and party size at constituency level. *Electoral Studies* 25 (4): 664–676.

Gerber, Alan S., and Donald P. Green. 2000. The effect of canvassing, direct mail, and telephone contact on voter turnout: A field experiment. *American Political Science Review* 94 (3): 653–663.

Johnston, Ron, and Charles Pattie. 2006. *Putting voters in their place: Geography and elections in Great Britain.* Oxford: Oxford University Press.

LeDuc, Lawrence. 2007. Realignment and dealignment in Canadian federal politics. In *Canadian Parties in Transition*, 3rd ed., ed. Alain-G. Gagnon and A. Brian Tanguay, 163–177. Peterborough, ON: Broadview Press.

Pattie, Charles J., and Ronald J. Johnston. 2003. Local battles in a national landslide: Constituency campaigning at the 2001 British general election. *Political Geography* 22 (4): 381–414.

Pattie, Charles, R. Paul Whiteley, Ron Johnston, and Patrick Seyd. 1994. Measuring local campaign effects: Labour Party constituency campaigning at the 1987 general election. *Political Studies* 42: 469–479.

Public Policy Forum. 2009. [Less] male, [even less] educated, [even less] experienced, and [even more] white. PowerPoint presentation at the Public Policy Forum, Ottawa. http://www.ppforum.ca/sites/default/files/MPs_Presentation_%20Updated.ppt#268,18,Political Work.

Rana, Abbas. 2008a. Tories, Libs to target all ridings lost by five per cent margin. *Hill Times*, February 25. http://www.thehilltimes.ca/html/index. php?display=story&full_path=2008/february/25/tories_libs_target_ridings/&c=2.

Rana, Abbas. 2008b. The 57 ridings that can change election's outcome. *Hill Times*, September 15.

Sayers, Anthony. 1999. *Parties, candidates, and constituency campaigns in Canada.* Vancouver: UBC Press.

Stanbury, W.T. 1991. *Money in politics: Financing federal parties and candidates in Canada.* Toronto: Dundurn Press.

Stokes, Donald E. 1975. Parties and the nationalization of electoral forces. In *The American party systems: Stages of political development*, ed. W.N. Chambers and W.D. Burnham, 182–202. Oxford: Oxford University Press.

Valpy, Michael. 2009. Liberals want to mirror Obama campaign brain. *Globe and Mail*, April 17.

Votepair.ca. 2008. Federal election 2008—Vote swap final report. http://www.votepair.ca/canada-2008/final-report/.

Ward, Ian. 2003. Localizing the national: The rediscovery and reshaping of local campaigning in Australia. *Party Politics* 9 (5): 583–600.

Whitely, Paul, and Patrick Seyd. 2003. Party election campaigning in Britain: The Labour Party. *Party Politics* 9 (5): 637–652.

Winsor, Hugh, and Stuart Soroka. 2008. Thinking strategically. *Globe and Mail*, October 10.

CHAPTER 7

Democracy and the Candidate Selection Process in Canadian Elections

Steve Patten

Introduction

Canadian elections are considered democratic because nearly every adult citizen has the right to cast a vote in support of the candidate they most want to represent their community in Parliament. No other principle or procedure associated with electoral democracy is more fundamental than our right to vote in free and fair elections that determine who, among the candidates vying for office, will take a seat in the House of Commons. But we should avoid becoming complacent about the quality of democracy our right to vote assures. After all, voting affords us nothing more than the right to choose from among a short list of predetermined candidates whose names appear on a ballot. Very few Canadians play any role whatsoever in determining who will stand for election as an official candidate.

The vast majority of individuals who put their names forward as candidates have been selected to run for office as the nominee of a registered political party, and almost all successful candidates represent one of Canada's major parties—the Conservatives, Liberals, New Democrats, or Bloc Québécois. It is not terribly unusual for unique local situations to result in the election of a few non-partisan independent members of Parliament. However, most Canadian politicians are partisan and enter public life by seeking the support of party members who gather at an electoral district association meeting to select their party's local candidate. As in most other liberal democracies, candidates are nominated by political parties in compliance with their own internally established rules and procedures.

Canadian voters have come to accept this situation as normal and legitimate. To most citizens, the candidate selection process seems to be of limited importance because electoral democracy is understood as a competitive political enterprise pitting parties, even more than individual candidates, against one another. Indeed, only about a quarter of the electorate report that their voting decisions are influenced by their local candidates. Voting decisions tend to be organized and motivated by assessments of the parties and their leaders—including where they stand on major issues of the day—rather than the relative merits of the individual candidates who are elected to serve in the House of Commons. Certainly, it is true that on election day our votes are cast for individual candidates in the electoral districts in which we live. But most of our political judgments will have been formed in relation to national-level parties, personalities, and events. Moreover, voters today often know very little about local candidates or the nominating conventions at which they are selected.

Admittedly, it is not surprising that Canadians know very little about nominating conventions. Even though these conventions represent one of the more significant opportunities for local party activists to play a meaningful role in the life of their party, they are typically small and uneventful. The news media often treat nominating conventions as private, internal party events that occur prior to the beginning of the election, and tend not to provide extensive media coverage of nomination contests unless they are marked by controversy. Sometimes it seems that the political press considers candidate selection to be newsworthy only when rules have been violated or candidates clash over controversial techniques used to sign up new members to attend and vote at the nominating convention. Academics are also guilty of largely ignoring candidate selection in their studies of Canadian elections. It can be argued, however, that there is good reason to understand candidate selection as an integral part of the election. The nominating convention is the first opportunity for widespread participation in the democratic processes that lead to the election of a new slate of parliamentarians. Moreover, as Richard Katz (2001) explains, by selecting the candidates who stand for election and then form our parties' parliamentary caucuses, the nomination process helps establish the ideological and sociological identity of our political parties.

It is important for students of elections and political parties to commit themselves to understanding and evaluating the processes through which Canadian parties nominate their candidates. We must never forget that the quality of electoral democracy depends, at least in part, on whether the processes parties use to nominate their candidates are themselves democratic. This chapter aims to provide some insight into democracy and the candidate selection process in Canadian elections. Candidate selection is analyzed on two key dimensions to assess the extent to which current processes are democratic: decentralization/centralization and inclusiveness/exclusivity. Specifically, is the nomination process decentralized and managed by local party associations, or is it characterized by centralized interventions that allow the party leader and appointed members of the national campaign team to undermine local autonomy? Do the decision processes and outcomes demonstrate a high degree of inclusiveness, or are they characterized by exclusivity and limitations on the ability of those outside the partisan elite to participate in selecting or becoming a candidate?

The consensus in the literature is that the candidate selection process used by Canadian parties is decentralized and inclusive—a depiction that has allowed observers to assume that candidate nominations are instances of strong, local democracy. This depiction is not entirely inaccurate. The majority of local nominating conventions occur without active central intervention, and anyone with a membership in the local electoral district association is usually allowed to vote at the conventions that select local candidates. Nevertheless, this chapter highlights the ways in which important aspects of the nomination process are, in fact, highly centralized and characterized by exclusivity. Through an examination of the three distinct phases in the candidate selection process—candidate search and screening, the nominating convention, and official candidate authorization—the chapter reveals that the quality of democracy in candidate selection is shaped by centralization and exclusivity as well as decentralization and inclusiveness. Although nominating conventions are decentralized local events that allow for very democratic and inclusive membership-based decisions, the processes of candidate search and candidate authorization are more centralized and reserve power for an exclusive segment of the party elite.

This mixed assessment will not surprise anyone who is familiar with the contradictory character of Canadian political parties. While internally democratic and committed to the principle of local autonomy, our political parties are centrally driven institutions with powerful national campaign teams and leaders (Carty 2004). Like a franchised business organization, the national party is responsible for the national brand and ad campaigns, but local associations are independent outlets responsible for the delivery of personnel and product. At the same time, competitive elections and the demands of the parliamentary party system seem to require party discipline and local compliance with centrally determined strategies and goals. These requirements create imperatives that run counter to a decentralized franchise organization, and the resulting contradictory tendencies within parties are played out across the three phases of the candidate selection process.

This chapter begins by establishing a framework within which we can understand political parties and analyze candidate selection. Separate assessments of candidate search and screening, the nominating convention, and the process of official candidate authorization follow. The final substantive section of this chapter explores the recurring issue of how the nomination process affects the extent of social diversity and representativeness in partisan and parliamentary institutions. While earlier sections of this chapter focus on inclusiveness in relation to opportunities to participate in nominating candidates, later sections examine inclusiveness in relation to social diversity and representativeness in nominating candidates. Leading experts agree that reforming the candidate selection process is key to achieving the inclusiveness associated with gender equity and minority representation in Canadian politics (Erickson

1993). What is most interesting—and challenging for strong democrats—is that the sorts of reforms that are needed to ensure greater representativeness in Canadian politics may involve interventionist central party initiatives that challenge local autonomy. These political realities certainly add to the complexity of any assessment of democracy in the candidate selection process in Canadian elections.

A Framework for Understanding Political Parties and Assessing Candidate Selection

Political parties are complex organizations comprising a variety of often competing tendencies. Kenneth Carty (2004) has described Canadian political parties as centrally driven but internally democratic organizations that value both autonomy for local units and the integral character of the party as a larger whole. As a result, there is a certain tension—perhaps even a contradiction—in how our parties organize and understand themselves. It is as if Canadian political parties were formed through an organizational bargain that strives to respect not only the value of local autonomy and initiative but also the efficiencies of standardization and strong leadership in the context of national electoral competition. As Carty explains, "organizational power and authority does not finally rest in any single place, or with any single set of individuals—it is (more or less) broadly shared" (9). But that sharing of power is under constant renegotiation, and the tension between centralization and local autonomy is never far below the surface of Canadian political parties.

In processes as complex and varied as candidate selection, both national and local imperatives and visions tend to operate simultaneously. To the extent that Carty is correct that our political parties are like franchised business organizations, the national party and local franchises have a shared interest in respecting the franchise agreement. The national party is responsible for defining the content and image of the national brand and delivering national ad campaigns (election campaigns). The local associations are independent outlets responsible for the delivery of personnel and product—that is, selecting and running a candidate, and connecting with local electors to get the vote out on election day. However, given that the national party and the local franchises rely on one another for their success, they continually desire a certain influence over one another. The national party, for example, wants to find ways of ensuring that local decisions regarding candidate selection and campaign planning are in line with and supportive of the national campaign and the leader's goals for establishing a parliamentary caucus (and, perhaps, a government).

As we turn to the task of describing how Canadian parties have selected candidates for elections, it is important to be cautious and nuanced. The process by which candidates are nominated has varied from electoral district to electoral district, party to party, and over time. Until very recently, the nomination process was left virtually untouched by public regulation. In Canada and the majority of advanced liberal democracies, there are very few laws telling parties how to select candidates (Rahat 2007, 157). In the first decades after Confederation, Canada's elitist cadre-style parties often lacked anything we might now call "candidate selection." The politicians who emerged from within the local elite were essentially self-selecting, and sometimes would not officially align themselves with a political party until after they were elected. As Canada's parties became more established toward the end of the 19th century, candidate selection became more formal, but the parties tended to leave decisions regarding the organization of the nomination process to the determination of local electoral district associations. In keeping with the logic of Carty's franchise metaphor, the Canadian party system became known for its decentralized approach to candidate selection.

In practice, however, the principle of decentralization in candidate selection has often been violated. Local autonomy in establishing rules of procedure for local nominating conventions has been the norm, but it has certainly not always been respected. In Newfoundland, for example, it has been reported that former Premier Joey Smallwood personally selected all but a few of the Liberal candidates who ran in federal and provincial elections from 1949 to 1968 (Williams 1981, 93). Smallwood was a uniquely powerful and autocratic leader. He simply let it be known that he expected local Liberals to acquiesce, and those with an interest in future involvement in the party accepted his decision on who would run as the local Liberal candidate.

Over the years, there have been numerous examples of party power brokers working behind the scenes to orchestrate the nomination of candidates who are favoured by the party establishment (Whitaker 1977, 143). In one infamous case a senior Liberal Party campaign official blocked all potential challenges to the renomination of a sitting MP by taking over the nomination process, and then opening and closing nominations before informing the local Liberal association. The MP was then acclaimed as the local Liberal candidate (Cross 2002, 376). As recently as 1993, a study of local versus central control of nominating conventions found that a significant minority of local associations reported some form of central party "interference" (Cross 2002, 374). This finding confirms the assessment that the local control assumed by the franchise metaphor is never absolute. Unfortunately, given the fact that central party direction has often been provided through informal relationships between party officials, high-level activists, and local notables, it has been difficult for academic observers to assess with certainty the extent to which meaningful local autonomy has been regularly realized (Bille 2001, 369).

The variation and complexity of approaches to nominating candidates become even more apparent once attention is drawn to the three distinct phases of the candidate selection process: (1) candidate search and screening, (2) the nominating convention, and (3) official candidate authorization (Williams 1981). (See Table 7.1.) Local nominating conventions are the most studied of the three phases, and it is in this phase that practice adheres most closely to the expectations associated with Carty's franchise metaphor. However, a meaningful assessment of candidate selection must consider all three phases, together and individually.

One challenge associated with assessing the quality of democracy in candidate selection is the range of issues that needs to be considered. We must examine whose participation is favoured by the established rules for conducting a candidate search and running nominating conventions, the possible existence of informal gatekeepers

TABLE 7.1   Analysis of the Three Phases of Candidate Selection

Phase of candidate selection	Decentralized versus centralized	Inclusive versus exclusive
1. Candidate search and screening	While the task of candidate search is decentralized to local committees, central party oversight and approval of the process has been institutionalized in formal party rules.	Membership on local candidate search committees is reserved for a fairly exclusive group of local political luminaries and, in some cases, representatives of the national campaign team.
2. The nominating convention	Nominating conventions are governed by centrally established rules, but they are run in a very decentralized manner. Local autonomy is rarely violated.	Although only those who purchase a membership prior to an established cut-off date may vote, there are almost no restrictions on who can join. Nomination decisions are made at very inclusive membership-based conventions.
3. Official candidate authorization	The legal requirement that party leaders authorize only one candidate in each electoral district is fundamentally very centralizing. It amounts to a legal power of veto over local nomination decisions.	The fact that the power to authorize (or veto) a candidate legally rests with the party leader, means that this phase of candidate selection is highly exclusive.

who have the capacity to determine who is likely to become a contestant, the extent of outside influence in the search and selection processes, and any barriers that may inhibit participation in these processes. Recent comparative scholarship has striven to develop a conceptual framework for the analysis of candidate selection. Rahat and Hazan (2001) suggest that approaches to candidate selection can be contrasted on four dimensions: (1) Who can be selected (open versus restricted)? (2) Who participates in the selection (inclusive versus exclusive)? (3) Where does selection take place (centrally selected versus locally selected)? (4) What decision rules are employed (appointment versus voting)?

All of these four dimensions are important in assessing candidate selection processes, and they are all addressed in this chapter. However, as is common in the literature on political parties, this chapter's examination of candidate selection emphasizes the issues of centralization versus decentralization and inclusiveness versus exclusivity (Pennings and Hazan 2001; Rahat 2007). A careful analysis of each phase of the candidate selection process follows.

The Three Phases of Candidate Selection

Candidate Search and Screening

Candidate selection begins with a search for politically attractive individuals who would be willing to stand as contestants at the party's local nominating convention. In anticipation of a coming election, electoral district associations are encouraged—in some cases required—to establish formal candidate search committees. The goal of these search committees is to identify well-known and respected individuals who have the capacity to strengthen the party's chances of winning the electoral district in which they would stand for election. In practice, however, the character of the task at hand depends on how likely it is that the political party in question can win the local electoral district. When the chances of victory are remote, interest in the nomination will be limited and the search committee may have to hunt long and hard to find an appropriate individual who is willing to stand for election. In safe seats where victory is likely, interest may be high and the search committee may actually serve more like a political filter designed to dissuade less attractive contestants and encourage those who are deemed more desirable. There is a lot at stake in a candidate search. Most obviously, the candidate search process determines the range of choices that are eventually put before the party "selectorate"—the selectorate being the party members who will gather to vote at the local nominating convention.

Participation in a candidate search provides a unique opportunity to exert significant influence at the earliest stages of an election. But who actually participates at this significant stage in the candidate selection process? Given the importance of identifying and encouraging the best possible individuals to seek the nomination, candidate search committees are typically staffed by a small group of local political luminaries, including key fundraisers, past candidates, and long-serving members of the electoral district association's executive board. These are individuals who have been involved in past campaigns. They are also likely to know key community leaders, civic politicians, and politically interested individuals with records of demonstrated success in their careers, politics, or other community engagement. They are the types of individuals who have the social stature required to approach and convince potential candidates to seek the nomination.

Until the 1990s, a candidate search was often conducted quite informally by an unofficial committee that emerged from among members of the local political establishment. There was often no formal search process. Even when there was, the real decision would often be made when the local social and political elite would "huddle together to decide on who would make a good candidate" (Scarrow 1964, 58). A candidate search, in this era, was a process of informal gatekeeping by well-connected members of the local political establishment. It was a highly exclusive process that lacked the transparency that is essential to democracy.

Over the past two decades the candidate search process has become more formalized and transparent, but local search committees remain quite small. They allow the involvement of only a fairly exclusive group of higher level local activists. Perhaps the most significant development to accompany the formalization of the candidate search has been the trend toward requiring that electoral district associations allow central campaign personnel or party staff to play a formal role in the local candidate search. Often this role amounts to the central party screening potential candidates through a formal application process that determines the eligibility of aspiring contestants. For example, the Liberal Party's "Green Light Process" empowers a committee of about a dozen members of the national campaign team to scrutinize and then grant or refuse potential contestants the right to contest a local nomination (Liberal Party of Canada 2009, 9–10).

The Conservative Party, for its part, now requires that every electoral district association appoint a four- to six-member candidate nomination committee to oversee the process of a candidate search. In each case, one member of this committee must be either the national campaign director or a designated political operations officer employed by the party's central office (Conservative Party of Canada 2009, 1). This condition is designed to ensure that channels are open for the provision of useful central input into the local candidate search process. But it also provides the national candidate selection committee with a window onto local developments, and this national committee has the power to veto any individual's candidacy. Thus, as is the case in other liberal democracies, the formalization of local candidate search committees moved parties away from the opaque and undemocratic candidate selection process of the past, but it also allowed central party authorities to institutionalize their capacity to condition the process (Hopkins 2001). Local and regional powerbrokers have, to a certain extent, been forced out of the backrooms by these potentially democratizing measures to formalize the search process, but the central party elite has been strengthened (Katz 2001). Moreover, unofficial backroom politics has not disappeared entirely. As Kenneth Carty and Munroe Eagles (2006, 52) recently observed, much of the competition among aspiring nominees continues to be resolved informally in political backrooms by local opinion leaders or, on occasion, by central campaign officials who let the wishes of the leader be known to local activists.

The concentration of power in the hands of a few influential partisans during the candidate search process is not without consequences. From the perspective of the party establishment, there is an obvious strategic logic to the centralized and exclusive process that has been institutionalized over the past two decades. Working together, local and central party officials can ensure that they are all aware of the local political scene and potential candidates as well as central campaign and party priorities. But there is good reason to ask whether exclusivity in candidate search and screening partially undermines the democratic significance of allowing an inclusive selectorate to vote at the local nominating convention. Moreover, given the limited range of political and cultural world views represented within the closed partisan world of those who dominate these search committees, we should not be surprised if there is only limited openness to non-traditional candidates. Some have also speculated that formally empowering local candidate search committees that have direct ties to the central party establishment is purposely designed to reinforce the power of the party's central elite; it allows the central elite to exclude rival factions from the party's slate of election candidates (Katz 2001). Whatever the case, there are reasons why those who are interested in electoral democracy might be concerned about the concentration of power and influence during the candidate search process. More light is being shone on the process than in the past, but participation remains restricted to a narrow range of influential partisans. We have also seen the institutionalization of the central party's capacity to manage the candidate search process.

The Nominating Convention

The second phase of candidate selection is the formal nominating convention. When there is a competitive race between contestants vying for the nomination, this phase of the process may include a period of campaigning to sign up new party members and secure the support of existing members who will attend and vote at the nominating convention. Not long ago, there were very few standardized rules governing nominating conventions. Most constituencies have held these conventions for as long as anyone can remember. But, as late as the 1980s, there were important differences in how these conventions functioned. In the vast majority of cases, the local electoral district association held a convention at which only existing party members had the right to vote. But there were some associations that lacked sophisticated membership lists, and in these cases the right to vote was granted to anyone willing to attend the nominating convention. There were also associations that were still following the decades-old practice of holding a delegated convention at which the local candidate was selected by delegates from polling subdivisions within the electoral district (Erickson and Carty 1991, 336; Williams 1981, 106). Variations in the makeup of the selectorate that would choose the local candidate existed precisely because Canadian parties lacked extensive national rules governing the conduct of nominating conventions, and the legal framework governing federal elections did not regulate the behaviour of parties or candidates during the nomination process.

By the 1990s, however, Canadian parties were developing more comprehensive and standardized regulations to govern local candidate selection. Interestingly, these regulations reflect the tension inherent in the "varying levels of mutual autonomy" that are associated with Canada's centrally driven yet democratic political parties (Carty 2004, 9). All the major parties now have formal processes for determining when electoral district associations will be granted permission to organize their nominating conventions, who will be eligible to vote, and what method of balloting will be used to determine which contestant will win the nomination. Many of these rules empower the central party to regulate local nominations. Still, the rules institutionalize an important dimension of local autonomy in candidate selection by demanding that in all but exceptional circumstances candidates will be nominated by votes at local nominating conventions. Reflecting on the nature of the modern nomination process, Carty (2004) has gone as far as to say that local associations "have direct and relatively unchallenged control over the selection of candidates" (19).

A recurring issue is whether sitting MPs should be subjected to a nominating convention to earn the right to remain the party's local candidate. In Canada, MPs are normally required to be renominated. But this requirement has, on occasion, been ignored. In 1993 Jean Chrétien decreed that sitting Liberal MPs who wished to run again would be automatically renominated. In 2009, the Conservatives changed their rules so that sitting MPs would only have to face a nominating convention if two-thirds or more of the membership in the local electoral district voted to hold a convention. Following a series of mail-in ballots in the spring of 2009, none of the 143 electoral districts with sitting MPs met that threshold, thus allowing all the Conservative MPs to be automatically renominated (Chase 2009).

The formal rules that Canadian parties have adopted for nominating conventions are designed to ensure that electoral district associations run closed but democratic conventions at which the selectorate includes all party members. Contestants for the nomination are given equal access to opportunities to contact existing members, sell new memberships, and address attendees at the nominating convention. The only restriction on a party member's right to vote is that he or she must have purchased a membership before a specified cut-off date—typically no more than one week to one month prior to the convention.

Interestingly, in contrast to the plurality voting system used to elect MPs, the balloting procedure for nominating conventions usually requires that a contestant obtain an absolute majority of votes (more than 50 percent) to win the nomination. If no contestant accomplishes this goal on the first ballot, it is most common for there to be a series of sequential ballots, each one held after removing the name of the candidate who received the least number of votes on the previous ballot. Sometimes, to hasten the process, the rules also stipulate that any candidate who failed to achieve a designated minimum percentage of votes is also removed from the next ballot. Alternatively, associations that prefer not to take the time to hold multiple ballots can opt to use a single preferential transferable ballot. This voting method allows members to rank their candidate preferences so that rather than conduct multiple ballots, officials are able to reassign the votes of those members who ranked a failed contestant as their first preference.

In 2004, the federal government implemented significant changes to Canada's campaign and party financing laws. One of the more interesting innovations involved extending public regulations to cover the financing of and spending by campaigns to secure local nominations. The new regulations put restrictive caps on the overall size of political contributions and stipulated that these caps included donations to nomination campaigns. They also limited spending on a nomination campaign to 20 percent of the limit allowed for a candidate's election campaign, or approximately $17,000 in a typical electoral district. While average nomination campaign expenses are well below this limit, many successful contestants in competitive electoral districts spend close to the legal limit. Thus, while implementation has not been flawless, the regulation of spending has the potential to restrict the capacity of contestants with wealthy backers to win the local nomination by funding a campaign that simply overwhelms potential challengers. Given past reluctance to regulate internal party affairs, these new rules may mark another step toward transforming political parties from private and autonomous voluntary organizations into quasi-public institutions—what Rahat (2007) refers to as "public utilities"—that are subject to democratic public regulation (Patten 2007).

To win a hotly contested nominating convention, a contestant must wage a well-orchestrated campaign on three distinct dimensions. First, a contestant's nomination campaign must win the support of local partisan opinion leaders who have extensive involvement in the electoral district association and recent election campaigns. The typical party member is not very active within the party. The majority attend fewer than two party activities per year, and play only a limited role at campaign time (Cross and Young 2006, 18). Members such as these tend to look to higher level local activists for cues on issues of importance, including candidate selection. In response, contestants for the local nomination work hard to win endorsements from the key activists who may influence the votes of less-engaged party members.

Securing these all-important endorsements usually requires that contestants avoid deviating from established visions of the party. In fact, the key to winning endorsements from members of the local partisan establishment is often not introducing new policy ideas or a new vision for the future of the party, but convincing key activists of two things: (1) that you are the contestant who has the capacity to win in a general election and (2) almost as important, that you want the activists you are courting to continue to play a prominent role within the local electoral district association. Nomination campaigns can be a source of new ideas and new blood. But there is a perverse dynamic in closed partisan networks; to win the support of the local party establishment, aspiring candidates must often avoid challenging the status quo.

Second, a contestant's nomination campaign must involve appeals for support from the existing membership base of the local electoral district association. The goal is not merely to convince party members to vote for the nomination contestant, but to secure active support that includes a willingness to publicly identify with the contestant. The ballot at the nominating convention will be secret, but in the context of a closed membership-based nomination process, conventions often take on the character of blocs of supporters gathering to see which team has the most voting strength. The process is "rarely deliberative" and "policy plays virtually no role" (Cross 2004, 62–63). Longer-term party members will have considered various alternative candidates in advance of the nominating convention. But, many of those who attend the convention will do so to vote for a specific candidate—and it will usually be the candidate that they believe has the best prospects of winning in a general election. Contestants need to arrive on convention night with a solid base of committed support and the capacity to demonstrate that their candidacy has momentum.

Public displays of support and a sense of momentum at the nominating convention are important because the decision might require two or more ballots. In situations where no contestant has the support of over 50 percent of those voting at the convention, it can be as important to be the second choice of those supporting other candidates as it is to have strong first preference support. As contestants are dropped from contention, those who remain must win over the supporters of those who are no longer in contention. The entire process requires subtle and nuanced appeals to a small and identifiable selectorate.

The reality, however, is that in a hotly contested nomination, the support of existing members is unlikely to be enough to ensure victory. Membership numbers fluctuate considerably in Canadian political parties, particularly in the Liberal and Conservative parties (Carty 2004). Unless recent political events have stimulated membership sales, it is not unusual for a local electoral district association to have fewer than 400 members when potential contestants first begin to consider a bid for the nomination—and not all of those will actually attend the convention (Cross and Young 2006). That is a relatively small pool of potential voters for a group of aspiring candidates to battle over. So, in most contested nominations the third, and sometimes most important, dimension of the nomination campaign is the contest to see which contestant can sell the most new memberships prior to the established cut-off date (usually one week to one month prior to the nominating convention).

The contest to sell party memberships is often the defining feature of a nomination campaign. It reinforces the importance of organizational capacity among the attributes that are essential to victory (Cross 2004). Contestants who are experienced partisan operatives and have the support of a well-organized team that can mobilize large numbers of new members will be significantly advantaged in a contested nomination. It is not unusual for membership numbers to increase 60 percent to 70 percent in an election year. But in electoral districts with hotly contested nominations, average local memberships often grow up to 300 percent (Carty, Cross, and Young 2000, 158). This means that winning contestants sell hundreds of new memberships. Experienced political organizers have learned that selling new memberships is most easily accomplished by campaigning within established groups and close-knit communities. Mobilizing social movement organizations, single-issue interest groups, and ethnic community organizations is a well-established, but controversial, method of drawing in new members to support a nomination contestant.

Attracting what have come to be known as "instant members" to support a nomination bid raises important issues about inclusiveness and who has the right to select a party's candidate for the general election. The trend in liberal democratic party systems has been toward greater inclusiveness (Bille 2001). Increasingly, it is considered unacceptable to restrict participation in candidate selection to an exclusive party agency. But there remain a range of views with regard to who should have the right to vote (Rahat and Hazan 2001). Should parties maintain the limited exclusivity of a closed primary in which only existing members are eligible to be selectors? Or, should they be more inclusive and move toward something approximating an open primary in which all voters have the right to attend and vote at a nominating convention?

Given that Canadian political parties have traditionally functioned like private voluntary associations that exist largely outside the purview of public regulation, it is not surprising that some partisans hold the view that the party belongs to its members and the right to participate in candidate selection should be reserved for those members. From this perspective, the practice of signing up new members to support a nomination contestant is a highly illegitimate practice, akin to allowing outsiders to take over the party. There are, however, activists who argue that bringing new members into the party is always beneficial. They contend that nomination contestants with the organizational capacity to sign up large numbers of supporters for the nominating convention are most desirable because these sorts of politicians will also attract campaign workers and donations come election time. From this perspective, being overly restrictive is detrimental to the interests of the party.

Some argue that deepening electoral democracy requires the most inclusive of candidate selection methods (Rahat 2007, 161). If political parties are to become more open public institutions that are willing to welcome the widespread involvement of all supportive voters, than they must be prepared to allow for open primaries in which anyone who is willing to attend the nominating convention should have the right to vote. From this perspective, outsiders cannot really take over a party because the party is like a public utility that belongs to all citizens who choose to get involved. Former Reform Party leader, Preston Manning, has argued that democracy might be enhanced by experimenting with some form of open primaries (Manning 2009). He points to the Conservative association in the British constituency of Totnes as an example of what might be done to involve more voters in candidate selection. In 2009 the Conservatives of Totnes used internal party processes to reduce an initial field of 11 contestants to just 3 front-runners. They then mailed ballots to all 69,000 eligible voters in the electoral district so that everyone who wanted to get involved could vote on who would be the Conservative candidate in the next election.

Canadian parties are known for an approach to candidate selection that is "very inclusive" in that there is considerable openness to new members participating in nominating conventions (Rahat 2001, 163). But the rules defining who is a member of the selectorate are tinged with elements of exclusivity. The practice of cutting off membership sales a week or more prior to the convention ensures that Canadian parties maintain a closed, membership-based procedure for candidate selection. This has meant that very few Canadians actually participate in party nominations. In 1993, for example, William Cross (2002, 378) estimated that the combined total of all the participants at nominating conventions for all of Canada's political parties was under 1,000 people per electoral district—or less than 2 percent of those eligible to vote in a general election. Thus, even with a decentralized and very inclusive process for candidate selection, only a narrow segment of the electorate participates in nominating conventions. The process is actually quite open and democratic, but a fairly select group of partisans still determines who has an opportunity to be elected to the Canadian House of Commons.

Official Candidate Authorization

The third and final phase of the candidate selection process is official candidate authorization. The authorization of local candidates has been particularly significant since the early 1970s, when party affiliation was added to the federal ballot. To ensure that the correct candidates are identified with each registered political party, Elections Canada now requires that party leaders formally authorize the candidacy of a single candidate in each electoral district. This power of endorsement amounts to giving the party leaders the power of legal veto (Carty, Cross, and Young 2000, 160). Of course, given that national party leaders prefer to avoid publicly rejecting a candidate who emerged successful from the local nomination process, candidate authorization is almost always a simple formality. All the same, the very existence of the authorization phase is fundamentally centralizing in character.

Most long-serving party leaders have used the authorization process to veto at least a few locally nominated candidates. These decisions are usually in response to information about prior ethical misconduct or views that are considered incompatible with party policy. Nonetheless, the decision to veto a locally selected candidate is seldom uncontroversial. To avoid having to make such decisions, party leaders rely on central campaign officials to monitor local candidate search processes and take effective interventions before questionable individuals can be selected by a local nominating convention. The power of veto associated with candidate authorization is used only as a last resort, but the threat of an eventual veto is sometimes used to dissuade unwanted individuals who are considering a bid for the nomination.

The picture that results from this review of the three phases of candidate selection supports a few competing interpretations. Given that anyone who purchases a membership prior to the established cut-off date is eligible to vote, the barriers to participation in the selectorate are quite minimal. Canadian parties have very inclusive and decentralized nominating conventions. However, in the same way that party nominations structure election ballots, the process of candidate search and screening structures the nomination contest. It is in the candidate search process that one finds initial evidence of exclusivity and centralization. Not only is participation in a candidate search restricted to a small group of higher level local activists, but also party rules reserve considerable space for centralization of decision making at the search and screening stage. Then, when it comes time for official candidate authorization, the legal decision on who will be the party's candidate is fully centralized, with power of authorization resting exclusively with the party leader.

Nominations, Electoral Choice, and Social Diversity

One of the perennial issues in the literature on candidate selection is the impact the process has on the representativeness of our partisan and parliamentary institutions. Because candidate selection structures electoral choice and determines who has an opportunity to be elected to serve in the House of Commons, the nomination processes of political parties can be more important to determining the extent of social diversity in Parliament than the actual vote on election day. This point goes to the heart of whether electoral politics fosters the sort of inclusiveness associated with democratic politics, gender equity, and meaningful minority representation. If the established parties are nominating individuals of similarly narrow social and economic backgrounds, voters have no way of making decisions that will break the established mould and redefine who can be successful in Canadian politics. Given this basic political reality, it is not surprising that feminist scholars with an interest in understanding and addressing the underrepresentation of women in Parliament have often focused their analysis on established practices for nominating candidates. Before concluding this chapter, it is useful to review the impact of candidate selection on electoral choice and social diversity in Canadian politics.

Pippa Norris and her colleagues (1990) have suggested that there are both demand and supply side explanations of the lack of social diversity in electoral and parliamentary politics. Simple demand-side explanations suggest that party selectorates discriminate against non-traditional contestants. These explanations suggest that those voting at nominating conventions are predisposed against supporting women, aspiring candidates from minority ethnic communities, and other atypical contestants. This is intuitively sensible given that the party members who gather to select candidates are not terribly representative of the general public, and that they likely have past candidates in mind when they begin to consider the type of person who would be most qualified to run in a general election. But the empirical evidence in terms of the actual willingness of party members to support women contestants suggests otherwise. When given the choice at a nominating convention, party members do not discriminate in favour of male candidates (Erickson 1991; Cheng and Tavits 2008). The problem is not that the parties' selectorates are discriminatory, but that too few women (and minority candidates) emerge as contestants aspiring to win at local nominating conventions. The problem, it seems, is rooted in events and choices that are made prior to the nominating convention.

If the party members who participate in nominating conventions are not universally predisposed against voting for—or "demanding"—women candidates, then our failure to achieve something closer to gender parity in electoral politics requires an explanation that focuses on the supply side of the equation. One way to approach this issue is to ask why more women (and minority contestants) don't step up to the plate as potential candidates. This question has led some feminist scholars to examine the social construction of women's political ambitions and interests, their sense of political efficacy, and the demands associated with the uneven distribution of domestic labour responsibilities. But there are also structural explanations that draw our attention to the nature of the candidate search processes, and it is these explanations that are of most interest to us here (Brodie 1991).

In his analysis of the representativeness of nomination contestants, William Cross (2004) argued that personal networks play an important role in identifying potential candidates and, given the social composition of local partisan elites, "members of minority groups are often not included within these networks" (69). This analysis echoes Harold Scarrow's much earlier speculation that when the "selection clique" that emerges from within the local party establishment is dominated by lawyers, businessmen, and other people of higher socioeconomic standing, we should expect that they will encourage people with similar social attributes to consider seeking the local nomination (Scarrow 1964, 58).

Christine Cheng and Margit Tavits (2008) examine what they call the "informal influences" in selecting political candidates. They contend that candidate search committees that are dominated by the party's proverbial old boys' network actually play an "inhibiting role" in terms of the attraction of women candidates. Party gatekeepers, they argue, will influence who will contest the local nomination. More specifically, using a data set for all parties and candidates in the 2004 and 2006 federal elections, they found that women were statistically more likely to be nominated when one particular gatekeeper—the local electoral district association president—was a woman rather than a man. It seems that the social composition of the committees charged with responsibility for candidate search is important in at least two ways. Not only can it expand and diversify the social networks within which such committees have the capacity to search for potential nomination contestants, but the very presence of women (and, presumably, racialized or ethnic minorities) sends a positive signal that plays a role in encouraging aspiring candidates.

It is this sort of analysis that convinced scholars such as Lynda Erickson that formalizing and improving candidate search processes is essential to achieving greater social diversity, inclusiveness, and equity of representation in electoral politics (Erickson 1991, 1993). Of course, we know that Canadian political parties have come a long way over the past two decades in terms of formalizing processes of candidate search within electoral district associations—indeed, the constitutions and centrally mandated candidate selection rules of the major parties now require the establishment of official search committees. But, on its own, the mere use of formal candidate search committees is not enough to ensure that a party achieves greater repetitiveness in its slate of candidates.

Erickson found that in 1988, prior to the widespread institutionalization of formal search committees, the presence of a local search committee was associated with an increased likelihood that a woman would seek the nomination (Erickson 1993, 76–78). Interestingly, however, this was not true across all the major parties. In electoral district associations without an incumbent, the use of a local search committee increased the likelihood of women aspirants from 28 percent to 52 percent for the New Democratic Party and from 34 percent to 37 percent for the Liberal Party. But the use of a formal candidate search committee by Progressive Conservative electoral district associations actually resulted in the decreased likelihood of there being women contestants. The percentage of Progressive Conservative electoral district nominations with women aspirants dropped from 30 percent when there was no search committee to 26 percent when there was one. Clearly, then, there are consequential differences in how the parties approach using these committees, and not all approaches result in greater representation of women among nomination contestants.

The approach of parties to increasing the number of women and minority candidates has varied from centrally driven and interventionist to more voluntarist and locally determined. Moreover, the choice of approach seems to be related to the party's ideological orientation and the perceived legitimacy of central versus local control over the candidate search process. While central campaign staff and organizers in all the major parties have been increasing their influence over the local candidate search process, some parties have been reluctant to intervene with prescriptive interventions designed to achieve greater inclusiveness in their slate of candidates. Erickson contends that decisions regarding how interventionist the central parties will be are shaped by partisan ideological differences. For example, and not surprisingly, the party that is most ideologically committed to the legitimacy of affirmative action—the New Democratic Party—has been the most interventionist in designing processes that ensure candidate search committees are doing all they can to encourage women and minorities to seek local nominations. The Conservative Party, on the other hand, has been slower to act and considerably more voluntarist in its approach (Erickson 1993, 66).

During the 1980s and 1990s, partisan activists concluded that to realize meaningful progress toward greater inclusiveness and social diversity, the central party must ensure that the local candidate search process is characterized by affirmative action in the form of outreach efforts, workshops, mentoring, and the provision of financial assistance to contestants with unique expenses or limited personal funds. While steps in these directions were taken by all parties, the Liberals and, in particular, the NDP went furthest. Under Jean Chrétien, the Liberal Party committed itself to a target of 25 percent women candidates. Both the Conservatives and the Liberals established funds to assist nominated women candidates. But, in 1997, the NDP adopted the most comprehensive affirmative action plan. The party set a number of goals, including the nomination of women in 60 percent of electoral districts where the party has a reasonable chance of victory, and candidates that "reflect the diversity of Canada" in a minimum of 15 percent of those electoral districts (Cross 2004, 70).

Analysis reveals that women and other atypical contestants for nomination more likely need to be approached multiple times, and even "talked into" seeking a nomination (Erickson 1993, 76). One of the most effective methods of persuading a reluctant candidate to seek the nomination is for the party leader, or someone close to the leader, to contact the person and offer direct personal encouragement. Of course, this requires fairly significant central party involvement in the local search, and there is the risk that encouragement may be taken as endorsement. But this is an example of how central party interventions can contribute to achieving greater inclusiveness in local candidate search processes.

Given the continuing lack of social diversity within partisan and parliamentary institutions, it is evident that innovation—even centrally driven intervention—is necessary to assure the extent of representativeness that is associated with deepening democracy. Throughout his tenure as Liberal Party leader, Jean Chrétien used this logic to justify his appointment of women candidates, even over the objections of party members who favoured local autonomy and democratic nominating conventions. The fact that Chrétien's appointments stood demonstrates the continued potential for central control of candidate selection. The fact that he, as leader, overrode local autonomy—and local democracy—to achieve the democratic goal of greater representativeness demonstrates how complicated the democratic equation in candidate selection can be.

Conclusion

Although the selection of candidates is properly understood as the first opportunity for participation in the democratic processes that culminate with the vote on election day, the process has remained largely outside the scope of public regulation. Political parties have been free to define their own rules and procedures for naming local candidates for general elections. Not surprisingly, the approach our parties have taken to managing candidate selection reflects the contradictory nature of power in our centrally driven but internally democratic party organizations. The important and visible events associated with nominating conventions are locally organized, very inclusive, and democratic. All the same, there is considerable central oversight and involvement during candidate search and screening. The candidate search process tends to be dominated by a fairly exclusive and unrepresentative group of higher level local activists and central campaign officials who are charged with ensuring that only approved individuals seek the party's nomination. Moreover, at the end of the candidate selection process, all candidates must be formally authorized by the party leader. Virtually all party leaders have, on occasion, used their power of authorization to veto locally selected candidates.

Given the typically shared interests of party officials—whether local or central—conflict between local and central views on who would make a good local candidate are not very common. Party leaders and campaign officials don't override local activists in more than a handful of cases in any given general election. But, as Cross discovered, as many as one-quarter to one-third of those directing the local candidate search will report some form of central party interference in the process (Cross 2002, 374). There is good reason, then, to avoid being overly complacent about democracy in candidate selection. The literature typically depicts candidate selection as decentralized and inclusive. But, clearly, features of centralization and exclusivity exist alongside the local autonomy that is considered important to democracy in candidate selection.

As Carty has observed, Canada's political parties are somewhat contradictory in character (Carty 2004). While internally democratic and committed in principle to local autonomy, they are centrally driven institutions with powerful national campaign teams and leaders. This basic political reality concerns many strong democrats. But, interestingly, those who are concerned with the extent of social diversity and representativeness in partisan and parliamentary institutions sometimes see opportunity in central power and authority. Many of the reforms designed to achieve greater inclusiveness and representativeness in Canadian politics have involved interventionist centralization in candidate selection. The democratic equation in candidate selection may not be as simple as one might initially expect.

DISCUSSION QUESTIONS

1. How would you explain to an average voter the way in which Canadian political parties select candidates for general elections? Discuss all three phases of the candidate selection process in your answer.
2. Canadian political and parliamentary institutions are not fully representative of the social diversity that exists in this country. How are the candidate selection processes of political parties implicated in this situation? What types of reforms to the candidate selection process would ensure greater inclusiveness and representativeness?
3. In what ways are aspects of the current candidate selection process shaped by both "decentralization and inclusiveness" and "centralization and exclusivity"?

FURTHER READING

Cross, William. 2002. Grassroots participation in candidate nominations. In *Citizen politics: Research and theory in Canadian political behaviour*, ed. Joanna Everitt and Brenda O'Neill, 373–385. Toronto: Oxford University Press.

Erickson, Lynda. 1993. Making her way in: Women, parties and candidacies in Canada. In *Gender and Party Politics*, ed. Joni Lovenduski and Pippa Norris, 60–85. London: Sage Publications.

Rahat, Gideon. 2007. Candidate selection: The choice before the choice. *Journal of Democracy* 18 (1): 157–170.

Williams, Robert J. 1981. Candidate selection. In *Canada at the polls, 1979 and 1980: A study of the general elections*, ed. Howard R. Penniman, 86–120. Washington: American Enterprise Institute for Public Policy.

REFERENCES

Bille, Lars. 2001. Democratizing a democratic procedure: Myth or reality? Candidate selection in Western European parties, 1960–1990. *Party Politics* 7 (3): 363–380.

Brodie, Janine. 1991. Women and the electoral process in Canada. In *Women in Canadian politics: Towards equity in representation*, ed. Kathy Megyery, 3–34. Toronto: Dundurn Press.

Carty, R. Kenneth. 2004. Parties as franchise systems: The stratarchical organizational imperative. *Party Politics* 10 (1): 5–24.

Carty, R. Kenneth, William Cross, and Lisa Young. 2000. *Rebuilding Canadian party politics*. Vancouver: UBC Press.

Carty, R. Kenneth, and Munroe Eagles. 2006. *Politics is local: National politics at the grassroots*. Toronto: Oxford University Press.

Chase, Steven. 2009. Sitting Tories to be automatically renominated. *Globe and Mail*, May 5.

Cheng, Christine, and Margit Tavits. 2008. Informal influences in selecting female political candidates. Paper presented at the annual meeting of the Canadian Political Science Association, Vancouver.

Conservative Party of Canada. 2009. Conservative Party of Canada candidate nomination rules and procedures. http://www.conservative.ca/media/NominationRules2009.pdf.

Cross, William. 2002. Grassroots participation in candidate nominations. In *Citizen politics: Research and theory in Canadian political behaviour*, ed. Joanna Everitt and Brenda O'Neill, 373–385. Toronto: Oxford University Press.

Cross, William. 2004. *Political parties*. Vancouver: UBC Press.

Cross, William, and Lisa Young. 2006. Are Canadian parties empty vessels? Membership, engagement and policy capacity. *Choices* 12 (4): 14–28.

Erickson, Lynda. 1991. Women and candidacies for the House of Commons. In *Women in Canadian politics: Towards equity in representation*, ed. Kathy Megyery, 101–126. Toronto: Dundurn Press.

Erickson, Lynda. 1993. Making her way in: Women, parties and candidacies in Canada. In *Gender and Party Politics*, ed. Joni Lovenduski and Pippa Norris, 60–85. London: Sage Publications.

Erickson, Lynda, and R. Kenneth Carty. 1991. Parties and candidates in the 1988 Canadian general election. *Canadian Journal of Political Science* 24 (2): 331–350.

Hopkins, Jonathan. 2001. Bringing the members back in? Democratizing candidate selection in Britain and Spain. *Party Politics* 7 (3): 343–361.

Katz, Richard S. 2001. The problem of candidate selection and models of party democracy. *Party Politics* 3 (3): 277–296.

Liberal Party of Canada. 2009. National rules for the selection of candidates for the Liberal Party of Canada. http://www.liberal.ca/pdf/englishrules.pdf.

Manning, Preston. 2009. Open primaries, open minds. *Globe and Mail*, July 27.

Norris, Pippa, R.K. Carty, Lynda Erickson, Joni Lovenduski, and Marian Simms. 1990. Party selectorates in Australia, Britain and Canada: Prolegomena for research in the 1990s. *Journal of Commonwealth and Comparative Politics* 28 (2): 219–245.

Patten, Steve. 2007. The evolution of the Canadian party system. In *Canadian parties in transition*, 3rd ed., ed. Alain-G Gagnon and A. Brian Tanguay, 55–81. Peterborough, ON: Broadview Press.

Pennings, Paul, and Reuven Y. Hazan. 2001. Democratizing candidate selection: Causes and consequences. *Party Politics* 3 (3): 267–275.

Rahat, Gideon. 2007. Candidate selection: The choice before the choice. *Journal of Democracy* 18 (1): 157–170.

Rahat, Gideon, and Reuven Y. Hazan. 2001. Candidate selection methods: An analytical framework. *Party Politics* 3 (3): 297–322.

Scarrow, Harold A. 1964. Nomination and local party organization in Canada: A case study. *Western Political Quarterly* 17: 55–62.

Whitaker, Reginald. 1977. *The government party: Organizing and financing the Liberal Party of Canada, 1930–1958*. Toronto: University of Toronto Press.

Williams, Robert J. 1981. Candidate selection. In *Canada at the polls, 1979 and 1980: A study of the general elections*, ed. Howard R. Penniman, 86–120. Washington: American Enterprise Institute for Public Policy.

CHAPTER 8

Campaign Strategy: Triage and the Concentration of Resources

Thomas Flanagan

Eine Operation ohne Schwerpunkt is wie ein Mann ohne Charakter.
[An operation without *Schwerpunkt* is like a man without character.]
—*Field Marshal Paul von Hindenburg*

Introduction

This chapter discusses the development of strategy for a political campaign, presenting the process analytically as a series of steps to define and build a winning coalition of voters. In an ideal world, campaign planners would go through all these steps logically and systematically, using each one as a platform for the next. In the real world, however, time is often in short supply and campaign planners are sometimes inexperienced and distracted with other tasks. For example, the Conservatives in 2004 had only two months between March 20, when Stephen Harper won the leadership of the party, and May 23, when the Governor General issued the writ for the election. In such circumstances, the execution of essential steps in the planning process is rushed, and phases get telescoped into each other or carried out simultaneously or out of sequence. But even if the real world is messier than the ideal one, there is still value in looking at an ideal process for developing campaign strategy.

The chapter is based heavily on my personal involvement in planning the Conservative campaigns of 2004 and 2005–6. I managed the former and worked in war room communications in the latter. Thus, many of the examples I use in this chapter refer to the Conservatives, but I believe the principles are generally applicable.

The central principle of campaign strategy is that, in a world of scarce resources and legislated spending limits, it is necessary to focus spending where it will do the most good. Competitive elections are won or lost at the margin, in battleground ridings and among swing voters. Effective strategy means relying on a clear-headed process of triage to determine which ridings and demographic groups can be considered safe in the coming election, which are hopeless (for the time being), and which are on the cusp but can be tilted in your direction with the application of extra effort. It is somewhat like the concept of *Schwerpunkt* (centre of gravity, or focal point) in the classic work *On War* by Carl von Clausewitz. The similarity is not surprising, for the political competition between parties is a domesticated version of warfare, and political and military campaigns have many things in common.

What Is a Political Campaign?

A *campaign*, in general, is a collective action project that seeks to coordinate the activities of people over a period of time to reach a predetermined objective. A military campaign tries to mobilize soldiers and equipment to defeat an enemy, a fundraising campaign seeks to raise money for a cause, an advertising campaign tries to inform consumers about a product and persuade them to buy. A *political campaign* is an attempt to mobilize a coalition of people to vote in support of a particular candidate or team of candidates. Fundraising and advertising campaigns are part of the larger political campaign, but they are subordinate to the overriding goal of success in the election.

Military and political campaigns are similar in that they both demand great dedication and intense effort, but there is an even more profound difference. Military campaigns use coercion against opponents, whereas political campaigns in a functioning democracy cannot use coercion and must rely on persuasion to mobilize supporters. Rhetoric makes up the weaponry of a political campaign.

The Importance of Rules

There is no such thing as a universal campaign model. A political campaign is always waged within a specific context of rules, which have a major effect in determining which strategies will be viable. Areas in which rules are important include the general institutional setting of the political system, the specific details of the electoral system, (for example, majority or proportional), and the regulatory framework for conducting elections as enforced by a body such as Elections Canada.

The institutional setting. The arrangement of political institutions makes a big difference in the conduct of campaigns. For example, winning a Canadian national or provincial election requires conducting dozens or hundreds of local campaigns in geographically defined electoral districts. In contrast, electing an American senator or the mayor of a Canadian city is essentially a "cattle drive" within one large jurisdiction. Victory comes from finding as many supporters as possible, regardless of where they live. These two different institutional settings demand very different electoral strategies. If you are fighting for votes in one big jurisdiction, you can keep building on your strength, whereas if you are fighting for votes in many electoral districts across a wide expanse of territory, you have to address the demands of minorities who may be insignificant in the big picture but regionally concentrated in a way that makes them pivotal in particular districts.

The electoral system. Broadly speaking, systems of proportional representation encourage parties to engage in "narrowcasting," that is, to deliver very clear messages to stable groups of core supporters. If no party expects to win a majority of seats, which is usually the case under proportional representation, a winning strategy is to cultivate the party's electoral base and keep lines of communication open with selected other parties in order to participate in a government coalition after the election. Negative campaigning against potential coalition partners would be counterproductive.

First-past-the-post, or single-member plurality (SMP), systems, by contrast, encourage parties to engage in "broadcasting" to assemble a wide coalition of voters in order to win a majority of seats in the legislature, or at least a large enough plurality of seats to form a government. Under that strategy, a party cannot limit itself to delivering clear messages to stable groups of core supporters; it must reach out in an attempt to persuade the undecided, which often leads to taking vague or fuzzy positions. Negative campaigning against opponents is also useful, because there is little likelihood of wanting to make a coalition with them later.

The regulatory framework. Democracies vary enormously in the rules they establish for the conduct of campaigns. Many countries prohibit or restrict television advertising. Japan also forbids Internet campaigning as well as door-to-door canvassing. In Canada, on the other hand, all methods of communicating with voters are allowed, though there are limits on the total amount of money that can be spent. Such differences have an obvious impact on communications strategy and choice of media. To cite another example, the fact that Australia has compulsory voting means that Australian parties do not have to spend money on GOTV (Get Out the Vote) to mobilize voters to show up at the polls on election day. They can dedicate their spending to persuasion, whereas Canadian parties must devote considerable resources to identifying supporters and getting them to the polls.

Given all these variables, it would require an entire book to discuss campaign strategy in the whole spectrum of legal contexts. In this chapter, I will concentrate on strategy for political parties running in Canadian federal and provincial elections, which have the following characteristics:

- multiple electoral districts
- a first-past-the-post (SMP) electoral system
- no restriction on means of communication
- a global cap on campaign spending

What Are a Party's Objectives?

Some parties, like the Liberals and Conservatives in federal politics, or the NDP and the Saskatchewan Party in provincial politics, are running to win. Their goal in every election is to win as many seats as are required to form the next government—a majority if possible, but at least a plurality. Other parties, however, may be running to pursue less exalted but still worthy goals. We can list the following possible goals, more or less in order of importance:

- form a majority government
- form a minority government
- become the Official Opposition
- become a recognized party (12 seats in the federal Parliament)
- elect one member to the legislature
- get enough votes to receive government funding (2 percent of the popular vote at the federal level)

Parties routinely exaggerate or understate their true goals for political reasons. Stephen Harper thought that talking about a majority government backfired in 2004, so in 2006 and 2008 he insisted that he just wanted to win enough seats to govern and refused to utter the dreaded "M-word." Jack Layton insisted in 2008 that the NDP was running to win government, but the NDP would have been delighted beyond its wildest dreams simply to get more seats than the Liberals and for the first time form the Official Opposition in Ottawa. The Greens in 2008 talked about winning enough seats to become a recognized party in Parliament, but they would have been deliriously happy to elect even one MP (which they have not yet managed to do).

Whatever party leaders may say in public about their objectives, it is crucial for campaign planners to design strategy around realistic objectives. There can and should be contingency plans if things start to look much better ("roll the dice") or worse ("save the furniture") than expected, but the main plan should be based on a sober assessment of what is realistically possible. In the rest of this chapter, we will focus on parties that have a credible chance of forming the next government, and therefore will try to win a majority of seats if possible, or at least a plurality.

Defining a Geographic Coalition

Winning a Canadian federal or provincial election means winning more seats than your rivals do. For strategic purposes, therefore, you should begin by performing a triage of seats into the following categories:

- seats that are safe for your party
- battleground ridings that could go either way (this will include seats you now hold but fear you could lose as well as seats you don't hold but think you might win)
- seats that are hopeless for your party (in this election, maybe not forever)

In the first attempt at an analysis, you can use what I call the "Rule of Ten." Canadian experience suggests that a strong local campaign backed up by a vigorous Direct Voter Contact (DVC) program can increase a party's vote share by as much as 10 percentage points over the results of the last election. That is, if a party got 30 percent of the popular vote last time in a riding, it might be able to raise that to 40 percent by going all out and pouring in resources to win. It is thus logical to designate as battleground ridings those in which the margin of victory (MOV) or margin of defeat (MOD) for your party was 10 points or less in the preceding election. If you lost by 10 points or less last time, you have a shot at winning this time; if you won by 10 points or less, you have to be afraid of losing.

However, this is just the first step in triage because it does not take sufficient account of candidacy factors. Canadian research suggests that, independently of the resources devoted to the struggle, the candidate can also make a difference of 10 percentage points, maybe even more. Incumbency is almost always an advantage unless the incumbent has become notorious for corruption, incompetence, or erratic behaviour. There are also "star candidates" who may be well-known to the public from a previous career in business, media, arts and entertainment, or public service. Thus, after making the first analysis of ridings based on past results, one should take a second look at ridings where candidates may make a difference. This is a case-by-case process with several factors involved, but we can consider a couple of examples to show how it might work. Let's say that in the last election an NDP challenger knocked off a Liberal incumbent by a margin of 5 percent. Normally that would be considered a battleground riding because of the Rule of Ten, but let's suppose that the new NDP incumbent has acquired a good reputation, the former Liberal incumbent has disappeared from the scene, and the Liberals have now nominated an unimpressive candidate whom no one has ever heard of. If resources are short, the campaign planner might tell the NDP incumbent that he's on his own and not to expect any special help from the national party. On the other hand, if the former Liberal incumbent has stayed politically active and is running again in an effort to win the riding back, the NDP will almost certainly designate this as a battleground riding and pour in extra resources to help its incumbent get re-elected.

Concentration of resources on battleground ridings is the essential strategic principle. Close elections are won or lost at the margin. The party must focus its efforts on ridings where the outcome is in doubt. This is not always easy to do, because almost all candidates running for a major party believe that they have a chance to win and demand as much help as they can get from the national party. But a party that fritters away its resources on hopeless contests will not win the election.

Concentration of resources can mean many different things, including some or all of the following:

- Transferring extra money from the national party to the targeted riding (remembering that local campaigns have their own spending limits that have to be observed)
- Offering organizational assistance, either by sending in experienced campaigners or by giving advice from the national war room
- Tilting the media buy so that advertising is heavier in targeted ridings. Media markets do not correspond perfectly with riding boundaries, but targeted

ridings often come in clusters (for example, the working-class areas of Toronto for the NDP) that fit into a single media market. Similarly, safe seats are often found in clusters (for example, the province of Alberta for the Conservatives or the West Island of Montreal for the Liberals). The Conservatives would be silly to spend more than the minimum on advertising in Alberta, and likewise for the Liberals in anglophone Montreal.

- Scheduling one or more visits from the leader's tour during the writ period of the campaign. In practice, this is often backed up by visits from other popular figures in the party—the so-called secondary or surrogate tour. Visits can attract local media attention and galvanize local party workers. However, they must be managed carefully because they can also be a distraction for the candidate and workers at times when they should be out door-knocking rather than entertaining visitors.

- Arranging a Direct Voter Contact program. I am speaking here of an organized and expensive program of identifying supporters, persuading the undecided one at a time, and getting out the vote at the end of the campaign. In theory and occasionally in practice, this can be done by the local campaign through a combination of direct mail, telephone calls, and door-to-door visits; but normally the national campaign will have to maintain the database while organizing and paying for the telephone calls and direct mail. There is just too much to be done in too short a period of time for most local campaigns to manage it properly. A good Direct Voter Contact program is the single most effective weapon available to the national campaign to deploy in battleground ridings.

To summarize, a geographic coalition is built by triaging ridings into safe, battleground, and hopeless categories. Candidates in safe seats (usually incumbents) will be expected to win their own ridings without special help from the national campaign. Candidates in hopeless ridings will be encouraged to do their best, and a few will actually win, since triage and prediction are never totally accurate. All candidates in these two categories will get the standard package—a platform, templates for advertising and signage, the party's training program, et cetera—but the special assistance will be reserved for where it can do the most good, in the battleground ridings.

Defining a Demographic Coalition

Just as a geographic coalition has to be defined in order to target organizational efforts, especially Direct Voter Contact, a demographic coalition has to be defined in order to guide policy formation and advertising. The basic principle of triage is applied here too, and voters are placed into the following categories:

- core supporters
- swing voters
- confirmed opponents

But if the basic principle of triage is the same in defining geographic and demographic coalitions, the method by which the triage is performed in each case is different. Geographic triage is carried out by analyzing past results at the riding level, overlaid with assessments of incumbency and candidate strength. Demographic triage is carried out with quantitative survey research, supplemented by qualitative research (focus and dial groups), especially to highlight the perceptions and views of swing voters.

Political parties poll regularly but should also commission a large baseline poll to prepare for an anticipated election. That poll must be carried out early enough that its results can influence the composition of the platform and the advertising creative work. Six months ahead of the election is about right, though it is not always easy to achieve that kind of precision in the real world. The sample size should be large—at least 2,500 and preferably more—because conclusions are needed about relatively small groups within the population; for example, conclusions are needed not just about women in general, but about married women in the suburbs of Toronto.

Triage is achieved by combining results from a number of different questions, such as the following:

- Which party did you vote for in the last election?
- If an election were held today, which party would you vote for?
- How committed are you to this choice? Very committed, committed, or not very committed?
- Which party would be your second choice?
- If undecided, are you leaning toward a particular party?
- Is there any party that you would never vote for?

There are different ways of adding up the results, but in general we can say that Liberal core supporters would be those who voted Liberal in the last election (if they were eligible to vote), would vote Liberal if the election were held today, and say they are committed or very committed to their choice. Committed opponents would be the mirror image, that is, they voted for another party in the last election, would vote for another party if the election were held today, are very committed or committed to their choice, do not have the Liberals as a second choice, and indeed say they would never vote Liberal.

In between lie the persuadable target voters, who are actually of the most interest to campaign strategists. These voters might fall into various subgroups, including the following:

- Those who voted Liberal last time but now say they support another party. The Liberal campaign will want to know why they have defected and what is necessary to get them back.
- Those who say they would vote Liberal today but are only weakly committed to their choice. Why are they wavering, and how can their support be solidified?
- Those who are undecided but say they are leaning toward the Liberals. What would cause them to make up their mind in the Liberal direction?

- Those who are supporting another party but have the Liberals as their second choice. What would make them switch to the Liberals?

The combination of core supporters and persuadable target voters is known as the party's "universe" of support. The universe is essentially the demographic realm within which a party is realistically justified in expending short-term resources to win votes. Voters outside the universe can still be approached, but they will require a long-term strategy that goes well beyond a single campaign. For example, the Conservative Party has been deliberately trying since early 2005 to get more support from visible minority voters. The effort has involved two campaign platforms and several policy innovations while the party is in government, plus innumerable outreach efforts by party leaders and staff. The attempt appeared to bear little fruit in the 2006 election but did seem to get results in 2008.

In short, a party will operate mainly within its universe but will probably also have one or more long-term growth initiatives. Within its universe, which constitutes the short-term horizon, a party will need to do two things: (1) keep its core supporters happy so they will not be tempted to go elsewhere; and (2) increase its coalition by bringing on board some of the persuadable target voters. There is an inevitable tension between these two objectives because offers to persuadable voters will probably involve policies that core supporters are not enthusiastic about, or perhaps actively dislike. But such ventures are necessary precisely because the swing voters have not yet been attracted by what appeals to core voters. Occasionally a party has so many core supporters that it hardly has to worry about attracting new supporters, but that is a rare luxury in competitive political systems. Normally, if the party hopes to win, its leadership will have no choice except to try to balance the expectations of core supporters against the demands of persuadable target voters.

Now that the party's researchers have defined their universe, they must also establish its demographic contours. What are the characteristics of core supporters, swing voters, and confirmed opponents? Using qualitative rather than precise quantitative terms, Table 8.1 shows some sample demographic aspects of the Conservative universe prior to the 2006 election.

The effect of these characteristics tends to be additive. Thus, the probability that a middle-aged, married, self-employed, Evangelical Protestant man living in a small town in Western Canada is a Conservative core supporter approaches 100 percent. By contrast, the probability that a young, unmarried, non-religious woman, living in downtown Toronto and working for a public sector employer, is a Conservative approaches 0 percent. Most people, of course, are not so extremely stereotyped; they have a mixture of characteristics, some of which are statistically associated with voting Conservative, while others are associated with supporting other parties. But the additive principle is still the key. The closer a person is to the demographic stereotype of Conservative voters, the more accessible that person is likely to be to Conservative appeals. In practice, this means that the best way to build a coalition is incrementally outward from core support rather than by making big leaps.

TABLE 8.1   Conservative Universe, 2005

Favouring Conservatives	Swing Voters	Favouring Opponents
Men	—	Women
Western	Ontario	Quebec and Atlantic
Evangelical Protestant	Mainstream Protestant; Roman Catholic	Non-religious
Married	Widowed, divorced	Never married
Self-employed	Employed; Private sector union	Unemployed; Public sector union
Rural	Suburban	Urban
Middle-aged	Seniors	Youth

Let's give some specific examples. The Conservative Party prior to the 2006 election, like other conservative parties around the world, had a "gender gap," that is, it tended to have less support among women than among men. If it was going to win, it needed to get more votes from women. That meant finding ways to appeal to female voters who were already closest to being Conservative supporters—for example, married, middle-class women in suburbs or small towns rather than young, unmarried women living in central cities. Or, in terms of religion, the Conservatives were doing very well with Evangelical Protestants, but not as well with Roman Catholics, who historically had been a Liberal support group. The party needed to get more Catholic votes, and that seemed like a more realistic possibility than getting more votes from atheists, because Roman Catholics—at least practising Catholics—share values and beliefs with Evangelical Protestants.

Going into the 2006 election, therefore, the Conservatives had a research-based strategy of trying to bring more married women and Roman Catholics over to their side, believing that these demographic categories contained many voters who resembled typical Conservative voters in other respects and just needed a little more encouragement to make the transition. In addition, the Conservatives also had a long-term strategy of trying to build support among certain ethnic and visible-minority voters. Again the additive principle was central. For example, even if Chinese voters had been overwhelmingly supporting the Liberal Party for decades, there were many Chinese voters whose demographic profile resembled that of typical Conservative voters—married, middle-class, middle-aged, self-employed, perhaps even Evangelical Protestant (for example, members of the Christian and Missionary Alliance). Such voters would be the logical place for the Conservatives to go prospecting.

Once target or non-target groups are established, strategists even give them nicknames to make them come to life. For example, in the leadup to the 2005–6 campaign, a Conservative strategist gave names to many groups that were of interest, either positive or negative, to his party. "Zoe" was his label for a group among which the Conservatives were unlikely to make much progress—young, single women in central cities. He even built a biography for "Zoe" to make her come alive. He depicted her as a recent sociology graduate living with her cat in downtown Toronto, doing yoga and eating vegetarian food. If she voted at all, it would probably be NDP or Liberal rather than Conservative. Such stereotyping helps those planning campaign communications visualize the people to whom they want to appeal and the types of communication that would reach them.

By itself, the additive principle leads only to intuitions about which demographic subgroups might be open to a party's appeals. These intuitions must be checked through survey research, by discovering how many members of demographic subgroups are leaning toward your party or have it as their second choice, testing their openness to the party's policies, and looking for breakthrough policies that might bring them on side. Qualitative research is also useful. Once quantitative analysis has isolated demographic targets, members can be recruited to join discussion groups, where they can talk about their perceptions of the party, their hesitations about supporting it, and their aspirations for what government can accomplish. It is, for example, crucial to learn whether members of a target group are hesitant because they don't like the leader or don't like the policies. If the leader is seen as too formal, he can be dressed in a sweater and open-necked shirt when shooting the advertisements. If the policies are wrong, the draft platform can be altered. Or maybe both changes need to be made.

In any case, it is essential to base decisions on research about what is likely to work with target voter groups. Research is particularly important because those who work for the party are loyalists; their views may be typical of the core supporters who keep the party going year in and year out, but they don't reflect those of the target voters whose support must be acquired to build a winning coalition. Party strategists cannot afford to trust their own intuitions, because they themselves are not typical of the people they are trying to attract.

I have discussed geographic and demographic triage separately for analytical purposes, but in the real world they are related. Ethnic groups, for example, are often geographically concentrated. If a party decides to make an appeal to a targeted ethnic group, that may bring certain ridings into play even though they do not seem winnable based on their history. Regionally defined groups are also, by definition, geographically concentrated. For example, the Liberal Party did not elect anyone in Alberta in 2006 and 2008, and in fact finished so far behind that it might not bother to target any ridings in the province in the next election. But the new Liberal leader, Michael Ignatieff, has made some effort to appeal to Alberta by talking reassuringly about the value of the oil sands to the Canadian economy. If he continues with this initiative, and if the polls show any movement, the Liberals might find it worthwhile to target one or two ridings in Alberta. If so, they would probably choose the ones where they came closest in 2008, even if the MOD was well behind 10 percentage points.

The Strategy of Persuasion

Defining geographic and demographic coalitions is the essential prerequisite for developing a communications strategy for the campaign. A campaign is an organized effort to persuade people to join your coalition, and communication is the means by which persuasion takes place. But for communication to be effective, the intended audience has to be known. You want to speak persuasively to your universe of voters, even more persuasively to undecided but potential supporters, and most persuasively to potential supporters in the battleground ridings that must be won to achieve victory in the election.

The platform is the most basic communications instrument. At one time the platform was printed and distributed in large quantities; now it is mainly posted on the party's website. In any case, the platform is read by only a small fraction of voters, but it is crucial because it guides all other communications, including advertising, leader's speeches, press releases, and responses to attacks.

The platform is conventionally understood as a set of policies that a party's elected representatives will implement if they form the government. That seems to imply that policy is the end and the campaign is the means. But that relationship is reversed from the standpoint of the campaign strategist, in whose eyes the platform and all its policies are a means to achieve the end of winning the election. From that perspective, parties don't try to get elected in order to implement their policies; they adopt policies in order to get elected.

As suggested above, the platform has to have some "red meat" items designed to hold the loyalty of core supporters. For example, the 2005–6 Conservative platform contained several promises of across-the-board tax cuts—reduction of the GST from 7 percent to 6 percent and then to 5 percent, lowering of corporate income taxes, and elimination of the capital gains tax under certain circumstances. These policies appealed strongly to Conservative core supporters, who tend to think that taxes—all taxes—are too high and should be lowered. But there were several highly targeted tax or grant policies, of which the Child Care Allowance—$100 per month for each child under six—was the most visible. The following tax and grant policies were also included in the Conservative platform:

- $1,000 Apprentice Incentive Grant
- Apprenticeship Job Creation Tax Credit
- Tools Tax Deduction
- increase from $1,000 to $2,000 in the pension income tax amount eligible for a federal tax credit
- exemption of the first $10,000 of student scholarship income from taxation
- $500 textbook tax credit
- $500 tax credit to parents for registration fees and memberships for physical fitness activities for their children
- federal tax credit for use of public transit

These platform items were an attempt to reach groups that had been targeted by campaign planners on the basis of research—parents of school and university age children, skilled workers, and retired people. These groups were open to voting Conservative but needed a little more inducement.

Targeting groups of voters is essential to building a winning coalition, but it can look like a crass appeal to self-interest. Hence the platform, and the party's whole communicative posture during the campaign, must also sound themes that appeal more broadly to voters' sense of the public interest. Here are three examples:

- Barack Obama made "change" the theme of his 2008 campaign for the presidency. "Change" was in fact a code word for several different things—electing the first black president in American history, replacing a Republican with a Democratic administration, transcending the highly polarized atmosphere that had marked American politics since the Clinton years of the 1990s, and perhaps many other things that voters might read into an amorphous concept such as "change."

- In 2005–6, the Conservatives made integrity in government a major theme because the Liberals were stuck with the blame for the "Adscam" abuses. The Conservatives proposed an "Accountability Act" as the first of their "Five Priorities" during the campaign.

- By the late 1970s, there was a widespread sense in Great Britain that the country was in decline and that the trade unions, some of which were led by Communists, were running wild. The Conservatives, led by Margaret Thatcher, thus turned the 1979 election into a veritable crusade against socialism. Thatcher previewed this theme almost as soon as she became leader, saying in 1976: "I call the Conservative Party now to a crusade. ... I appeal to all those men and women of goodwill who do not want a Marxist future for themselves or their children or their children's children."

Failure to sound a convincing overarching theme can make even the most carefully constructed platform difficult to sell. In 2004, the Canadian Conservatives had a detailed platform with a lot of appeal to targeted groups, but the overall thematics were rather mushy. What exactly did the campaign slogan "Demand Better" mean? Stephen Harper did not repeat this mistake, as he emphasized integrity in the 2005–6 campaign and leadership in 2008, making the latter campaign not so much about policy as about his alleged superiority as a leader over then Liberal leader Stéphane Dion.

A useful tool in establishing the major theme of a campaign is the so-called SWOT analysis, which is also often used in the business world. SWOT is an acronym for *s*trengths, *w*eaknesses, *o*pportunities, *t*hreats. Typically, a group of strategists, numbering anywhere from five to twenty, will spend half a day reviewing the situation, not just from their own perspective, but from the viewpoint of their major opponent. Table 8.2 presents a fraction of what a SWOT analysis might have shown prior to the 2008 election campaign.

TABLE 8.2   Partial SWOT Analysis of 2008 Election Campaign

Strengths

Conservatives	Liberals
Leader respected for competence	Best-established party brand
Lots of money for pre-writ ads	

Weaknesses

Conservatives	Liberals
Leader widely mistrusted	Leader widely seen as incompetent
	No money for pre-writ ads

Opportunities

Conservatives	Liberals
Spend money on negative ads against Liberal leader	Somehow heighten mistrust of Conservative leader

Threats

Conservatives	Liberals
Economic downturn could cause voters to turn against government	Leader's preoccupation with environmental policy could backfire

I don't know if the Conservative strategists actually carried out this SWOT analysis, but they acted as if they had. They used their financial advantage to run negative ads attacking Stéphane Dion's competence and his "Green Shift" policies as well as positive ads showing Stephen Harper looking casual in a blue sweater and speaking in friendly, reassuring tones. They also pre-empted the threat of an economic downturn by calling an early election, even though that required Harper to ignore his own fixed-election-date legislation (see Chapter 4 on election law by Heather MacIvor). The Liberals, by contrast, seemed less strategic. Dion emphasized the "Green Shift" even though a lot of polling data showed that voters were turning against it, and did not come up with anything compelling to take advantage of Harper's potential personality weaknesses. The Liberals almost got lucky when the economic downturn became manifest in the last two weeks of the campaign, but by then the Conservatives had done so much damage to Dion's image, and he had associated himself so totally with environmental themes, that he could not make himself seem a plausible leader for an economic emergency.

The Mechanics of Persuasion

Once the platform and thematics are in place and some version of a SWOT analysis has been conducted, the strategist must consider the mechanics of "getting the message out." The national campaign will conduct the "air war" in the media while leaving the "ground war" of personal contact to the local campaigns, with the important exception of the Direct Voter Contact campaign in targeted ridings. The media campaign will have two branches: advertising, which has to be paid for, and news coverage, which is earned primarily through the leader's tour.

Paid advertising may or may not be the most important part of a campaign—that will depend on circumstances—but it is usually the most expensive. A fully funded national campaign ($20 million in 2008) may well spend about 60 percent of its budget on advertising. Creation and production of the ads may cost $1 million or even more, while the rest will go to the media buy. The media buy is so large because television, the most effective form of political advertising, is so expensive. National campaigns rely largely on television, with sometimes a little radio and/or full-page newspaper advertising. Viral marketing on the Internet is becoming more and more important but tends to complement and reinforce television advertising rather than replace it. "Outdoor" advertising—signs and billboards—is generally left to the local campaigns.

The media buy, which may make up as much as half the entire campaign budget, should be driven by the geographic and demographic coalitional analysis. Geographically, it is vital to make the media buy heavier where there are targeted ridings. Some aspects of this are easy to achieve. For example, the Conservatives and Liberals both spend little on advertising in Alberta—the Conservatives because they expect to win every seat and the Liberals because they don't expect to win any. But it is harder to focus the media buy when target ridings are scattered. In cases like that, particularly in remote rural ridings, radio can be a cost-effective tool because the reach of a radio station may correspond more or less with the boundaries of a targeted riding.

Demographically, the objective is to place ads on the shows ("properties," as they are called in the business) that are watched by the sorts of viewers the campaign is trying to reach. News and public affairs programs are important in that the people who watch them are likely to vote, and so advertising there is not wasting money on people who are not interested. Beyond that, professional media buyers have access to exhaustive statistics on the demographics of television audiences. Some of the science is pretty obvious. To reach male voters, choose hockey, golf, fishing, and other sports shows (except figure skating); to reach female voters, go to the "soaps" (for stay-at-home moms) or dramas about personal relationships. But media buyers can go far beyond the obvious by breaking down the demographics of a media property by all the usual demographic variables, including gender, age, income, marital status, and place of residence.

The advertising creative process should also be driven by the coalitional analysis. Ads designed to reach a young, hip audience (good for selling cellphones but a waste of money in Canadian politics since young people are less likely to vote) would be different from ads designed to reach mom and pop relaxing at home after an exhausting day of work and coping with children. Most of the people who do advertising creative are young, hip urbanites, but their job is to understand their clients' needs, and that is where the research comes in. If the creative team knows the demographics of the target groups the party is trying to bring into its coalition, they should be able to reach that audience.

Earned media is garnered largely through the organized madness of the leader's tour, in which the party rents a combination of planes and buses to haul the leader, staff, and media people around the country for the length of the campaign. The leader might bring 20 to 30 staff members along, and there might be a similar number of print journalists, columnists, and electronic reporters with their microphones and camera crews. Media companies pay as much as $10,000 a week for a seat on the leader's tour, so they expect it to generate headline stories for their newspapers or broadcasts.

If the leader's tour is going to be effective, it must be meticulously planned, and the planning must be driven by an understanding of the party's coalition and target voters. The principle of triage applies to choosing geographic destinations. While the campaign will want to touch down in all major media markets of the country at least once, it will want to spend most of its time in battleground ridings, not in safe or hopeless seats. Thus, the Conservatives will probably stop only once in Calgary, even though it is Prime Minister Harper's home city. Reporters accompanying the tour will interpret it as a sign of weakness if the tour starts to visit ridings previously thought to be party strongholds and will start filing unflattering stories about the tour; nonetheless, it may be necessary to "save the furniture" in the late stages of the campaign if the polls are unpromising. Correspondingly, if the party seems to have captured a wave, it may send the leader to ridings previously thought unwinnable. But in spite of these potential variations, the best course is usually to concentrate on the battleground ridings designated as such when the campaign was planned.

It is not enough to visit the right places; the leader's tour must also dramatize its messages in ways calculated to reach target demographic groups. It has to generate the right photo ops. For example, when Stephen Harper announced tax credits for children's sports programs in 2005, he staged the announcement in a dojo where kids were taking karate lessons. Perhaps he should not have worn a suit, but at that time he had a weight problem and looked better in boxy business attire than in casual clothes. In any case, the setting and the resulting visuals were arresting enough to get on front pages of newspapers and to be played in TV news broadcasts, thus attracting the attention of parents everywhere in Canada who were the target of this particular policy.

Enormous effort goes into planning the leader's tour. It is no small feat to schedule the correct ridings and then find locations for announcements and photo ops that will fit both the geographic location and the demographics of the target groups. You would not announce Wheat Board policy in Toronto, because you want to be surrounded by farmers and tractors, and you would not announce immigration policy in rural Saskatchewan, because you want to be surrounded by visible minorities when you make your statement. All this is perfectly obvious and yet not always easy to achieve when you have to combine it with the demands of keeping to schedule, maintaining security, and satisfying local party organizers who want the leader at a rally.

Sticking to the Script

Campaigns are dynamic in nature, so there must be some flexibility in the plan, to allow for changing circumstances. An issue may unexpectedly arise, causing the leader's tour to change its itinerary so that the issue can be addressed in an appropriate location. Opponents may come up with hard-hitting negative ads requiring response ads to blunt their effectiveness. Revelations about something the leader said or did years ago may divert the campaign from getting out its own message. To cope with such contingencies, the campaign must have a process for crisis management, allowing the war room managers to discuss things with the leader and key advisers who are on the tour.

But while acknowledging the importance of flexibility and crisis management, it is usually best to stay as close as possible to the script. If the campaign is properly planned, it is based on months of thinking and hundreds of thousands of dollars of research. What are the odds of coming up with a better plan on the spur of the moment under great pressure during the heat of a campaign? Let me give a couple of examples from personal experience with Conservative campaigns:

- In 2004, Conservative polling numbers soared after Stephen Harper performed well in the English leaders' debate, and we decided to go for broke, hoping that talk of winning a majority government would create a bandwagon effect. But instead of a self-fulfilling prophecy we produced a self-induced train wreck. Voters began to look more skeptically at Harper once we were talking about winning a majority of seats, and an unfortunate press release caused the whole bubble to burst. The lesson? We were not working from a plan to win a majority of seats, so we should not have suddenly started to talk about it late in the campaign.

- The Conservatives were doing everything right in the first three weeks of the 2005 campaign, rolling out new policy every day, and the media were saying that our campaign was the best. Yet our polling numbers, measured in terms of the ballot question ("If the election were held today, which party would you vote for?") barely moved. Many of us in the war room, including me, started to get nervous, worrying that we needed to do something, anything, else. But campaign manager Doug Finley stood fast, saying, "Stick to the plan." He was right. We were in fact making progress as voters were becoming aware of our positions, and that eventually led to a change in voting intentions.

The Permanent Campaign

We used to think of political campaigns as episodes, spasms of energy every four or five years. About a year before an election was expected, a party would appoint a campaign committee and a manager to get ready. Planning and preparation were required, and there might be a brief period of pre-writ advertising before the election was called; but the campaign itself was basically a five-week phenomenon. However, several factors have come together recently to shift Canadian federal politics in the direction of the "permanent campaign" model. One is that we have had minority governments since 2004 and will probably see more of the same as long as the Bloc Québécois is able to hold its vote in Quebec. Under minority government, you never know when the writ might be dropped, so you have to have the campaign machine ready to go on short notice. Also, Canada's electoral finance regime has produced a situation in which parties can raise more money than they are able to spend in the writ period. Parties are not investment clubs; if they have extra money, they will spend it during the pre-writ period to improve their electoral prospects.

This tendency has become most noticeable in the Conservative Party. The Conservative campaign team never rests. A campaign manager reporting directly to the leader, not to a committee, is always in place. Voter identification linked to fundraising goes on 363 days a year (Christmas and Easter excepted). With the cash flow from such aggressive fundraising, the party can afford to spend millions on advertising, even years in advance of the writ, and to fund other activities such as the Conservative University, which trains candidates and workers, especially in the use of its Direct Voter Contact program and the associated electronic database. Activities funded by the House of Commons can also be channelled to political purposes—travel to targeted ridings and ethnic communities, mail outs with a response card for voter identification, public opinion research to find policies that will resonate with target demographic groups. All parties do some of these things some of the time, but the Conservatives are ahead of the pack in the scale on which they operate. They now coordinate all their activities, starting years before an anticipated election, to concentrate their resources on the *Schwerpunkt*—the swing ridings and target demographic groups where the election will be won or lost.

If the Conservative example spreads to other parties, campaigning will become a fully institutionalized feature of a party's activities. Just as corporate marketing departments are always engaged in advertising or other promotional campaigns, political parties may also have to make their campaign machinery a permanent part of their organization. The campaign manager may become more like a vice-president of marketing, responsible for selling the party to the public on an ongoing basis. We are not there yet, but it is a possible outcome if current trends persist.

DISCUSSION QUESTIONS

1. How would Canadian campaigns change if Canada were to adopt proportional representation? What, if any, would be the impact on platform development, advertising, leaders' tours, and Direct Voter Contact?

2. This chapter gives an idea of geographic and demographic coalitions of support for the main federal parties. Can you sketch out the corresponding coalitions for the main parties in the province in which you live?

3. Have you seen any negative ads on television? Do you think they are effective? Why or why not?

4. This chapter says nothing about social networking sites such as Facebook and Twitter. What impact do you think they have on campaigning?

FURTHER READING

Clarkson, Stephen. 2005. *The big red machine: How the Liberal Party dominates Canadian politics.* Vancouver: UBC Press. An anatomy of Liberal campaigns from 1974 through 2004. The triumphalist tone is now out-of-date, but it has much valuable information.

Duffy, John. 2002. *Fights of our lives: Elections, leadership, and the making of Canada.* Toronto: HarperCollins. An illustrated popular history of Canadian campaigning since 1867, with emphasis on crucial realigning elections.

Flanagan, Tom. 2009. *Harper's team: Behind the scenes in the Conservative rise to power.* Montreal: McGill-Queen's University Press. A detailed account of Stephen Harper's two leadership campaigns as well as the Canadian elections of 2004, 2006, and 2008.

Johnston, Richard. 1992. *Letting the people decide: Dynamics of a Canadian election.* Montreal: McGill-Queen's University Press. This classic academic analysis of the 1988 election pioneered the use of tracking polls.

Kinsella, Warren. 2007. *The war room: Political strategies for business, NGOs, and anyone who wants to win.* Toronto: Dundurn Press. Public relations and advertising in Canadian politics, based on Kinsella's personal experience with Liberal campaigns.

Laschinger, John, and Geoffrey Stevens. 1992. *Leaders and lesser mortals: Backroom politics in Canada.* Toronto: Key Porter. A portrait of Canadian campaigning in the 1970s and 1980s by John Laschinger, Canada's most experienced campaign manager. Technology has changed since then, but the principles remain the same.

Luntz, Frank. 2007. *Words that work: It's not what you say, it's what people hear.* New York: Hyperion. An American pollster on how to use research to craft political rhetoric.

Pammett, Jon H., and Christopher Dornan, eds. 2009. *The Canadian federal election of 2008.* Toronto: Dundurn Press. A collection of scholarly papers on the election and campaign. Part of a series of similar books extending back to the 1984 election.

Raymond, Allen. 2008. *How to rig an election: Confessions of a Republican operative.* New York: Simon and Schuster. Autobiography of a professional consultant who went too far with dirty tricks and ended up in jail.

CHAPTER 9

Still Waiting for an Internet Prime Minister: Online Campaigning by Canadian Political Parties

Tamara A. Small

Introduction

The use of Facebook, Twitter, and YouTube has dramatically changed the landscape of electoral politics. This point was amply demonstrated during the 2008 US election, in which Barack Obama was dubbed the "Internet president" by the media (Harnden 2008). Obama's use of the Internet has been likened to John F. Kennedy's use of television; JFK's masterful performance on television in the 1960 election, especially the infamous debate with Richard Nixon,[1] was critical to his success (Taras 1990, 168). JFK ushered in the era of the "television president," and marked a transformation in election campaigns. Television forced campaigns to focus more on visual image and less on the spoken word as a means of communicating with voters. To some, Obama's groundbreaking Internet use was crucial to his victory in the 2008 presidential election. One media commentator suggests that Obama "showed other politicians how to harness the power of the Web in 2008, bringing political campaigns kicking and screaming into the 21st century" (Gross 2008). Consider the evidence:

- YouTube users spent 14.5 million hours watching official Barack Obama videos.
- Obama's Facebook page had 2.6 million supporters.

- 123,000 people followed Obama on Twitter, making the page the leading Twitter page for much of 2008.
- 3.2 million people donated through BarackObama.com.
- More than 70 percent of the $750 million raised by the Obama campaign was from online donations (Wagner 2008; Vargas 2008).

It remains to be seen how integral the Internet actually was to Obama's victory, especially since similar claims about the power of the Internet have been made in previous elections. For instance, Howard Dean was considered the JFK of the Internet in the 2004 election. Hindman (2005) noted, "Dean's candidacy is thus the best evidence to date that the Web matters for politics" (127). Like Obama, Dean made innovative use of the technology and raised significant amounts of money online. However, the clear difference between Dean and Obama is that the latter was successful not only in the primaries[2] but also in the general election. Scholarly assessment of Obama's online campaign is still forthcoming.

The American election was not the only election in 2008. Canadians also went to the polls that year. Like their American counterparts, Canadian political parties have been using the Internet for campaigning since the early 1990s. However, proclamations of innovative and successful use of the Internet are practically non-existent in Canadian politics. Indeed, both popular and scholarly assessments of online campaigning are critical. This chapter examines the use of the Internet in the 2008 federal election. It argues that the approach of Canadian political parties to online campaigning has changed little from previous election campaigns, despite the introduction of a new environment for online campaigning: the social networking site. The use of such sites by Canadian parties is reminiscent of online campaigning in previous federal elections.

This chapter begins with an overview of the role of the Internet in democratic politics. A brief history of online campaigning in Canadian federal elections follows. Then, the online context of the 2008 federal election is considered. The environment of online campaigning has evolved with the introduction of Web 2.0 and social networking sites, which are more collaborative and interactive. Campaigning on three very popular social networking sites—YouTube, Facebook, and Twitter—by Canada's five main political parties is then described and assessed.[3] Even though Internet technology may have evolved, online campaigning by Canadian political parties has not. Some innovative online campaigning did occur in 2008. Indeed, the campaign witnessed uses of Web 2.0 by individual Canadians that captured the attention of the media and the electorate. However, inventive online campaigning is generally not in the purview of Canada's political parties.

Internet Politics: Potentials and Perspectives

Regarding politics and the Internet, a guiding question of political scientists and Internet researchers is this: "is the Internet changing how we do politics and how we think about politics?" (Chadwick 2007, 1). Embedded in this question is the assumption that the Internet could and should change democratic politics, and that this change would be for the better. This is because the Internet "is seen to possess what may be broadly termed 'democratic' potentials untraceable in the traditional media" (Bentivegna 2002, 54). Similarly, Klotz (2004) notes that the Internet "offers the potential to do things that were impossible before. … As a medium for politics, it offers advances over previous media" (4).

FIGURE 9.1   Elizabeth May's Facebook Page, September 2008

The use of social media tools in Canadian political campaigns, such as Elizabeth May's Facebook page, remains in its infancy. Parties still tend to treat the Internet primarily as a modern marketing tool for one-way communication.

Interactivity is often cited as a "democratic potential" of the Internet. Through email, instant messaging, and message boards, the Internet provides users with direct and instantaneous communication with other users. As such, the Internet is unmatched in its capacity to allow citizens to engage in discussions with political officials and/or other citizens compared with other mass media. The Internet is also an extremely inexpensive communication medium. It is very cost-effective in terms of technical production and transmission. Videos on YouTube cost little to nothing to produce, and can be viewed by millions. Moreover, users have access to free email, websites, and blogs. These services can increase political participation because they lower entry barriers into politics. Decentralization is another factor that can increase political participation. The "Internet would provide the technology required to link a politically active cyber civil society and more formal decision-making processes once controlled by elite gatekeepers" (Chadwick 2007, 22). As a decentralized space, the Internet reduces the power of intermediaries (journalists, political parties, legislatures) because it allows any individual or group to directly participate in politics. The Internet also has the potential to be a space for marginalized voices. Moreover, the Internet "transcends physical proximity" (Bimber 1999, 409), which means that individuals can communicate beyond their locale. Users all over the world can view a website, blog, or YouTube video. Additionally, they can communicate with one another. The Internet's reach has the potential to deterritorialize politics, putting into question the old adage "all politics is local." Finally, the Internet allows for narrowcasting, that is, "the practice of sending particular political messages to particular people" (Howard 2005, 158). The Internet lets politicians, groups, or citizens target their messages.

These and other characteristics of the Internet lead some to suggest that the Internet has the capacity to revolutionize and reinvigorate democratic politics by enhancing public participation and efficacy. Howard Dean's campaign manager and self-proclaimed cyber-utopian Joe Trippi (2005), believes that the Internet is "the best tool we have ever created" to help achieve full participation in democracy (226). Cyber-utopians claim that because all political organizations have the same potential to reach citizens online, the Internet has the capacity to equalize the playing field between major and so-called fringe political actors—a claim known as the *equalization hypothesis*. The *mobilization hypothesis*, on the other hand, states that at an individual level, the informational and interactive capabilities of the Internet have the potential to mobilize the disengaged, including young people and political minorities.

This is just one perspective on Internet politics, however. Little consensus exists in the literature about the nature of the change that the Internet might bring. Some question the deterministic view of digital democracy presented above. For example, Richard Davis (1999) asks how the additional cost, involvement, and time commitment incurred by Internet politics would make people more politically efficacious (173). Andrew Chadwick (2007) contends that instead of withering away, intermediaries have "found their skills highly relevant in the Internet age" (22). These skeptics do not deny that the Internet will change politics. However, they do question the scope and nature of the change. According to the *normalization hypothesis*, the main beneficiaries of the Internet are not the disenfranchised groups and individuals, but traditional institutions:

> [A]s the Internet develops, patterns of socioeconomic and political relationships on-line come to resemble those of the real world. Applied to political parties, this hypothesis implies that just as the major parties dominate the sphere of everyday domestic politics, so they come to dominate cyberspace. (Margolis and Resnick 2000, 26)

Cyber-skeptics consider that the Internet reinforces, not alters, levels of participation and efficacy. For them, politics on the Internet will be "politics as usual" (Margolis and Resnick 2000).

Finally, some scholars suggest that the Internet will have negative repercussions for democracy. Cass Sunstein (2004) argues that "many people are increasingly engaged in the process of 'personalization,' which limits their exposure to topics and points of view of their own choosing" (58). The concern with this *cyber-balkanization* is that "in a free society, citizens aspire to a system that provides a range of experience—with people, topics, and ideas—they would not have selected in advance" (Sunstein 2004, 59). Worse yet, others argue that the Internet could be employed as a tool to oppress, dominate, and surveil citizens. For instance, the Reporter Without Borders website reports that almost 500 bloggers worldwide were arrested because of their online activities in 2008. The very same aspects of the technology that make it democratic can be used against citizens. When considering the role of the Internet in Canadian elections, we should keep all of these perspectives in mind. In doing so, we can avoid technological determinism and the assumption that the Internet, in and of itself, will make politics more democratic.

A History of Online Campaigning in Canadian Federal Politics

Online campaigning in Canadian politics began in 1993. In the 1993 election, the National Capital FreeNet established forums for parties to post information and communicate with voters (Kippen 2000, 36). The Liberal Party was the only party to make use of the FreeNet, and became the first federal party to enter cyberspace. Grant Kippen (2000) notes that the discussion forum feature "proved to be very disappointing … dominated by a small group of individuals with very entrenched viewpoints" (37). By the next federal election in 1997, all major Canadian parties had established an online presence, as did some local candidates. Party websites were far more tech-savvy than the average Canadian Internet user, which led Kenneth Carty, William Cross, and Lisa Young (2000) to describe this use of the Internet as "very much in its infancy" (208). The 2000 federal election is considered Canada's first real Internet election. By that time, the majority of Canadians had access to the Internet, and it was commonplace among parties at all levels of government. Nevertheless, commentators again concluded that the Internet had not significantly altered the campaign. Party campaign sites were little more than "electronic brochures." Attallah and Burton (2001) conclude that Canadian parties had "not fully thought through [the Internet's] true political utility or value" (227–28).

Our scholarly understanding of Internet politics was greatly enhanced after the 2004 federal election. Several studies on the topic were published by scholars (see Barney 2005, 2007; Kernaghan 2007; Small 2004, 2006; Small, Taras, and Danchuk 2008) and other organizations (Hillwatch 2004). Tamara Small, David Taras, and David Danchuk (2008) conclude that party websites "were no longer the electronic version of lawn signs. They had become multi-media platforms that were used to organize campaign activities, get out campaign messages quickly and collect valuable data" (130). Though the websites of Canadian parties were technologically sophisticated and far more integrated in the overall election strategies, assessments of the online campaign remained skeptical. First, party websites were used to perform traditional campaign activities (Small 2006; Kernaghan 2007). They serves as a depository for campaign information for both voters and journalists. Parties did do a better job of trying to get people involved in the campaign compared with the previous campaign. Visitors to party websites could quickly join the party, volunteer to help with the campaign, or donate money online. Viral campaigning features such as "send to a friend" were commonplace. However, campaign emails focused on the same traditional campaign activities: information dissemination and calls for volunteers and donations. Hillwatch (2004) was critical and suggested that parties "offer no substantive means through which party grassroots can organize, mobilize, share practices, download key campaign tools, and coordinate outreach." Kenneth Kernaghan (2007) concludes that far from being transformative, the Internet was merely "supplementary" to offline campaign activities (215).

Another reason the 2004 federal election did not meet the threshold suggested by cyber-optimists was that parties did not use their websites to engage with the electorate. Indeed, as Kernaghan (2007) notes, "Online interactivity in the narrow sense of direct two-way communication between a voter and a party or candidate site has been uncommon in Canadian elections" (215). The parties did not even incorporate the online engagement tool that dominated American politics at the time—the campaign blog. Blogging was central to online campaigning in the 2004 US presidential primaries, especially Howard Dean's Blog for America. Blogs are both "interactive and interconnected," allowing for a "dialogue between bloggers [authors] and readers, and readers with other readers" (O'Brien 2004, 4). Despite the centrality of blogging to US presidential politics, "Canadian parties did not jump on the blogwagon in 2004" (Small 2006, 67). Based on interviews, Small and colleagues (2008) concluded that Canadian parties "feared that online discussions could knock them off message by raising controversial issues or tarnish their image bringing attention to the 'crazies' that might invade or be planted in party chat rooms" (9). Overall, online campaigning in the 2004 federal election was mainly unidirectional, from the campaign to voters.

Significant developments in online campaigning did not occur in the 18 months between the 2004 and 2006 federal campaigns. Small and colleagues (2008) suggest, "In most ways the 2006 cyber campaign was a replay of the 2004 campaign. Websites were mostly static and conservative except that they had become a bit more advanced in their uses of technology" (126). Hillwatch's (2006) follow-up report came to a similar conclusion about Canada's political party websites: "they continue to be very much like lawn signs—they still inform, but don't engage" (1). As in 2004, the online strategy of Canadian parties was heavily focused on information dissemination and media relations. Online engagement tools remained scant. "Despite more strategic use of the Internet in 2004 and 2006, Canadian party Web sites lag behind their American counterparts when it comes to online citizen engagement" (Small 2006, 68).

The Online Context of the 2008 Federal Election

Canadians continue to be among the heaviest Internet users worldwide: approximately three-quarters of Canadians are regular users of the Internet. This said, politics is not a significant area of online interest for Canadians (Zamaria and Fletcher 2008, 215). Research by the Canadian Internet Project shows that even though the majority of Canadian Internet users have accessed online government information, they rarely engage in other aspects of online politics (Zamaria and Fletcher 2008). In 2007, only 21 percent of Internet users reported visiting the website of a Canadian political party or individual politician (226). Nineteen percent of Internet users had communicated with a Canadian elected or bureaucratic official, while only 14 percent had ever provided feedback to an online government survey or consultation (226). Moreover, when asked about the potential of the Internet to empower citizens, Canadians are skeptical: "fewer than one in four thinks the Internet can give them more political power or influence over government" (Zamaria and Fletcher 2008, 228). A CBC/Environics (CBC News 2008a) pre-election survey provides similar data on the disengagement between citizens, politics, and the Internet. Just over 52 percent of Canadians report that they frequently or sometimes use the Internet for information or opinion about politics and public issues. Almost 30 percent of Canadians never use the Internet for political information. Those who use the Internet for political information typically visit the websites of media organizations. Just over 50 percent of these users frequently or sometimes obtain political information from media websites. Obtaining political information from other types of sites is rare. Only 6 percent reported using a blog or YouTube for political information. Indeed, the majority of Canadians that use the Internet for political information have never used a blog or YouTube for such purposes. Going into the 2008 federal election, Canadian political parties faced quite a challenge in engaging Canadians online.

Another important consideration in assessing online campaigning in 2008 is the nature of the technology itself. Over the history of online campaigning, the Internet has evolved. Indeed, Obama's success has been attributed to his ability to capitalize on social networking sites. Social networking is part of a broader technology trend called *Web 2.0*. According to Murugesan (2007) "Web 2.0 is the second phase in the Web's evolution" (34). Compared with its predecessor, Web 2.0 changes the nature of participation online to "read/write," that is, "where the online audience moves beyond passive viewing of Web content to actually contributing to the content" (Sweetser and Weaver Lariscy 2008, 179). "Web 2.0 harnesses the Web in a more interactive and collaborative manner, emphasizing peers' social interaction and collective intelligence, and presents new opportunities for leveraging the Web and engaging its users more effectively" (Murugesan 2007, 34). In addition to social networking, blogging, micro-blogging, online video sites, wikis and social bookmarking are part of the Web 2.0 environment. This is not to say that participation and collaboration were non-existent in the pre–Web 2.0 period. Indeed, websites, chat rooms, message boards, and blogs did facilitate self-expression, communication, and interaction. However, according to Yana Breindl and Pascal Francq (2008), "the massive increase of Web surfers in recent years is changing the dynamic of the internet. 'Web 2.0' describes therefore principally the period characterised by an easiness in content production and publication on the internet" (19).

Social networking sites are central to the Web 2.0 phenomena. According to danah boyd and Nicole Ellison (2007, n.p.), social network sites are web-based services that allow individuals to (1) construct a public or semi-public profile within a bounded system, (2) articulate a list of other users with whom they share a connection, and (3) view and traverse their list of connections and those made by others within the system.

YouTube, MySpace, Friendster, Facebook, and Twitter are all social networking sites. Online social networking has grown rapidly. Between 2007 and 2008, comScore (2008) reported a 25 percent increase in the use of social networking sites worldwide, that is, almost 600 million unique visitors used various social networking sites in 2008. The Canadian Internet Project suggests that social networking sites have become an important part of the online routines of many Canadian Internet users. Almost 40 percent of Canadian Internet users visited a social networking site in 2007. One year later, an M2 Universal social media survey showed that 59 percent of online Canadians have created a social networking profile (Powell 2008).

Given the popularity of social networking sites and their successful use in Obama's campaign, it should not be surprising that Canadian parties have jumped on the Web 2.0 bandwagon. Table 9.1 identifies the Web 2.0 sites used by each of Canada's parties in the 2008 federal election.[4] Many of the parties added icons of their Web 2.0 sites to the home page of their official website. By clicking on an icon, the user would be taken directly to the party's profile. Canadian parties are found across the Web 2.0 universe. In addition to social networking sites (Facebook, Twitter, MySpace, YouTube), some parties had social bookmarking (Delicious), social news (reddit, Hugg, Digg), news aggregator (FriendFeed), and image-sharing (Flickr) pages. Canadian parties now operate an online network, in addition to the Web 2.0 sites in Table 9.1, and all parties continue to campaign on their official party websites. A few parties also operated secondary websites in the 2008 federal election, including the Conservative's Not a Leader site, the NDP's Orange Room site, and the Liberals' This Is Dion and Scandalpedia sites.[5] Indeed, one of these sites was the subject of a gaffe during the campaign. The Conservative attack site Not a Leader added a graphic of a puffin flying across the screen, pooping on the shoulder of the Liberal leader. The gaffe, known as the "pooping puffin" incident, received considerable media attention, pushing the Conservatives "off message." In response, the prime minister apologized for the puffin ad, and that ad along with many of the site's negative advertisements (such as the "Dion excuse generator") were removed from the site.

Although the 2008 online campaign by Canadian parties was extensive, this chapter will focus on the parties' use of three very popular social networking sites: YouTube, Facebook, and Twitter. Williams and Gulati (2007) suggest that social networking sites are different from traditional campaign websites:

> Candidates control both the content of the web site as well as how users interact with it. Social networking sites, on the other hand, allow users to contribute or even control content and to initiate contact with other users. Sometimes the struggle for control over the message or access to supporters forces campaigns to respond. (4)

As such, we might expect that online campaigning would be different in 2008 because of the inclusion of social networking.

Tubing the Trail

Founded in 2005, YouTube is the pre-eminent online video website. Consistent with the slogan "Broadcast Yourself," the site allows for the free posting and sharing of videos. In 2007, YouTube launched a Canadian version of the site to promote Canadian-generated content. In addition to being a video-sharing platform, YouTube is also a social networking site. YouTube offers users their own profile page called a "channel" to post content. Once a channel is established, the user can subscribe to other channels or be subscribed to in the same way one is a "friend" on Facebook. Anyone can watch videos, whether they have an account or not; however, having a YouTube account allows a user to comment on and rank videos. According to YouTube, "hundreds of millions" of videos are viewed daily, and "hundreds of thousands" of videos are uploaded daily. The site claims that "every minute, ten hours of video is uploaded to YouTube." Canadians are avid viewers of online videos; according to comScore (2009), 21 million Canadians viewed online videos, spending an average of ten hours over the month in February 2009.

The "YouTube-ization" of politics began in the 2006 American election (Lizza 2006). Central to this was the "macaca moment," where Republican Senator George Allen, running for re-election, referred to a campaign volunteer of his opponent as a "macaca" at a campaign stop. (The word *macaca* is considered a racial slur.) The speech was filmed and posted on the YouTube page of Allen's opponent, Jim Webb, where it became one of the most-viewed videos (Lizza 2006). To date, the video has been viewed some 700,000 times. The video, which became a media scandal after it created a "viral buzz" (Carlson and Strandberg 2008, 6) in the blogosphere, is credited as part of the reason for Allen's defeat in the election. "The costs of making and disseminating the video were negligible, but millions of dollars in traditional television advertising could not heal the wound it inflicted" (Perlmutter 2008, 106). The "macaca moment" demonstrates the reach and power of YouTube during an election. It also establishes the "campaign videographer" as an important member of a campaign team (Zusman 2007, 2). Online videos garnered considerable attention during the 2008 presidential campaign. YouTube created a portal called "Face the Candidates," where candidates established their own online video page that included television advertising and other videos. Additionally, non-campaign videos such as *I've Got a Crush on Obama* and *Vote Different* have been viewed by millions of people.

Official campaigns can post videos on YouTube. Gueorguieva (2008) suggests a number of benefits in using YouTube, including "access to voters, the advertising campaign, fund-raising, and the budget" (5). Despite the benefits, there are also drawbacks. Carlson and Strandberg (2008) note that with YouTube, the campaign surrenders control over the message because viewers are able to comment on videos posted by the campaign (3). Additionally, campaigns also give up their pre-eminence. In traditional media such as television, major political parties are the only game in

TABLE 9.1   Web 2.0 Sites Used by Canadian Parties in the 2008 Federal Election

Party	Facebook	YouTube	Twitter	Digg	Delicious	Flickr	MySpace	Blogging	FriendFeed	StumbleUpon	Hugg	Reddit
BQ	X	X	X					X				
CPC	X	X	X	X	X	X	X					
GPC	X	X	X	X	X			X		X	X	X
LPC	X	X	X	X	X	X	X					
NDP	X	X	X	X	X	X			X			

Note: BQ = Bloc Québécois, CPC = Conservative Party of Canada, GPC = Green Party of Canada, LPC = Liberal Party of Canada, NDP = New Democratic Party of Canada.

TABLE 9.2   YouTube Use in the 2008 Federal Election, by Party

Party	Videos uploaded			Videos watched			Subscribers			Channel views		
	Pre-election	Election day	% Increase	Pre-election	Election day	% Increase	Pre-election	Election day	% Increase	Pre-election	Election day	% Increase
BQ	177	269	52.0	295	453	53.6	35	86	145.7	1,959	4,205	114.7
CPC	7	33	371.4	78	148	89.7	211	358	69.7	24,093	38,508	59.8
LPC	21	157	647.6	511	1,986	288.6	140	369	163.6	4,341	21,244	389.4
NDP	21	117	457.1	n/a	n/a	n/a	148	447	202.0	3,068	13,026	324.6
Total	226	576	154.9	884	2,587	192.6	534	1,260	136.0	33,461	76,983	130.1

Note: BQ = Bloc Québécois, CPC = Conservative Party of Canada, LPC = Liberal Party of Canada, NDP = New Democratic Party of Canada.

town in terms of political advertising. However, one of the most intriguing aspects of online political videos is the level of amateurism. Not only are political parties and candidates creating online videos, but because of the decentralized and inexpensive nature of the Internet, independent groups and individuals are also creating online political videos (see Darr and Barko 2004).

Online videos are not new to Internet campaigning in Canada. Indeed, political parties made extensive use of online video in the 2004 federal election. As the television ads were released over the airwaves, they were also posted on main party websites, as were videos from campaign events. According to Small (2006), the use of multimedia features, such as video, was an indicator of the technological progress made from the previous online campaign: "If the campaign sites of 2000 were static electronic brochures, the sites of 2004 moved beyond text-based communications and were far more dynamic" (228). All five main political parties established YouTube channels in 2007. In the 2008 federal election, the parties continued to upload video to their website as well as to YouTube and Facebook.

Despite having YouTube channels for more than a year, most parties made little use of them prior to the campaign. However, the dropping of the writ initiated considerable activity on the channels—by the parties themselves and channel viewers. The lone exception was the Green Party: despite having a YouTube channel, the party did not use it during the campaign. The other four parties were very committed to their YouTube channels; comparing total number of videos on election day to the pre-election, the parties uploaded a total of 353 videos over the campaign (see Table 9.2). Indeed, there was almost a 50 percent increase in the number of videos posted over the 37-day campaign. The Liberals were the most active party, uploading 139 videos. Their channel was a mix of television ads and informal videos of Stéphane Dion's Campaign Diary. The most popular video on the Liberal channel was *Stephen Harper Copies Australian Prime Minister John Howard*. At a press conference, Bob Rae accused Harper of plagiarizing a speech by former Australian Prime Minister John Howard by showing a video of the two speeches side-by-side. The video was also posted on the Liberals' official website and YouTube. This Conservative gaffe garnered considerable media attention, and to date more than 150,000 views of the video have been recorded.

Two main types of videos appeared on the parties' YouTube channels: television ads and campaign videos. As in previous elections, television ads were posted on YouTube and official party websites. Posting TV ads to YouTube could be viewed as the integration of online and offline campaigns. However, it could also be viewed as nothing more than an "information dump" (Teinowitz 2007). Campaign videos, which are more interesting, provide a behind-the-scenes look at the hustings, showing viewers what it is like to be a part of the leader's tour. Dion's Campaign Diary is illustrative. According to the party,

> The campaign diary is a chance for Mr. Dion to speak directly to Canadian voters, unfiltered by the national media. Each day he shares his thoughts, insights and experiences on the campaign and the Liberal vision for our country. (Liberal Party of Canada 2008)

Campaign videos of speeches or announcements at rallies across the country were found on all channels. The Bloc Québécois YouTube channel focused not only on the national campaign but also on local candidates. The site featured video introductions of Bloc candidates as well as a few videos capturing Bloc candidates going door-to-door in their ridings. The Conservative campaign videos also featured local candidates as Harper crossed the country. The BQ, NDP, and Liberals made extensive use of campaign videos, as seen by the number of videos posted on YouTube, compared with the Conservatives. Clearly, the campaign videographer has become integral to Canadian elections.

Campaign videos can be considered an important innovation in Canadian online campaigning because they allow viewers to see and hear aspects of the campaign they do not normally see in the mainstream news. News reports, print or broadcast, tend to be brief. David Taras (1990) has noted that the "average news story is roughly nine-seconds long and contains no more than 150–250 words" (102). As such, the rationale or philosophy that underlies a policy announcement is reduced to a short sound bite or quotation. On YouTube, viewers can watch a complete speech or announcement by a party leader, regardless of where in Canada the speech took place. In this way, the parties are taking advantage of the democratic potential of decentralization. Through YouTube, the parties take control over the messages provided to the public. Thus, they curtail the role played by journalists as intermediaries, substantially increasing the unfiltered information available to voters. These videos are also important because they contribute to the freshness of the channel. Freshness refers to the frequency with which a site is regularly updated. The Institute for Politics, Democracy and the Internet (2002) suggests that voters will downgrade a website that is not regularly updated (12). Although a limited number of television ads can be uploaded to YouTube, no such restriction applies to campaign videos. Endless content can be uploaded as the leader's tour criss-crosses the country. In the 2008 federal election, viewers constantly found new content on the party channels (especially those of the NDP, Liberal Party, and BQ) because of campaign videos.

Voters were also moderately active on the parties' YouTube channels when we consider the number of subscribers, channel views, and videos watched over the campaign (see Table 9.2). Since the Green Party channel was all but dormant during the campaign, it is not included in Table 9.2. Although the numbers may seem quite modest, significant increases in viewership and subscribers took place over the 37 day campaign. As Table 9.2 shows, the total numbers of videos watched increased by 192 percent, subscribers increased by 136 percent, and channel views increased by 130 percent for the four parties combined. Indeed, YouTube.ca listed the channels of the Liberals and the Conservatives on the "Most Viewed" page each week of the campaign. This implies that the election campaign did generate YouTube buzz, and over the five weeks more and more people became interested in the YouTube campaign.

Campaign Faceoff

Facebook is not only one of the most popular social networking sites but also one of the world's most trafficked websites. Founded in February 2004, Facebook is a social utility that helps people communicate with others. Facebook claims that there are more than 200 million active users of the site, 11.5 million of whom are Canadian (Zinc Research 2009). According to Facebook, users spend more than 3.5 billion minutes on the site daily. As a social networking site, Facebook lets individuals create a personal profile and form links with other users called "friends."

Politics is popular on Facebook. Like other Facebook users, politicians can provide information about themselves, post photographs or videos, post notes to their supporters, and interact with supporters on their "wall." In the United States, if the "YouTube-ization" of politics began in the 2006 election, the "Facebook election" began in the 2008 election. Chris Hughes, one of Facebook's co-founders, was hired by Barack Obama to coordinate his online campaign. Several million people "friended" the Democratic presidential candidate. During the election, some 500 Facebook groups dedicated to Obama were established, including the popular One Million Strong for Barack group. Sanson (2008) notes that "Barack Obama has had the strongest Facebook presence of all of the candidates this election cycle. … What has made the Obama campaign's use of Facebook most successful is its creation of groups as a means for education, mobilization and fundraising" (167).

Conducting a campaign on Facebook has a number of clear benefits. First, Facebook can increase exposure at a low cost or no cost. Moreover, this type of exposure is unmediated. Second, Facebook provides access to the millennial generation—those born between 1980 and 2000. Some argue that Facebook provides millennials, who are increasingly apathetic about politics, "with meaningful opportunities to become engaged" (Sanson 2008, 171). This point is particularly relevant to Canadian politics given that a study by the Dominion Institute (2008) showed that four in five young Canadians, aged 18 to 25, had a Facebook profile in 2008. Third, because Facebook requires users to request to become a "friend" or supporter of a campaign, it provides a ready-made online database that campaign workers can access to seek contributions and recruit volunteers. Moreover, Facebook allows for narrowcasting; access to user profiles provides information that can be extracted to create tailored campaign messages. According to Sanson (2008, 168–169), the Obama campaign hired the firm Strategic Telemetry to microtarget messages from information extracted from Facebook. Finally, Facebook's interactivity allows direct communication between voters and campaign workers as well as among voters.

All Canadian parties have two Facebook pages: one for the national party and one for the party leader. Nevertheless, Facebook seemed to be the most underutilized social networking site in the 2008 federal campaign. Unlike the material on YouTube and Twitter, where most parties were very active posting new content, the Facebook profiles of Canadian leaders were static and had little information. Few leader Facebook pages included content that was not already available to voters on other social networking sites like Flickr and YouTube. Most leader Facebook pages provided basic information about the leader and contact information. Beyond that, "friends" were privy to some interesting facts about Canada's party leaders: for example, *Hockey Night in Canada* is Stéphane Dion's favourite TV show, and Stephen Harper is writing a book on the early history of professional hockey. The Conservative Party was the least enthusiastic in its use of Facebook as a campaigning tool. It had limited posts on the walls of its leader's page. Similarly, the NDP seemed less enthusiastic about Facebook than about other social networking sites. Its posts were often recycled information from the party's website and Twitter feed. The video section included a collection of TV ads, but the ads were just a subset of the party's YouTube page. Stéphane Dion's Facebook page was essentially an image-sharing site, posting campaign photos from the leader's tour—despite the fact that the Liberals already had an image-sharing account on Flickr. Elizabeth May posted a number of notes on her Facebook page. These notes, however, were simply reproductions of posts from her blog (see Figure 9.1).

Very few Canadian party leaders used Facebook to narrowcast or microtarget as Obama did. Jack Layton sent out two messages: one to recruit volunteers and another to raise funds. Stéphane Dion engaged in viral campaigning once: he asked supporters to "help us spread the message" by sending a message to others and encouraging them to become a "friend" of the Liberal leader. The Bloc Québécois Facebook page was the most innovative in that some authority over the page was given to the youth wing of the party. In a few instances, the BQ Facebook page was used to inform supporters of national and local events and encourage them to attend. Beyond these examples, direct appeals for support via Facebook were non-existent in the Canadian campaign. Obama's success in fundraising via social networking sites suggests the lack of microtargeting was a lost opportunity for Canadian political parties during the last election. Arguably, a Facebook "friend" would be the very type of person that would be willing to donate or volunteer. Overall, Facebook was used minimally during the 2008 federal campaign, and when it was, it was used as an information dump more than anything else.

Whereas 2.6 million people "friended" Barack Obama, Canadians did not clamour to become friends with the leaders of Canadian political parties. Table 9.3 shows that just over 65,000 people chose to "friend" a leader. If Facebook "friends" are indicative of popular support, Jack Layton would have won the election. As interest in the social networking campaign grew, so too did the number of Facebook "friends" (they increased by 39 percent over the campaign) (Small 2008).

Web 2.0 gave parties the ability to use the Internet to boost participation in the campaign. Supporters could contribute campaign content and interact with the party and other supporters. Generally, Facebook was not used for this purpose. Even though friends of Elizabeth May and Jack Layton were able to submit "fan" photos and videos, only a small number of people did so. The Facebook wall is also important in this respect. On the wall, others can write messages: "The wall is a public writing space so others who view your profile can see what has been written on your wall. Once you have received a wall message, you can respond directly back to the friend who left it using the 'wall-to-wall' mode" (webopedia 2009). Analysis by Sweetser and Weaver

TABLE 9.3   Facebook Use in the 2008 Federal Election, by Party Leader

Party leader	"Friends"	Wall posts
Stéphane Dion	14,263	1936
Gilles Duceppe	2,383	133
Stephen Harper	17,903	0
Jack Layton	25,127	835
Elizabeth May	5,377	521
Total	65,053	3425

Lariscy (2008) on Facebook in the 2006 American election suggests that "for some potential voters writing on candidate walls is an engaging activity" (192). "Friends" of the leaders used this feature sparingly. The prime minister's profile did not feature a wall; there was no two-way interactivity on his page. Over 3,000 wall comments were posted to the leader profiles by the end of the campaign. This finding implies that the engagement in Facebook is limited. Sweetser and Weaver Lariscy (2008) found that few candidates responded to wall comments in the US House and Senate campaigns during the 2006 mid-term election (193). The same was true in the 2008 federal election in Canada. The wall allows "friends" to post comments and potentially communicate with other supporters. Neither the party leaders nor campaign workers were involved in this type of communication. Becoming a "friend" does not in any way signify broader engagement with the party or the campaign.

All A-Twitter

Twitter is a social networking and microblogging site that was founded in 2006. Microblogging lets users "describe their current status in short posts distributed by instant messages, mobile phones, email or the Web" (Java et al. 2007, 1). Like other social networking sites, a user sets up a profile. Twitter allows subscribers to write a 140-character status update called a "tweet" to the question, "What are you doing?" There are two types of relationships on Twitter: "following" and "followers." On Twitter, *following* refers to the list of people whose updates you have signed up to receive, while *followers* are the people who have signed up to receive your updates. Being followed and following can allow for a reciprocal relationship between Twitter users. In February 2008, Nielsen News reported that Twitter had almost 500,000 users; within a year, that number had increased 1,382 percent (McGiboney 2009). Another study shows that in 2009, almost 50 percent of Canadians were using Twitter (6S Marketing 2009).

Prior to the 2008 federal election, Stephen Harper established a Twitter profile on September 2, 2008, making him the first party leader to do so. Within ten days, the other four major party leaders established profiles. However, there were also some imposter profiles on Twitter, better known as cybersquatters. Cybersquatting refers to "the deliberate registration of a domain name with the intent to profit by either ransoming the name to the highest bidder or diverting web traffic" (Sanderson 2009, 6).

If an individual searched for the profiles of Harper and Dion, they may have followed the wrong individual. The "StephenJHarper" page, which even featured a photo, was not the prime minister's profile. The official Dion page was called "liberaltour," since "stephanedion" was taken, complete with an unflattering photo of the Liberal leader. According to Sanderson (2009), cybersquatting, which has affected political officials worldwide, can have commercial motivation or be the result of the "desire to criticize, parody, inconvenience, or impersonate a political candidate" (10). Inconveniencing the candidate appears to be the motivation of the Harper and Dion squatters, as neither posted any tweets during the election campaign. However, both had more than 100 followers. Canadians searching for the profiles of Harper and Dion may have been confused.

As was the case with Facebook, Canadians did not interact with their party leaders on Twitter in the same way that Americans interacted with Barack Obama on Twitter. During the last week of the campaign, there were just over 4,000 followers of Canada's party leaders led, again, by NDP leader Jack Layton (see Table 9.4).

According to Table 9.4, each campaign varied in its twittering activity. Jack Layton and Elizabeth May twittered the most, posting over 100 tweets over the 37-day campaign. It was not uncommon for leaders to post more than once per day. Analysis from a study entitled *Why We Twitter* suggests that there are four main uses of Twitter: "daily chatter, conversations, sharing information and reporting news" (Java et al. 2007, 2). Campaign tweets in the 2008 federal election could be assessed in a similar manner. According to Java and colleagues (2007) "daily chatter" is the most common use of Twitter, where users tweet about their daily routine or what they are currently doing. "Daily chatter," in this election, was in the form of campaign updates. The tweets informed followers of what the party leaders or the campaign had done, were doing, or were going to do that day. For instance, on September 8, Jack Layton wrote, "we're on our way to Regina after tar sands event and another in Vancouver." Harper wrote, "Speaking to supporters in Regina about Saskatchewan's future." Though most campaign updates were related to campaign events, some were a bit more personal.

TABLE 9.4   Twitter Use in the 2008 Federal Election, by Party

Party	Twitter profile name	Followers	Tweets
BQ	GillesDuceppe	241	85
CPC	pmharper	1,042	58
GPC	ElizabethMay	648	114
LPC	liberaltour	896	73
NDP	jacklayton	1,247	138
Total		4,074	468

Note: BQ = Bloc Québécois, CPC = Conservative Party of Canada, GPC = Green Party of Canada, LPC = Liberal Party of Canada, NDP = New Democratic Party of Canada.

Elizabeth May tweeted that she was "enjoying fair trade coffee before the press conference in Halifax" and was "packing for the debates in Ottawa." Given the nature of this technology, it is difficult to really know whether the party leader or a staff member is twittering. The lone exception was the Liberals. In the bio section, it was made clear that Dion was not twittering. Rather, National Director Greg Fergus, who travelled with Dion, was the author of the Liberal tweets.

Another function of Twitter during the campaign relates to what Java and colleagues (2008) call "sharing information/URLs." The campaigns used Twitter to direct followers to relevant digital content including videos, photos, favourable newspaper articles, news updates, and policy statements on their websites. For example, the Harper tweet "Announced plan to protect natural resources and building a clean energy superpower" included a link to the related policy plank on the Conservative main party website. While a tweet may only be 140 characters, the URL allows the party to provide more and detailed information. This use of Twitter demonstrates an integration of all aspects of the online campaign. In this sense, the campaign is a network where Twitter users, through the hyperlink, can seamlessly move from one part of the online campaign to another. Some campaigns, especially the NDP's, used Twitter as a method of encouraging supporters to get involved with the campaign. In several instances, they encouraged followers to find out how they can help with the campaign and posted a link to locate the nearest riding headquarters.

Twitter can be conversational and interactive. Although Twitter does not allow for the instantaneous communication of an instant-messaging application, followers can respond to the tweets of those they are following, which are called "@replies." This feature, however, was rarely used during the 2008 federal election. One might interpret this as meaning that Canadians were uninterested in interacting with the party leaders. However, a more probable explanation is that the campaigns had disabled the response function by selecting the "No @replies" setting. By selecting this setting, the replies of followers are not posted on the site. As Twitter notes, "If you're not interested in Twitter as a conversational thing, you may not need to see tweets directed to others." Only the pages of May and Duceppe allowed for @replies during the campaign. Otherwise, Twitter was used in a unidirectional manner, and parties did not permit followers to respond to or provide feedback on tweets.

During the two leaders' debates, the NDP made the most inventive use of Twitter. While the other parties used the site to announce the English language debate, on the day of the event jacklayton tweeted, "Check the NDP Twitter updates regularly tonight for the latest on the leaders debates." During both debates, the NDP used its tweets to clarify or dispute the facts made by the other leaders in real time. During the English language debate, tweets included "FACT CHECK: Dion wrong on carbon tax" and "FACTCHECK: Oil companies did benefit from Harper's economic policies." There were ten tweets posted during the English language debate and eleven during the French language debate. During the live televised debates, the party leaders are constrained by speaking order and time limits, but Twitter allowed the NDP to publish instant responses to comments made by the other party leaders in real-time to their followers. The NDP use of Twitter during the debate is reminiscent of the use of the Internet during the presidential debates between Al Gore and George W. Bush in 2004. The Bush campaign announced that it was conducting real-time fact checking of statements made by Gore on www.debatefacts.com. The Gore campaign responded by indicating it would do the same. These "e-buttals" were posted online and emailed to journalists. E-buttals or tweet-buttals represent a wholly web-exclusive campaign technique, as this type of rapid response would be practically impossible in any other medium. This application of Twitter was a missed opportunity for the other parties in the 2008 federal election.

Conclusion

What does the use of YouTube, Facebook, and Twitter by Canadian political parties in the 2008 federal election tell us about the trajectory of online campaigning in Canada? The main conclusion that can be drawn from this analysis is that even though the technology may have evolved since the last campaign, the use of the Internet by Canadian political parties has not. Although social networking sites provide campaigns with additional opportunities to build collaborative and interactive relationships with the electorate, collaboration and interaction are not terms that describe the use of the Internet in the 2008 federal election. Rather, past patterns of Internet use during campaigns appear to have become regularized. Despite claims by cyber-optimists, the Internet has not contributed to a greater participatory ethos for Canadian parties. Interaction and collaboration between parties and the electorate remain rare. Parties continue to use the Internet (whether through their official websites or social networking sites) mainly to provide information to voters. Essentially, parties treat the Internet primarily as a modern marketing tool for one-way communication.

This examination of the use of the three key social networking sites during the last federal election appears to replicate what scholars have noted in previous campaigns. First, there was little innovative use of social networking sites. YouTube, Facebook, and Twitter simply afforded the parties with another online venue to share press releases, photos, and online videos. These sites were largely used as information dumps. Campaign videos on YouTube were the only web-exclusive content. Although campaign videos did exist in previous campaigns, YouTube contributed to their proliferation in the 2008 federal campaign. Moreover, these videos allowed parties and voters to bypass the media. Second, like previous campaigns, two-way interactivity was rare. Supporters were able to comment on the parties' Facebook and YouTube pages (with the exception of the Conservative Party's pages), which was certainly unprecedented compared with previous campaigns. However, the level of engagement between the parties and supporters remained the same. Supporters could make comments on videos or other campaign issues, other users might respond, but the party leaders and campaign workers remained silent. Finally, this analysis indicates that the social networking campaign did not generate much excitement among Canadian voters. Of the three key social networking sites, Facebook was the most popular. Nevertheless, the parties' Facebook "friends" represent only a small proportion of the Canadian electorate—less than 1 percent of those that showed up at the polls on election day. Barack Obama's masterful use of social networking sites is considered to have won him the presidency, but Canadian parties' use of social networking sites in the last election did not contribute to a fundamental shift in online campaigning in Canada.

This chapter would be remiss to suggest that Web 2.0 was irrelevant in the 2008 federal campaign. The use of YouTube, Facebook, and Twitter by Canadian parties may have lacked innovation overall, but the NDP proved to be extremely inventive with its secondary website, The Orange Room. The site, whose slogan is "Create. Share. Be a Part of It.," was dedicated to the read/write quality of Web 2.0. According to the site, "The Orange Room is the one-stop shop for anyone looking to find—and share—digital media related to the New Democrat campaign in this election." Once an account has been created, the site allows NDP supporters to upload content including videos, photos, and news stories. For example, during the election the site featured a "Caption Challenge," which featured a photo (usually of the prime minister) under which users could write a (usually mocking) caption. Those who submitted content received points, "and moving up the ranks earns you bragging rights—and a shot later at some special prizes" (NDP 2008). The Orange Room was also linked to Facebook. The "Orange Room FB" was a Facebook version of the Orange Room that included user-generated campaign videos. The Facebook page also included activities. For example, users could invite "friends" to add Orange Room FB to their own page. Users could also "Send Gifts," such as a photo of Tommy Douglas or the NDP campaign bus, to a "friend." Should the "friend" accept the gift, it would appear on the profile page, thereby promoting the party.

The Orange Room was a continuation of the NDP's pioneering e-strategy. Very late in the 2004 campaign, the NDP launched the "NDP e-Campaign." Supporters could download Jack Layton wallpaper or add an NDP banner to their websites. "Most important, the party was able to galvanize an undisclosed number of activists into establishing their own fund-raising networks. According to one campaign official, the party was able to attract 'dozens and dozens of people who never left their home offices and they raised thousands and thousands of dollars for the campaign'" (Small, Taras, and Danchuk 2008, 123). Although innovative, the user-generated, collaborative aspects of the Orange Room were moderate at best. Users uploaded 35 percent of the videos on the site. Most of the videos were uploaded by the NDP campaign and were similar to those found on YouTube. Only 13 percent of images were user-generated. Despite moderate use, the NDP's Orange Room certainly stands out in the 2008 campaign in terms of its embodiment of Web 2.0 principles.

Web 2.0 and social networking sites were not just used by political parties. Thousands of candidates across Canada posted profiles on Facebook. Several hundred Facebook groups were launched related to the election. Subscribers posted thousands of election-related clips on YouTube. Mashline.com released the song "I've Got a Crush on Harper." Indeed, many of the interesting Web 2.0 moments in this campaign had little to do with Canada's political parties. The Facebook group Anti-Harper Vote Swap Canada and the *Culture en péril* YouTube video best illustrate this.

Anti-Harper Vote Swap Canada formed on Facebook shortly after the writ dropped. The group promoted an "Anything But Conservative" (ABC) vote, that is, they sought to ensure that the Harper Conservatives did not form the next government. Using a Facebook application, the group offered opportunities to those whose preferred candidate had a slim chance of winning to swap votes with those in other constituencies. The swap would ensure that two votes would be strategically cast against the Conservatives. Vote swapping is not new to online campaigns. Indeed, the Internet "is a perfect medium for such distant transactions" (Coleman and Hall 2001). Vote swapping sites existed in the 2000 and 2004 American elections; supporters of Al Gore and Ralph Nader could swap votes in an attempt to thwart the election of George W. Bush. According to Hartvigsen (2006), approximately 36,000 American voters participated in vote swapping in the 2000 election, and 21,000 participated in the 2004 election. In the 2001 UK election, Coleman and Hall (2001) argue that there is "strong evidence" that vote swapping was successful in two British constituencies. Vote swapping rose to prominence in the 2008 election with the Anti-Harper Vote Swap Canada Facebook page and www.voteforenvironment.ca.[6] Both attracted significant media attention and prompted the establishment of opposition Facebook groups such as Anti-Anti-Harper Vote Swap and Voters Against Vote Swapping. The rise in attention given to vote swapping even prompted an Elections Canada investigation, which determined that vote swapping is legal and does not violate any electoral laws. More than 13,000 users had joined the Facebook group by the end of the campaign. However, the success of vote swapping is unclear given the Conservative minority victory on election day.

Culture en péril was a video posted on YouTube by popular Quebec singer Michel Rivard on September 18, 2008. The video protests the Conservative government's arts funding policy. Prior to the election, the Conservative government announced $45 million in cuts to arts and culture funding. The decision was widely criticized and became an election issue. In the video, Rivard plays for an English-speaking federal arts committee. The committee rejects Rivard's funding request due to confusion over words in the song, which they believe are obscene. The original French language video and an English subtitled version were exceptionally popular during the campaign; according to the Infoscape Research Lab, it was the top election-related video on YouTube from September 22 to October 3 (CBC News 2008b). By election day, there were more than half a million views of the video. The success of *Culture en péril* is a key moment in the history of online campaigning in Canada. It demonstrates the power and reach of a political message from a single individual, using technology freely available—something that could not exist in the pre-Internet world.

This chapter shows that unlike Barack Obama in the last US presidential election, Stephen Harper was not the "Internet prime minister" of this election. Indeed, none of Canada's party leaders followed in Obama's footsteps. Is an Internet prime minister just around the corner? It is difficult to predict what the future holds for online campaigning in Canada. The Internet is constantly evolving, as we can see from the advent of Web 2.0. The focal technology appears to change from election to election. Online

FIGURE 9.2   Culture en péril, YouTube

"Culture en péril," a YouTube video by Quebec singer Michel Rivard, became wildly popular during the 2008 election campaign. The Harper government's $45 million cut to cultural funding became an election issue, and online media tools provided a quick and inexpensive way for arts groups to voice their objections to the cuts.

campaigns elsewhere, especially in the United States, have also evolved. Compare Obama's use of the Internet in the 2008 campaign with assessments of the 1996 American campaign, where scholars generally agree that attempts to engage citizens through the Internet were lacking (Stromer-Galley 2000). Just as American online campaigns have become more interactive over time, so too may Canadian ones. Perhaps we should not gather too much from a comparison between Obama's experience with online campaigning and that of Canada's political parties. Given the differences in the US and Canadian political systems, perhaps the contrasting results should not be surprising. Whereas Canada has a party-centred regime, the United States has a candidate-centred regime. The two countries have vastly different regulatory and media environments. These factors undoubtedly shape how candidates and parties campaign online. Stephen Ward (2008) suggests that systematic factors, organizational-institutional factors including parties, and individual-level factors all contribute to shaping online campaigning and its variations across countries. Another factor worth considering is the limited number of Canadians that engaged in the online campaign. Both technological and political factors will structure the likelihood of a Canadian party leader becoming the "Internet prime minister" during the next federal election.

NOTES

1. The Kennedy–Nixon debate, which occurred on September, 26 1960, was the first ever televised debate in an American presidential campaign. Americans who listened to the debate on the radio pronounced Republican Richard Nixon the winner. However, Americans who watched the debate on television concluded that John F. Kennedy was the victor. Clean-cut, tanned, and charismatic, JFK appeared much more comfortable on television compared with his rival. Television viewers focused on what they saw, rather than what they heard.

2. In part because of the Internet, Vermont Governor Howard Dean was considered an early front-runner for Democratic presidential nomination in the 2004 election. Despite a 20 percent lead in the polls, Dean came in third place in the all-important Iowa caucus, the first vote of the primary season. The loss ultimately doomed Dean's candidacy.

3. This analysis is based on original data collected by the author during the 2008 campaign. The author thanks Erik Johnson for his research assistance.

4. Note that the parties established profiles on many of these sites prior to the 2008 election.

5. Not a Leader was an attack website aimed entirely at Liberal Leader Stéphane Dion. The site was made famous during the campaign due to the "pooping puffin" incident. The Orange Room was a social networking site for NDP supporters. This Is Dion profiled Liberal leader Stéphane Dion, while Scandalpedia, similar in format to Wikipedia, chronicled the scandals of the Conservative Party. Not a Leader existed prior to the 2008 campaign, but the other three sites were launched during the campaign.

6. Like the Facebook page, www.voteforenvironment.ca promoted an ABC vote.

DISCUSSION QUESTIONS

1. Why is the Internet considered a democratic technology? Does the Internet have any characteristics that work against democracy?

2. Why isn't politics a significant area of online interest for Canadians?

3. Can the Internet combat voter apathy?

4. Is building collaborative and interactive relationships with the electorate on the Internet too risky for Canadian political parties and leaders?

5. How could Canada's parties make better use of the Internet?

6. What is microtargeting?

7. Why would non-party actors be more innovative online campaigners than political parties?

8. Is an "Internet prime minister" forthcoming? What would have to happen for one to emerge?

FURTHER READING

Barney, Darin. 2005. *Communication technology*. Vancouver: UBC Press.

Bentivegna, Sara. 2002. Politics and the new media. In *The handbook of new media*, ed. Leah A. Lievrouw and Sonia M. Livingstone, 50–61. London: Sage Publications.

Chadwick, Andrew. 2007. *Internet politics: States, citizens, and new communication technologies*. London: Oxford University Press.

Davis, Richard, Diana Owen, David Taras, and Stephen Ward. 2008. *Making a difference: A comparative view of the role of the Internet in election politics*. Lexington, SC: Lexington Press.

Small, Tamara A. 2004. parties@canada: The Internet and the 2004 cyber-campaign. In *The Canadian general election of 2004*, ed. Jon H. Pammett and Christopher Dornan, 203–234. Toronto: Dundurn Press.

Small, Tamara A., David Taras, and Dave Danchuk. 2008. Party Web sites and online campaigning during the 2004 and 2006 Canadian federal elections. In *Making a difference: A comparative view of the role of the Internet in election politics*, ed. Richard Davis, Diana Owen, David Taras, and Stephen Ward, 113–133. Lexington, SC: Lexington Press.

REFERENCES

6S Marketing. 2009. Survey says … Canadians are crazy about social media. News release, March 18. http://www.6smarketing.com/survey-sayscanadians-are-crazy-about-social-media-2/.

Attallah, Paul, and Angela Burton. 2001. Television, the Internet and the Canadian federal election of 2000. In *The Canadian general election of 2000*, ed. Jon H. Pammett and Christopher Doran, 215–242. Toronto: Dundurn Press.

Barney, Darin. 2005. *Communication technology*. Vancouver: UBC Press.

Barney, Darin. 2007. The Internet and political communications in Canadian party politics: The view from 2004. In *Canadian parties in transition*, ed. Alain-G. Gagnon and A. Brian Tanguay, 371–382. Peterborough, ON: Broadview Press.

Bentivegna, Sara. 2002. Politics and the new media. In *The handbook of new media*, ed. Leah A. Lievrouw and Sonia M. Livingstone, 50–61. London: Sage Publications.

Bimber, Bruce. 1999. The Internet and citizen communication with government: Does the medium matter? *Political Communication* 16 (4): 409–428.

boyd, danah m., and Nicole B. Ellison. 2007. Social network sites: Definition, history, and scholarship. *Journal of Computer-Mediated Communication* 13 (1). http://jcmc.indiana.edu/vol13/issue1/boyd.ellison.html.

Breindl, Yanah, and Pascal Francq. 2008. Can Web 2.0 applications save e-democracy? A study of how new Internet applications may enhance citizen participation in the political process on-line. *International Journal of Electronic Democracy* 1 (1): 14–31.

Carlson, Tom, and Kim Strandberg. 2008. Riding the Web 2.0 wave—Candidates on YouTube in the 2007 Finnish national elections. *Journal of Information Technology and Politics* 5 (2): 159–174.

Carty, R. Kenneth, William Cross, and Lisa Young. 2000. *Rebuilding Canadian party politics*. Vancouver: UBC Press.

CBC News. 2008a. *Pre-election poll: Full results*. http://www.cbc.ca/canada/story/2008/09/07/f-full-poll-results.html.

CBC News. 2008b. *Canada votes 2008—Top 5 YouTube videos*. http://www.cbc.ca/news/canadavotes/campaign2/ormiston/top_5_youtube_videos/.

Chadwick, Andrew. 2007. *Internet politics: States, citizens, and new communication technologies*. London: Oxford University Press.

Coleman, Stephen, and Nicola Hall. 2001. Spinning on the Web: E-campaigning and beyond. In *2001: A cyber space odyssey: The Internet in the UK election*, ed. Stephen Coleman. London: Hansard Society. http://www.hansardsociety.org.uk.

comScore. 2008. Social networking explodes worldwide as sites increase their focus on cultural relevance. News release, August 12. http://www.comscore.com/press/release.asp?press=2396.

comScore. 2009. Canada ranks as a global leader in online video viewing. News release, April 21. http://www.comscore.com/Press_Events/Press_Releases/2009/4/Canada_Leads_World_in_Online_Video_Viewing.

Darr, Carol, and Julie Barko. 2004. *Under the radar and over the top: Independently-produced videos in the 2004 presidential election.* Institute for Politics, Democracy & the Internet. http://www.ipdi.org/UploadedFiles/under_the_radar_and_over_the_top.pdf.

Davis, Richard. 1999. *The web of politics: The Internet's impact on the American political system.* New York: Oxford University Press.

Dominion Institute. 2008. *2008 youth election study.* http://www.dominion.ca/Youth_Survey_September%2024_v04P.pdf.

Gross, Grant. 2008. Obama transforms web-based politics. *PC World*, December 22. http://www.pcworld.com/businesscenter/article/155917/obama_transforms_webbased_politics.html.

Gueorguieva, V. 2008. Voters, MySpace, and YouTube: The impact of alternative communication channels on the 2008 election cycle and beyond. *Social Science Computer Review* 26 (3): 288–300.

Harnden, Toby. 2008. Barack Obama will be America's first "internet president." *telegraph.co.uk*, November 11. http://www.telegraph.co.uk/news/worldnews/northamerica/usa/barackobama/3443143/Barack-Obama-will-be-Americas-first-internet-president.html.

Hartvigsen, David. 2006. Vote trading in public elections. *Mathematical Social Sciences* 51 (1): 31–48.

Hillwatch. 2004. *Political web sites: Strategic assets or virtual lawn signs?* http://www.hillwatch.com/Publications/Research/Virtuallawnsigns.aspx.

Hillwatch. 2006. *Still virtually lawn signs. Benchmarking Canadian political web sites during the 2006 campaign.* http://www.hillwatch.com/Publications/Research/Still_Virtually_Lawn_Signs.aspx.

Hindman, Matthew. 2005. The real lessons of Howard Dean: Reflections on the first digital campaign. *Perspectives on Politics* 3 (1): 121–128.

Howard, Philip N. 2005. Deep democracy, thin citizenship: Digital media and the production of political culture. *Annals of the American Academy of Political and Social Science* 597 (1): 153–170.

Institute for Politics, Democracy and the Internet. 2002. *Online campaigning 2002: A primer.* http://www.ipdi.org/UploadedFiles/onlinecampaigning2002.pdf.

Java, Akshay, Tim Finin, Xiaodan Song, and Belle Tseng. 2007. Why we Twitter: Understanding microblogging usage and communities. Proceedings of the Joint 9th WEBKDD and 1st SNA-KDD Workshop 2007, August 12, 2007, San Jose, California.

Kernaghan, Kenneth. 2007. Moving beyond politics as usual? Online Campaigning. In *Digital state at the leading edge*, ed. Sandford Borins, Kenneth Kernaghan, David Brown, Nick Bontis, Perri 6, and Fred Thompson, 183–223. Toronto: University of Toronto Press.

Kippen, Grant. 2000. *The use of new information technologies by a political party: A case study of the Liberal Party in the 1993 and 1997 federal elections.* Vancouver: SFU-UBC Centre for the Study of Government and Business.

Klotz, Robert. 2004. *The politics of Internet communication.* Lanham, MD: Rowman and Littlefield Publishers.

Liberal Party of Canada. 2008. *Stéphane Dion's daily video "campaign diary" gives personal account of campaign.* News release, September 26.

Lizza, Ryan. 2006. The YouTube election. *New York Times*, August 20. http://www.nytimes.com/2006/08/20/weekinreview/20lizza.html?_r=2.

Margolis, Michael, and David Resnick. 2000. *Politics as usual—The cyberspace "revolution."* Thousand Oaks, CA: Sage Publishing.

McGiboney, Michelle. 2009. Twitter's tweet smell of success. *Nielson Online*, March 18. http://blog.nielsen.com/nielsenwire/online_mobile/twitters-tweet-smell-of-success.

Murugesan, San. 2007. Understanding Web 2.0. *IT Professional* 9 (4): 34–41.

NDP. 2008. Earning points. *Orange room.* http://orangeroom.ca/points.

O'Brien, Barbara. 2004. *Blogging America: Political discourse in a digital nation.* Wilsonville, OR: William James & Co.

Perlmutter, David D. 2008. *Blogwars.* New York: Oxford University Press. .

Powell, Chris. 2008. Canadians love their online video: M2 study. *Marketing*, May 2. http://www.marketingmag.ca/english/news/media/article.jsp?content= 20080502_777333_2459.

Sanderson, Matthew T. 2009. Candidates, squatters, and gripers: A primer on political cybersquatting and a proposal for reform. *Election Law Journal* 8 (1): 3–29.

Sanson, Angela. 2008. Facebook and youth mobilization in the 2008 presidential election. *Gnovis Journal* 8 (3): 162–174.

Small, Tamara A. 2004. parties@canada: The Internet and the 2004 cyber-campaign. In *The Canadian general election of 2004*, ed. Jon H. Pammett and Christopher Dornan, 203–234. Toronto: Dundurn Press.

Small, Tamara A. 2006. A tale of two cyber-campaigns: Election engagement in North America. *International Journal of Technology, Knowledge and Society* 2 (5): 63–74.

Small, Tamara A. 2008. The Facebook effect? On-line campaigning in the 2008 Canadian and US elections. *Policy Options* 29 (10): 85–87.

Small, Tamara A., David Taras, and Dave Danchuk. 2008. Party web sites and online campaigning during the 2004 and 2006 Canadian federal elections. In *Making a difference: A comparative view of the role of the Internet in election politics*, ed. Richard Davis, Diana Owen, David Taras, and Stephen Ward, 113–133. Lexington, SC: Lexington Press.

Stromer-Galley, Jennifer. 2000. On-line interaction and why candidates avoid it. *Journal of Communication* 50 (4): 111–132.

Sunstein, Cass R. 2004. Democracy and filtering. *Communications of the ACM* 47 (12): 57–59.

Sweetser, Kaye D., and Ruthann A. Weaver Lariscy. 2008. Candidates make good friends: An analysis of candidates' use of Facebook. *International Journal of Strategic Communication* 2 (3): 175–198.

Taras, David. 1990 *The newsmakers: The media's influence on Canadian politics.* Scarborough, ON: Nelson Canada.

Teinowitz, Ira. 2007. YouTube in '08: Kingmaker and heartbreaker. *Advertising Age*, April 30.

Trippi, Joe. 2005. *The revolution will not be televised: Democracy, the Internet, and the overthrow of everything.* New York: Regan Books.

Vargas, Jose Antonio. 2008. Obama raised half a billion online. *Washington Post*, November 20. http://voices.washingtonpost.com/44/2008/11/20/obama_raised_half_a_billion_on.html.

Wagner, Mitch. 2008. Obama election ushering in first Internet presidency. *InformationWeek*, November 5. http://www.informationweek.com/news/government/ showArticle.jhtml?articleID=212000815.

Ward, Stephen. 2008. Introduction. In *Making a difference: A comparative view of the role of the Internet in election politics*, ed. Richard Davis, Diana Owen, David Taras, and Stephen Ward, 1–14. Lexington, SC: Lexington Press.

webopedia. 2009. *Facebook wall.* http://webopedia.com/TERM/F/Facebook_wall.html.

Williams, Christine B., and Girish J. "Jeff" Gulati. 2007. Social networks in political campaigns: Facebook and the 2006 midterm elections. Paper presented at the annual meeting of the American Political Science Association Chicago, Illinois, August 30–September 2.

Zamaria, Charles, and Fred Fletcher. 2008. *Canada online! The Internet, media and emerging technologies: Uses, attitudes, trends and international comparisons 2007.* Toronto: Canadian Internet Project.

Zinc Research. 2009. *11.5 million and counting—Facebook dominates competitors in Canada.* News release, March 5. http://www.zincresearch.com/pressroom.htm.

Zusman, Amanda. 2007. Got rhythm? Rhyme? Turn it into a web video that can change the election. *Campaigns and Elections*, August 1.

CHAPTER 10

Polling as Modern Alchemy: Measuring Public Opinion in Canadian Elections

André Turcotte

Introduction

The ancient practice of alchemy has been defined as the endeavour to find the key to the transformation of chemical substances, especially of base metals into silver and gold; and beyond that, to find "the elixir of immortality."[1] This forbidden practice was perceived as scientific by alchemists but was generally described as part art and part science.[2] During its heyday in the 15th and 16th centuries, alchemy attracted both the disillusioned and the eminent, among them Sir Isaac Newton, probably the greatest scientist that ever lived.[3] In some ways, today's political pollsters can be described as modern-day alchemists trying to find the key to the transformation of basic opinions and sentiments into votes, and beyond that, to find the elixir of political longevity. As was the case for alchemy in the Middle Ages, polling is attracting both the opportunist and the illustrious. Moreover, this modern craft has a strong scientific basis, but most would concede that it has an important artistic dimension in the interpretation of results. As well-known pollster Daniel Yankelovich once wrote: "I have never conducted a public opinion survey that did not surprise me in one way or another" (Yankelovich 1991, xi).

In this chapter, I will look at the art and science of public opinion polling with a special emphasis on how it is practised in modern Canadian elections. The starting point of this overview is a short examination of the changing nature of our understanding of public opinion and its dynamics. The way in which public opinion has been conceptualized over time has affected how it is measured and how its role is perceived in the political process. This point will become clear when the early efforts to gauge public opinion in Canada are discussed. I will then review the different types of polls and focus on the context within which they are conducted. It should be noted that a "poll" and a "survey" are different: a poll is a general inquiry into public opinion, and a survey tends to be a more comprehensive assessment. However, this distinction is highly technical and will be largely ignored for the purposes of this discussion. It is equally important to note that I do not subscribe to the criticism directed against polls as lacking in accuracy and integrity; polls have a purpose, and students of public opinion must understand what that purpose is. Finally, I will examine the ways in which public opinion is currently quantified as well as the challenges in quantification and what they mean for democracy in Canada.

Defining Public Opinion

Interest in understanding and defining public opinion predates attempts to measure it. While this section does not present an exhaustive examination of the origins and evolution of the concept of public opinion, it does present key developments in the concept that pertain to our discussion of polling. The origins of the concept of public opinion can be traced back to the 17th and 18th centuries. William Shakespeare referred to public opinion as a "mistress of effects," while Blaise Pascal described it as the "queen of the world" (Speier 1950, 377). In the works of Helvétius (1759), Rousseau (1761), and D'Holbach (1770), public opinion was defined as a form of social pressure imposed on individual behaviour. As democracy established itself as a form of government, public opinion was increasingly "cherished as a safeguard of morality in politics" (Speier 1950, 377). Jacques Necker (1784) appears to have been the first to popularize the expression "public opinion" in Europe in the leadup to the French Revolution, and increasingly public opinion was perceived as a way to express dissatisfaction with government authority. This licence to criticize rulers contributed to the downfall of the French monarchy.

L'Affaire Dreyfus was one of the first instances in which public opinion was mobilized and used in the public arena. While the details of this political crisis that shook France between 1894 and 1906 are beyond the scope of this chapter,[4] it is important to note that *l'Affaire Dreyfus* showed the clout of mobilized public opinion in defending against what was generally perceived as an injustice perpetrated by the government of the day. Relying on public opinion, the supporters of Captain Alfred Dreyfus were able to circumvent the prevailing mechanisms for political representation to prove Dreyfus's innocence. While it would take several decades for public opinion to become fully integrated in the public arena, *l'Affaire Dreyfus* ushered in a re-evaluation of public opinion as being both sovereign and potentially mobilized if not manipulated. Henceforth, scholars began to define public opinion as a source of influence above all others. In this vein, William Bryce (1911) described public opinion as a permanent tribunal of the exercise of power and as unexpressed and sometimes unconscious opinion whose power rests in the fact that it emerges from the masses. Bryce's characterization was reminiscent of the one articulated by Jeremy Bentham more than a century before.[5] John Dewey (1927) echoed Bryce to the extent that he conceived of public opinion as a judgment rendered by the public on the affairs of the state. But not everyone was enthusiastic about this new source of influence.

Nineteenth-century German statesman Otto von Bismarck was largely indifferent to public opinion and its apparent moral claims. For him, public opinion was primarily dependent on mood and sentiment and largely incapable of the calm calculations necessary for good government (Speier 1950, 385). Similarly, Gustave Le Bon suggested that the "unconscious action of crowds had replaced the conscious activity of individuals" (1960, 24). For Le Bon, crowds were impressed only by images, and mass opinion was the artifact of simple reasoning by association and sentiment rather than logic.

A seminal but divergent study of public opinion was released in the period preceding the emergence of scientific polling. Published in 1922, *Public Opinion* proposed a conceptual framework that influenced several generations of scholars. Its author, Walter Lippmann, did not concentrate on the sovereign dimension of public opinion but rather on the potential and necessity to manipulate it. For Lippmann, public opinion is primarily "a moralized and codified version of the facts" (1922, 82). People are unable to fully know or understand the complexity of the environment they live in. Accordingly, they have to rely on an approximation of that environment—what Lippmann called "the pictures in our heads or the pseudo-environment" (10)—to try to make sense of a world that is too complex and too fleeting for direct understanding. In building that pseudo-environment, people rely on codes, symbols, and stereotypes. Accordingly, Lippmann argued that "the analyst of public opinion must begin by recognizing the triangular relationship between the scene of action, the human picture of that scene, and the human response to that picture working itself out upon the scene of action" (11). One implication is that we can never really know how people think or will behave in response to a policy, a fact, or argument. All we really can know is how they will respond to their inadequate picture of the policy, fact, or argument. Another implication, which is central to Lippmann's argument, is that if the elite understand the symbols and stereotypes used by the public, they will have the capacity to manipulate public opinion and to "manufacture consent" (158).

Lippmann's conceptualization of public opinion was set aside with the development of the polling industry and the quantification of public opinion. The pioneers of this industry, namely George Gallup, Elmo Roper, and Archibald Crossley in the private sector, as well as Henry Wallace and Rensis Likert in the government at the US Department of Agriculture (Converse 1987, 15), successfully promoted a "one person, one vote" definition of public opinion. I will return to a number of these pioneers in the next section, but in terms of their impact on our notion of public opinion, their early successes in predicting the outcome of presidential elections and the publicity their predictions generated meant that by the 1940s, public opinion was understood as what is measured by surveys (Blondiaux 1998, 11). This understanding of public opinion was a departure from previous ones because it introduced an egalitarian dimension to the concept. Unlike V.O. Key Jr.'s definition of public opinion as "those opinions held by private persons which governments find it prudent to heed" (Key 1961, 4), early pollsters stressed the importance of each individual opinion. This fresh view elevated the sovereignty of public opinion—as measured by new instruments—and gave a voice to the people. In this vein, George Gallup argued that polls were the salvation of democracy (Wheeler 1976, 78). These developments were captured by William Kornhauser in *The Politics of Mass Society* (1959), in which he defined public opinion as "the transitory general will" (23). According to Kornhauser, mass society implies a situation in which rule by the masses dislodges aristocratic rule leading to "equality of voice in the determination of social policy" (1959, 27). Accordingly, public opinion was regarded primarily as public communication from citizens to their government, with the former claiming the right to have their opinions hold some influence on the actions of their government (Speier 1950). This conceptualization of public opinion would irretrievably guide public opinion research for several decades, and pollsters ensconced themselves in the role of neutral recorders of public opinion and virtual spokesperson for the people (Kornhauser 1959, 29). As Leo Bogart noted:

> The world of public opinion in today's sense really began with the Gallup Polls of the mid-1930s, and it is impossible for us to retreat to the meaning of public opinion as it was understood by Thomas Jefferson in the eighteenth century, by Alexis de Tocqueville and Lord Bryce in the nineteenth—or even Walter Lippmann in 1922. (1985, 14)

However, recent developments in our understanding of public opinion borrow to some extent from Lippmann's framework. There is no denying the secured position of public opinion as the sovereign voice of the people. In democratic societies, few would object to the "one person, one vote" our understanding of the concept represents. However, studies focusing on public opinion formation—that is, not so much on what people believe in but on how people arrive at the opinions they hold—have led to renewed interest in the capacity to influence the formation of those opinions. The literature on this subject is varied and multidisciplinary. It encompasses fields as varied as psychology, cognition sciences, political science, psychology, and communication. In this chapter, I concentrate on the contribution of three specific authors and their works: Daniel Yankelovich's *Coming to Public Judgment* (1991), John R. Zaller's *The Nature and Origins of Mass Opinion* (1992), and Samuel L. Popkin's *The Reasoning Voter* (1994). Together, they provide the foundation for our contemporary understanding of public opinion.

The contributions by Yankelovich and Popkin are largely influenced by the fact that both were able to combine practical and scholarly insights into the topic. Yankelovich is a Harvard and Sorbonne-educated public opinion researcher whose professional career spans over 50 years. Popkin holds a Ph.D. from MIT and is professor of political science at the University of California at San Diego. His academic understanding of public opinion polling is complemented by his experience as a political consultant—most notably for George McGovern, Jimmy Carter, Bill Clinton, and

Al Gore. Accordingly, Yankelovich and Popkin have been involved not only in trying to understand and measure public opinion but also in seeking to influence public opinion for the benefit of their clients. In *Coming to Public Judgment*, Yankelovich developed a framework to enhance the quality of public opinion. It is this enhanced state that he calls *public judgment* (1991, 5). Accordingly, public judgment is a form of public opinion that exhibits more thoughtfulness, more weighing of alternatives, and more genuine engagement with the issues. It puts more emphasis on the normative, valuing, and ethical side of questions than on the factual and informational side. An important lesson from his framework is the suggestion that public opinion formation goes through specific stages. According to Yankelovich, there are three stages of evolution when moving from mass opinion to public judgment:

- Stage 1: consciousness raising
- Stage 2: working through
- Stage 3: resolution[6]

While one might dispute Yankelovich's typology, the main lesson for the measurement of public opinion rests in the realization that polling needs to take into account at which stage of development members of the public at large may be at a given point in time. It follows that the public requires different kinds of information about an issue, depending on their level of understanding of it and their stage in the process of opinion formation. While Yankelovich suggested that his framework should be used to enhance the quality of the opinions held by the citizenry and ultimately improve democracy, his framework also points to the possibility of effectively influencing opinion formation through a better comprehension of its dynamics. A specific example from the 2008 federal election can be used to illustrate the strategic implications of Yankelovich's contribution.

When Stéphane Dion became leader of the Liberal Party in late 2006, polls indicated that the environment was emerging as a very important issue. A poll conducted by Environics in November 2006 found that 13 percent of Canadians believed the environment was the most important issue facing the country, second only to health care at 16 percent. Just as many notables in the Middle Ages were lured by the alchemists' gold, Dion saw those polling results as a panacea for his flagging leadership and developed his "Green Shift" policy as a way to capitalize on the changing priorities of Canadians. Voters were in the "consciousness raising" phase about the environment—as defined by Yankelovich—and were receptive to the arguments put forth by Dion. For their part, the Conservatives understood they could not yet counter the rise in interest about this important issue. The Green Shift had a positive impact on the electoral fortunes of the Liberal Party. In January 2007, the Liberals were only three points behind the Conservatives in voting intentions (Leger Marketing 2007). But unfortunately for the Liberals, the election was still several months away.

As voters were "working through" their issue priorities, the Conservatives began to present the Green Shift as a policy that would increase taxes for Canadians. Voters became conflicted between their concern over the environment and their aversion to higher taxes. By the time the 2008 federal election was called, Canadians had come to a "resolution" about the Green Shift that was by then negatively perceived as a "carbon tax" that would hurt the economy. Looking at Table 10.1, we see that the Conservatives were more effective than the Liberals at managing opinion formation about the environment. The issue had lost most of its salience by the time voters went to the polls.

Popkin figuratively delved into the minds of voters to try to understand how they think about politics. Inspired by academic research in cognitive psychology, he presented a low-information rationality model to describe opinion formation. According to Popkin,

> voters actually do reason about parties, candidates, and issues. They have premises, and they use those premises to make inferences from their observations of the world around them. They think about who and what political parties stand for; they think about the meaning of political endorsements; they think about what government can and should do. And the performance of government, parties, and candidates affects their assessments and preferences. (1994, 7)

Popkin did not suggest that decisions are made by voters who are very knowledgeable and fully engaged in the process. However, he rejects the notion that low information necessarily equals a lack of rationality in making decisions. In *The Reasoning Voter*, Popkin proposed that voters rely on relatively stable heuristics—or judgmental shortcuts[7]—in forming their opinions, and these shortcuts allow most *to reason* through the opinion formation process. Accordingly, the polling function extends beyond the simple reporting of opinions to incorporate an understanding of those stable heuristics voters rely on in making their decisions. Questions about voters'

TABLE 10.1 Most Important Issues in the 2008 Federal Election

	Percent
General economic concerns	22.9
Health care	18.6
General social welfare issues	10.2
Environmental concerns	8.5
Unemployment	3.5
Taxes	3.0
Integrity	2.3
Debt/deficit	1.7
National unity	0.6
US/foreign influence	0.3
Need for majority government	0.3
General other issues	13.6
None	14.5

$N = 3,247$

Source: 2008 Canadian Election Study.

values and beliefs, their socioeconomic background and political predispositions, as well as personal characteristics become analytical tools to be used in predicting how the electorate would work its way through different policy initiatives.

John Zaller offers a different perspective from Yankelovich's and Popkin's, and his view complements our current understanding of public opinion. Zaller reaffirmed the primacy of the role of elites in the dynamics of opinion formation in ways that are at times reminiscent of the arguments made by Walter Lippmann in 1922. The author's main thesis is that "across a very wide range of issues, variations in the information carried in elite discourse, individual differences in attention to this information, and individual differences in political values and other predispositions jointly determine the contours of public opinion" (Zaller 1992, 6). Zaller made several important contributions to the scientific study of public opinion—too many to be able to adequately review them here. Of particular interest to this discussion is the suggestion that since citizens do not typically carry around in their heads fixed attitudes on an issue but construct "opinion statements," they make greatest use of ideas that are most salient to them or "top of mind" (1). Therefore, the possibility exists to "prime" voters to think about specific issues over others and to suggest specific "ideas" to guide them through the opinion formation process. Polling becomes particularly effective in tracking the emergence of top-of-mind issues and the factors that influence them. Priming is different from manipulation because voters keep control of the process, but it forces us to reconsider whether polls are "the salvation of democracy" as George Gallup once espoused. Rather than simply reporting the opinions of the public, polls have infiltrated the dynamics leading to the formation of such opinions. The ways in which this influence has changed public opinion polling will be the focus of the remainder of this chapter.

BOX 10.1

Ten Scholars Who Have Shaped the Concept of Public Opinion

- William Bryce (*The American Commonwealth*, 1911)
- Walter Lippmann (*Public Opinion*, 1922)
- John Dewey (*The Public and Its Problems*, 1927)
- William Kornhauser (*The Politics of Mass Society*, 1959)
- Gustave Le Bon (*The Crowd*, 1960)
- V.O. Key Jr. (*Public Opinion and American Democracy*, 1961)
- Daniel Yankelovich (*Coming to Public Judgment: Making Democracy Work in a Complex World*, 1991)
- John R. Zaller (*The Nature and Origins of Mass Opinion*, 1992)
- Samuel Popkin (*The Reasoning Voter: Communication and Persuasion in Presidential Campaigns*, 1994)
- Leo Bogart (*Finding Out*, 2003)

Early Efforts to Measure Public Opinion in Canada

Before exploring the first attempts to measure public opinion in Canada, a quick look at the origins of polling will put the Canadian experience in perspective. While we know that this practice in Canada began in the 1940s, one must look back almost 200 years to find the first systematic measures of public opinion. In 1745, the controller general in France commissioned a study to gather sociodemographic and economic data on and measure general attitudes toward a potential increase in land taxes in the country (Blondiaux 1998, 52). Then, between 1793 and 1794, the French minister of the interior mandated regional commissioners to administer questionnaires to gather information about *l'esprit public* (the public mood) of the nation. By 1802, France had established a government structure to measure systematically and on a regular basis the mood of the French public (53–54). It is important to note that the information gathered through these early efforts was kept in strict confidence and used only for the benefit of the governing elite.

It is generally accepted that the first known published poll was conducted by the *Harrisburg Pennsylvanian* on July 24, 1824 (Hoy 1989, 12). That poll predicted that Andrew Jackson would beat John Quincy Adams in the US presidential race. This was an ominous beginning for polling: Adams won the presidency that year and Jackson had to wait four years before he moved to the White House. During the presidential elections of 1908 and 1912, the *New York Herald* teamed up with other newspapers (the *Cincinnati Enquirer*, the *Chicago Record-Herald*, the *St. Louis Republic*, the *Boston Globe*, and the *Los Angeles Times*) to conduct a national poll on voting intentions but failed to make accurate predictions (Hoy 1989, 12). These early polls were known as "straw polls" and as their lack of success demonstrated, they were methodologically flawed. At that time, no efforts were made to ensure that the sample of opinions was representative of the population. Undeterred, the *Literary Digest* published the results of a straw poll giving Alf Landon a commanding lead (57.1 percent to 42.9 percent) over Franklin Delano Roosevelt in the 1936 presidential election. However, FDR beat Landon in a landslide victory with 62.5 percent of the vote, making the *Digest*'s 19.6 percentage-point error the largest ever registered in a national poll in a presidential election (Lachapelle 1991, 2–3). The *Literary Digest* folded less than a year after this debacle (Wheeler 1976, 84), and it appeared that the practice of election polling would be short-lived.

Intellectual advancements in statistics and the science of sampling rejuvenated the polling industry. The roots of scientific polling emerged from the debates that took place at the International Institute of Statistics where the Norwegian A.N. Kiaer unsuccessfully presented his method of representative sampling in 1895, 1897, and again in 1901. Finally, in 1903, the Institute accepted the validity of Kiaer's methodological claims (Lachapelle 1991, 4). Subsequently, polling relied on variations of Kiaer's sampling method to make inferences about the behaviour of a given population. It is important to define what a representative sample is since it constitutes the cornerstone of modern polling. In simple terms, a representative sample is "one in which every major attribute of the larger population from which the sample is drawn is present in roughly the proportion or frequency with which those attributes occur in the larger population ... a truly representative sample is a microcosm—a smaller, but accurate, model—of the larger population from which it is taken" (Manheim et al. 2008, 119). The guiding principle to guarantee representativeness is that the sample be randomly selected. To ensure randomness, the sample must be chosen in such a manner that each and every individual in the entire population has an equal opportunity to be selected for analysis (Manheim et al. 2008, 122).

Representative sampling entered the realm of political polling when George Gallup relied on scientific polling to help his mother-in-law become the first woman to hold the position of secretary of state in Iowa in 1932. Gallup's doctoral thesis on sampling techniques led to the founding of the polling industry in 1935 as he and two other early pollsters, Archibald Crossley and Elmo Roper, began conducting polls on a regular basis (Sabato 1981, 69). The expansion of the industry suffered a setback in 1948 when the three major American polling firms predicted a victory for presidential candidate Thomas E. Dewey over the eventual winner, Harry S. Truman. However, this setback was temporary. Newspaper editors realized that the reading public liked polls, and their publication increased readership and generated publicity. Hence, polls continued to be published in newspapers while pollsters expanded their influence and scope of activities. In 1958, Gallup worked for the Eisenhower campaign helping to design television advertisements, but it was Lou Harris who really put polling on the map with the John F. Kennedy election of 1960.

In Canada, marketing research began with the founding of Canadian Facts in 1932 (Butler 2007, 40). William Lyon Mackenzie King was the first prime minister to rely on public opinion polling. Faced with the stalemate of the plebiscite on conscription, King secretly commissioned Gallup through his Canadian affiliate—the Canadian Institute of Public Opinion (CIPO)—to gather information destined to reconcile the growing schism between the two founding nations (Magnant 1980, 19). Gallup conducted a poll for the King administration in September 1942 (Hoy 1989, 17), and political polling was born in Canada. Jean Lesage is generally believed to have been the first Canadian leader to use polls systematically in the 1960 Quebec election. At the federal level, both the Liberals and PCs relied on the strategic advice of American pollsters in the 1960s and early 1970s; notably, Lou Harris was hired by the Pearson Liberals, and Robert Teeter was hired by the Progressive Conservative Party. It was during the 1965 federal election that political polling began to appear in the Canadian media.

Then, in the early 1970s, the federal Liberals hired Martin Goldfarb as their party pollster. Goldfarb is important for three reasons. First, he was Canadian. The Liberals became the first of the federal parties to realize the incongruity of relying on American experts to understand the mood of Canadians. Second, Goldfarb became the first of what Butler called "pollstars" (Butler 2007, 35). Third, Goldfarb was educated in anthropology and sociology, and this influenced his conceptualization of public opinion. His role was that of a "seer"; his strength was his ability to understand the general mood of the electorate and explain it to his political clients. This is in line with the "one person, one vote" interpretation of public opinion espoused by the early pioneers.

The Tories also recognized that they should rely on a Canadian to measure the opinion of Canadian voters. They ditched Robert Teeter after the 1974 election and hired Allan Gregg, a doctoral student in political science at Carleton University. Once called "the punk pollster" (Sawatsky 1987, chap. 8), Gregg brought much more than style to the political polling profession. Beyond the leather jackets and the long hair, Gregg had a solid education in quantitative analysis and a rigorous understanding of methodology. Before the 1979 election, Gregg spent some time in the United States with experts such as Peter Hart, Pat Caddell, Lance Torrence, Stu Spencer, and, more important, Richard Wirthlin (Sawatsky 1987, 109). Wirthlin was about to establish an enviable reputation for his role in the election of Ronald Reagan as president of the United States.[8] His winning approach relied on large-scale tracking surveys[9] and a unique and very specific way to segment the electorate. For Wirthlin, not all voters were created equal in the sense that a presidential campaign had to focus on consolidating its base of support and understand those voters who may be persuaded to vote for the candidate. Accordingly, the pollster was no longer a seer but became more like a surgeon, dissecting public opinion to focus only on those voters who are instrumental to victory and to comprehend those arguments that might sway them. Wirthlin may or may not have been the first to understand this approach, but he certainly was the first to push it as the keystone to electoral strategy—and Gregg was listening. As Sawatsky explained:

> Gregg was convinced that tracking represented the biggest breakthrough in election campaigning since television. It could virtually dictate the details of an election campaign, by uncovering moods and divulging trends. When public opinion shifted during the campaign the party could reposition itself to meet the change. A party could emphasize some issues and drop others with pinpoint effect as the campaign developed. (1987, 110)

BOX 10.2
Allan Gregg on Polling

When we first started Decima, the principal focus of our political research was simply finding out where you stood, in terms of political preference—the horse race stuff. Very rapidly however, it become clear, once you knew you were ahead, you needed to develop strategies to find out how to consolidate your existing support, and if you were behind, you had to determine how to expand your vote by identifying those voters who were most likely to switch. This turned our focus to "targetting" and developing composite variables that would allow us to segment the population into finer and finer slices. Throughout the years this has become the "starting point" of most political research. Today, we now incorporate segmentation analysis into much more sophisticated multi-variant analysis, so we can determine not only who are the "most pursuadable" elements of the population but also what messaging, issues, or dimensions of image are most likely to trigger a change in voting behaviour.

Allan Gregg is the founder of Decima Research.

Gregg demonstrated the proficiency of this new approach by helping Ontario Premier Bill Davis win his elusive majority in 1981 and by helping Brian Mulroney become prime minister in 1984 and again in 1988. Soon enough, another emerging "pollstar" pushed aside the old Liberal guard and helped the Liberals return to power. Like Gregg, Michael Marzolini relied on daily tracking surveys and was strongly committed to rigorous methodology. He also brought an uncanny expertise in evaluating the effectiveness of campaign communications among key segments of the electorate. In the leadup to the 1993 election, his research largely contributed to the development and design of the Liberal Red Book, which most political experts consider as a stroke of genius.[10] With Gregg and Marzolini, the foundations of the contemporary approach to measuring public opinion were in place.

BOX 10.3
Michael Marzolini on Polling

The measurement and interpretation of public opinion is not some "black art." It is both a profession and a public trust. Surveys are simply public consultation—a means by which the public can be included in the decision-making process. People's needs, concerns, attitudes, perceptions and preferences are important inputs for all decisions, whether at the corporate or the government level. These decisions should never be dictated by polls, but consulting the public on important matters usually leads to better products, services, and policy decisions, and a better relationship between the public and the decision-makers.

For government, polling brings the public to the table, and facilitates a dialogue between the public and their elected representatives. It is not a replacement for individual consultation, or indeed leadership, but is a fast, accurate and cost-effective way of listening to voters who don't always write letters to their MP when they disagree or agree with government policy. These reasons are why we conduct surveys, and broadcasting the benefits of our work should be one of our industry's goals.

Michael Marzolini is chairman of Pollara Strategic Pubic Opinion and Market Research.

Polls Don't Lie, But They Have a Purpose

One of the most contentious public policies in recent years is whether same-sex couples should be allowed to marry. By the end of 2004, the Supreme Court of Canada unanimously ruled in favour of allowing same-sex marriages. In the leadup to the court's decision, Canadians were inundated with polling results that often seemed contradictory. This particular issue will allow for an examination of the factors affecting poll results and their interpretation.

In January 2004, Ipsos Reid conducted a poll showing that 48 percent of Canadians believed the then Prime Minister Paul Martin should not amend Canada's marriage laws to include same-sex marriages, while 47 percent said he should (Ipsos Reid, January 15, 2004). Three months later, 43 percent of Canadians were in favour of same-sex marriages, while 47 percent were opposed (Leger Marketing, April 6–11, 2004). By June 2004, support for allowing same-sex couples to marry rose to 57 percent (Environics Research, June 16–21, 2004). In November of the same year, 39 percent of Canadians felt that same-sex marriages should be fully recognized and equal to conventional heterosexual marriage (Ipsos Reid, November 19–22, 2004). One month later, 60 percent of Canadians supported the heterosexual definition of marriage (Nordic Research Group, December 11–16, 2004). On the surface, it would appear that within a year, Canadians went from being ambivalent about same-sex marriages to being fully supportive and finally rejecting the idea. The details of the polls tell a different story.

Canadians were not consistently asked about their support or opposition to same-sex marriages. While the January 2004 poll was about same-sex marriages, the question asked pertained to allowing Paul Martin to amend Canada's marriage law to include same-sex marriage. While fairly similar, the April 2004 poll asked whether Canadians were "in favour or not of same-sex marriages" while in June, they were asked if "same-sex couples should be allowed to marry." In November 2004, Canadians were not asked if they supported same-sex marriages but whether such unions "should be fully recognized like a heterosexual marriage" or in other ways such as a civil union. The December poll asked if Canadians "support or oppose keeping the definition of marriage as a union of a man and a woman." While the polling results on this issue seemed to have varied widely, the variations were the byproduct of changes in the wording of the questions. In fact, if we look at polls conducted by Ipsos on this issue between 1999 and 2004, we see that, when asked the same question—"Do you support or oppose same-sex couples being able to marry and register their marriage with their provincial government?"—Canadians have been fairly consistent:

- 1996: 46 percent of Canadians support same-sex marriage
- 1999: 55 percent support
- 2003: 49 percent support
- 2004: 54 percent support[11]

This example points to the importance of question wording and the extent to which findings are affected by changes in the words used. In general, short questions are better than longer ones. It is also important to limit the amount of factual information included in the wording of the questions. However, when necessary, it is essential to present both sides of the issue to allow respondents to provide an unbiased answer. When comparing poll results, it is necessary to evaluate questions with similar wording and also know the purpose of the poll.

As I mentioned earlier, I do not agree with those who criticize polls as being generally inaccurate and performing an illegitimate function in our democracy. In fact, polls published during election campaigns have proven to be generally accurate in predicting the outcomes. For instance, the last three polls released in the 2008 federal election accurately predicted both the outcome and the vote share for each political party within the margin of error. But as all opinions are not created equal, neither are polls. In broad terms, polls can be conducted for academic purposes, specific clients, or media release.

Polls conducted for academic purposes seek to understand people's beliefs, values, and attitudes, and how these relate to their behaviour. Such polls provide opportunities to evaluate theories and assumptions about behaviour which, at times, does not withstand the close scrutiny of empirical research. Although academic polling has been conducted since the 1930s,[12] the tradition of academic survey research was firmed up by a group of academics from Columbia University who sought to understand how voters make decisions. *The People's Choice* was a study of presidential voting in Erie County in 1940 (Lazarsfeld, Berelson, and Gaudet 1944). From that election onward, academics have looked at elections as a way to understand behaviour. Those efforts have not been limited to studying electoral behaviour, but elections have often proven to be useful signposts around which academic surveys are organized.[13] In Canada, the first election studies were conducted in 1965 and 1968. They largely replicated the approach followed by the Michigan School (Gidengil 1992, 221) and *The American Voter* (Campbell et al. 1960). The purpose of polls conducted by academics is not to predict outcomes, but to develop a body of research to allow generations of scholars to better understand issues related to individual behaviour. As Elisabeth Gidengil put it, "any attempt to assess the contribution of the Canadian National Election Studies (NES) must bear in mind that secondary analysis is the primary use of surveys in a situation of scarcity" (1992, 220).

Polls conducted for specific clients attract the ire of critics who decry the undue influence of polling. In politics, such polls are commissioned by political parties and candidates to help them get elected. In market research, such polls are commissioned to convince customers to buy certain products or services. As Chapter 8 by Thomas Flanagan indicates, polls play an important role both prior to the election campaign as well as during the writ period. As they plan their campaign strategy, political parties spend large amounts of money to gauge the appeal of various campaign themes; to assess the familiarity with and impressions of candidates and potential opponents; to assess the appeal of the leaders' appearance and demeanour; and, most important, to conduct electoral segmentation to classify voters into different demographic and psychological categories with a view to persuading them to support a particular candidate. The sole purpose of such polls is to help political parties better understand how to win elections. The approach in conducting these polls increasingly reflects the current understanding of public opinion as highly segmented and susceptible to being primed.

Media polls are most controversial, mainly because they are the most visible. Right from the start, George Gallup understood the media appeal of public opinion polls and more than 70 years later, there is little sign that the media appetite has been satiated. For instance, between the federal elections of January 2006 and October 2008, a total of 288 political polls were published in various Canadian media outlets—an average of more than eight political polls per month. The attraction goes both ways. Pollsters could never decide which function suited them best, hesitating between the roles of university researcher, journalist, and expert (Blondiaux 1998, 25). When a pollster decides to publish a poll independently, the main and only purpose is to generate publicity for himself or herself and the polling firm. This is not to suggest that the findings of such polls are inaccurate, but they are designed to maximize media exposure. The main element in achieving this objective is timing. In simple terms, a poll about gun control would yield different results if conducted immediately after a high-profile shooting. While academic surveys would avoid conducting a study within a frenzied atmosphere and client-proprietary polls would seek to track the lasting impact of the event, a media poll would seek to capitalize on the heated environment as a way to ensure that the findings are published on the front page of newspapers or presented as the lead story on television. It is important to reiterate that the findings are accurate, but they reflect opinions held in the aftermath of a high-profile event. In a speech to the Professional Market Research Society conference in 2000, Michael Marzolini criticized the reporting of media polls with the following story:

> We all remember that poll for Hydro-Québec during the ice storm a few years ago, a telephone survey asking Quebecers how good a job the hydro company was doing at dealing with this disaster, when many people were without power. The newspapers reported that 80 percent of respondents thought they were doing a great job. The only problem was that all the respondents they telephoned had to have electricity and phone service to answer the survey. The less satisfied respondents were over-nighting in the public shelters.

What Marzolini failed to mention is that the poll was front page news to the delight of the firm that conducted it. However, Marzolini's criticism is well founded since such polls, which are conducted by opportunistic pollsters, have a negative impact on the reputation of the polling industry. Such criticisms have led to demands to regulate the polling industry in general and the publications of public opinion polls in particular. Guidelines to regulate the publication of polls have been put forth since the late 1970s, first by the *Comité des sondages du Regroupement québécois des sciences sociales* and later by Guy Lachapelle in his report to the Royal Commission on Electoral Reform and Party Financing in 1991. The aim of the recommendations is to ensure that the public gets all the necessary information about the conduct of polls and their findings. Accordingly, the publication of survey results should include the following:

1. The name of the sponsor of the poll
2. The name of the polling institute
3. The interview period
4. The data collection method used
5. The size of the original sample
6. The number of non-eligible respondents
7. The rejection and response rates
8. The number of respondents
9. The margin of error
10. The sampling method
11. The wording of the questions (Lachapelle 1991, 114)

With this information, citizens would have the opportunity to judge, if not the accuracy, at least the legitimacy of the information they are being influenced with.

The Challenges of Measuring Public Opinion in Modern Canadian Elections

In the 2008 federal election, only 59 percent of eligible voters decided to exercise their right to vote—the lowest turnout ever in Canadian federal elections. This marked the sixth consecutive election when less than 70 percent of Canadians voted[14] and this is the starting point of our concluding discussion about the challenges of measuring public opinion in Canadian elections. When only 59 percent of Canadians vote, that means 41 percent are not interested enough to do so. If one is tasked to measure the opinion of Canadian *voters* in the lead up to an election, the first challenge is to find a way to segregate between the opinion of those who matter (voters) and those who do not (non-voters). Moreover, if one has to help design a campaign strategy to win an election, the second challenge is to focus only on those voters who can help win the election and discount the opinions of others. The challenges of measuring public opinion are both methodological and analytical.

From a methodological perspective, the newest challenge is the declining response rate in telephone polls. According to the latest data available, over the last four years refusal rates in Canada have increased from 67.8 percent to 77.4 percent, a 9.6-point difference. Moreover, participation rates on omnibus telephone surveys currently hover around 20 percent to 25 percent. Analysis of client studies, which are more varied in questionnaire length and field practices, also shows an increase in refusal rates, but a more moderate one—from 65.9 percent to 67.9 percent, a 2 percent increase over a four-year period. Participation rates for such studies are therefore 32 percent (Professional Marketing Research Society). Another challenge pertains to the data collection method. Back in the 1980s, survey organizations realized that door-to-door interviewing was becoming increasingly unreliable as more and more people were uncomfortable opening their doors to strangers to answer their questions in face-to-face interviews. To overcome declining response rates, polling firms eventually switched to telephone interviewing, where people are randomly called at home and asked to answer a few questions. The polling industry is at a similar crossroads. As mentioned, response rate in telephone interviewing is so low that it now threatens accuracy.[15] Also, more people no longer have regular telephone lines and only use cellphones—making them almost impossible to reach. However, the alternative of Internet-survey methodology remains problematic because representativeness—a key element for accuracy—cannot be achieved through this method.[16] As explained earlier, the key to guarantee representativeness is for the sample to be drawn to ensure that each and every individual in the entire population has an equal opportunity to be selected for analysis. While a majority of Canadians have access to the Internet, that access still does not extend to the whole population. More important, respondents in Internet surveys have been pre-selected for their willingness to participate in such studies and are often offered a financial incentive to do so. Unlike telephone survey methodology, which can track down respondents who are underrepresented in surveys, there is no way to reach Internet voters who are unwilling to participate.

From an analytical perspective, the main challenge is to design polls that reflect the contemporary understanding of public opinion as defined by Yankelovich, Popkin, and Zaller. The importance is to capture as much of the opinion formation process as possible. The key to overcoming this challenge is accurate segmentation and sophisticated tracking of the dynamics of opinion formation. As Flanagan describes in Chapter 8 of this book, political parties are increasingly focusing only on those few voters who will make the difference between winning and losing. While convincing targeted voters to support a specific party has always been the objective of election campaigns, the shrinking electorate has rendered this endeavour particularly challenging. This point should not be lightly dismissed. Assuming that the winning party gets 40 percent of the vote—this research strategy implies that a party will dismiss the opinions of 60 percent of the voting electorate. Assuming again that only 60 percent of eligible voters are part of that voting electorate, the focus is on less than 25 percent of eligible voters. When Jean Chrétien won his second consecutive majority in 1997 with a record low 38 percent of the vote, the fact that voter turnout was 67 percent meant that the Liberals managed to form a majority government with the support of 25 percent of eligible voters. In 2008, Stephen Harper was able to form a minority government with the support of 22 percent of eligible voters. Needless to say, the consequences of this new reality are contrary to the principles of democracy, which seek to represent the views of the majority.[17] From an analytical perspective, each party pollster has its own proprietary approach to solving this challenge. Several are inspired by the successful approach developed by the Harris Tories in 1995 and used by the Reform Party in 1997 and subsequently by the Canadian Alliance. Based on the analysis by American consultant Mike Murphy, the Harris campaign focused on what it called "gap voters" who were defined as voters who should be voting for the Harris Conservatives—based on positive evaluations of party policies and of the party and leader—but did not. The polling strategy was therefore to zero in on understanding those few gap voters and overcome their obstacles to support the Tories. This approach was taken one step further by the Reform Party and the Canadian Alliance, which used polling to identify the "lights in the window"—namely the policies that the party should promote to attract the gap voters—even if they may not support the other party policies.

Conclusion

As I mentioned at several points throughout this chapter, the new ways to measure public opinion are not without consequences. The current reality suggests that public opinion is still conceptualized as sovereign but no longer equal since the views of fewer strategically important voters are given undue prominence. Pollsters did not create this new reality but have astutely adapted their expertise to expand their role and influence in it. George Gallup's pioneering efforts have created a social phenomenon that has evolved beyond his expectations. Gallup's legacy has not only redefined the concept of public opinion as something that can be measured and quantified but also introduced important challenges into the practice of democracy. The pollster, as a modern-day alchemist, tries to reconcile diverse methodological and analytical challenges and transform them into a coherent understanding of the dynamics of opinion formation and, in the process, turn opinions into votes.

NOTES

1. Adapted from Bowker (1997).
2. See, for example, Cobb and Goldwhite (2002), especially chapters 4 and 5.
3. For a readable and entertaining biography of Newton, see White (1999).
4. For a recent English version of this episode, see Bredin (2000).
5. See Bentham (1986). In this book, originally published in 1789, Bentham referred to the "tribunal of public opinion."
6. For a full discussion of the characteristics of each stage, see Yankelovich (1991, Part II).
7. The use of judgmental shortcuts is similar to Lippmann's use of stereotypes.
8. For a fascinating look at Wirthlin's role in that election and his approach to measuring public opinion, see Perry (1991).
9. Unlike typical surveys, tracking surveys are usually conducted on a daily basis with the view not only to understand public opinion but also to "track" how it is evolving.
10. For a full discussion of that campaign and how effective the Red Book was for the Liberals, see Frizzell and Pammett (1997) and Clarkson (2005).
11. Data from various polls conducted by Ipsos Canada (http://www.ipsos.ca).
12. One of the earliest examples is LaPiere (1934).
13. Examples of other long-running academic studies not linked to elections are the World Values Survey, the International Social Survey Programme, and the General Social Survey.
14. See the Elections Canada website: http://www.elections.ca.
15. For a full discussion of this issue and new ways to overcome low response rates, see Lepkowski et al. (2007).
16. See, for example, Lightfoot (2008).
17. On the significance of this new focus on only certain parts of the electorate, see Galbraith (1992).

DISCUSSION QUESTIONS

1. Imagine that you are launching a new product and want to ascertain the potential demand for it. Design a short survey and administer it to about 20 randomly selected neighbours on your street. Then administer the same questionnaire to about 20 students from your cohort. Compare the results. What do the results indicate about the process of segmentation described in this chapter?
2. Find a poll published in the newspaper. How do the reported findings compare with the guidelines for the publication of polls discussed in this chapter?
3. Select a contentious public policy issue such as abortion, euthanasia, death penalty or others. Find ten published polls from different polling firms on the issue. Do the findings differ? Identify potential explanations for any differences.

FURTHER READING

Butler, Peter M. 2007. *Polling and public opinion: A Canadian perspective.* Toronto: University of Toronto Press.

Lippmann, Walter. 1922. *Public opinion.* New York: Free Press.

Popkin, Samuel. 1994. *The reasoning voter: Communication and persuasion in presidential campaigns,* 2nd ed. Chicago: University of Chicago Press.

Sabato, Larry J. 1981. *The rise of political consultants.* New York: Basic Books.

Yankelovich, Daniel. 1991. *Coming to public judgment: Making democracy work in a complex world.* Syracuse, NY: Syracuse University Press.

Zaller, John R. 1992. *The nature and origins of mass opinion.* Cambridge: Cambridge University Press.

REFERENCES

Bentham, Jeremy. 1986. *Introduction to the principles of morals and legislation.* Bethesda, MD: Legal Classic Library. (Orig. pub. 1789.)

Blondiaux, Loic. 1998. *La fabrique de l'opinion.* Paris: Seuil.

Bowker, John. 1997. Alchemy. *The concise Oxford dictionary of world religions.* Oxford: Oxford University Press. http://www.encyclopedia.com.

Bredin, Jean. 2000. *The affair: The case of Alfred Dreyfus.* London: George Braziller Publishers.

Bryce, William. 1911. *The American Commonwealth.* London: MacMillan.

Butler, Peter M. 2007. *Polling and public opinion: A Canadian perspective.* Toronto: University of Toronto Press.

Campbell, Angus, Philip E. Converse, Warren E. Miller, and Donald E. Stokes. 1960. *The American voter.* New York: Wiley.

Clarkson, Stephen. 2005. *The big red machine.* Vancouver: UBC Press.

Cobb, Cathy, and Harold Goldwhite. 2002. *Creations of fire.* New York: Basic Books.

Converse, Philip. 1987. *Changing conceptions of public opinion in the political process. Public Opinion Quarterly* 51 (2): S12–S24.

Dewey, John. 1927. *The public and its problems.* New York: Holt.

D'Holbach, Baron. 1770. *System of nature.*

Frizzell, Alan, and Jon H. Pammett, eds. 1997. *The Canadian general election of 1997.* Ottawa: Dundurn Press.

Galbraith, John Kenneth. 1992. *The culture of contentment.* Boston: Houghton Mifflin and Company.

Gidengil, Elisabeth. 1992. Canada votes. *Canadian Journal of Political Science* 25 (2): 219–248.

Helvétius, Claude Adrien. 1759. *Essays on the mind.*

Hoy, Claire. 1989. *Margin of error.* Toronto: Key Porter Books.

Key, V.O., Jr. 1961. *Public opinion and American democracy.* New York: Knopf.

Kornhauser, William. 1959. *The politics of mass society.* New York: Free Press.

Lachapelle, Guy. 1991. *Polls and the media in Canadian elections.* Ottawa: Supply and Services Canada.

LaPiere, Richard T. 1934. Attitudes vs. actions. *Social Forces* 13 (2): 230–237.

Lazarsfeld, Paul F., Bernard Berelson, and Hazel Gaudet. 1944. *The people's choice: How the voter makes up his mind in a presidential election.* New York: Columbia University Press.

Le Bon, Gustave. 1960. *The crowd.* New York: Viking Press.

Leger Marketing. 2007. The Leger federal election monitor, January 24.

Lepkowski, James M., Clyde Tucker, J. Michael Brick, Edith D. De Leeuw, Lilli Japec, Paul J. Lavrakas, Michael W. Link, and Roberta L. Sangster. 2007. *Advances in telephone survey methodology*. Hoboken, NJ: Wiley-Science.

Lightfoot, William. 2008. *A comparative study of research methodologies*. Saarbrucken, Germany: VDM Verlag.

Lippmann, Walter. 1922. *Public opinion*. New York: Free Press.

Magnant, Michel. 1980. *Les sondages d'opinion*. Ottawa: Supply and Services.

Manheim, Jarol, Richard C. Rich, Lars B. Willnat, and Craig Leonard Brians. 2008. *Empirical political analysis*. New York: Pearson Education.

Marzolini, Michael. Speech presented at the Professional Market Research Society Conference 2000, Toronto, June 6, 2000.

Necker, Jacques. 1784. *De l'administration des finances de la France*. Paris.

Perry, Roland. 1991. *Hidden power: The programming of the president*. Mansfield, OH: Rainbow Publishing.

Popkin, Samuel. 1994. *The reasoning voter: Communication and persuasion in presidential campaigns*, 2nd ed. Chicago: University of Chicago Press.

Professional Marketing Research Society (former website).

Rousseau, Jean-Jacques. 1761. *La nouvelle Héloïse*.

Sabato, Larry J. 1981. *The rise of political consultants*. New York: Basic Books.

Sawatsky, John. 1987. *The insiders*: Government, business and the lobbyists. Toronto: McClelland & Stewart.

Speier, Hans. 1950. Historical development of public opinion. *The American Journal of Sociology* 55.

Wheeler, Michael. 1976. *Lies, damn lies, and statistics*. New York: Liveright.

White, Michael. 1999. *Isaac Newton: The last sorcerer*. New York: Basic Books.

Yankelovich, Daniel. 1991. *Coming to public judgment: Making democracy work in a complex world*. Syracuse, NY: Syracuse University Press.

Zaller, John R. 1992. *The nature and origins of mass opinion*. Cambridge: Cambridge University Press.

PART FOUR
The Canadian Voter

CHAPTER 11

Overview of Voting Behaviour Theories

Andrea Perrella

Introduction

Guess how the following four people voted in the 2006 federal election. Here is what we know of them:

- Voter #1: Protestant male, lives in Alberta, with a total household income greater than $100,000
- Voter #2: Toronto man, Catholic, of Italian descent
- Voter #3: Francophone 26-year-old female in a common-law relationship living in Eastern Quebec
- Voter #4: Middle-aged married woman, somewhat religious in her Protestant faith, whose household income ranges from $70,000 to $79,000, living in a rural area of southwestern Ontario

Here are the obvious answers: Voter #1 must have cast a ballot for the Conservatives; Voter #2 for the Liberals; Voter #3 for the Bloc Québécois; and Voter #4 for the Conservatives. Now here is what really happened: Voter #1 supported the Liberals; Voter #2 the Conservatives; Voter #3 the Conservatives; and Voter #4 the New Democratic Party.

The four people are actual voters who participated in the Canadian Election Study survey. The initial and, as it turns out, incorrect answers are not based on faulty thinking. Many of us would have given the same incorrect answers because most higher-income males who live in Alberta *do* indeed support the Conservatives, most Italians who live in Toronto *do* vote Liberal, and so forth. Demographics—key statistical categories that place people into social groups (for example, ethnicity, sex, income, region of residence)—may identify some general voter tendencies, but the fact that general tendencies do not always explain voting behaviour suggests that a more complex process is at play.

This chapter examines some of the forces that affect voting behaviour according to the main theoretical pillars of voting research, particularly those that relate to two key behavioural concepts: mobilization and conversion. Mobilization involves "getting out the vote," that is, party workers identify potential supporters and encourage them to vote. Conversion involves persuading a supporter of one party to consider voting for another. As one can imagine, it is easier to mobilize than to convert. But modern campaigns, particularly with all their negative ads and daily tracking of poll numbers, give the impression that elections are all about converting votes. Despite this impression, much of the evidence supports the view that elections are an exercise in mobilization. Conversion is rare, for reasons that may become apparent after this chapter's overview of voting behaviour theories.

The Evolution of Voting Research

Voting research spans at least as far back as the 1940s, and still, to this day, there remain debates as to what makes voters tick. Early research indicates that demographics is key to vote choice (Lazarfeld, Berelson, and Gaudet 1948). Later research indicates that more sociological and psychological factors are key to vote choice (Campbell et al. 1960). Demographics, as it turns out, is a remote contributor to what is a fairly complex process with countervailing forces that pull voters toward one party or another. This complex process renders the exercise of understanding voting behaviour quite challenging.

Another branch of voting research focuses attention on the individual voter and his or her individual interests. Based on the notion of rationality (Downs 1957), voters sort through different choices to select the candidate or the party that would best serve their interests, whatever they may be. There is some possibility for conversion, assuming that a party can transmit a convincing message that adequately appeals to a voter's key concerns and interests, many of which can be analyzed through a survey of issue priorities, voter perceptions of a governing party's performance (for example, handling of the economy), and the prospects for an opposition party to perform any better.

Evidence exists to support each of these three general families of theories, although no one theory can claim to explain *all* voting behaviour. In many cases, the validity and applicability of a theory depends on context, be it institutional (for example, electoral formula, party system), sociological (for example, relationship among the key social divisions, or "cleavages"), or individual (for example, the level of a voter's political sophistication).

In addition, much of the foundation of these general families of theories was developed before our tumultuous modern times, which are characterized by a growing sense of alienation and cynicism, major structural economic upheaval, urbanization, globalization, rapid developments in media, and so forth. It is hard enough to get a handle on these developments on their own; understanding the role they play in voting behaviour seems next to impossible. In many instances, these developments have challenged the theories, forcing voting researchers to re-examine how different factors mix together into a more complete and holistic understanding of what moves a particular person to cast a ballot for a particular party, and why sometimes that same person may change his or her mind in a subsequent election.

Indeed, making sense of the simple act of voting seems daunting, with so many factors to consider. Voting research has succeeded in explaining *most* voting behaviour, and it is even capable of explaining many exceptions to the rule, such as our four voters who appear to behave contrary to expectations. Research on voting behaviour spans a considerable amount of time, so while there is still much to learn, a great body of knowledge already exists. The four voters we examined above may deviate from expectations, but that is because we failed to take into account all other relevant factors.

The rest of this chapter provides an overview of the evolution of voting research and the contribution each theory has made to our understanding of voting behaviour. It includes a brief discussion of seminal works from the United States, which is where most voting research hails from, and from Canada.

Demographics

An explanation of voting behaviour according to membership in demographic groups formed the first important body of work related to electoral research. The Columbia School perspective, named after the university that hosted the study, considered that for the most part, a person's vote choice is determined long *before* the start of a campaign (Lazarfeld, Berelson, and Gaudet 1948). People who belong to certain demographic groups predictably and consistently support certain parties. For example, African-Americans overwhelmingly support the Democratic Party whereas Southern whites overwhelmingly support the Republican Party.

This model points to mobilization as a key determinant of voting behaviour. People who belong to certain demographic groups tend to associate with others in the same group, forming a social network that can be easily mobilized by community leaders. These social networks make it difficult to convert voters.

Later research adds a psychological dimension to the explanation of voting behaviour. Membership in any one demographic group implies *socialization*. People are socialized into a particular milieu, and acquire the traits and attitudes that predominate in that context. Children grow up in households headed by parents who traditionally follow the same religion, and often belong to the same ethnic group and social class. Parents also typically share similar values (which is presumably why they married) and, by extension, political preferences. These values and political preferences are transmitted to offspring, and are reinforced if shared by neighbours and other members of the community. Consequently, affiliations people have with political parties are deeply ingrained, leading voters to remain loyal to those parties toward which they were socialized into identifying.[1]

Canadian voters also fit neatly into various demographic categories. Researchers have found that the following demographic categories are very important to voting behaviour: region, ethnicity, religion, and gender. Class, too, has been studied, but findings suggest that class has far less of an impact on vote choice. Let's examine each category in more detail.

Region

Region is perhaps one of the most stable predictors of vote choice (Gidengil et al. 1999). Where you live in Canada goes a long way toward explaining the party you prefer. For example, the Liberals do better in Ontario than in Saskatchewan, and the Conservatives are stronger in Alberta compared with Quebec.

When a party does well in a region, it does *very* well, and generally it continues to do well for a long time. For example, most of the seats in Quebec went to the Liberals from the time the party had been led by Wilfrid Laurier in the 1890s until the large electoral sweep of the Progressive Conservatives under Brian Mulroney in the 1984 and 1988 elections (a pattern reminiscent of John Diefenbaker's breakthrough in Quebec in 1958). Since the 1990s, the Bloc Québécois have held most of the seats in Quebec. We can find similar patterns of regional-level party dominance elsewhere, which tempts us to assume that we can predict how people will vote simply by knowing where they live. A glance at the electoral map suggests that the Conservatives can count on nearly all the seats in the Prairies, while the Liberals have a lock on Toronto, save a few seats held by the NDP. But even in so-called strongholds, many voters cast a ballot for a party that is not regionally strong. In Quebec, for instance, 38 percent of the votes in 2008 were cast for the Bloc Québécois, with the remainder—the majority— dispersed among other parties (for example, 22 percent for the Conservatives, 24 percent for the Liberals, 12 percent for the NDP). And within any one riding, rarely does a candidate win with more than 50 percent of the vote. But the overall trend does suggest that voters in a particular region have a strong tendency to lean the same way.

Why is that? What is so special about region that influences voting preference? While no one disputes the relevance of region as a determinant of the vote, there is no consensus on an explanation. Regional political culture has been cited as a possible cause.

Regional Political Culture

Political culture can be defined as a set of generally shared broad principles, values, and assumptions about expectations of politics. These attributes are transmitted through socialization, that is, through the influence of parents, schools, peers, literature, the media, and so forth. Culture defines what a society believes to be a legitimate course of action. One can analogize political culture as the "personality" of a society. In fact, our individual personalities incorporate elements of political culture. Our personality defines how we behave in a particular situation; political culture defines how we respond to a particular political situation.

This social-psychological notion of voting behaviour has a long history. The empirical study of political culture goes back to the years following the Second World War, when political scientists wondered aloud why highly advanced societies, such as Germany, could fall into the hands of brutal dictators. Could there be something about the personality of Germans, the way they were raised, that led them to regard Nazism as a legitimate response to the political and economic crisis of the 1930s? Gabriel Almond and Sidney Verba's *The Civic Culture* (1963) reports findings of a cross-national survey of individuals in Germany, Britain, the United States, Italy, and Mexico. Their early study developed a typology of three cultures: *the parochial culture*, in which individuals hardly consider or think about the state and may even view it with some disdain; *the subject culture*, in which individuals are aware of the state but hold no expectations to participate in political deliberations (typical of an authoritarian regime); and *the participant culture*, in which individuals are aware of the state and expect to play some part in its decisions. While no one society is purely any of these cultures, Britain and the United States exemplify a more participant culture.

Almond and Verba's seminal work led to considerable research on political culture, which has produced diverse answers to the same general question: Do societies reflect political "personality" traits that explain why people behave the way they do, and, more concretely, vote the way they do?

Few people in Canada hold anti-democratic values; within our democratic political culture subcultures do exist, each with a different view of politics. Some of these differences coincide with the general views of political parties. In other words, some attributes of culture "bond" with the values projected by different parties. Subcultures need not exist in geographical terms. Members of the Internet generation will tell you that they belong to virtual communities of like-minded individuals who share similar values, beliefs, attitudes, dreams, and so forth, but who live in different cities and countries. But geographically defined subcultures hold a special place in Canadian politics as political parties that "bond" with a particular subculture can more easily mobilize potential voters who live generally close to each other. A province is one convenient aggregation of such a subculture.

Quebec is perhaps the province that best exemplifies a provincially defined subculture within Canada. The phrase "distinct society" has been captured by nationalist Quebeckers, but the phrase can easily apply to many other parts of Canada.[2] While Quebec may have institutional features that render it different from the rest of Canada, one can argue that a diversity of political cultures exists across Canada (Simeon and Elkins 1974).

The Hartzian perspective is a classic take on regional political culture (Hartz 1955; Horowitz 1966, 1978). Louis Hartz studied the "new world" societies such as Canada, the United States, South America, and Australia. Each society traces its origins to European colonists, and thus, can trace its culture back to these roots. Different parts of Canada were populated by different waves of migration. The first wave came from feudal France in the 1500s, with many settlements in and around Quebec City and beyond forming what was then New France. After New France fell to the British in 1763, migrants settled into other areas and established the social framework for societies that include Ontario. The American Revolution in the 1770s saw a migration of what now can be considered refugees, British loyalists fleeing the American colonies amid threat of persecution. They settled primarily along the Canadian shores of the

St. Lawrence River and also in Atlantic Canada. Meanwhile, within British North America that is now Canada, migrants from Britain continued to arrive. From 1815 to 1850, about 1 million settlers from Britain arrived in Canada, most of whom settled into what is now Ontario. The migration from Britain occurred during an era when liberalism and the ideals of a free market dominated political thought in Europe.

The result was a society with fairly diverse ideological fragments. Each major migratory wave brought with it fragments of the dominant culture at that time. Early settlers in New France brought with them the dominant ideas and cultural norms that defined feudal France; British settlers brought with them the ideas and cultural norms that defined the emerging liberal revolution; Loyalists fleeing the American Revolution brought with them the ideas and cultural norms that defined an earlier "Tory" era. These cultural fragments took root in new places, spawning a society with norms, institutions, and ideas that reflected the ideas that defined the societies from where (and when) settlers departed. As a result, Quebec, Ontario, New Brunswick, as well as other provinces each characterize different cultural norms that can be traced back to these originating fragments.

The diversity of political cultures, particularly the natural conflict between "Tory" and "liberal" ideologies, permitted a dynamic that allowed socialism to emerge as a synthesis (Horowitz 1966, 1978). For this reason, Canada has seen the rise of a modest socialist movement in the form of the Co-operative Commonwealth Federation, founded in 1932, which offered a socialist response to the Great Depression. The party later became the more moderate New Democratic Party in 1961, which has since remained a fixture of the opposition benches in the House of Commons. In contrast, the European experience has seen social-democratic parties displace centrist parties, and left-of-centre parties now regularly occupy office. In Canada, the dominance of the Tory and liberal fragments seem to express themselves quite effectively through the Conservative and Liberal parties, respectively, with the NDP never quite able to emerge as a viable governing party. On this score, the NDP has not even been able to attain the same status as some of the other "third parties" that have sprouted, mostly as a response to regional discontent. One such third party was the Progressives (not to be confused with the Progressive Conservatives) in the early part of the 20th century. This Western-based party captured a quarter of the seats in the House of Commons and decimated the Conservative Party's electoral base. More recently, the Bloc Québécois in 1993 and the Reform Party in 1997 won enough seats in their respective regional strongholds to become the official opposition. The NDP never attained such success, with a nationwide social-democratic movement unable to compete against strong regionally based flare-ups.

While performance at the federal level is somewhat constrained, the NDP and the social-democratic Parti Québécois have succeeded provincially, but it is unclear whether any socialist tendency among the electorate propelled these parties to power or whether it was factors related to government performance. The PQ's rise to power in the 1976 Quebec election occurred after the governing Liberals faced severe labour unrest and within a context of rising support for separatism (Fraser 1984; McRoberts and Posgate 1984). Federally, many Quebec voters have thrown their support behind the Bloc Québécois since the 1990s, but not necessarily because of the BQ's left-of-centre views. The Bloc Québécois's support derives from its nationalist appeals following the 1990 failure of the Meech Lake Accord, which, had it been ratified, would have addressed some of Quebec's traditional demands. When support for sovereignty waned recently in Quebec, the beneficiaries were the Conservatives!

The same pattern explains the unique cultural norms of other provinces, such as Saskatchewan and Alberta, two neighbouring provinces, with the former influenced by European fragments and the latter by fragments of American settlers (Wiseman 1981, 1996). Saskatchewan can accommodate ideas of state intervention (which is why the NDP does well there) whereas Alberta regards the state as an intervening obstacle to progress (which is why Conservatives and "populist" parties do well there). The Progressives, Social Credit, Reform (later Alliance), and even the Cooperative Commonwealth Federation (later the NDP) all had their origins in the Prairies, a region of Canada with a political culture that is more conducive to the development of an ideologically based party that is dissonant with the prevailing parties in Central Canada.

While fragment theory gives some insight into the regional fractionalization of Canadian voting, it is not a complete and perfect explanation.

First, migration to Canada has not stopped. Canada has seen wave after wave of immigrants to the point that Canada's popular image of itself is as a country of immigrants. The continual inflow of migrants brings new "fragments" that make it difficult for any one dominant political culture to take hold. In addition, the countries and regions of origin have shifted considerably. The original waves of settlement from France and Britain made way for other European immigrants, and now non-European immigrants. What is particularly interesting about immigrants from these more recent waves is their propensity to support the Liberal Party, for reasons that are not obvious. This topic is examined in more detail in a later section.

Second, the idea of provincial political cultures can only go so far. Other political cultures exist in provinces, and they produce distinctive voting patterns as well (Henderson 2004). The most obvious example is the difference between urban and rural voters. Toronto and Montreal are more alike than Toronto and North Bay. In fact, some parts of Ontario resemble some parts of New Brunswick! Is there an "urban" culture and a "rural" culture? If yes, do these cultures produce distinctive ideological norms that lead people to align themselves with particular parties? What is an "urban" ideology? Here, the answers are not all that clear. It just may be that individuals vote less according to ideological views that germinated from some distant cultural fragment and more according to proximate, short-term concerns that touch on issues and problems prevalent in their region. For instance, public transit is a far more important issue to people who live in cities than to people in rural areas, and public transit is also favoured by parties of the left. Conversely, gun control is more controversial in rural areas, where hunters are not only more numerous, but farmers often rely on firearms to ward off predators from their livestock. Consequently, rural voters tend to oppose restrictions on gun ownership, while urban voters, faced with a steady diet of firearm-related crimes, tend to favour more restrictions.

Third, despite the previous points, regional political cultures may exist, and these cultures may produce distinctive regional ideologies. But do political parties pay attention and distinguish themselves accordingly? A solid argument can be made that Canadian political parties generally avoid taking a distinctive ideological stand. Part of the reason is the brokerage party system, where successful parties strike (that is, broker) various broad coalitions across the country to secure blocks of votes. Blocks can be defined regionally (for example, the "Western vote"), ethnically (for example, French voters), or along other broad dimensions. Consequently, a party that wins an election does so by bringing together into one large electoral "tent" different groups of voters with different ideological views, but the "tent" rarely includes ideologically charged discussions.

Ethnicity

Ethnicity is a basic demographic trait that defines a person's membership in a greater social whole. It has also been the basis of many violent political conflicts. Civil wars and genocides are frequently about ethnically defined social divisions, or cleavages. In a democratic setting such as Canada's, ethnic divisions can express themselves in the form of troublesome political movements, but often they meld into the existing party system, in a predictable pattern.

The most predictable pattern is the division between the two founding ethnic groups in Canada. The English and the French had, and to a great extent still have, distinctive voting preferences. While the English traditionally have lent more support to the Conservative Party, the French have lent more support to the Liberal Party. This pattern has not been unbreakable, but it has remained a fixture of Canadian politics right up to the emergence of the Bloc in Quebec, after which many francophones in Quebec aligned more with that party than with the Liberals.

However, when one looks only at federalist francophone Quebeckers (and even francophones outside of Quebec), the traditional high support for Liberals persists. Why this pattern emerged in Canada has a lot to do with history. At Confederation, the traditional lifestyle of Quebec's Catholic and "Tory" culture fit nicely with the Conservative Party's ideals (Underhill 1935). However, a series of setbacks, such as Louis Riel's hanging, left the Conservative Party in tatters among the French.

Louis Riel, a Métis who helped found the province of Manitoba, led a rebellion against the Canadian government in 1885, partly motivated by concern over French language rights. He was captured and later hanged for treason. Many French Canadians saw this execution as an attack against them, and consequently perceived the Conservative Party as an English imperialist party with intolerance for the French.

Meanwhile, in 1887 Wilfrid Laurier became the leader of the Liberal Party, which he quickly set out to reorganize. A Quebec-born and Montreal-educated French-speaking political leader, he was able to promote the Liberal Party effectively among French-speaking voters, particularly in Quebec. Support from this block of voters helped the Liberals win their first majority government in 1896. Quebec support also remained secure for the Liberals, right up to the early 1980s, helping the party dominate Canadian politics and establishing the Liberal Party of Canada as one of the most successful parties in the democratic world.

Another block of voters with a distinctive voting pattern is immigrants. Canadian Election Study respondents whose mother tongue is neither English nor French, the so-called allophones, have consistently and overwhelmingly supported the Liberals. For example, in the 1970s, 60 percent of the allophone vote went to the Liberals. In the 1980s, the Liberals still had an edge, although the Progressive Conservative Party's electoral gains under Brian Mulroney helped narrow that edge to 54 percent in 1984. In 1988, allophones were equally likely to have voted for one major party as the other. In the 1990s, the allophone vote returned to traditional patterns, with more than 45 percent of this group's support going to the Liberals. This pattern persisted in subsequent elections. Although allophones in 2006 threw more of their support, 41 percent, to Stephen Harper's Conservatives, 37 percent (still a substantial margin) supported the Liberals under Paul Martin. Voter #2, described at the beginning of the chapter, may follow this pattern. Italians, who have normally voted Liberal, like most immigrant voters, have begun to show greater diversity in their political preferences.

Outside of Quebec, the ethnic group that provides the largest support to the Liberals remains the French: 44 percent voted for the Liberals in 2006. The Conservatives continue to receive strong support from the English, but in 2006 new inroads were made in support from non-French and non-English voters: more than 47 percent voted for the Conservatives. In addition, visible minorities, normally Liberal voters, have begun to consider other parties, such as the NDP and Conservatives (Gidengil et al. 2009).

The role ethnicity plays in Canadian elections remains an open question (Blais 2005). While francophone and immigrant voters typically throw their support behind the Liberals, the reasons why are not all that obvious. Is the Liberal Party more pro-immigrant than the Conservative Party? Some may perceive that as being the case, but there is no evidence that the Liberals have a much better track record on the treatment of immigrants compared with the Conservatives. Nonetheless, immigrant voters do show some tendency to regard the Liberals as the party most able to address concerns that are important to them (Kim and Perrella 2008).

A major obstacle in researching immigrant voters is the survey method; most of what we know about voting behaviour relies on election surveys. While the Canadian Election Survey series is a rich mine of information, sample sizes for any one election year number around 2,000 to 3,000, with a small proportion of these respondents being immigrants. This makes it difficult to study immigrant voters closely and to establish clear generalizations.

Religion

Religion rivals region as an important driver of voting behaviour. Catholics and non-Christians, in particular, tend to support the Liberals in high proportions whereas

Protestants are more divided, albeit showing a greater tendency to support the Conservatives. Why these tendencies arose does not lend itself to easy answers (Blais 2005). Although we can make some sense of region, religion tends to confound.[3]

In Canada, the Catholic and Protestant pattern of Liberal and Conservative voting is often ascribed to tensions between the rival religions of an earlier time. The fall of New France came with harsh British rule to outlaw the French culture and its Catholic faith. Eventually, this policy was reversed, but some antipathy between the two general Christian groups may have persisted. And even after any ill feelings had long dissipated, Catholics and Protestants remain fairly consistent in their distinctive voting patterns. Why?

One can argue that the English/French/immigrant electoral divide in Canada can be summarized by religion. That is, the main reason the English have traditionally shown greater support for the Conservatives is the predominance of Protestantism among the English, while Liberal support among the French may be connected to the fact that most francophones are Catholic. Immigrant support for the Liberals may also be tied to the fact that most immigrants, especially the newer waves, are not Christian. Perhaps there is some truth to this argument, as the tie of religion and politics is never fully severed, even after centuries of attempts to throw the "church" out of politics and to turn public institutions into fully secular bodies. Although it is possible for institutions to "secularize," it is not equally possible to force voters to forget their religious ties.

Many countries have an electorate that is split over religion. One prominent example is the United States, in which the "Christian right" has come to dominate the Republican Party and, during the presidency of George W. Bush, obtain some success in dominating the political agenda. In Europe, many countries have parties with clearly religious names and mandates, such as the Christian Democrats. Electoral divides occurred during the secularization of Europe, with a markedly ideological dimension. Seculars tended to side with left-of-centre social democratic parties whereas the religious tended to side with conservative Christian parties. The same patterns exist today.

But Canada was not founded by Quakers. It did not undergo a Reformation. Canada's founding was, if anything, very civil, very legal. In addition, distinct Catholic-Protestant voting behaviour is not merely an artifact of the French–English linguistic divide: Catholics in English Canada are also pro-Liberal (Blais et al. 2002).

In fact, attempts to explain, or explain away, the religious cleavage have succeeded only when one takes into account socialization (Irvine 1974). Attitudes that led to religion-based antipathies between the two Christian groups were transmitted from generation to generation and from parents to their children, even though the religion-based reasons for the conflict are no longer very relevant.

Other explanations suggest that religion emerges as a salient vote determinant when other factors are weak. Matthew Mendelsohn and Richard Nadeau (1997) have found that religion yields a null effect on the vote when one takes into account exposure to the media, at least as it pertains to the Catholic–Protestant divide. Religion becomes less important politically among those who consume a lot of media. Richard

BOX 11.1
Election Surveys: Seeing the Big Picture

Knowledge of voters generally is gained from surveys, a technique that has become a familiar part of any election campaign. While public opinion polls commissioned by various news organizations ask few questions and are mostly interested in knowing which party is in the lead, more academic surveys employ batteries of questions to identify the causal dynamics of voting behaviour. Surveys include questions that measure political attitudes, values, and a host of other dimensions.

What is remarkable about the survey technique is that with a few thousand participants, it can paint a fairly complete picture of a country's electorate, the population of which can number in the millions. But this remarkable ability to reflect accurately the general population depends on several factors.

Key among these factors is the random selection of participants. Random selection prevents bias and ensures that opinions are representative of the population. One technique used in telephone surveys is random-digit dialing, where a computer randomly generates telephone numbers to determine who will be invited to participate.

Once randomness is assured, the mathematical principle of the Central Limit Theorem enters the picture. This theorem proves why a sample of about 1,000 people is usually enough to draw fairly accurate generalizations of a population that may number in the millions. While it is too cumbersome to describe how this theorem works, it is grounded in the assumption of randomness and follows probability theory.

From a randomly gathered sample, estimates can be calculated. For instance, if 38 percent of a sample of 1,000 voters indicated that they would vote for the Liberal Party, does that mean that 38 percent of *all* Canadian voters would do the same? Here is another question: if the same sample of 1,000 voters show men more likely to vote Conservative than women, would a similar pattern emerge if we studied the entire Canadian electorate? With sufficiently large samples, we can answer both questions with high confidence, expressed by a margin of error. So, while a sample of 1,000 suggests support for the Liberals at 38 percent, we can be fairly confident (95 percent sure) that Canada-wide that level of support is expected to range ± 3 percentage points, that is, anywhere between 35 and 41 percent. We are not 100 percent sure that this range is correct, but 95 percent certainty is usually good enough.

Calculating the margin of error is a key objective of analysis based on the Central Limit Theorem. The wider the margin, the less accurate the estimates. While small samples produce wide margins, a remarkable property of the Central Limit Theorem is that a sample of 1,000 is usually accurate, with increases in sample sizes improving margins of error ever so slightly.

However, samples in election surveys designed by academic researchers generally number in the 2,000 to 4,000 range. This permits a study of subsamples. For example, one can use a Canadian Election Study's national sample of about 2,000 voters to compare how voters in Atlantic Canada differ from those in the Prairies, with subsamples numbering in the hundreds.

Granted, analysis based on such smaller subsamples produces estimates with wider margins of errors. This is not always a problem. Even samples that number in the hundreds can sometimes produce important findings. And again, we feel confident about the validity of these findings simply because everything was done to ensure the sample is free from bias. Randomness achieves this objective, and achieving randomness is the most difficult part of survey design.

Johnston (1985) found that the "religious cleavage" sustained its link to the vote when it was geographically salient. For example, Catholics voted like Catholics when they resided in areas with large Catholic populations. But when Catholics lived in areas not marked by large Catholic populations, class considerations grew in importance along the union/non-union cleavage (see also Pammett 1991). In a more recent test of that hypothesis, Paul Bélanger and Munroe Eagles (2006) found similar effects, especially with respect to Catholic concentrations, with the union/non-union cleavage having a little less support.

If these findings point to any explanation, it is to the degree to which socialization continues to regenerate antiquated cleavages and party identifications. Those exposed to influences other than their pastor or their neighbourhood are less prone to behave according to patterns suggested by their religious affiliation. In other words, it is not religion and religious doctrine that propels one to vote a certain way but the simple fact that without some sort of override, people default to predispositions that have already been etched into their collective memories.

The Catholic-Protestant divide may have been temporarily bridged in 2006, with Catholics outside Quebec voting evenly for the Liberals and the Conservatives, and Catholics in 2008 leaning even more toward the Conservatives (Gidengil et al. 2009). Even non-Christians appear to have shifted away from their "default" leanings, with their support for the Liberals in 2006 at 27 percent, behind the 33 percent of non-Christians that had voted Conservative—results that might reflect an anti-Liberal antipathy in light of the sponsorship scandal. But among Protestant voters, there was no shift; they supported the Conservatives in fairly large proportions, although members of the more Evangelical denominations were far more likely to support the Conservatives than members of more "mainstream" Protestant denominations such as the Anglican, Presbyterian, and United churches (Kay, Perrella, and Brown 2009).

Gender

One sweeping generalization about gender as a vote determinant is that women are seen as more supportive of social programs, and not necessarily entirely convinced about the merits of free-market capitalism as the solution to economic and social problems (Gidengil 1995; Gidengil et al. 2005). This so-called gender gap explains why at present women are less likely than men to support the Conservatives and more likely than men to vote Liberal or NDP. In 2006, 36 percent of women voters cast a ballot for Harper's Conservatives, while the proportion among males was much higher, 44 percent. Similar results are apparent for 2008, although the Conservatives may have lost some ground among men, but male voters are still far more likely than women to have voted for Harper.[4]

But an aversion to parties of the right has not always characterized female voters. Prior to the 1980s, women were generally more *conservative* than men (Inglehart and Norris 2003). This inclination was true not only for Canadian women but also for women throughout much of the industrialized world. Several reasons may account for it. As noted by Elisabeth Gidengil (2007), women tended to occupy roles as domestic housewives and tended to be active with the church. Together, these factors combined to constrain the influence of views contrary to the dominant "masculine" political culture.[5]

But Gidengil (2007) also notes that the nature of the gender gap should not focus exclusively—or even primarily—on women, because whatever gap that has emerged recently has a lot to do with changing voting patterns among *men*. The rise of the industrial economy employed many men in trades and on unionized assembly lines. Since membership in a union facilitates support for union-friendly parties, it is therefore not at all surprising to see more men than women support parties such as the NDP. Organized labour has declined in strength over the last few decades. Alongside emerged the "new right" parties, with their anti-union, anti-immigrant, and anti-welfare policy stances. These stances resonate with men who are increasingly vulnerable in an economic climate that offers few opportunities for high-paying jobs (Fieschi and Heywood 2004). As a result, men tilted right. One notable example is the recent rise of the Reform Party in Canada.[6] The Reform Party emerged in Canada as a regional party, but its supporters were more likely to be men. The Canadian Election Study shows that about 60 percent of Reform/Alliance voters were men in 1993. This trend continued into the 2000 election, when Reform changed its name to the Alliance Party. In more recent elections, men are still more likely than women to support the Conservative Party, although the gender gap has narrowed, with 2004 showing an anomalous—and from all accounts, temporary—reversal, with Conservative voters being mostly female.

But another pattern unfolded throughout this period. Women increasingly joined the workforce, which exposed them to economic cycles. They did not take up unionized, high-paying jobs but instead found work in the growing but lower-paid services sector. As a result, and as governments restrained welfare programs, women often found themselves in economically vulnerable situations. Naturally, they became more inclined to support parties that addressed those concerns. Whether the Liberal Party has a successful track record on addressing economic hardship is a matter for debate, but clearly the Conservative parties (and, prior to them, the Reform/Alliance) took a very different position on the state's role in the economy compared with the NDP, which typically favours the expansion of welfare programs.

Class

The history of political science is often intertwined with the history of class struggles: revolutions, the emergence of communism, and the Cold War all have class as a central theme. Marxists and other thinkers of the "left" would have no problem with this assertion, but in Canada explaining voting behaviour based on class has been a challenge. While class-based voting has been detected in Canada (Alford 1963; Kay 1977; Lambert et al. 1987), it is nowhere nearly as significant as it is in many other industrialized countries. Yes, the NDP is a socialist party that (sometimes) appeals to class, but the party has never attained much more than third-party status, and electoral gains have often come about after the party downplayed its socialist and class-oriented program to resemble a middle-of-the-road party. Why does class matter so little in Canada? Let's examine three possibilities.

First, as mentioned earlier, the brokerage style of Canada's political parties makes it difficult to demarcate voters along class lines. Picking favourites along class lines is a good way to lose an election. Given that parties make no outright claims to stand for this or that class, voters, consequently, align themselves with parties for reasons other than class.

Second, perhaps the brokerage party system itself is the reason class matters so little (Brodie and Jenson 1988). As noted earlier, parties broker coalitions along many different lines (ethnic, regional, religious), but avoid class. The avoidance of class could reflect the fact that the two major parties in Canada embrace the main principles of capitalism, so there is no need to stake out political ground along owner-worker lines. As a result, campaigns pay little attention to class interests.

Third, Canada's defining cleavage structures are more ethnically and regionally based. Lipset and Rokkan (1967) point to two possible "revolutions" that can develop cleavages in a country. An "industrial revolution" produces a capitalist system that pits owners against workers, a classic class struggle. A "national revolution" leads to the emergence and consolidation of nation states. The history of states is not always a pretty story of the coming together of people who share similar views, practise similar religions, and speak the same language. If anything, the history of nation states is the complete opposite. It is a history of conquest and violent repressions, where people in different regions were told to speak a particular language (other languages and dialects were outlawed), practise a particular religion, and so on. Forced assimilation may have had some measure of success, but almost every country has its fair share of regional separatist movements, such as the Basques, the Catalans, the Corsicans, Scots, and so forth.[7] These movements date back to a national revolution that failed to assimilate everyone, consequently leaving behind a region with a completely different set of ideas that are often at odds with the central government. Canada is not much different. Conflict in Canada is more defined by its national revolution than by an industrial revolution. That could be why regional divisions, particularly when they overlap linguistic and religious clusters, are more important to the vote than are ideological or class differences.

Party Identification

The preceding look at sociological and demographic factors suggests that membership in any one group is not, on its own, enough to explain the vote. First, people can belong to many primary groups, and it is not always easy to determine which primary group is central to the vote, and how "cross-cutting memberships" attenuate the vote decision process. A *cross-cutting membership* is defined as membership in more than one primary group. For example, a person can be Catholic, living in Alberta, female, and of Irish ancestry. Cross-cutting memberships among voters are common, and how a voter resolves these potential opposing "pulls" is not obvious. Recall Voter #4, a somewhat religious Protestant woman living in southwestern Ontario. Of all of her cross-cutting memberships, perhaps being female is more important to her support for the NDP. Perhaps her other attributes, such as her religion (and religiosity!) are less important.

In addition, membership in a sociological group comes with a package of thoughts and ideas that may align more with one particular party. When this occurs, psychological attachments develop that persist well beyond the relevance of the original reasons. For example, conflicts between Protestants and Catholics have long been relegated to the dustbin of Canada's history. Yet, Catholics and Protestants still vote in distinct ways. Why?

While mobilization is certainly a factor that explains how membership in particular groups can align voters around certain parties, a lot of the evidence suggests that the nexus between socio-demographic factors and party choice often hinges on attitudes and values. In other words, region, ethnicity, religion, and gender are electorally important because of how membership in these groups affects how we learn about and understand politics, and how we perceive various parties in light of that understanding. Voting preferences do not just magically appear. They are formed through socialization, be it through influence from parents, schools, peers, and so forth. One grows "into" what is referred to as "party identification," a central concept in voting behaviour studies.

Party identification can be defined as the party with which one most closely associates at a psychological level. This is not too dissimilar from sports fans who identify with a particular team. They don't just "follow" or support a team, they genuinely feel a membership to some greater family, and respond with a shared abhorrence toward a historical rival. The Maple Leafs–Canadiens hockey rivalry is a clear sports example, where the fan base for each team is strong and persistent. Even if fans move away from their home city to a rival city, they retain that identification: that is, even if Canadiens fans move to Toronto, they remain loyal to Montreal. Party identification is akin to this phenomenon. Partisans identify with a party and remain loyal to that party through thick and thin, regardless of the party's fortunes nationally, and regardless of the party's viability locally.

An important attribute of party identification is the manner in which it can define the relative stability of voting behaviour. The concept emerged out of election studies conducted at the University of Michigan (Campbell et al. 1960), and has henceforth carried the name the Michigan School. However, as we all know, and as the opening of this chapter suggests, stability is not synonymous with constancy. Voters who identify with a particular party can switch, even if only temporarily. However, it appears that Canadian voters switch more frequently and with greater ease than the theory would expect.

Why Canadian voters switch party identification has attracted significant debate and inquiry. Is partisanship in Canada weak? Related to the first question, is partisanship in Canada unstable? Finally, is weak and unstable partisanship attributable to forces such as changes in attitudes, values, and socioeconomic conditions that have seen voters in other countries detach from party loyalties? Let's examine each of these questions.

The Strength of Partisanship

Partisanship is generally measured with survey questions that ask respondents to select the party with which they identify most and to indicate how strongly they feel about that party. One of the earliest studies of Canadian voting has shown that for the most part, partisanship in Canada is weak. Several reasons account for this finding.

First, Canada's brokerage party system constrains the development of strong, durable partisan ties. Voters are more likely to hold strong identification with parties that have clear ideological positions. This is true of the current Conservative Party and the NDP (Merolla, Stephenson, and Zechmeister 2008). But typically, Canadian parties optimize their chances of winning elections by forging widespread national coalitions across many groups, and this approach makes it hard for partisan attachments to form (Clarke et al. 1979, 1984, 1991, 1996). As a result, Canadians derive their ephemeral party identifications from evaluations of party leaders and whatever issues the parties raise during a campaign.

Second, different configurations of the party system at the federal and provincial levels make it possible for a strong national party to have weak regional bases and vice versa. The Liberal Party struggles to gain acceptance in the West. The NDP struggles as a national party, although it can gain seats in various pockets around the country. However, the BC Liberal Party and the Saskatchewan NDP are by no means failures. Discrepancies between national and provincial party systems encourage voters to identify with one party nationally, but a different party provincially (Uslaner 1989, 1990). This "split" identification may give the impression that, overall, voters hold weak and contradictory partisan attachments. But in fact, it may mask a stronger partisan leaning, one that takes into account not only the party label but also the party's regional viability.

The Stability of Partisanship

The instability of partisanship among Canadian voters has been noted in very early research. It appears that Canadians change party identification quite readily. At the very least, partisanship is more volatile among Canadian voters than among American voters (Kornberg and Clarke 1992; see also Stephenson, Scotto, and Kornberg 2004, and Stewart and Clarke 1998).

While it is not rare for people to switch their votes from one election to the next (although this should not happen too regularly), survey research shows that voters also switch party identification. As noted by John Meisel (1973), both voting and partisanship move together, opening the possibility for the partisanship/vote relationship to be, in fact, reversed: people's partisan identifications are justified *after* the vote choice.

While the brokerage party system may account for some of this volatility, another plausible reason exists. Early American research that developed into what is now known as the concept of party identification took place in a fairly peaceful, ideologically free period, namely the period before the 1960s and 1970s. The experience of the Second World War, which marked the end of a very ideologically charged period of upheaval, may have shaken voters and parties and caused them to think and act more pragmatically. The post-war consensus of Keynesian economic doctrine also seems to have muted much of whatever remained of the ideological clashes. Keynesian economics, inspired by British economist John Maynard Keynes in his famous book *The General Theory of Employment, Interest and Money* (1936), is based on the idea that governments can play an important role in economic management. Government expenditures and taxes can stimulate or slow down the economy, as needed. This doctrine challenged the laissez-faire free-market economic thinking that dominated prior to the Great Depression, and offered a more attractive solution than the other alternative that was quickly gaining credibility: socialism. Socialism, communism, and other ideologies of the "left" blamed the Great Depression on the core principles of capitalism. This led to a "right" versus "left" political debate. In Canada, it was during the Great Depression that two new parties emerged: the right wing Social Credit and the left wing Co-operative Commonwealth Federation. Keynesianism mediated this conflict by providing a middle way. Government expenditures (for example, on building bridges and roads) can stimulate employment growth, thereby kick-starting a new economic growth cycle, all the while retaining the capitalist structure pretty much intact.

The success of Keynesianism undermined much of the credibility of both traditional laissez-faire and left wing political views. Even the NDP accepted the doctrine of Keynesianism. Consequently, parties hovered toward the centre, and voters tended to remain stable party loyalists, if only because there was no compelling reason to change.

But by the 1960s, many advanced industrial societies began to witness political upheaval. Partisan attachments became weaker, more unstable. It was around this time that Canadian researchers started to conduct election studies and, consequently, it was around this time that voters manifested contradictory behaviours. One possible reason for these behaviours was the rise of a new value system that challenged the notion of the political party as the key vehicle of democratic participation.

The Influence of Post-Material Forces

Since the politically turbulent 1960s, researchers have noted a shift in attitudes that cannot be easily attributed simply to "the times." A new generation emerged that did not look at politics quite the same way as their older cohorts, and this phenomenon carried across borders. The political activism that characterized the "hippy" movement in the United States had parallels in other Western countries. Inglehart (1977, 1990) took a closer look at this phenomenon and found that this baby-boom cohort, born in the years that followed the end of the Second World War, had noticeably distinct attitudes. Unlike their parents, members of this new cohort do not regard voting as the be all and end all of democratic participation. They do not hold the same level of respect for authority. More accurately, they do not hold the same level of blind deferential respect for authority. Instead, they eagerly challenge authority and hierarchical power structures. They challenge the political system by voting with their feet in the form of protest marches, petitions, sit-ins, and so forth. In addition, their expectations of the state are different. They demand that the state put more emphasis on "post-material" issues such as rights, the environment, and lifestyle instead of the more conventional and "material" issues of economic management, law and order, and national defence. In sum, this cohort exhibits an entirely different political culture, one that has not neatly jibed with the status quo.

Neil Nevitte (1996) found similar patterns among Canadian voters. Not only do Canadians reflect post-material attributes, they are also less likely to hold party identifications, a trend with parallels in other countries (Dalton 2002). In fact, one of the main consequences of post-materialism is the corrosion of party identification. While previous cohorts had little problem latching on to one party and remaining loyal, newer cohorts are more prone to shop around. But this is not due to the fickle nature of post-materialists. Since post-materialists are less likely to regard voting as the main and sole means of political participation, they are less prone to invest as much psychological energy in any one party. Instead, they may remain more loyal to certain core ideals, and behave accordingly.

Campaign Effects on Voting

Election campaigns are often portrayed as a competition for votes, similar to a free market of businesses out to attract potential buyers. Such a perspective suggests that voter conversion is possible: voters can potentially be persuaded to vote for a particular party, just as consumers can be persuaded to purchase a certain product. After all, voters, even stable partisans, can switch parties. Election polls during a campaign often show volatile swings in popular support for various parties, which suggests that voters are being persuaded back and forth. Were conversion and persuasion not possible, then why else would parties expend so much energy and resources on campaigning? Surely, there is more to a campaign than just mobilizing your own supporters.

Even if campaigns can dislodge a partisan voter to cast a ballot for another party, nothing suggests that a voter forever rejects the party she has grown accustomed to supporting. It only means that during a campaign, a flurry of activities and events can conspire to lead a voter to think twice. Perhaps she returns to her partisan leanings in the next election. But that is a different campaign, a different bundle of forces, and consequently a different vote calculus. Although many campaign-specific elements can affect voting behaviour, two are among the most influential, or at least the most talked about: issue salience and leader evaluations.

Issue Salience

Elections take place in a context. They are not simply an opportunity for voters to be reminded of their party loyalties. They are a test of each party's ability to respond to current pressing concerns and problems. The term *salience* is used to describe the perceived importance of an issue. For example, if more people become concerned about health care, this issue rises in salience. Election campaigns, then, become a fight over what issues the parties wish to see salient, and what issues they wish to see dormant. Despite such efforts, there are some issues that remain consistently salient.

The economy is certainly one of them. Economic conditions are generally a major driver of voting behaviour in just about every democratic election worldwide, with many voters looking at the state of the economy to determine whether the incumbent deserves to be re-elected or ousted (Lewis-Beck 1988). The prospect for such a link has produced an extensive body of research on "economic voting."[8]

While much of the research is based in the United States and other countries, research into Canadian economic voting has not been sparse, with the results fairly consistent with patterns found elsewhere (Nadeau and Blais 1995; Nadeau et al. 2000). In sum, when an election is held during a time of economic decline, voters tend to withdraw support from the incumbent and shift it toward the opposition. The link between economics and voting seems obvious. But a closer look shows that the relationship is not clear-cut.

First, we must distinguish whether we are talking about the national economy or a voter's personal "pocketbook" financial situation. Which one is more important? One would rationally expect changes to personal finances to have a greater effect on the vote than changes to the national economy (see, for example, Downs 1957), but the evidence does not bear this out. It appears that voters are more responsive to changes in *national* economic conditions, regardless of personal circumstances. This theory is called "sociotropic voting" (Brody and Sniderman 1977; Kinder and Kiewiet 1981).

While the consensus is that sociotropic voting is more widespread than pocketbook voting, there are instances in which personal finances emerge as more important. Welfare regimes in particular are noted for a higher level of pocketbook voting. Two reasons explain this effect. First, the predominant culture in places with relatively weak welfare regimes, such as Canada, Britain, and the United States, gives the impression that a person's economic gain flows from individual effort (Feldman 1982, 1985). But in northern European and Scandinavian societies, the state's greater role in economic matters provides a clearer connection between public policy and personal finances (Nannestad and Paldam 1995, 1997).

Second, economic voting can be backward looking ("retrospective") or forward looking ("prospective"). Both approaches have merit. In general, voters respond to changes in economic conditions that have taken place before election day (Fiorina, 1978), because information about the past is readily available and predictions hold some risk of being off target. Retrospective voting is more prevalent when voters are faced with a sitting incumbent who has an economic record to defend (Nadeau and Lewis-Beck 2001). The unemployment rate and a lagging economic indicator are very important to the vote (Nadeau and Blais 1993). For example, concerns over a rise in unemployment contributed to some of the lost votes incurred by the Liberals in the 1997 federal election (Nadeau et al. 2000). As for prospective voting, some debate exists over whether it's even possible, given that the future is unknown; perhaps the best a voter can do is look at a party's past record, assuming that it was in government. Prospective economic voting more commonly occurs in contexts in which *neither* candidate is a sitting incumbent, as was the case in the 2008 American presidential election (Nadeau and Lewis-Beck 2001).

During a campaign, different factors can contribute to the salience of an issue. Sometimes, an issue can be related to a contemporary event. For example, an election held during a time of urban violence and escalating gang violence will naturally lead voters and party leaders alike to talk about crime and guns. A case in point is the December 2005 Boxing Day shooting in downtown Toronto that resulted in the death of an innocent bystander, teenager Jane Creba. Despite statistics that clearly show a general long-term decline in violent crime in Canada, this incident, along with a string of other gang-related shootings in Toronto, raised the issues of both crime and gun control, causing the parties to provide some sort of response.

Other times, an issue can be strategically manipulated by party leaders and party strategists so that it becomes salient. For example, in 1988, the Liberals under John Turner decided, as a strategic move, to oppose the Canada–US Free Trade Agreement (Johnston et al. 1992) whereas the governing Conservatives under Mulroney were naturally in favour of it. Sometimes, an election gives the appearance of having only a single issue of contention. For example, government corruption was an important issue in the 2006 federal election, contributing to the loss of the Liberal Party and the election of the Conservative Party. But typically, elections are fought on several issue dimensions. Health care and the environment are two fairly recent issues that often compete with other issues (for example, the economy, crime, terrorism).

However, there are indications that no matter what issues parties and leaders try to push in a campaign, and no matter how cleverly crafted a negative ad, voters may not be fully attentive (Clarke et al. 1996). The reasons this is so may have more to do with the relatively low level of knowledge Canadians have about politics and political issues (Fournier 2002). In other words, for an issue to matter in an election, voters must be aware of it and consider it important. Despite assertions made by Downsians, it seems that only a small percentage of the population cares enough about elections to take into account issues as a means to determine which party to support (Mutz 1998).

Leader Evaluations

Canadian political parties are often defined by their leaders. For example, we hear about the "Chrétien Liberals" and the "Harper Conservatives." Political parties give a high amount of prominence to the person they select as leader. A discussion on why this is the case falls outside the parameters of this chapter. However, clearly the ascendency of the Prime Minister's Office (PMO) as *the* centre of power in Canada has turned the party leader into an individual with considerable influence. The public spectacle of Question Period in Parliament is generally viewed by citizens as the main (and perhaps *only*) functioning aspect of the Canadian government. However, this is far from the truth. As authors on Canadian government have noted (see, for example, MacIvor 2006, 300), the PMO has emerged as central to the governing process. The PMO is staffed by individuals appointed by the prime minister, and they are most definitely partisan to the PM's party. While members of the PMO are unelected, they hold significant power in that they have direct, daily contact with the prime minister, providing advice on numerous matters related to policy and day-to-day decisions. The PMO often directs the policy agenda that is imposed on Cabinet, which generally comprises elected members of Parliament.[9] Some regard this "presidential" model of governing as troublesome, arguing that decision-making power over the policy agenda has shifted away from elected members of Parliament and the public deliberations in the House of Commons to unelected prime ministerial appointees (often close friends) whose discussions are never held in public. All of this boils down to a considerably powerful role for the prime minister, and, by extension, for a party leader. A party leader is not just the spokesperson of a collective political movement, but the individual who, if elected as prime minister, will direct, perhaps even micromanage, key government decisions.

As a result, the vote often follows leader evaluations, and party strategists often focus campaign communication on the leader. There have been exceptions to this rule, such as the 1993 federal election. In the early 1990s, many Canadians thought Jean Chrétien's profile in Canada was generally weak (Nadeau and Blais 1995) and would therefore impede the Liberals' return to power. As a result, Liberal party strategists in the 1993 campaign focused attention away from Chrétien and directed it to the Liberal team, to indicate that the party's competencies should be recognized in other members, not just its leader. But this exception proves the rule. Since voters, by default, look to the leader as one of the main bases on which to decide whether to support a party, the Liberal message sought to minimize that default to raise the profile of the party.

Perhaps the most visible and concrete determinant of leadership evaluations is the much-hyped televised debate. Here, voters can see for themselves in an unfiltered context what each leader has to offer, and how each leader stands up to rivals. In many ways, the debates are often portrayed as a bout, with an expected winner and expected "knock-out" punches.

Indeed, some debates have proven somewhat influential in the vote. The leaders' debate during the 1988 campaign was dominated by the divisive issue of free trade. The Liberals decided to make free trade an election issue (Johnston, et al. 1992) and their leader, John Turner, used the televised debate as an opportunity to turn free trade into a hot-button issue that touched on threats to Canadian sovereignty and culture. Evidence suggests that this strategic decision succeeded in raising the Liberal vote, although it was not enough to turn the tide completely against the Progressive Conservatives, which were returned to office with another majority.

Influential debates, however, are rare. Debates, as a campaign event, are not likely to move voters much. If anything, debates are likely to improve the overall image of the party leaders, especially candidates who are less known (Blais and Perrella 2008). They are also likely to reinforce and mobilize partisans (Leduc and Price 1985) rather than convert voters. In other words, those who identify with a particular party are more likely to view the performance of their party leader favourably. This perception bias among partisans diminishes the ability of a debate to actually convert anyone.

Strategic Voting

Canada's plurality electoral system renders most voters as losers. Parties can win a majority of seats, thereby locking their hold on Parliament, with about 40 percent of the popular vote, and in some cases, even less than that. Within each riding, candidates generally need a similar proportion of votes, 40 percent, to secure a win. This tendency is not unusual, but a normal consequence in Canada. Only in a pure two-party or two-candidate race would a winner need a true majority of at least 50-percent-plus-one of the votes. Canada has a more diverse party system, and seats in Canada are contested by many candidates. In 2008, the average number of candidates per riding was 5.2. While typically there are no more than two viable candidates,[10] the fact remains that few winners are elected with a majority. How would a voter respond to this situation when she would like to support a candidate with little hope of winning? What should a Liberal voter do in a Saskatchewan riding where the Conservative candidate is bound to win, with the NDP candidate in second place? What would a Conservative voter do in downtown Toronto? How about an NDP voter in east-end Montreal? Or how about a supporter of one of the many marginal and fringe parties, such as the Libertarian, Communist, Family Law, and Green parties? When voters realize that their preferred candidate is bound to lose, they have a choice: vote sincerely, that is, vote for their first choice that leads to a wasted ballot (for example, a ballot that has no effect on the final result) or vote for whichever candidate is likely to beat that one candidate they dislike most. That second option is referred to as strategic voting.

Strategic voting is one of the possible scenarios within the body of rational choice voter research. It assumes that voters have enough information about the relative competitiveness of the candidates and parties, and also that they know how they feel about each one. Therefore, such rational voters would be able to make the right choice to optimize utility (that is, gains) and minimize losses. Gains are defined as the net benefit of having a particular candidate winning, that is, the net benefit in feeling good about the choice and its possible ultimate result.

The problem with strategic voting is that it assumes voters have a great deal of information. Not only would voters need to know the relative prospects of each of the major parties, they would also need to know how they feel about each one. This approach assumes that voters know their own interests, which candidate is most likely to advance those interests, and which candidate is most likely to get in the way of those interests. We already noted research that suggests Canadians have a relatively low level of knowledge about politics and political issues (Fournier 2002). During the heat of a campaign, such information can become blurred. First, all of the major parties may give the appearance of being viable. Canvassing, all-candidates debates, and door-to-door campaigning give the impression that all candidates are alive and well, and ready for a fight. Second, all parties make all kinds of promises that either confuse voters or lead them to believe that parties spew exaggerated empty promises. Either way, it is difficult for voters to think and act strategically. And in fact, few do. Research has shown that a very miniscule percentage of the electorate engages in strategic voting (Blais et al. 2002; Nevitte et al. 2000). In 2004, 11 percent of voters claimed to have cast a strategic vote, reflecting strong efforts by the Liberals to encourage NDP voters to convert (Clarke et al. 2005). Most voters, it turns out, are quite prepared to vote sincerely, even when faced with the stark reality that such a vote will, at the end of the day, have no effect on the ultimate outcome. What else would explain why, in 2008, almost 10 percent of the electorate (that's 110,000 votes) voted for fringe parties or why 24 percent of Albertans voted for either the Liberals or NDP?

Conclusion

Let's return to our original four voters to explain their vote choices. If you recall, we had some prior expectations, which ultimately proved false, assuming that we placed a great deal of weight on the Columbia School perspective. How well can we explain individual vote choices based on relevant information obtained from their responses to survey questions?

1. Voter #1 is a Protestant male who lives in Alberta, with a total household income greater than $100,000. We expected him, an Albertan of higher income, to vote Conservative, but instead he voted Liberal. Even though he voted Liberal in 2004, he does not appear to be a Liberal partisan, or a partisan of any party. He is certainly not new to Alberta, having lived in his Calgary-area neighbourhood for at least ten years. But his top concerns are child care and the environment, two issues with which the Liberals sought to associate strongly in the 2006 campaign. Voter #1 is a clear case of issue-based voting, even though he is fully aware of the low prospect of the Liberal candidate winning in his riding (he pegged the riding as Conservative). While we can understand why he voted Liberal, why does he hold *no* partisan leanings, let alone weak ones? It is plausible that this voter questions the whole validity of partisanship, given that he was born in 1949, making him a baby boomer, and thus, a member of the post-material generation. Or, perhaps he is a member of a "mainstream" denomination, such as the Anglican Church, where support for the Liberal Party is not rare.

2. Voter #2, the Italian Canadian living in Toronto, was expected to vote Liberal, as do most Italians and most Torontonians. But instead, he voted Conservative. He is a fairly strong Conservative partisan, having voted Conservative in 2004, and identifying corruption and taxation as his two most important issues in the 2006 campaign. The first issue, corruption, surely caused him to turn away from the Liberals, while concerns about taxation naturally led him to the Conservatives, given their strong message about reducing the GST. Voter #2 felt the Conservatives were best able to handle both issues, making this another classic case of issue-based voting. While we can understand why his issue concerns and partisan leanings led him to cast a ballot for the Conservatives, what may have contributed to someone in his situation having such strong Conservative partisan leanings? Keep in mind that the Conservative Party in 2006 was still fairly new and being led by someone whose party roots are

grounded in the former Reform/Alliance party of Alberta. This voter's occupation as a sales representative may be telling. While we do not know the nature of his work precisely (the Canadian Election Study is not that detailed), we can imagine that someone who works in sales may be sensitive to the issue of taxation on commission earnings, which is a far less stable stream of revenue than wage earning. If such a person considers that the Conservatives are more responsive to his concerns, then it makes more sense why this voter sided with the Harper Conservatives in the 2004 and 2006 elections.

3. Voter #3, the 26-year-old francophone female in Eastern Quebec, might have been expected to vote Bloc, as did many of her neighbours. But she opted for the Conservatives. Why? Here is what else we know of her: the most important issue to her was social programs and health care, issues regarding which the Liberals can claim to have some credibility,[11] at least far more than the Conservatives. She did express some worries about Quebec sovereignty, so this may explain why the Bloc did not appear as an attractive option. She does not normally identify with any of the parties. Her assessment of the economy is that it has remained about the same over the one-year period before the election campaign, and is optimistic about the near future. She recognizes the Bloc has the best chance of winning in her riding, and the Liberals have the second-best chance. Although Voter #3 indicated that she is a weak Liberal identifier who voted Liberal in 2004, she revealed some inclination toward the Conservatives, because she would prefer seeing a Conservative *majority* government. Consequently, she voted Conservative. What explains her vote? Was she swayed by campaign ads, the debate, or other campaign events? Was her vote strategic? All are viable possibilities.

4. Voter #4, a somewhat religious middle-aged married woman, lives in a rural Southwestern Ontario area. We expected a Conservative vote from her, but she instead supported the NDP. Similar to Voter #3, Voter #4's main concern during the 2006 election was social programs and health care, issues that are quite important to women. But unlike Voter #3, Voter #4 is a very strong NDP identifier and believes that the NDP is best able to handle these issues. Consequently, her vote is fairly straightforward: she is a solid NDP backer who has remained loyal to the NDP, all for the right reasons.

There are many voters like these four all over Canada. But it should be emphasized that for the most part, all voters in Canada behave predictably. We can understand how people vote by taking into account demographics, social psychology, and campaign-specific and short-term factors. In addition, we can better understand how people vote when we incorporate all of these factors into a complete model. André Blais et al. (2002) proposed a multi-stage vote model (based on a similar model developed in Warren Miller and Merrill Shanks 2006), which distinguishes factors as remote (such as demographics), intermediate (such as values and party identification), and proximate (such as issues and leaders). One of the main contributions of this more elaborate model is that it acknowledges that each factor, on its own, may help explain some voting behaviour. That is, region, religion, and gender can already account for some degree of voting behaviour. These remote factors can then be used to explain values and attitudes that shape partisan identifications (intermediate factors). While these intermediate factors can also explain an individual vote, they help explain how voters respond to factors that are "closer" to the vote: issues and campaign messages. Overall, then, to understand how people vote, one must take into account a fairly wide array of influences, and then map them out in a manner that proceeds to a plausible explanation.

NOTES

1. This is a very skeletal summary of the Columbia School's contribution to our understanding of voting behaviour.
2. In Quebec, "distinct society" often refers to the main pillars of Quebec society that distinguish it from the "rest of Canada," such as its French language and Napoleonic civil-law legal system (as opposed to the British common-law system that prevails in English Canada). It can also refer to a general tendency of Quebec to exhibit a "collectivist" culture that gives precedence to group rights over individual rights, in contrast to English Canada and its emphasis on individual rights over group rights.
3. The role religion plays in Canadian voting has typically focused on the Catholic–Protestant divide. Studies of non-Christians suffer from a lack of sufficient data, although some newer research has begun to overcome this challenge. See, for example, Kay, Perrella, and Brown (2009).
4. Data was drawn from the Ipsos Reid election-day online survey.
5. See O'Neill (2002) for a discussion on political culture and how it relates to gender.
6. The Reform Party of Canada was a milder version of such parties. More radical and intolerant brands are found in Europe.
7. Even non-democratic countries, such as China, face similar regional movements, with Tibet being a well-known case.
8. For a bibliography on economic voting, see http://www.wlu.ca/lispop/ecovoting.
9. On rare occasions, a senator can be appointed to Cabinet. Sometimes, a minister is appointed from outside of Parliament, but that minister usually moves quickly to find a riding within which to run and, presumably, win a seat in the House of Commons.
10. The propensity of the first-past-the-post electoral system to permit no more than two viable candidates is referred to as "Duverger's Law," a principle developed by Maurice Duverger (1954).
11. This chapter does not discuss "issue ownership," whereby certain issues are generally associated as having some credibility with certain parties. For a discussion of this concept, see Bélanger and Meguid (2008).

DISCUSSION QUESTIONS

1. Identify your own personal partisan leanings (for example, the party you generally prefer) and find out how they compare with the partisan leanings of your parents and friends.
2. How do you think negative advertising will affect future election campaigns? Will it turn off voters? Will it polarize voters?
3. Do regional voting patterns spell trouble for national unity?

FURTHER READING

Websites

Canada Research Chair in Electoral Studies: http://www.crcee.umontreal.ca.
Canadian Election Study: http://ces-eec.mcgill.ca.

Books

Blais, André, Elisabeth Gidengil, Richard Nadeau, and Neil Nevitte. 2002. *Anatomy of a Liberal victory: Making sense of the vote in the 2000 Canadian election.* Peterborough, ON: Broadview Press.

Clarke, Harold D., Jane Jenson, Lawrence LeDuc, and Jon H. Pammett. 1996. *Absent mandate: Canadian electoral politics in an era of restructuring.* Toronto: Gage.

Nevitte, Neil, André Blais, Elisabeth Gidengil, and Richard Nadeau. 2000. *Unsteady state: The 1997 Canadian federal election.* Don Mills, ON: Oxford University Press.

REFERENCES

Alford, Robert R. 1963. *Party and society: The Anglo-American democracies.* Chicago: Rand McNally.

Almond, Gabriel A., and Sidney Verba. 1963. *The civic culture: Political attitudes and democracy in five nations.* Boston: Little, Brown and Company.

Bélanger, Éric, and Bonnie M. Meguid. 2008. Issue salience, issue ownership, and issue-based vote choice. *Electoral Studies* 27: 477–491.

Bélanger, Paul, and Munroe Eagles. 2006. The geography of class and religion in Canadian elections revisited. *Canadian Journal of Political Science* 39: 591–609.

Blais, André. 2005. Accounting for the electoral success of the Liberal Party in Canada: Presidential address to the annual meeting of the Canadian Political Science Association. *Canadian Journal of Political Science* 38: 821–840.

Blais, André, Elisabeth Gidengil, Richard Nadeau, and Neil Nevitte. 2002. *Anatomy of a Liberal victory: Making sense of the vote in the 2000 Canadian election.* Peterborough, ON: Broadview Press.

Blais, André, and Andrea M.L. Perrella. 2008. Systemic effects of televised candidates' debates. *International Journal of Press/Politics* 13: 451–464.

Brodie, Janine, and Jane Jenson. 1988. *Crisis, challenge and change: Party and class in Canada revisited.* Ottawa: Carleton University Press.

Brody, Richard A., and Paul M. Sniderman. 1977. From life space to polling place: The relevance of personal concerns for voting behaviour. *British Journal of Political Science* 7: 337–360.

Campbell, Angus, Philip E. Converse, Warren E. Miller, and Donald E. Stokes. 1960. *The American voter.* Chicago: University of Chicago Press.

Clarke, Harold D., Jane Jenson, Lawrence LeDuc, and Jon H. Pammett. 1979. *Political choice in Canada.* Toronto: McGraw-Hill.

Clarke, Harold D., Jane Jenson, Lawrence LeDuc, and Jon H. Pammett. 1984. *Absent mandate: The politics of discontent in Canada.* Toronto: Gage.

Clarke, Harold D., Jane Jenson, Lawrence LeDuc, and Jon H. Pammett. 1991. *Absent mandate: Interpreting change in Canadian elections.* Toronto: Gage.

Clarke, Harold D., Jane Jenson, Lawrence LeDuc, and Jon H. Pammett. 1996. *Absent mandate: Canadian electoral politics in an era of restructuring.* Toronto: Gage.

Clarke, Harold D., Allan Kornberg, John MacLeod, and Thomas Scotto. 2005. Too close to call: Political choice in Canada, 2004. *PS: Political Science and Politics* 38: 247–253.

Dalton, Russell J. 2002. *Citizen politics.* New York: Chatham House.

Downs, Anthony. 1957. *An economic theory of democracy.* New York: Harper & Row.

Duverger, Maurice. 1954. *Political parties.* New York: Wiley.

Feldman, Stanley. 1982. Economic self-interest and political behavior. *American Journal of Political Science* 27: 446–466.

Feldman, Stanley. 1985. Economic self-interest and the vote: Evidence and meaning. In *Economic conditions and electoral outcomes: The United States and Western Europe,* ed. Heinz Eulau and Michael S. Lewis-Beck, 144–166. New York: Agathon Press.

Fieschi, Catherine, and Paul Heywood. 2004. Trust, cynicism and populist anti-politics. *Journal of Political Ideologies* 9: 289–309.

Fiorina, Morris. 1978. Economic retrospective voting in American national elections: A micro-analysis. *American Journal of Political Science.* 22: 426–443.

Fournier, Patrick. 2002. The uninformed Canadian voter. In *Citizen politics: Research and theory in Canadian political behaviour,* ed. Joanna Everitt and Brenda O'Neill, 92–109. Don Mills, ON: Oxford University Press.

Fraser, Graham. 1984. *René Lévesque and the Parti Québécois in power.* Toronto: Macmillan.

Gidengil, Elisabeth. 1995. Economic man—social woman? The case of the gender gap in support for the Canada–US Free Trade Agreement. *Comparative Political Studies* 28: 384–408.

Gidengil, Elisabeth. 2007. Beyond the gender gap: Presidential address to the Canadian Political Science Association. *Canadian Journal of Political Science* 40: 1–17.

Gidengil, Elisabeth, André Blais, Richard Nadeau, and Neil Nevitte. 1999. Making sense of regional voting in the 1997 Canadian federal election: Liberal and reform support outside Quebec. *Canadian Journal of Political Science* 32: 247–272.

Gidengil, Elisabeth, Patrick Fournier, Joanna Everitt, Neil Nevitte, and André Blais. 2009. The anatomy of a Liberal defeat. Paper presented at the annual meeting of the Canadian Political Science Association, Ottawa.

Gidengil, Elisabeth, Matthew Hennigar, André Blais, and Neil Nevitte. 2005. Explaining the gender gap in support for the new right: The case of Canada. *Comparative Political Studies* 38: 1–25.

Hartz, Louis. 1955. *The Liberal tradition in America.* New York: Harcourt Brace.

Henderson, Ailsa. 2004. Regional political cultures in Canada. *Canadian Journal of Political Science* 37: 595–615.

Horowitz, Gad. 1966. Conservatism, liberalism, and socialism in Canada: An interpretation. *Canadian Journal of Economics and Political Science* 32: 143–171.

Horowitz, Gad. 1978. Notes on conservatism, liberalism and socialism in Canada. *Canadian Journal of Political Science* 11: 383–399.

Inglehart, Ronald. 1977. *The silent revolution.* Princeton, NJ: Princeton University Press.

Inglehart, Ronald. 1990. *Culture shift in advanced industrialized society.* Princeton, NJ: Princeton University Press.

Inglehart, Ronald, and Pippa Norris. 2003. *Rising tide: Gender equality and cultural change around the world.* New York: Cambridge University Press.

Irvine, William P. 1974. Explaining the religious basis of the Canadian partisan identity: Success on the third try. *Canadian Journal of Political Science* 7: 560–563.

Johnston, Richard. 1985. The reproduction of the religious cleavage in Canadian elections. *Canadian Journal of Political Science* 18: 99–113.

Johnston, Richard, André Blais, Henry E. Brady, and Jean Crête. 1992. *Letting the people decide: Dynamics of a Canadian election.* Montreal: McGill-Queen's University Press.

Kay, Barry. 1977. An examination of class and left–right party images in Canadian voting. *Canadian Journal of Political Science* 10: 127–143.

Kay, Barry J., Andrea M.L. Perrella, and Steven D. Brown. 2009. The religion enigma: Theoretical riddle or classificational artifact? Paper presented to the annual meeting of the American Political Science Association, Toronto.

Keynes, John Maynard. 1936. *The general theory of employment, interest and money.* London: MacMillan and Company.

Kim, Jiyoon, and Andrea M.L. Perrella. 2008. Beyond the Liberal Party: Immigrant voting behaviour in Canada. Paper presented to the annual meeting of the Canadian Political Science Association, Vancouver.

Kinder, Donald R., and Roderick Kiewiet. 1981. Sociotropic politics: The American case. *British Journal of Political Science* 11: 129–161.

Kornberg, Allan, and Harold D. Clarke. 1992. *Citizens and community: Political support in a representative democracy.* New York: Cambridge University Press.

Lambert, Ronald D., James E. Curtis, Steven D. Brown, and Barry J. Kay. 1987. Social class, left/right political orientations and subjective class voting in provincial and federal elections. *Canadian Review of Sociology and Anthropology* 24: 385–406.

Lazarfeld, Paul F., Bernard Berelson, and Hazel Gaudet. 1948. *The people's choice: How the voter makes up his mind in a presidential campaign.* New York: Columbia University Press.

LeDuc, Lawrence, and Richard Price. 1985. Great debates: The televised leadership debates of 1979. *Canadian Journal of Political Science* 18: 135–153.

Lewis-Beck, Michael S. 1988. *Economics and elections: The major Western democracies.* Ann Arbor: University of Michigan Press.

Lipset, Seymour M., and Stein Rokkan. 1967. *Party systems and voter alignments.* New York: Free Press.

MacIvor, Heather. 2006. *Parameters of power: Canada's political institutions.* Toronto: Thomson Nelson.

McRoberts, Kenneth, and Dale Posgate. 1984. *Quebec: Social change and political crisis.* Toronto: McClelland & Stewart.

Meisel, John. 1973. *Working papers on Canadian politics.* Montreal: McGill-Queen's Press.

Mendelsohn, Matthew, and Richard Nadeau. 1997. The religious cleavage and the media in Canada. *Canadian Journal of Political Science* 30: 129–146.

Merolla, Jennifer L., Laura B. Stephenson, and Elisabeth J. Zechmeister. 2008. Can Canadians take a hint? The (in)effectiveness of party labels as information shortcuts in Canada. *Canadian Journal of Political Science* 41: 673–696.

Miller, Warren E., and J. Merrill Shanks. 1996. *The new American voter.* Cambridge, MA: Harvard University Press.

Mutz, Diana. 1998. *Impersonal influence: How perceptions of mass collectives affect political attitudes.* Cambridge: Cambridge University Press.

Nadeau, Richard, and André Blais. 1993. Explaining election outcomes in Canada: Economy and politics. *Canadian Journal of Political Science* 75: 775–790.

Nadeau, Richard, and André Blais. 1995. Economic conditions, leader evaluations and election outcomes in Canada. *Canadian Public Policy* 21: 212–218.

Nadeau, Richard, André Blais, Neil Nevitte, and Elisabeth Gidengil. 2000. It's unemployment, stupid! Why perceptions about the job situation hurt the Liberals in the 1997 election. *Canadian Public Policy* 26: 77–97.

Nadeau, Richard, and Michael S. Lewis-Beck. 2001. National economic voting in U.S. presidential elections. *Journal of Politics* 63: 159–181.

Nannestad, Peter, and Martin Paldam. 1995. It's the government's fault! A cross-section study of economic voting in Denmark, 1990/93. *European Journal of Political Research* 28: 33–62.

Nannestad, Peter, and Martin Paldam. 1997. From the pocketbook of the welfare man: A pooled cross-section study of economic voting in Denmark, 1986–92. *British Journal of Political Science* 27: 119–136.

Nevitte, Neil. 1996. *The decline of deference: Canadian value change in cross-national perspective.* Peterborough, ON: Broadview Press.

Nevitte, Neil, André Blais, Elisabeth Gidengil, and Richard Nadeau. 2000. *Unsteady state: The 1997 Canadian federal election.* Don Mills, ON: Oxford University Press.

O'Neill, Brenda. 2002. Sugar and spice? Political culture and the political behaviour of Canadian women. In *Citizen politics: Research and theory in Canadian political behaviour,* ed. Joanna Everitt and Brenda O'Neill, 40–55. Don Mills, ON: Oxford University Press.

Pammett, Jon H. 1991. The effects of individual and contextual variables on partisanship in Canada. *European Journal of Political Research* 19: 399–412.

Simeon, Richard, and David J. Elkins. 1974. Regional political cultures in Canada. *Canadian Journal of Political Science* 7: 397–437.

Stephenson, Laura B., Thomas J. Scotto, and Allan Kornberg. 2004. Slip, sliding away or *le plus ça change* … : Canadian and American partisanship in comparative perspective. *American Review of Canadian Studies* 34: 283–312.

Stewart, Marianne C., and Harold D. Clarke. 1998. The dynamics of party identification in federal systems: The Canadian case. *American Journal of Political Science* 42: 97–116.

Underhill, Frank. 1935. The development of national political parties in Canada. *Canadian Historical Review* 16: 367–387.

Uslaner, Eric M. 1989. Multiple party identifiers in Canada: Participation and affect. *Journal of Politics* 51: 993–1003.

Uslaner, Eric M. 1990. Splitting image: Partisan affiliations in Canada's "two political worlds." *American Journal of Political Science* 34: 961–981.

Wiseman, Nelson. 1981. The pattern of prairie politics. *Queen's Quarterly* 88: 298–231.

Wiseman, Nelson. 1996. Provincial political cultures. In *Provinces,* ed. C. Dunn, 21–62. Peterborough, ON: Broadview Press.

CHAPTER 12

Voter Turnout

Lawrence LeDuc and Jon H. Pammett

Introduction

Voter turnout occupies an important place in the study of elections. Analysts of particular elections often cite turnout as one of the factors leading to the outcome of an election. When one party or candidate is more successful in motivating potential supporters to cast a ballot, an advantage over its opponents can thereby be gained. Similarly, if one's potential voters turn out in smaller than expected numbers, an unexpected setback might occur. For these reasons, most books or anthologies dealing with specific elections in Canada and other countries typically contain a chapter on voter turnout.[1]

But turnout can also matter in other, more fundamental, ways than simply as one of several factors that might help to explain the outcome of a particular election. A high turnout of voters enhances the democratic legitimacy of the electoral process, while a low turnout can call it into question. If only a minority of eligible voters participate in an election, how then can it be said to represent the will of the majority of citizens? Declining turnout in many countries, including Canada, invariably raises questions about the health and strength of a country's democracy. We will have more to say on this subject later in this chapter.

Turnout patterns can also have an influence on the manner in which electoral campaigns are conducted. Politicians, so to speak, "know where the votes are." Social groups with a reputation for high voter turnout often find the issues that they care most about receiving greater attention during a campaign, and their voices listened to more consistently. The political clout of union members, senior citizens, or strategically placed ethnic minorities, to mention only a few examples, is often enhanced in this way.

Voter Turnout in Canada

Historically, Canada has been a country of relatively high voter turnout. From Confederation until the Second World War, around 70 percent of eligible voters could be expected to cast a ballot in a federal election. Over that long period, turnout fluctuated from one election to another only within a fairly narrow band. The high and low points were both recorded around the beginning of the 20th century—63 percent in the 1896 election and 77 percent four years later in 1900. After 1945, turnout in federal elections rose slightly, reaching 79 percent in the 1958 election and typically registering levels of about 75 percent up until 1993.[2]

Turnout in provincial elections has varied somewhat more widely, both over time and among the different provinces. In many provinces (for example, Quebec, British Columbia, New Brunswick, Newfoundland) turnout in provincial elections has generally been higher than at the federal level.[3] Ontario and Alberta were, for a time, the only provinces in which turnout in federal elections was consistently higher than that in provincial ones.[4] In more recent years however, federal and provincial turnout in a number of provinces has begun to converge—often at lower levels than were recorded either federally or provincially in the past.[5]

Fluctuations in turnout from one election to another are often difficult to fully account for. Sometimes, one political party may have been more successful than its competitors in mobilizing voters, or a particularly compelling issue or set of events may galvanize the electorate. But such variations, sometimes exaggerated in post-election analyses, are typically small. Turnout was high (75 percent) in the wartime election of 1917 that was won by the Borden Union government, but only slightly above the average for the period. It also reached 75 percent in the free trade election of 1988, but this was actually 1 percentage point below the election of 1979 in which the Conservatives led by Joe Clark defeated the Liberal government of Pierre Elliott Trudeau. Seasonal variations between elections can also play a role. Turnout was lower than average (69 percent) in the unexpected February election of 1980, in which the Clark government was defeated, and also in the August election of 1953 (68 percent), held during the traditional summer vacation period. However, it is also evident from past studies of elections that turnout fluctuations can be partly accounted for by voters moving into and out of the electorate on a more or less random basis. Although in any given election, a quarter or more of eligible Canadians do not vote, they are not consistently the same non-voters. In previous research, we used the term "transient voters" to describe this segment of the electorate in order to emphasize that this group did not constitute a permanently disconnected and politically alienated part of the population.[6] Rather, Canadians have generally tended to conform to the idea that voting was a kind of "civic duty" and, even if they were unable to vote in a particular election, they generally expressed their intention to vote in the next one. Often, this intent was realized, in that non-voters in one election drifted into the electorate subsequently, and some voters for a variety of reasons (often short-term personal ones) did not get to the polls. We therefore concluded that the distinctions between voters and non-voters in any given election were in fact relatively minor, and that the circulation of transient voters into and out of the electorate generally had only modest effects on election outcomes.[7] These tendencies, however well documented in survey research in previous elections, may well be changing. Turnout patterns in both Canada and other countries over the past two decades have shifted abruptly, and the political and social implications of these changes are only beginning to be fully understood.

Measuring the Voter Turnout Decline

It has now been more than two decades since political scientists began to take note of the decline in voter turnout in a number of Western democracies. Seen within the context of a particular country, hypotheses about the factors accounting for a decline in turnout from one election to another were often election specific. But as evidence has mounted over time that the decline in turnout is much more systematic and sustained than can be explained by such short-term factors, scholarly interest has increasingly turned to more fundamental possible causes.

In Canada, turnout in federal elections declined from a rather reliable level of about 75 percent in the mid-1980s to levels at around 60 percent—depending upon the years chosen, a decline of 10 to 15 percentage points occurring over a relatively short time (see Figure 12.1). Prior to 1993, declines in turnout in Canada were relatively few, and were typically explained by seasonal fluctuations owing to the absence of a fixed election timetable. But, in 1993, turnout declined abruptly to below 70 percent. At the time, it was thought that this dip might have been due to the unusual character of that election, which produced a major shift in the Canadian party system. But after

FIGURE 12.1   Turnout in Federal Elections, 1945–2008

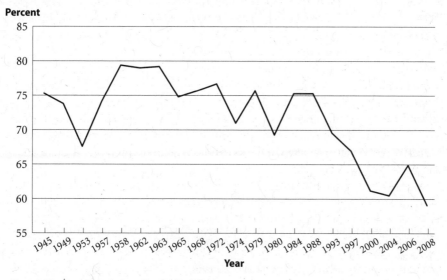

Source: Elections Canada. http://www.elections.ca.

1993, turnout in Canadian federal elections continued to decline, reaching new lows successively in 1997, 2000, and 2004, and rebounding slightly (to 65 percent) in the 2006 election. However, the pattern of decline was quickly reestablished, as turnout again registered a new historic low (59 percent) in the 2008 federal election. With hindsight, it is clear that the 1993 decline had less to do with the specific characteristics of that election than it appeared at the time. In the same period of less than 20 years, the turnout in many of Canada's provincial elections has been declining as well.[8]

Canada is not alone among established democracies in experiencing a sustained decline in voter turnout in recent years, but its decline has been among the largest (see Table 12.1). As similar patterns of turnout decline have been observed in numerous

TABLE 12.1   Recent Voter Turnout in 20 Democracies Compared with 1980s Average

Country	Electoral system	Turnout		
		Last election[a]	1980s average	Net change
Denmark	PR	87	88	−1
Brazil	PR	83	84	−1
Austria	PR	82	91	−9
Italy	mixed	81	89	−8
Sweden	PR	81	89	−8
Netherlands	PR	81	84	−3
Germany	mixed	78	87	−9
Norway	PR	77	83	−6
Spain	PR	76	73	+3
Greece	PR	74	83	−9
Japan	mixed	68	69	−1
Ireland	STV	67	74	−7
Finland	PR	65	74	−9
Israel	PR	64	79	−15
Britain	plurality	61	74	−13
France	majority-plurality	60	73	−13
Canada	plurality	59	73	−14
India	plurality	58	60	−2
United States[b]	plurality[c]	58	52	+6
Switzerland	PR	48	48	0

[a] Most recent election to December 31, 2008. Lower house of legislature, unless otherwise noted.

[b] November 2008 presidential election. Comparison is with 1984 and 1988 presidential elections. Statistic is percentage of voting age population.

[c] Majority of electoral college votes in presidential elections.

Source: International IDEA. n.d. Voter turnout. http://www.idea.int/vt.

countries, explanations that highlight institutional or other country-specific characteristics appear increasingly unsatisfactory. Comparative research confirms the intuitive notion that "institutions matter," but also demonstrates that patterns of decline have emerged under a variety of different institutional settings.[9] Countries with systems of proportional representation have generally tended to have higher turnout in elections, but many of these have also experienced declines. For example, Sweden continues to have higher turnout in its elections than many other European countries, but turnout in Swedish parliamentary elections has nevertheless declined by about 8 percentage points since the early 1980s (see Table 12.1). Austria, Germany, and Greece display similar patterns. Israel, which has one of the most proportional electoral systems in the world, experienced a decline of 15 percentage points over this period, from an average of 79 percent in the 1980s to 64 percent in the 2006 election.

The turnout decline has not taken place at the same rate, or at exactly the same times in all countries. In US presidential elections, for example, the decline began in the mid-1960s, accelerated in the 1970s, and appeared to bottom out at a level of about 50 percent of the voting age population in 1988.[10] Although it made another new low in 1996, turnout recovered somewhat in the next two US presidential elections, and increased sharply to a level of about 58 percent of the voting age population in the 2008 presidential election. Many observers of that election attributed the increase to the success of the Obama campaign in mobilizing support among groups that in the past have had lower rates of participation in elections. The decline in Britain mirrors that of Canada almost exactly. Britain experienced a steep decline to just below 60 percent over two elections (1997 and 2001) before showing a very slight recovery to 61 percent in the 2005 election (Whiteley et al. 2001; Curtice 2006).

Turnout in provincial elections has declined in tandem with that in federal elections, and in some instances even more steeply (see Table 12.2). Turnout in the 2008 election in Quebec, for example, established a record low of 57 percent—a decline of 22 percent from the average levels of the 1980s. In Alberta, a new historic turnout low of 41 percent was recorded in the 2008 provincial election—a decline of 16 percentage points from the already low average of 57 percent two decades earlier. In almost every instance, turnout in the most recent provincial election established an historic low. Only Prince Edward Island has been successful in maintaining high turnout levels in provincial elections, although federal turnout in PEI dropped sharply in 2008, as it did in all other provinces (see Table 12.2).

Explaining the Voter Turnout Decline

Of course, aggregate data can tell only a small part of the story. They can identify similarities or differences between countries and time periods, regional and some demographic patterns, or institutional and other correlates. But such data cannot answer the fundamental question posed by Wattenberg (2002): "Where have all the voters gone?" Survey research moves us a step closer to an explanation, but relatively few survey questions are directed toward non-voters, and the number of cases available for analysis in many national surveys is often too small to provide a detailed

TABLE 12.2   Voter Turnout in Recent Provincial and Federal Elections Compared with 1980s Average, by Province

	Provincial			Federal		
	Last election[a]	1980s average	Net change	2008 election	1980s average[b]	Net change
Prince Edward Island	84	84	0	70	85	−15
Saskatchewan	76	83	−7	62	78	−16
New Brunswick	68	82	−14	63	77	−14
Newfoundland	62	79	−17	48	66	−18
Nova Scotia	60	72	−12	61	75	−14
British Columbia	58	77	−19	61	78	−17
Manitoba	57	71	−14	57	74	−17
Quebec	57	79	−22	61	76	−15
Ontario	53	64	−11	59	75	−16
Alberta	41	57	−16	53	72	−19
Mean decline			−13			−16

[a] To December 31, 2008.
[b] Federal average of 1984 and 1988 elections.

Source: Elections Canada; provincial sites. http://www.elections.ca/content.asp?section=lin&dir=url&document=index&lang=e&textonly=false.

profile of the disappearing voters. Nevertheless, standard voting surveys have been valuable in identifying some of the sociodemographic correlates of non-voting—for example, age, gender, education, income—as well as attitudinal or behavioural correlates such as partisanship or political efficacy. But such studies are at best suggestive as to the true causes underlying the turnout decline.

A number of demographic and attitudinal factors help to explain non-voting.[11] Length of residence in the respondent's current location is important, since this provides familiarity with the local context and personalities of candidates. Household income is a more important demographic factor than education, but both tend to be related in some degree to voting. Mobilization by groups, parties, or candidates is also correlated with voting; this is true not only for direct personal contact by party campaigners but also for remembering party contact by a phone solicitation or a literature delivery. Finally, two other factors are related to voter turnout. A more competitive political environment helps to boost turnout, since people report being more likely to go to the polls if they feel that their vote would make a difference in the outcome of an election. In addition, feelings of general political trust in elected representatives, as well as of political efficacy, have some relationship with voting.

When survey respondents are asked to give their reasons for failing to vote in any given election, these typically fall into two broad categories (see Table 12.3). Personal

TABLE 12.3   Reasons for Not Voting in Federal Elections

	2000	2004
Political or institutional reasons	59%	43%
Not interested in election/politics		
Vote has no meaning, makes no difference		
Election a foregone conclusion		
Parties/politicians all the same		
Didn't know who to vote for		
Personal reasons	38%	40%
Too busy with work/school/family		
Away, on vacation, not available		
Forgot, didn't know where to vote		
Couldn't get there, no transportation		
Physical or health reasons; illness		
All other; don't know; no reason given	3%	17%

$N = 1,036$.

Source: 2000 data from Elections Canada Survey (Pammett and LeDuc 2003b). N (non-voters) = 968; 2004 data from Canadian Election Study. N (non-voters) = 418.

reasons (for example, "too busy," "away," "forgot") are a common theme, although these can in some instances simply be convenient excuses. More telling however is the somewhat larger number of responses that indicate some degree of dissatisfaction with the political system itself. The feeling that the vote is not meaningful or that there is no one worth voting for recurs with some frequency. To some degree, this is a function of the institutions within which voting in Canada takes place. Canadians cast only a single vote for a local member of Parliament, and in many parts of the country or in certain constituencies, this is not perceived as a particularly meaningful choice. Since 1993, when the party system suddenly became more regionalized, this tendency to regard the vote as devoid of any real meaning has been reinforced by political realities. Why would a Liberal voter in Alberta or a Conservative voter in Toronto feel that their vote has any real meaning? While the election in the aggregate may be more competitive, the actual voting choice presented at the constituency level can often be little more than a foregone conclusion.

Survey evidence also suggests that non-voters do not necessarily see their decision *not* to vote as a fixed decision. Like voters, the decision not to vote is often made late in a campaign (see Table 12.4) and can be as much a function of circumstance as a conscious determination to tune out the world of politics completely. Of course, political interest plays a role in this process. Citizens who are attentive to politics may nevertheless decide not to vote for a variety of personal or political reasons. But others for whom politics seems largely irrelevant or uninteresting may well lack the incentive to vote as election day approaches.

TABLE 12.4   Time of Voting (Non-Voting) Decision

"When did you decide how to vote?" "When did you decide not to vote?"	Voters	Non-voters
Before the campaign began	48%	27%
During the campaign	37%	18%
Election day	14%	36%
Don't know; never really decided	1%	19%

Source: 2004 Canadian Election Study. http://ces-eec.mcgill.ca/surveys.html#2004. *N* (voters) = 2,383; *N* (non-voters) = 418.

Age and (Non-)Voting

Two characteristics of contemporary non-voters in Canada stand out. Almost half of all non-voters in the 2000 federal election were under 30 years of age. A majority expressed little interest in politics. Non-voters assigned less importance to the act of voting than did voters, and the young non-voters do not have as strong a sense of "civic duty" with respect to voting as do older respondents. Thus, the broader explanation of the turnout decline is to be found more in the normal processes of population replacement that have been taking place over a number of years than in the failure of the electoral system or party system to provide meaningful choices for Canadians. A steady growth in the proportion of the population with little interest in politics and a belief that voting is not all that important has been driving turnout down in each successive election.

Figure 12.2 dramatically illustrates the pattern of decline in turnout across the generations that has been at work in the Canadian electorate over the past decade or more. The levels of non-participation for the three cohorts of newly eligible voters entering the electorate in each of the past three federal elections are striking.[12] Even those who entered the electorate much earlier (for example, 1974–1980) voted in 2000 at a lower rate than those in the older age groups. For those who became eligible to vote in 1984 or 1988 (aged 30 to 37 in 2000), the overall percentage casting a ballot in 2000 was just 54 percent.

It is not unusual to find lower rates of voting participation among the young. Such patterns are well documented in the literature on non-voting in Canada and in other countries (see Franklin, Lyons, and Marsh 2004; Gidengil et al. 2003; Lyons and Alexander 2000; Park 2004; Rubenson et al. 2004; and Wass 2007). But lower participation rates among the young have generally been interpreted as a pattern associated with specific behavioural characteristics of the life cycle. As people age, they become more politically aware and engaged. Therefore, it is to be expected that voting rates should increase over time with these normal life-cycle changes. They should also increase with rising levels of education. Our evidence suggests, however, that such changes are occurring more slowly than they have in the past, and that voters, when they do begin to enter the electorate, are doing so later in life and in fewer numbers.[13]

FIGURE 12.2   Estimated Voting Participation Rates by Age Cohorts, 2000 Federal Election

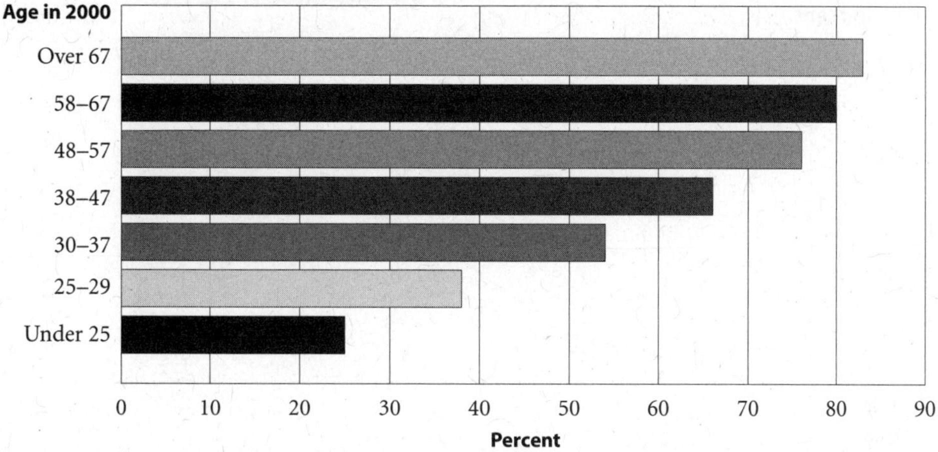

Source: Elections Canada Survey (Pammett and LeDuc 2003b, 20). Weighted $N = 2,467$.

Since the mid to late 1970s, each newly eligible cohort of voters has been increasingly disinclined to believe that elections are important or meaningful—a view that stands in stark contrast to that of the generations that entered the electorate before 1974 (see Figure 12.3). Accompanying this growing disbelief in the efficacy of elections is a propensity to disengage, which displays a similar trend across the cohorts of young voters for the past two decades. While this trend appears to moderate slightly among the youngest cohort (18- to 20-year-olds), that group was also the one that had the lowest participation rate of any of the cohorts in the federal election that took place just prior to the time of the survey. If only about one in five newly eligible voters can be expected to vote in the first election for which they are eligible, there is little doubt that voter turnout in Canada will continue for some time yet on its long-term downward path. But the responses shown in Figure 12.3 should not be given an entirely negative interpretation. In no age group, even those in the younger age categories, does a majority of Canadians think that voting in elections is not in some sense "important." And a majority of Canadians in every age group, even the youngest ones, say that they are likely to vote in the next election. We may interpret these responses with some skepticism, but they do not indicate a determination to turn away completely from the political process on the part of young voters. The pattern suggests disengagement, not alienation.

Probing Young Non-Voters

The survey data discussed above tell us a good deal about *who* is not participating in federal elections, but they provide only a hint of the reasons *why* younger voters may be disengaging from electoral politics in such large numbers. To obtain further insight

FIGURE 12.3   Importance of Elections and Probability of Voting, by Age Cohorts

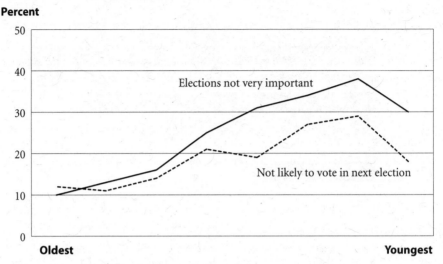

Source: Elections Canada Survey (Pammett and LeDuc 2003b, 71–72). Weighted N = 2,467.

into the attitudes of young voters, we conducted two small group studies in which respondents were able to discuss more openly their feelings about politics and attitudes toward elections and voting.[14] Participants in these studies were asked a range of open-ended questions designed to probe issues related to voting behaviour, including perceptions of politics and political campaigns; political interest; socialization influences with respect to voting; politics; and civic duty. Participants were also asked for recommendations on increasing engagement and projections about future voting. As a consequence of the small group sizes, these discussions are best regarded as simply producing insights into the thought processes of the participants. But combined with the more statistically reliable findings of the surveys, these data shed considerable light on some of the forces driving the larger demographic processes.[15]

Three principal themes emerged from the small group studies, which help to reveal some of the attitudinal factors that lie behind the typical reasons given for not voting in elections. The first of these is a clearly discernible *lack of personal connection* to the political world, and a feeling that electoral politics as practised in Canada may have little relevance to the lives of younger people. Wattenberg (2008) compared attempting to engage uninterested young people in politics to "getting someone who doesn't follow sports to watch a football game." This lack of connection is reinforced by peer group influences and practices. Among the observations of our young respondents regarding politics were comments such as, "the topic of politics rarely if ever comes up with friends" or "talking about politics is incredibly boring for me." This tendency to tune out the political world leads to a self consciousness of a lack of knowledge and information. "I do not think I am very politically informed," one of our young focus group respondents admitted, adding that "I need to look into it more. I want to know more if I vote."

Another observed: "I wouldn't know who to vote for and I don't want to just take my parent's side." While many young people do not talk about or relate to politics now, there is nevertheless a recognition among many of them that they will do so at some time in the future. "As we get older we'll have more responsibility; right now I don't have to think about what my parents think about when they look at parties. I'll probably get more involved." To some extent this is a function of what young people *do* see when they encounter the world of electoral politics. "I can't blame the politicians, because we are not important. There are different stages of your life; in your twenties, job security, in your thirties, child care, in your forties, pensions.... Statistically politicians use the campaign to attract the biggest population, and I'm not the biggest population."

The feeling among many young people that politics as practised in the Canadian electoral arena has little relevance for them is reinforced by what they see around them. Politicians "know where their voters are," and the issues that they tend to emphasize most during election campaigns are not those to which young people can readily relate. Several of the participants in our small group discussions emphasized this point. "I would get involved if issues were related to us. Most of the stuff they talk about doesn't affect us. … Mostly what they talk about doesn't relate to us … not a massive impact. I'm not interested." Or more pointedly: "I think that a lot of them [political parties] have given up on us. What have they done? A hundred bucks says they stop at a seniors home—what about a university? They are not going to do it. They have no interest, and they don't even try."

Youth have not necessarily made up their minds that politics is irrelevant, but many currently cannot make the connection, and instead the focus of their attention is on other things. They have radically different media habits than previous generations who were exposed to political debate more regularly (Wattenberg 2008).

A second major theme that emerges from the small group studies—one also found repeatedly in the larger surveys—is the adverse reaction of many Canadians to the *negativity* of modern electoral politics. While older respondents are also put off by the negativity of modern electoral politics, younger people tend to be even less accepting of such practices: "pretty negative … when I think of it, it's dirty and politicians shouldn't be trusted. It's hard to take what they say seriously … lying … and the commercials are disrespectful to Canadians. It's all garbage." Or, "When I think of the commercials I hear, or anything political, I think it's negative. I am not learning anything, and it does influence me. I don't know what to do." "The candidates are just bashing each other every chance they get and they are only saying what we want to hear. It seems like whoever is elected never follows through with their promises and we end up suffering in the end. In all honesty it reminds me of a high school popularity contest." "All the commercials are pointing at flaws … poor sportsmanship. It turns me off."

And, as is made clear by the following comment of a 20-year-old first-time voter, the negativity is not just a reason to dislike politics. It also provides a rationale for ignoring it altogether. "I see a lot of negative finger-pointing by all the parties. As well, most of the things each party says they will do just seem really dishonest. I mean, none of those things will ever actually get done; they're just ways to get more votes. I really don't like that."

Finally, non-voting for our younger respondents does not carry the sense of social stigma that is more typically found in the older age groups. While many younger respondents agree that people ideally *should* vote in elections, they are not as likely to criticize those who come to the opposite conclusion. As one of our Facebook respondents put it, "During election campaigns, citizens should vote. But, it's not necessary for them to do so." Rather, many of our younger respondents place greater emphasis on an *informed* vote. Hence, the lack of attention to politics, coupled with a lack of necessary information, provides an acceptable rationale for non-participation. "I'm not informed. I don't know anything. My vote would not be informed." Or, as one respondent put it more succinctly, "I believe that a citizen should vote if one feels that they know what they are voting for, if you are unsure then you should not vote because that one vote could decide our future in the wrong way." While older generations are more likely to emphasize the *civic duty* aspect of voting, the younger age groups approach participation in elections more pragmatically. Civic duty alone is not enough to persuade newly eligible voters to go to the polls if they do not feel sufficiently informed or connected.

Conclusion

The demographic processes that are driving the turnout decline are relentless and slow moving, and the current pattern of decline is therefore unlikely to be easily or quickly reversed. If the age of the electorate is rising even faster than that of the population more generally, it will not be surprising to find governments under increasing pressure to pay ever more attention to issues such as health care and pensions than to education or employment. Younger voters are thus increasingly likely to feel, with some justification, that issues of greater concern to them are not addressed in election campaigns. But, it is also true that if younger voters continue to exit the electorate in large numbers, their voices will not be heard, their issues will not be addressed, and their candidates will not be elected. These types of linkages tend to create a type of "vicious circle" of non-participation that is largely self-reinforcing (see Figure 12.4).[16] Non-voting among the young simply encourages politicians to give even greater attention to the concerns of older voters. The same may be said with respect to the increasing negativity of electoral campaigns or the declining sense of voting as a civic duty. Continued high voting rates among the older age groups, driven in part by their stronger sense of voting as a civic duty, encourages political parties and candidates to target those groups during election campaigns. If non-voting is more acceptable to younger generations than it has been to older cohorts of voters, then the age gap among voters in elections is more likely to widen rather than to narrow.

Thus, the disengagement of young voters from the electorate has many implications for the kinds of issues addressed in the political arena, the types of candidates

FIGURE 12.4   "Vicious Circle" of Non-Participation in Elections

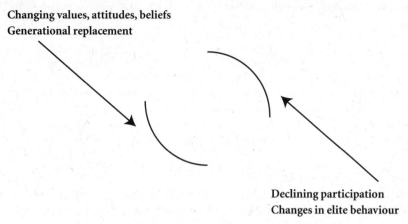

Changing values, attitudes, beliefs
Generational replacement

Declining participation
Changes in elite behaviour

who seek election, the positions taken by political parties, and the formation of public policy. In the longer term, there may also be serious implications for the health of electoral democracy itself. However, it is also clear that younger age cohorts, while more disengaged from the contemporary world of electoral politics than their elders, remain open to future political engagement. This sense of openness to the possibility of future participation could conceivably provide a rare opportunity for politicians who are willing to reach out and build less combative, inclusive, and meaningful bridges to younger voters. The increased engagement of youth in the 2008 US presidential election, although it may not be replicated elsewhere, at least suggests this possibility.

Although turnout in elections in Canada, both federal and provincial, may settle at levels that are considerably lower than in the past, it is likely to remain an important topic of study related to elections. In fact, lower turnout in the aggregate means that changes in turnout patterns over the course of an electoral cycle may be even more important in their electoral effects than they have been in the past. While parties and candidates may continue, as they always have, to target the most consistently reliable voting groups, lower turnout introduces greater uncertainty and potentially greater volatility. In a close election, or a competitive riding, relatively small changes in turnout could well be decisive.

NOTES

1. For examples, see LeDuc and Pammett (2006) and Curtice (2006).
2. For a complete listing of turnout rates in all federal elections from 1874 to 2006, see LeDuc and Pammett (2006, 306).
3. During the 1980s, for example, turnout in Newfoundland provincial elections averaged 13 percentage points higher than in federal ones (79 percent versus 66 percent). In Quebec over the same period, provincial turnout was about 3 percentage points higher (79 percent versus 76 percent), and in New Brunswick about 5 percentage points higher (82 percent versus 77 percent).

4. In Ontario, turnout in provincial elections during the 1980s averaged about 64 percent, compared with 75 percent in federal ones. In Alberta, the differential was even wider (57 percent versus 72 percent).

5. In Ontario, for example, turnout in the 2000 federal election was 58 percent—the same as in the 1999 provincial election. In Alberta, the turnout in the 2001 provincial election was 53 percent, compared with 54 percent in the province in the 2000 federal election.

6. See Clarke et al., *Political choice in Canada* (1979; 1980) for an exposition of this argument. See also Clarke et al., *Absent mandate* (1984; 1991; 1996) by the same authors for a continuation of this analysis in subsequent elections.

7. Ibid.

8. For example, in the 2008 Quebec election, turnout registered at a historic low of 57 percent. In the 2007 Ontario provincial election, turnout was 53 percent—the lowest ever recorded in the province. And, in the 2008 provincial election in Alberta, turnout reached an astonishing historic low of 41 percent.

9. For a discussion of comparative turnout patterns, see Milner (1997); Blais and Dobrzynska (1998) and Franklin (2004). A more comprehensive comparative treatment can be found in International Institute for Democracy and Electoral Assistance (2003). See also Rose (1997).

10. American turnout data are not strictly comparable to those from most other countries because of the absence of a national voters' list or central electoral authority in the United States. The statistics cited here are based on "voting age population," which is calculated from census data. Other methods of calculation may produce slightly higher estimates. On turnout patterns in US presidential elections, see Teixera (1992); Lyons and Alexander (2000); Gray and Caul (2002).

11. Here, we report findings from a survey conducted by the authors for Elections Canada in April 2002. The sample design used in this survey called for a short screening interview with a large number of randomly selected Canadians (5,637) as well as a longer interview with 988 reported voters in the 2000 federal election and 968 reported non-voters. The findings of this study are reported in detail in Pammett and LeDuc (2003b). See also Pammett and LeDuc (2003a; 2005).

12. The cohorts displayed in Figure 12.2 are structured according to the particular election at which a respondent first became eligible to vote. To have been eligible to vote in the 1988 federal election for example, a respondent would have to have been at least 30 years old in 2000.

13. An analysis of pooled data from the Canadian Election Studies confirms this pattern. Such an analysis clearly shows that, across a number of elections spanning more than 30 years, each generation of newly eligible voters participates at lower rates and begins to enter the electorate at a higher age. See Pammett et al. (2001).

14. The first of these consisted of two focus group studies conducted at the time of the 2007 Ontario provincial election. One group discussion involved ten potential first-time voters (aged 18 to 20), and the other was comprised of seven participants (aged 20 to 24) who had been eligible to vote in a previous election. A more detailed report of this study can be found in LeDuc, Pammett, and Bastedo (2008).

15. A second qualitative project was conducted at the time of the 2008 federal election. In this study, 33 respondents under the age of 26 were recruited on Facebook, and invited to share their views of politics and the election campaign in blogged responses over a period of four weeks. For a detailed report of this study, see Bastedo et al. (2009).

16. This theme is pursued in greater detail in Pammett and LeDuc (2004).

DISCUSSION QUESTIONS

1. Does voter turnout help us to explain the outcome of an election? Why or why not?
2. Voter turnout in elections in Canada and in most other Western democracies has been falling off in recent years. Why? What are some of the implications of the turnout decline?
3. In some provinces, voter turnout in provincial elections tends to be higher than in federal elections. Which provinces? What are some of the factors that may lead to higher provincial turnout?
4. Voter turnout in elections may have an influence on the conduct of election campaigns. In what ways? Why does this matter?
5. Voter turnout increased in the 2008 US presidential election. Why? Do you think that we may see a similar increase in turnout in the next federal election in Canada? Why or why not?

FURTHER READING

Blais, André. 2006. What affects voter turnout? *Annual Review of Political Science* 9: 111–125.

Franklin, Mark N. 2002. Electoral participation. In *Comparing democracies 2: New challenges in the study of elections and voting*, ed. Lawrence LeDuc, Richard G. Niemi, and Pippa Norris, 148–168. Thousand Oaks, CA: Sage Publications.

International Institute for Democracy and Electoral Assistance. 2003. *Voter turnout from 1945 to 1997: A global report.* 3rd ed. Stockholm, Sweden: International IDEA. http://www.idea.int.

Johnston, Richard, J. Scott Matthews, and Amanda Bittner. 2007. Turnout and the party system in Canada. *Electoral Studies* 26: 735–745.

Milner, Henry. 2002. *Civic literacy: How informed citizens make democracy work.* Lebanon, NH: University Press of New England.

Norris, Pippa. 2002. *Democratic phoenix: Reinventing political activism.* Cambridge: Cambridge University Press.

REFERENCES

Bastedo, Heather, Nicole Goodman, Lawrence LeDuc, and Jon H. Pammett. 2009. "Facebooking" young voters in the 2008 federal election campaign. Paper presented at the annual meeting of the Canadian Political Science Association, Carleton University, Ottawa.

Blais, André, and Agnieszka Dobrzynska. 1998. Turnout in electoral democracies. *European Journal of Political Research* 33: 239–261.

Clarke, Harold D., Jane Jenson, Lawrence LeDuc, and Jon H. Pammett. 1979. *Political choice in Canada.* Toronto: McGraw-Hill Ryerson.

Clarke, Harold D., Jane Jenson, Lawrence LeDuc, and Jon H. Pammett. 1980. *Political choice in Canada.* abr. ed. Toronto: McGraw-Hill Ryerson.

Clarke, Harold D., Jane Jenson, Lawrence LeDuc, and Jon H. Pammett. 1984. *Absent mandate.* Toronto: Gage.

Clarke, Harold D., Jane Jenson, Lawrence LeDuc, and Jon H. Pammett. 1991. *Absent mandate.* 2nd ed. Toronto: Gage.

Clarke, Harold D., Jane Jenson, Lawrence LeDuc, and Jon H. Pammett. 1996. *Absent mandate.* 3rd ed. Toronto: Gage.

Curtice, John. 2006. Turnout. In *Britain votes: 2005*, ed. Pippa Norris and Christopher Wlezien, 776–785. Oxford: Oxford University Press.

Franklin, Mark N. 2004. *Voter turnout and the dynamics of electoral competition in established democracies since 1945*. New York: Cambridge University Press.

Franklin, Mark N., Patrick Lyons, and Michael Marsh. 2004. The generational basis of turnout decline in established democracies. *Acta Politica* 39 (2): 115–151.

Gidengil, Elisabeth, André Blais, Neil Nevitte, and Richard Nadeau. 2003. Turned off or tuned out? Youth participation in politics. *Electoral Insight* 5 (2): 9–14.

Gray, Mark, and Miki Caul. 2002. Declining voter turnout in advanced industrial democracies, 1950–1997: The effects of declining group mobilization. *Comparative Political Studies* 33: 1091–1122.

International Institute for Democracy and Electoral Assistance. 2003. *Voter turnout from 1945 to 1997: A global report*. 3rd ed. Stockholm: International IDEA.

LeDuc, Lawrence, and Jon H. Pammett. 2006. Voter turnout in 2006: More than just the weather. In *The Canadian federal election of 2006*, ed. Jon H. Pammett and Christopher Dornan, 318–342. Toronto: Dundurn Press.

LeDuc, Lawrence, Jon H. Pammett, and Heather Bastedo. 2008. The problem of young voters: A qualitative and quantitative analysis. Paper presented at the annual meeting of the American Political Science Association, Boston.

Lyons, William, and Robert Alexander. 2000. A tale of two electorates: Generational replacement and the decline of voting in presidential elections. *Journal of Politics* 62: 1014–1034.

Milner, Henry. 1997. Electoral systems, integrated institutions and turnout in local and national elections: Canada in comparative perspective. *Canadian Journal of Political Science* 30: 89–106.

Pammett, Jon H., and Lawrence LeDuc. 2003a. Confronting the problem of declining voter turnout among youth. *Electoral Insight* 5: 3–8.

Pammett, Jon H., and Lawrence LeDuc. 2003b. *Explaining the turnout decline in Canadian federal elections: A new survey of non-voters*. Ottawa: Elections Canada. http://www.elections.ca.

Pammett, Jon H., and Lawrence LeDuc. 2004. Four vicious circles of turnout: Competitiveness, regionalism, culture and participation in Canada. Paper presented at the Joint Sessions Workshops of the European Consortium for Political Research, Uppsala, Sweden.

Pammett, Jon H., and Lawrence LeDuc. 2005. Behind the turnout decline. In *The Canadian general election of 2004*, ed. Jon H. Pammett and Christopher Dornan, 338–360. Toronto: Dundurn Press.

Pammett, Jon H., Lawrence LeDuc, Erin Theissen, and Antoine Bilodeau. 2001. *Canadian voting turnout in comparative perspective*. Report prepared for Elections Canada, Ottawa.

Park, Alison. 2004. Has modern politics disenchanted the young? In *British social attitudes: the 21st report*, ed. Alison Park, Professor John Curtice, Katarina Thomson, Catherine Bromley, and Miranda Phillips, 23–47. London: Sage Publications.

Rose, Richard. 1997. Evaluating election turnout. In *Voter turnout from 1945 to 1997: A global report on political participation*. 2nd ed. Stockholm: International IDEA.

Rubenson, Daniel, André Blais, Patrick Fournier, Elisabeth Gidengil, and Neil Nevitte. 2004. Accounting for the age gap in turnout. *Acta Politica* 39: 407–421.

Teixeira, Ruy. 1992. *The disappearing American voter*. Washington, DC: Brookings Institution.

Wass, Hanna. 2007. The effects of age, generation and period on turnout in Finland: 1975–2003. *Electoral Studies* 26: 648–659.

Wattenberg, Martin P. 2002. *Where have all the voters gone?* Cambridge, MA: Harvard University Press.

Wattenberg, Martin P. 2008. *Is voting for young people?* New York: Pearson Longman.

Whiteley, Paul, Harold D. Clarke, David Sanders, and Marianne Stewart. 2001. Turnout. *Parliamentary Affairs* 54: 775–788.

CHAPTER 13

Patterns of Party Identification in Canada

Joanna Everitt, Elisabeth Gidengil, Patrick Fournier, and Neil Nevitte

Introduction

Election researchers have long debated the degree to which voters hold strong party attachments (Schickler and Green 1997). This debate has been particularly vigorous in Canada (Gidengil 1992). Early scholars of voting behaviour argued that the concept of party identification was indistinguishable from vote choice: when people changed their vote, they appeared to change their party identification as well (Meisel 1975, 67). Others have argued that only a small portion of Canadian voters hold durable party allegiances. In other words, the majority should be considered flexible partisans who are influenced by short-term forces such as leaders, issues, or campaign events that lead them to change their identification from one election to another (Clarke et al. 1979, 1984, 1991, 1996; LeDuc et al. 1984). More recently, scholars have argued that better survey instruments reveal higher levels of party identification than were previously thought to exist (Johnston 1992; Blais et al. 2001): between one-half and two-thirds of the Canadian electorate are considered to be fairly strong or very strong party identifiers. This chapter argues that a substantial portion of the Canadian electorate holds enduring party allegiances and that this partisanship plays an important role in structuring voters' views on the different political parties and party leaders, and can influence the choices voters make at the ballot box.

Research on partisanship often relies on measures of party identification that are constructed from data gathered during a single election campaign and focus on strength of identification and consistency across levels of government. Due to the lack of panel data, research is seldom able to provide good measures of the stability of these partisan attachments.[1] Furthermore, it is seldom able to demonstrate how this stability might relate to other important factors in election campaigns, such as vote choice and leader evaluations. The 2004, 2006, and 2008 Canadian Election Studies (CES) allow us to address this weakness in the party identification literature by creating a new measure of party identification that is based on voters' party identifications at five different points in time in three different election campaigns.

These panel data are particularly important because they allow us to examine party attachments during an important transition period in Canadian electoral history. By the 2004 election, the transformation of the Canadian party system that had occurred during the 1990s was complete. The Canadian Alliance, previously the Reform Party, had merged with the Progressive Conservatives to form the Conservative Party of Canada. The new party faced the electorate for the first time in 2004. This consolidation of the parties on the right along with the fallout of the sponsorship scandal broke the Liberal dominance of the turn of the century and ushered in a period of successive minority governments and considerable electoral instability. No party managed to win enough votes during this period to form a majority government, which has raised questions about the degree to which Canadians maintain their party allegiances.

Using the panel component of the CES, we were able to assess partisan stability by distinguishing stable partisans (those who consistently identify with the same political party) from those whose partisan attachments are weaker. We were then able to use this measure to explore the degree to which party identification conditions other important election assessments such as voting behaviour and the manner in which voters evaluate the various parties and their leaders. In short, we discovered that the number of Liberal Party identifiers dropped considerably from 2004 to 2008, and the number of Conservative partisans increased. Furthermore, we found a strong relationship between the stability of party identification and party and leadership evaluations and vote choice.

The Debate Surrounding Party Identification in Canada

Popularized by the Michigan school of electoral analysis, party identification represents an enduring psychological attachment or a feeling of affinity to a political party (Campbell et al. 1960). As Elisabeth Gidengil (1992) has argued, it involves "a feeling of closeness to a political party; just as people identify with their religious group or their ethnic group they identify with a political party" (231). Although voters may be drawn away from their natural political predispositions by short-term forces such as current political issues, new party leaders, or campaign events, the theory suggests that they will inevitably be drawn back to their true political home. Along with making voters more predisposed to vote for a particular party, party identification may also condition voters' views on policy issues and party leaders (Miller and Shanks 1996). Voters who feel close to a party may also be likely to view that party and its leader more favourably than do those who have no identification with that party or whose identification is weaker.

When researchers first started to use party identification to explain the voting be-haviour of the Canadian electorate, they concluded that it was a meaningless concept because few respondents indicated an identification that differed from their vote choice. Since it was obvious from the aggregate results that voters changed their vote from one election to another, these scholars argued that when Canadians change their vote, they must change their identification at the same time (Meisel 1975, 67). In other words, party identification seemed to travel with the vote. This tendency un-dermined the expectation that party identification was the measure of a stable and strong attachment to a particular party because the concept seemed to be tied to short-term electoral preferences.

In an effort to provide more nuance to this concept, Clarke and his colleagues de-veloped the categories of durable partisans and flexible partisans. *Durable partisans* were defined as voters whose identification was strong, stable across federal and pro-vincial jurisdictions, and consistent across time. *Flexible partisans* were defined as voters who failed to meet one or more of the aforementioned criteria (Clarke et al. 1979, 1984, 1991, 1996; LeDuc et al. 1984). Based on studies conducted during the 1970s and the early 1980s, these authors concluded that only between a quarter and a third of Canadians could be considered to be durable partisans. The majority of voters were flexible partisans.

This conclusion—that partisanship among the Canadian electorate was highly unstable—was challenged on a number of grounds. The durable partisan requirement that voters identify with the same party across federal and provincial jurisdictions did not acknowledge the complexity of the federal system in Canada (Blake 1982). Not all parties are competitive (or even present for that matter) at both the federal and provincial levels in all parts of the country. For example, the Social Credit Party in British Columbia and the Parti Québécois in Quebec do not have federal counter-parts. This difference in federal and provincial party systems made it difficult, if not impossible, for voters to hold the same party identification across orders of govern-ment, which caused the number of stable partisans to be underestimated.

Another challenge came from those who argued that the high level of partisan in-stability found by Clarke and his colleagues (1979, 1984, 1991, 1996) is the result of how their question measuring party identification was worded (Johnston 1992; Blais et al. 2001). Early election studies typically asked, "Generally speaking, in federal politics do you usually think of yourself as Liberal, Conservative, NDP or what?" The framing of this question limited respondents' choices to one of the main parties and did not offer them the option of indicating that they identified with none of the par-ties. Since 1988, the CES have addressed this flaw in the survey instrument by including a "none of these" option. By using this new measure and considering only those who indicated that they "fairly strongly" or "very strongly" aligned with a party, the survey has revealed that a much larger number of voters appeared to have stable partisan attachments. In fact, the number of eligible voters in Canada who could be defined as party identifiers increased to about two-thirds in 1988 (Johnston et al. 1992). This number was smaller in the 1997 and 2000 elections (51 percent and 56 percent, respectively), a period during which a considerable transition took place in the Canadian party system: new regionally based parties were being established and reconfigured, and traditional partisan allegiances were being challenged (Nevitte et al. 2000; Blais et al. 2002).

Party Identification, Party Evaluations, Leadership Evaluations, and Vote Choice

Party identification, as originally conceived by the Michigan school, is of great interest to election researchers because it is one of the strongest predictors of party evaluations and leadership evaluations, which are regularly related to vote choice. As Warren Miller, Martin Wattenberg, and Oksana Malanchuk (1986) have argued, "the attitude consistency theory underlying this model suggested that party identification acts as a perceptual screen, and that the human need for consistency results in attitudes toward less central political objects, such as candidates, being brought into harmony with party identification" (522). In other words, those who strongly identify with a party are likely to view factors connected to that party such as the party itself or the party leader more favourably than those who do not identify with it or identify with it only weakly. This is not to say that contextual factors such as a party's performance or a leader's personal characteristics will not affect voters' responses at a particular time. However, we would expect voters that have a more stable identification with a particular party to be more predisposed to supporting that party and its leader, and more likely to vote for that party.

There is little debate about the degree to which party identification can affect attitudes toward parties and their records. John Zaller (1992), among others, has argued that strong party identifiers are more likely to resist negative information about their preferred party or candidates and be receptive to positive information about them. In his research on partisan bias, Bartels (2002) found that Republican voters were more likely than Democrat voters to assess George H.W. Bush's economic performance positively, and that these two viewpoints moved in parallel over the course of Bush's term in office. Bartels argued that if it were not for partisan bias, the attitudes of Republicans and Democrats would converge as voters gathered more information about politicians and objective conditions. He concluded that "partisan bias in political perceptions plays a crucial role in perpetuating and reinforcing sharp differences in opinion between Democrats and Republicans" (Bartels 2002, 139).

Studies that have looked at the public's attitudes toward parties over time indicate a downward trend in party evaluations since 1968 (Clarke and Kornberg 1993; Gidengil and Blais 2007). Clark and Kornberg (1993) have argued that "average feelings about the three federal parties decreased by 0.4 points per year across the 1968 and 1990 period" (300). This finding translated into approximately a 9 percentage point drop in the average sentiment toward political parties during this period.

Evaluations of political parties are not usually included in voting models (Johnston 1992; Blais et al. 2002; Nevitte et al. 2000; Clarke et al. 2008) because they are viewed as being too close to the party identification measure. However, it is important to note that the relationship between party identification and party evaluation is not perfect and is likely to vary from one election to another. Party identification is a general and enduring predisposition, whereas party evaluations should reflect voters' reactions to a party during a particular election campaign. Nonetheless, it is reasonable to expect that individuals who identify with a party are likely to view that party more positively than those who support other parties. The stronger and more consistently people identify with a party, the more positive we might expect their evaluation of that party to be.

Party identification is also very important in helping explain other aspects of political behaviour such as leadership evaluations. Many have argued that party leaders have become increasingly important in electoral politics (Hayes and McAllister 1997). Arguments for the importance of party leadership are supported by the increased media attention directed toward leaders rather than issues, policies, and other candidates (Mendelsohn 1993; Wattenberg 1991), as well as by the preoccupation with slight shifts in leadership evaluations in election-period public opinion polls (Graetz and McAllister 1987). Parties and politicians believe that leaders and their personalities influence election outcomes. As a result, they seek to frame their leaders in the best possible manner while often resorting to attack ads to undermine the credibility of their opponents. All of these factors point to the salience of leaders in Canadian election campaigns.

Although the attention to party leaders does not necessarily translate into leader-centred voting behaviour (Gidengil and Blais 2007), there is little doubt that leadership evaluations affect party preferences (Blais et al. 2002; Graetz and McAllister 1987; Nevitte et al. 2000; Stewart and Clarke 1992). Furthermore, there is evidence that party identification, particularly for strong and stable partisans, is even more likely to condition leadership evaluations (Blais et al. 2001). The reason, as is the case for party evaluations, is that strong and stable party identifiers tend to be more favourably predisposed to their own party leader than are voters who support other parties.

In a cross-country comparison of Britain, Canada, and the United States, André Blais and his colleagues (2002) found that the strength of party identification was related to leadership evaluations: the weaker the identification of voters with a political party, the lower their evaluations of that party's leader (13). Although the results for Canada were not as clearcut as they were for the other countries, they indicate that further research needs to be conducted, perhaps with better measures of partisan attachments.

Finally, party identification is considered an important factor in explaining election outcomes (Blais et al. 2002). While not all partisans vote for their party, a substantial number do. It is because of their traditionally stronger partisan base that the Liberals have been so successful in past elections (Blais et al. 2002; Gidengil et al. 2006). As Blais and his colleagues (2002) have argued, partisanship acts as a form of inertia. While party identifiers do not vote in a predetermined way, their attachment to a party makes them far more likely than non-identifiers to vote for that party (Blais et al. 2002). However, their degree of support may vary from one election to another, depending on campaign dynamics (Johnston et al. 1992).

Data and Methods

The panel design of the 2004, 2006, and 2008 CES[2] allows us to track the same respondents' party identification over three elections during a four-year period.[3] The 2004 and 2006 CES comprised a campaign survey and a post-election survey, while the 2008 study only re-interviewed panel respondents after the election. Because of panel attrition, the number of respondents used in this analysis is smaller than the overall number of respondents in the 2004 CES. Only 1,025 people responded to the party identification question in all five waves of the study.[4]

Because of the unique panel characteristics of these data, this analysis is able to use a different measure of party identification than past studies, which have typically relied on respondents' strength of identification with a party at one time. First, it focuses on voters' responses in all five waves of the panel study to the question, "In federal politics, do you usually think of yourself as a Liberal, Conservative, NDP, Bloc Québécois, Green Party, or none of these?"[5] Using these responses, we were able to create a measure of the stability or consistency of party identification that is not affected by recall error or the issue of reciprocal causation (that is, the likelihood that individuals might identify with a party simply because they like the current leader or intend to vote for it in that election). Respondents were assigned to one of four categories for each party. Voters who consistently identified with the same party in all five waves of the panel study were labelled *stable partisans*. Voters who identified with their party only three or four times over the three elections were labelled *unstable partisans*. Voters who identified with a party only once or twice were labelled *visitors*. Voters who never indicated an attachment to a party were labelled *non-identifiers*. Second, because the analysis is based on a more demanding measure of identification, it does not rely on the strength of identification question, as was commonly the case in past studies of partisanship that only included responses from those who "fairly strongly" or "very strongly" identified with a party.

This new robust measure of party identification was then compared with the three key questions in the 2008 CES. Because of the small sample of panel respondents from Quebec, we only examined results for the Conservatives, Liberals, and the NDP in this analysis. We began by analyzing the stability and consistency of party identification across the five surveys. Then, we compared the mean ratings for each party in 2008 according to the stability and consistency of its party identifiers across the five surveys. We did the same for the mean leader evaluations.[6] Finally, we compared the vote choice distribution for each category of party identification.

Results

While vote choice may shift from one election to another, party identification should remain far more stable. A first glance at Table 13.1, which includes the cross-sectional results of each wave of the survey, suggests that this is indeed the case. When asked in successive waves of the election studies how they viewed themselves, voters were fairly consistent in their aggregate responses.[7] Between 23.5 percent and 30.2 percent of respondents identified with the Liberals during the last three federal elections, with

TABLE 13.1   Party Identification Across the 2004, 2006, and 2008 Federal Election Campaigns (Percentage of the Electorate)

	2004 campaign	2004 post	2006 campaign	2006 post	2008 campaign	2008 post
Other	1.0	0.8	0.6	0.6	1.2	0.9
Liberal	28.5	29.7	30.2	29.1	23.5	25.4
Conservative	18.0	21.1	20.6	24.8	22.7	25.7
NDP	7.3	8.9	8.9	10.0	9.6	11.0
Bloc Québécois	8.3	8.4	8.7	8.6	8.4	8.5
Green Party	0.2	0.6	0.4	0.4	2.6	2.8
None of these	29.0	26.1	23.7	22.7	24.4	18.8
Don't know	4.0	1.4	3.7	1.4	4.4	2.3
Refused	3.7	3.2	3.3	2.4	3.2	4.7
$N =$	4,290	3,137	4,035	3,215	3,241	2,469

Note: Columns may not total 100.0 due to rounding.

Source: 2004, 2006, and 2008 Canadian Election Studies.

the percentage at its lowest in the 2008 election. Between 7.3 percent and 11 percent of voters identified with the NDP, and roughly 8 percent identified with the Bloc. Only the Conservatives saw any substantial shift in the number of voters who identified with them over this period. The percentage of Conservative Party identifiers grew steadily over the last three elections and reached a high of 25.7 percent of the electorate in the post-election wave of the 2008 election study.

Table 13.1 also shows that more than two-thirds of the electorate is prepared to indicate a feeling of closeness with a party when asked by survey researchers. These results are slightly higher than those found in other election analyses, which is likely due to the fact that previous studies factored strength of identification into their measures. Thus, this preliminary assessment of party identification may capture weak identifiers who regularly move between one party and another or between identification and non-identification. In other words, although it would appear that there were only slight changes that occurred in the percentage of respondents who identified with the various parties from one election to the next, parties have no guarantees that they can regularly count on this support since some respondents may feel only weakly attached to the parties with which they have identified.

In fact, some shifting goes on—even during the course of a single election campaign. This point becomes clear when we move from the aggregate level to look at the consistency of individual responses. In both 2004 and 2006, consistent Liberal identifiers composed only 18 percent of the electorate. Consistent Conservative identifiers composed 14 percent in 2004 and 17 percent in 2006; consistent NDP identifiers composed 5.5 percent in 2004 and 6.3 percent in 2006; and consistent Bloc identifiers composed 4.8 percent in 2004 and 6.3 percent in 2006. The number of respondents who indicated that they either had no attachment to a political party or had switched political parties between the pre- and the post-election surveys was 58 percent in 2004 and 52.4 percent in 2006.

When responses are compared across all five waves of the panel study, the percentage of voters who consistently identified with a party drops even further. Table 13.2 shows that a total of 31.6 percent of the respondents in the panel data were stable partisans who identified with the same party in all five waves of the survey. Meanwhile, 15.7 percent indicated that they identified with the same party in four of the five waves.

Despite starting with a smaller proportion of the electorate in 2004, the Conservatives managed to retain more of their partisans than the other parties did. Just over 13 percent of respondents indicated that they identified with the Conservatives in all five waves of the study; that is, 5 percentage points fewer than had identified with them in the campaign wave of the 2004 CES, but only slightly fewer than had identified with them in both the pre- and post-campaign waves of the 2004 CES. As might be anticipated from their drop in the aggregate data, Liberal partisans were less stable. The Liberal Party saw its proportion of identifiers drop by more than half; they went from 28.5 percent in the campaign wave of the 2004 CES to 11.7 percent when responses to all five waves of the study were considered. This drop was substantial for a party whose past electoral success was attributed to the fact that half of voters who identified with a party identified with the Liberals (Blais et al. 2002). Both the NDP and the Bloc also saw their percentage of party identifiers decrease when stronger conditions of consistency were imposed. The NDP identifiers dropped from 7.3 percent in the campaign wave of the 2004 CES to 4 percent in the aggregate data. The Bloc fell from 8.3 percent to 2.7 percent.

Unstable partisans often identify with their party, but on occasion they assume a non-partisan identity or shift their identity to another party. Most often, when unstable partisans move away from their own party, they move to a non-partisan position. In all, 22.4 percent of the Liberals' unstable partisans in the post-campaign wave of the 2008 election indicated that they no longer identified with a political party, 16 percent identified with the Conservatives, and 1.6 percent identified with the NDP. A full

TABLE 13.2   Consistency of Respondent Identification Across the 2004, 2006, and 2008 Federal Election Campaigns

	Number of times the respondent identified with a party (percentage)					
	0	1	2	3	4	5
Conservative	64.9	9.6	4.0	3.7	4.5	13.2
Liberal	61.2	9.3	5.3	5.4	7.0	11.7
NDP	83.6	4.9	2.6	2.6	2.3	4.0
Bloc Québécois	91.6	1.9	1.2	0.7	1.9	2.7
Total		25.7	13.1	12.4	15.7	31.6

Source: 2004, 2006, and 2008 Canadian Election Studies.

59 percent remained true to the Liberals. In all, 20 percent of the Conservatives' unstable partisans shifted to a non-partisan identification, 1 percent identified with the Liberals, and 2 percent identified with the NDP. A full 73 percent of the Conservatives' unstable partisans maintained a Conservative identity in this election. The NDP's unstable partisans were more evenly divided among their primary opponents (10.2 percent for each of the Liberals and Conservatives) and a non-partisan position (18.4 percent).

These results suggest that by 2008 the partisan base of the Conservatives had grown. More voters were beginning to identify with the party and, as a result, the proportion of respondents who could be categorized as Conservative unstable partisans was larger than it had been in earlier elections. Because a number of voters were shifting to the Conservatives, the party's unstable partisans appeared more loyal. Both the Liberals and the NDP saw just over half of their unstable partisans continue to identify with them. Those who had identified with these parties in earlier elections were less likely to identify with them in 2008. The only consolation for the Liberals in these results is that their percentage of unstable partisans (those who identified with the Liberals in at least three of the five surveys) is higher (13.4 percent) than that of the Conservatives (8.2 percent). This finding suggests that if the Liberal Party were to run a strong election campaign with a popular party leader, it might be able to draw these "sometimes" identifiers back to the fold.

The Conservatives currently have a larger base of consistent party supporters than the Liberals; however, questions arise about either party's ability to win enough support to form a majority government. If stable and unstable partisans were combined, 24.1 percent of voters would support the Liberals and 21.4 percent would support the Conservatives. Neither the NDP nor the Bloc would gain much support from their unstable partisans. Even if all of their slightly weaker identifiers supported them, the NDP and the Bloc would trail the two larger parties with 8.9 percent and 5.3 percent of voters, respectively.

Although party identification is considered an enduring attachment, short-term factors such as party performance and leadership evaluations can, in an election, lead voters to abstain from voting or shift their vote to another party. Nonetheless, we would still expect that those who identify strongly with a party to be predisposed to support it. As Figure 13.1 shows, this is in fact the case. This figure presents the results when mean scores are compared for each type of party identifier. All differences in this table are statistically significant. The first column for each party reflects the mean scores given to the party for the full panel sample. The subsequent columns represent stable partisans, unstable partisans, visitors, and non-identifiers. These results indicate that the Conservative Party was viewed more favourably than the Liberals and the NDP; however, none of the parties received enthusiastic support across the full panel sample. The Conservatives just barely broke the neutral 50 percent mark, and the Liberals and NDP were 6 and 8 percentage points behind that mark, respectively.

More interesting in this analysis is the pattern of results that appears when the average ratings are compared for each type of party identifier. As expected, in the case of all three parties, those who have identified, even fleetingly, with a party in the last

FIGURE 13.1   Party Evaluations, 2008 Federal Election

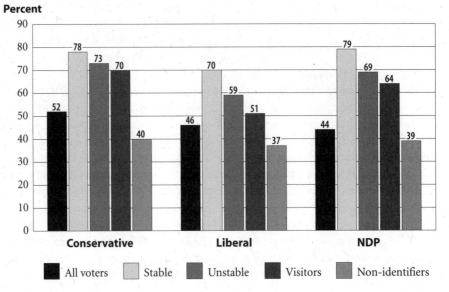

Source: 2008 Canadian Election Survey.

three elections viewed that party more positively than have those who had never identified with it. Clearly, stable partisans held the most positive views of their parties. However, even those whom we have classified as visitors have views that are still substantially more positive than are the views of those who have never identified with a party. The Liberal Party saw the greatest variation among stable partisans, unstable partisans, and visitors, which may reflect the fact that its partisan base declined the most over the last three election campaigns.

Another important short-term factor influencing the 2008 federal election campaign was the ranking of the party leaders among the electorate. While Stephen Harper, leader of the Conservatives, and Jack Layton, leader of the NDP, had headed their parties prior to the 2004 election, Stéphane Dion had become Liberal leader in the fall of 2006. He replaced Paul Martin, who stepped down as Liberal leader after the Liberals lost the 2006 election. Shortly after Dion won the Liberal leadership, the Conservatives began to air a series of attack ads aimed at undermining his credibility as a leader in an effort to reduce his support among the public. These ads continued until the 2008 election and helped generate an image of the Liberal leader as weak and ineffective. By the election, two-thirds of the respondents to the 2008 CES considered Dion a weak leader and awarded him the lowest leadership evaluations of any leader in an election since 2000. In contrast, both Stephen Harper and Jack Layton received higher overall evaluations than they had in the previous two campaigns (Gidengil et al. 2009).

Figure 13.2 shows that while none of the leaders scored a particularly positive evaluation among the whole panel sample (Harper scored a neutral 50 percent), it is

FIGURE 13.2   Leader Evaluations, 2008 Federal Election

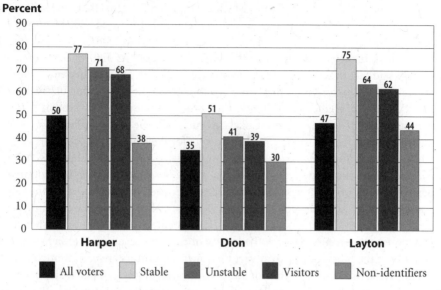

Source: 2008 Canadian Election Survey.

clear that the leaders were more popular with their own identifiers than with sup-porters of other parties. The highest leadership evaluations for all leaders came from their party's stable partisans.

Even Dion, who scored extremely poorly among the sample as a whole, received a slightly positive 51 percent score among those who consistently identified themselves as Liberals. However, his low general evaluations were not just due to the negative attitudes of non-Liberals. Even the most stable Liberal partisans viewed Dion more critically than the other parties' stable partisans viewed their leaders. Harper received a score of 77 percent from his party's stable partisans, and he even received a 68 percent score from visitors. Layton scored 75 percent from his party's stable partisans and 62 percent from visitors. While there is little doubt that those who had flirted at one time or another with a party identification were likely to view that party's leader more fa-vourably than were those who had never felt such an affiliation, there is also little doubt that these evaluations are conditional on a leader's performance. The impact of party identification is relative, not absolute. Weak leaders will receive low ratings, although their ratings will be a little less negative among their party's stable and un-stable partisans.

Although it is obvious from these results that party identification is related to voters' evaluations of political parties and party leaders, ultimately all elections are decided by vote choice. One of the reasons for John Meisel's (1975) earlier concern about party identification in Canada was that it was so strongly correlated with vote choice that these two variables seemed to be measuring the same thing. Subsequent scholars have suggested that there is definitely a strong relationship between party identification and voting behaviour, in part because party identification has an impact on party and leadership evaluations, which are short-term factors that can lead voters to look elsewhere in a given election. This was certainly the case in 2008.

While the responses of the panel participants in the 2004 to 2008 CES do not exactly match the actual election outcomes, they are fairly close.[8] As Figure 13.3 shows, 42 percent said that they voted for the Conservatives, 27 percent said they voted for the Liberals, and 17 percent said they voted for the NDP. When the voting behaviour of respondents is examined according to their type of partisanship, a familiar pattern appears: stable partisans are most likely to vote for their party, while those whose identification is less stable are less likely to vote for their party.

Two observations need to be made about these data. First, stable Conservative partisanship is almost perfectly correlated with Conservative voting behaviour: 95 percent of the Conservatives' stable partisans indicated that they voted for the Conservatives in the 2008 election. The Liberals could only count on the support of 85 percent of their stable partisans, while the NDP's stable partisan support fell between the two (at 90 percent). Second, the loyalty of the Conservative identifiers and the inability of the Liberal Party to attract their own supporters are even more obvious among those who are less stable identifiers or just flirting with a particular partisan identity. Whereas 81 percent of the Conservatives' unstable partisans and 73 percent of their visitors said they voted for the Conservatives, only 45 percent of the Liberals' unstable partisans and 35 percent of their visitors said they voted for the Liberals. Again, the NDP partisans fell in between, with 52 percent of stable partisans and 48 percent of their visitors saying they voted for the NDP.

FIGURE 13.3 Vote Choice, 2008 Federal Election

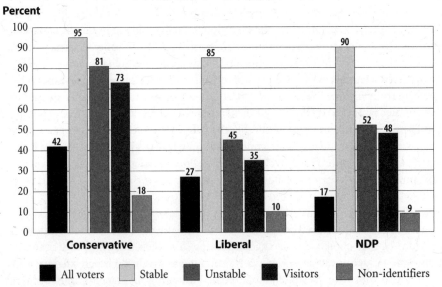

Source: 2008 Canadian Election Survey.

Conclusion

The results of these analyses suggest that party identification does represent a real and meaningful attachment to a political party. Even during a period of considerable electoral instability, almost a third of Canadian voters remained loyal enough to a political party to identify with it at five different points in time. A further 15.7 percent of identifiers were unfaithful to their party or provided a response of "none of these" only once during the period under study. It is also clear that voters, when they moved away from a party, were as likely to move to a non-partisan position as they were to switch to another party identification.

Furthermore, as we anticipated, this analysis indicates that a strong and clear relationship exists between partisan identification and the way that voters evaluate parties and their leaders and end up voting in an election. While partisanship is not a perfect predictor of responses to these items, the relationships are easy to observe. Stable party identifiers are likely to view their party and the party's leader more positively than unstable party identifiers and those who have occasionally identified with the party. More important, these results indicate that party identification is an independent political concept. Partisans are willing to continue to identify with their party, even while voting against it. Although short-term political forces that often come into play during an election campaign may mediate the "homing" effects of party identification, even visitors to a party's fold are more likely to have positive views of that party and its leader and are more likely to vote for that party than those who have never felt any attachment to it.

These results suggest that the Conservative Party has been the most successful between 2004 and 2008 in maintaining the loyalty of its partisans and broadening its base of support. It has clearly managed to develop an identity that is distinct from the old Progressive Conservative and Canadian Alliance parties that splintered the right during the 1990s. While the data used in this chapter do not enable us to account for why voters have been drawn to the Conservative Party, other work analyzing the basis of party support in recent elections suggests that the Liberal Party has been losing support among the two groups that have traditionally formed its core voters: visible minorities and Catholics. In 2008, the key beneficiary of this move away from the Liberals was the Conservatives. Visible minorities were almost as likely to vote for the Conservative Party in this election as they were for the Liberal Party. The shift to the Conservatives was even more pronounced among Catholic voters (Gidengil et al. 2009). Although it is too soon to determine whether this shift represents a permanent realignment of visible minority and Catholic support, it certainly leaves the Conservative Party in a much more competitive electoral position than they have been in for almost two decades.

While the NDP has made few gains or losses over the last three elections, the Liberals, on the other hand, have seen their partisan base whittled away. The cumulative impact of the sponsorship scandal in 2004, the Gomery Commission revelations in 2006, and a weak leader in 2008 has reduced the number of Liberal stable partisans to a proportion of the electorate that is now similar to that of the Conservatives. An optimistic response to this trend would be that despite these challenges, which have helped erode the party's base of support, Liberal partisans have not completely disappeared. They remain, albeit in fewer numbers, attached to their party and more likely to vote for it than for any other party. Furthermore, there is still a large base of Liberal unstable partisans and Liberal visitors who may be persuaded under the right conditions to return to the party's fold. A more pessimistic response would be that the Liberal electoral dominance that has marked much of the history of the 20th century in Canada can no longer be counted on.

NOTES

1. An exception would be the work by LeDuc et al. (1984), which used panel data from the 1974, 1979, and 1980 Canadian Election Studies to examine the stability of party identification. However, since the party identification question in these surveys did not include a "none of these" option in the list of parties individuals could identify with, it probably overstated the flexibility of voters during this period.
2. The Canadian Election Studies were funded by the Social Sciences and Humanities Research Council of Canada and Elections Canada. The field work was conducted by the Institute for Social Research at York University.
3. Eighteen months separated the end of the 2004 election and the beginning of the 2006 campaign. Thirty-three months separated the 2006 and the 2008 elections.
4. These panel respondents were slightly unrepresentative of the general public in that they were on average older (only 14 percent of the sample were under the age of 40), slightly more female (52.2 percent as opposed to 51 percent in the electorate), better educated (almost twice as likely to have a university degree), and more Protestant than the average voter (10 percentage points more Protestant and 7 percentage points less Catholic).
5. These data are based on the initial question, "In federal politics, do you usually think of yourself as a Liberal, Conservative, N.D.P., Bloc Québécois, or none of these?" They do not include respondents who answered the follow-up question, "Do you generally think of yourself as being a little closer to one of the federal parties than to the others?" and if so, "Which one is that?"
6. Party evaluation questions asked respondents to identify how they feel about each political party on a scale from 0 to 100: "0" means that they really dislike the party and "100" means that they really like the party. Leader evaluation questions asked respondents to identify how they feel about each party leader on a scale from 0 to 100: "0" means that they really dislike the leader and "100" means that they really like the leader.
7. These aggregate responses likely overstate the stability of party identification.
8. In the 2008 election, the Conservatives received 37.7 percent of the popular vote, not the 42 percent that they received from the panel respondents. The Liberals received 26.3 percent of support from the electorate and 27 percent from the panel. The NDP received 18.2 percent of support from the electorate and 17 percent from the panel.

DISCUSSION QUESTIONS

1. How does the measure of party identification used in this chapter differ from previous measures of party identification?
2. How do stable partisans behave differently from unstable partisans, visitors, and non-identifiers?

3. Imagine that you are a political adviser to the Conservatives, Liberals, or NDP. How might the information in this chapter help your party prepare for an upcoming election campaign?

FURTHER READING

Blais, André, Elisabeth Gidengil, Richard Nadeau, and Neil Nevitte. 2001. Measuring party identification: Canada, Britain, and the United States. *Political Behavior* 23: 5–22.

Blais, André, Elisabeth Gidengil, Richard Nadeau, and Neil Nevitte. 2002. *Anatomy of a Liberal victory: Making sense of the 2000 Canadian election.* Peterborough, ON: Broadview Press.

Canadian Election Study. http://ces-eec.mcgill.ca/ces.html.

Clarke, Harold D., Jane Jenson, Lawrence LeDuc, and Jon H. Pammett. 1979. *Political choice in Canada.* Toronto: McGraw-Hill Ryerson.

Meisel, John. 1975. Party images in Canada: A report on work in progress. In *Working papers on Canadian politics*, 2nd enlarged ed., ed. John Meisel, 63–126. Montreal: McGill-Queen's University Press.

REFERENCES

Bartels, Larry. 2002. Beyond the running tally: Partisan bias and political perceptions. *Political Behavior* 24 (2): 117–150.

Blais, André, Elisabeth Gidengil, Richard Nadeau, and Neil Nevitte. 2001. Measuring party identification: Canada, Britain, and the United States. *Political Behavior* 23: 5–22.

Blais, André, Elisabeth Gidengil, Richard Nadeau, and Neil Nevitte. 2002. *Anatomy of a Liberal victory: Making sense of the 2000 Canadian election.* Peterborough, ON: Broadview Press.

Blake, D.E. 1982. The consistency of inconsistency: Party identification in federal and provincial politics. *Canadian Journal of Political Science* 15: 691–710.

Campbell, Angus, Philip E. Converse, Warren E. Miller, and Donald Stokes. 1960. *The American voter.* New York: Wiley.

Canadian Election Study. http://ces-eec.mcgill.ca/ces.html.

Clarke, Harold D., Jane Jenson, Lawrence LeDuc, and Jon H. Pammett. 1979. *Political choice in Canada.* Toronto: McGraw-Hill Ryerson.

Clarke, Harold D., Jane Jenson, Lawrence LeDuc, and Jon H. Pammett. 1984. *Absent mandate: The politics of discontent in Canada.* Toronto: Gage.

Clarke, Harold D., Jane Jenson, Lawrence LeDuc, and Jon H. Pammett. 1991. *Absent mandate.* 2nd ed. Toronto: Gage.

Clarke, Harold D., Jane Jenson, Lawrence LeDuc, and Jon H. Pammett. 1996. *Absent mandate: Canadian electoral politics in an era of restructuring.* 3rd ed. Toronto: Gage.

Clarke, Harold D., and Allan Kornberg. 1993. Evaluations and evolution: Public attitudes toward Canada's federal political parties, 1965–1991. *Canadian Journal of Political Science* 26 (2): 287–311.

Clarke, Harold D., Allan Kornberg, and Thomas J. Scotto. 2008. *Political choices: Canada and the United States.* Toronto: University of Toronto Press.

Gidengil, Elisabeth. 1992. Canada votes: A quarter century of Canadian national election studies. *Canadian Journal of Political Science* 25: 219–248.

Gidengil, Elisabeth, and André Blais. 2007. Are leaders becoming more important to vote choice? In *Political leadership and representation in Canada: Essays in honour of John Courtney*, ed. Hans Michelmann, Donald Story, and Jeffrey Steeves, 39–59. Toronto: University of Toronto Press.

Gidengil, Elisabeth, André Blais, Joanna Everitt, Patrick Fournier, and Neil Nevitte. 2006. Back to the future? Making sense of the 2004 Canadian election outside Quebec. *Canadian Journal of Political Science* 39: 1–25.

Gidengil, Elisabeth, Patrick Fournier, Joanna Everitt, Neil Nevitte, and André Blais. 2009. The anatomy of a Liberal defeat. Paper presented at the annual meeting of the Canadian Political Science Association, May, Ottawa.

Graetz, Brian, and Ian McAllister. 1987. Popular evaluations of party leaders in the Anglo-American democracies. In *Political elites in Anglo-American democracies: Changes in stable regimes*, ed. Harold D. Clarke and Moshe M. Czudnowski, 44–64, DeKalb, IL: Northern Illinois University Press.

Hayes, Bernadett, and Ian McAllister. 1997. Gender, party leaders and electoral outcomes in Australia, Britain and the United States. *Comparative Political Studies* 30 (1): 3–26.

Johnston, Richard. 1992. Party identification measures in the Anglo-American democracies: A national survey experiment. *American Journal of Political Science* 36: 542–559.

Johnston, Richard, André Blais, Henry E. Brady, and Jean Crête. 1992. *Letting the people decide: Dynamics of a Canadian election.* Montreal: McGill-Queen's University Press.

LeDuc, Lawrence, Harold D. Clarke, Jane Jenson, and Jon H. Pammett. 1984. Partisan instability in Canada: Evidence from a new panel study. *The American Political Science Review* 78 (2): 470–484.

Meisel, John. 1975. Party images in Canada: A report on work in progress. In *Working papers on Canadian politics*, 2nd enlarged ed., ed. John Meisel, 63–126. Montreal: McGill-Queen's University Press.

Mendelsohn, Matthew. 1993. Television's frames in the 1988 Canadian election. *Canadian Journal of Political Science* 26: 149–171.

Miller, Warren E., and J. Merrill Shanks. 1996. *The new American voter.* Cambridge: Harvard University Press.

Miller, Warren, Martin Wattenberg, and Oskana Malanchuk. 1986. Schematic assessments of presidential candidates. *American Political Science Review* 80 (2): 521–540.

Nevitte, Neil, André Blais, Elisabeth Gidengil, and Richard Nadeau. 2000. *Unsteady state: The 1997 Canadian federal election.* Don Mills, ON: Oxford University Press.

Schickler, Eric, and Donald Green. 1997. The stability of party identification in Western democracies: Results from eight panel surveys. *Comparative Political Studies* 30 (4): 450–483.

Stewart, Marianne, and Harold D. Clarke. 1992. The (un)importance of party leaders: Leader images and party choice in the 1987 British election. *The Journal of Politics* 54 (2): 447–470.

Wattenberg, Martin. 1991. *The rise of candidate-centred politics: Presidential elections of the 1980s.* Cambridge, MA: Harvard University Press.

Wattenberg, Martin. 2003. Electoral turnout: The new generation gap. *British elections and parties review* 13: 159–173.

Zaller, John R. 1992. *The nature and origins of mass opinion.* New York: Cambridge University Press.

CHAPTER 14

Greater Than the Sum of Its Parts: Political Cultures and Regions in Canada

Ailsa Henderson

Introduction

Canada is a large country with distinct geographical regions and a population that is ethnically, linguistically, socially, and culturally diverse. The physical variation in territory and a geographically dispersed and heterogeneous population make for all manner of natural and man-made regions. It is no surprise, then, that political scientists are interested in exploring the political consequences of regionalism. As we might imagine, people whose livelihoods are dominated by access to different resources or whose communities are preoccupied by markedly different types of concerns develop distinct policy needs and preferences. It is therefore understandable that governments respond to this variation by differentiating groups of people by their needs and wishes. It is also understandable that people living in different regions might respond to the same policies in distinct ways. The causes of political differentiation are relatively clear, but the consequences of this differentiation on the relationship between citizens and the state continue to captivate political scientists. Does the existence of political regions and the different political treatment meted out to different groups of individuals across the country lead to varying levels of political support, participation in political life, efficacy, and public confidence in government?

We know that a link exists between region or province of residence and aspects of electoral behaviour, such as partisan preference or participation. But what drives regional variations in attitudes and behaviours? Are they affected by nothing more than the characteristics that define a region, or do regions themselves exert an independent impact on political behaviour? Studying such variations offers more than an understanding of the parts that constitute the whole of Canadian political life; it does more than highlight the existence of regions. Instead, it offers us insight into the operation of the wider "system" of political life, which both reflects and creates regional variations in attitudes and behaviours. It was to this very Canadian debate on regionalism in politics that the article reprinted below, "Regional Political Cultures in Canada," sought to contribute when it was published in 2004. Its republication at the end of this chapter provides an opportunity to re-examine its arguments, fleshing them out in light of questions and comments made by colleagues in the intervening years.

"Regional Political Cultures in Canada"

The original article was by no means the first to examine multiple political cultures in Canada. It was not even the first to employ that title, nor the first to employ it in the *Canadian Journal of Political Science* (Simeon and Elkins 1974). However, it attempted to build on previous studies and mark a new direction in such research by highlighting that provinces are not the only or main source of territorial variation in attitudes in Canada. The other contribution of the article was that our traditional east-west understanding of regionalism in Canada has ignored the considerable north-south dimension to our politics. The demographic dominance of the south has tended to blind us to the provincial and territorial north, regions that are less exotic but more interesting than southern academics might have imagined. But how do such regional political cultures operate?

We know, of course, that sociodemographic variables such as gender, age, education, and income are associated with attitudinal and behavioural variability. Younger people vote less frequently than do older people, and those with higher levels of education tend to be more trusting of government than individuals who left school earlier. We know also that place matters, that a woman in Vancouver and one in Baker Lake might have different evaluations of government, just as a university graduate in Rimouski and one in Windsor might have different partisan preferences. Political scientists have typically grounded these differing preferences in the sociodemographic variation that exists across provinces. In addition, the provincial governments themselves have helped to structure political attitudes and behaviours. Even two neighbouring provinces, such as Alberta and Saskatchewan, have different approaches to taxes, health care, and auto insurance.

In other words, governments behave differently because of the populations they find themselves governing, and so variations in resources, or the linguistic, social, and cultural characteristics of electorates can lead to different policies, which in turn spark particular expectations and perceptions on the part of the public. In this interpretation, provinces are the engines of attitudinal and behavioural heterogeneity in Canada, their borders creating multiple political cultures, one for each province (and presumably one for each territory, although these jurisdictions are typically not discussed explicitly). This important finding, that the substate political level has the capacity to instill attitudes and behaviour and serves as a unique agent of socialization, is often underestimated in wider political science in a kind of empirical state-ism. Before the popularity of the multilevel literature, Canadian scholars had clearly established the significance of the substate level. Carefully detailing just how and why it affects cross-level political participation, general political attitudes, or voting in federal elections has been a more recent concern (Cutler 2008a, 2008b; Anderson 2008; Henderson 2008).[1]

Economic, cultural, and social variations affect the way in which provincial governments respond to the perceived needs of their electorates. Likewise, the Canadian government responds to and facilitates regionalism in two ways. First, it delivers policies targeted at particular populations and regions. Policies aimed at revitalizing the fishing industry or the agricultural sector, or ones that improve funding for cities may be of universal benefit to all Canadians indirectly, but have a direct effect on those employed in particular industries, or those living in particular regions. Second, by virtue of the varied nature of the country, policies designed to treat the entire country uniformly will not have equal effect or be received in a similar manner by all. Policies lauded and welcomed in some quarters will seem irrelevant or a pernicious intrusion in others. Differing evaluations of the federal government can stem from both policy that targets a specific group or policy that is intended to have universal applicability and appeal, but suits or fits some groups better than others. In other words, social and cultural variations within the population can prompt government treatment that is regionally specific in intent or effect, which in turn can prompt regionally specific political reactions in terms of partisan preference, trust in government, and voter participation. It is in this cycle of action and reaction that we can see how regional political cultures operate in Canada. Regional political cultures do not replace provincial political cultures, they co-exist alongside them. They are the territorial variants of Canadian political culture. The Canadian political system sets the boundaries for a Canadian political culture, and the Canadian government is the object of support or distrust, satisfaction or antipathy within that political culture. Provincial and territorial political cultures, by contrast, operate within the different substate jurisdictions in Canada. Although the findings in the article demonstrate that regional political cultures do a better job of explaining attitudinal variation in Canada, the article does not intend to suggest that provincial political cultures do not exist or do not exert a powerful socializing force on individuals: the two political cultures exist in tandem. Depending on the particular region or province in question, they can either reinforce each other or act at cross purposes.

A Way Forward

In response to such claims, one might pose two questions. First, just how stable are regional political cultures? Does their location change over time either subtly or drastically and, in either case, what is "cultural" about them, particularly if they lack an independent agent of socialization? Second, how, if at all, does the location or presence of regional political cultures help to explain individual-level participation? The following section responds to each question in turn.

Regional political cultures are the territorial variants of Canadian political culture. Their location is relatively stable over time, in the sense that it has been identified according to variables such as economic activity, the ethnic and linguistic characteristics of the population, population mobility, and social structure. To the extent that such variables are stable over time, so too will be the location of the regional variants. They are not likely to be static, however, and this quality does not detract from their "cultural" nature. Their existence is a function of the "system" of Canadian political life. They are parts of a culture; they are not stand-alone cultures. The Canadian political culture is distinct, not because of how the modal response or median voter can be compared with those in other states, but because of what occurs internally.

The impact of regional political cultures on individual-level political behaviour requires similar careful treatment, for it encourages us to think of political culture as a possible independent variable, which some political culture research clearly counsels against (Elkins and Simeon 1979). The article argues that regional political cultures exist and indicates where they are located. It presents them as independent variables in a final table solely to demonstrate that they are better able to account for certain variables than province of residence is. It does not employ them in a model to account for individual attitudes; overall, the article treats political culture as a dependent variable. For some political scientists, it is helpful to employ political culture as an independent variable. For example, a large and developed literature in the United States seeks to determine whether and how Daniel Elazar's (1984) three political cultures account for variations in political attitudes, electoral behaviour, state budgets, and policies.[2] I would argue, however, that research seeking to employ regional political culture as an independent variable must first identity how it will address four questions:

1. Is it appropriate to use political culture, which is a property of the aggregate, to explain individual-level behaviour, or in so doing does it become a last ditch catch-all variable used to account for deficiencies in models of behaviour?

2. Is political culture being used as a measure of contextual effects (a characteristic of the system as a whole) or compositional effects (a summary variable for the aggregated ethnicity, linguistic diversity, or social structure of a region)?

3. How can we distinguish the influence of regional political culture from the influence of provincial political culture?

4. How can we distinguish the impact of political culture from the impact of individual characteristics such as age, gender, and education?

The second question is of most relevance to the article reprinted below, which aggregated statistics to identify the location of regional political cultures. These aggregated statistics are examples of compositional variables (Hutchison 2007). The political cultures themselves, however, are contextual variables.

The mechanics of conducting research that pits individual-level variables against regional and provincial political cultures is relatively straightforward. Multilevel analysis using software such as MLwiN is able to determine the impact of individual-level and aggregate-level variables. Of greater concern is the conceptual distinction among aggregate-level variables and the theoretical model that accounts for political culture's impact. Such research would be received well by those seeking to account for individual-level attitudes and behaviour but received with caution by some political culture researchers. The article avoided the four issues raised above by determining the existence of and identifying the location of regional political cultures. It tells us not about individual behaviour, but about Canadian political culture as a whole. Canada is more than just 13 separate substate political cultures. Its political culture has created and now includes clear regional variants: it is greater than the sum of its parts.

NOTES

1. A special panel at the 2008 Canadian Political Science Association conference addressed this issue, revisiting the arguments in Elkins and Simeon's *Small Worlds*, published in 1980.
2. "Regional Political Cultures in Canada" contains a discussion of typical examples of such research.

DISCUSSION QUESTIONS

1. If you had to identify the regions of Canada, how many regions would you identify and where would they be? What characteristics would distinguish them?
2. Considering the presence of both regional and provincial political cultures in Canada, can we speak of a single Canadian political culture?
3. Are regional political cultures merely descriptive or can they help us predict variations in political attitudes and behaviour?

FURTHER READING

Elazar, Daniel. 1984. *American federalism*. 3rd ed. New York: Harper & Row.

Elkins, David, and Richard Simeon, eds. 1980. *Small worlds: Provinces and parties in Canadian political life*. Toronto: Methuen.

Henderson, Ailsa. 2007. *Hierarchies of belonging: National identity and political culture in Scotland and Quebec*. Montreal and Kingston: McGill-Queen's University Press.

Henderson, Ailsa. 2007. *Nunavut: Rethinking political culture*. Vancouver: UBC Press.

Nevitte, Neil. 1996. *The decline of deference*. Peterborough, ON: Broadview Press.

Putnam, Robert. 1993. *Making democracy work*. Princeton: Princeton University Press.

REFERENCES

Anderson, Cameron. 2008. Region and policy preferences in Canada: 1979–2006. Paper presented at the annual conference of the Canadian Political Science Association, Vancouver.

Cutler, Fred. 2008a. One voter, two first-order elections. *Electoral Studies* 27: 492–503.

Cutler, Fred. 2008b. The space between worlds: Intergovernmental policy and elections in Canada. Paper presented at the annual conference of the Canadian Political Science Association, Vancouver.

Elazar, Daniel. 1984. *American federalism.* 3rd ed. New York: Harper & Row.

Elkins, David, and Richard Simeon. 1979. A cause in search of its effect, or what does political culture explain? *Comparative Politics* 11: 127–145.

Elkins, David, and Richard Simeon, eds. 1980. *Small worlds: Provinces and parties in Canadian political life.* Toronto: Methuen.

Henderson, Ailsa. 2008. "Small worlds" as predictors of generalized political attitudes. Paper presented at the annual conference of the Canadian Political Science Association, Vancouver.

Hutchison, Dougal. 2007. When is a compositional effect not a compositional effect? *Quality and Quantity* 41 (2): 219–232.

Simeon, Richard, and David Elkins. 1974. Regional political cultures in Canada. *Canadian Journal of Political Science* 7 (3): 397–437.

Regional Political Cultures in Canada

Ailsa Henderson

Canadian Journal of Political Science 37 (3): 595–615 (2004).
Reprinted with the permission of Cambridge University Press.

Research on political attitudes and behaviour in Canada tells us that Canadian political culture is not what it used to be. Canadians are becoming less deferential than they once were. Depending on which research you read Canadians are either becoming more like Americans (Nesbitt-Larking, 1998; Nevitte, 1996) or less like Americans (Adams, 1998; 2003; Lipset, 1990; Peacock, 1998). Voter turnout is down, cynicism is up, confidence in leaders is down, distrust is up. The fundamental tenets of Canadian political culture, to the extent that we believe what they had to say about Canadian political attitudes, appear to be shifting. If these attitudes are changing, we have reason to believe that other tenets, such as regionalism, are also not static. This article argues first that interprovincial differences in political attitudes are either stable or declining, depending on the indicator. Second, it demonstrates that on measures of trust and efficacy, regional rather than provincial affiliations account for variations among Canadians.

Regionalism is one of the accepted facts of Canadian political life. The distinct fragments in eastern Canada and present-day Quebec are credited with tempering Canadian liberalism with a Tory or feudal touch (Horowitz, 1966; McRae, 1964; Lipset, 1968). Our understanding of the brokerage system of political life in Canada hinges on the existence of regional demands. Literature on different political approaches in various provinces has received considerable attention and has linked social practices and demography to the development of party politics.[1] For the most part these works were neither comparative nor quantitative, but rather efforts to account for the tenor of political life in a particular region or province.[2]

Systematic attention to quantitative data on regional political cultures owes much to Richard Simeon and David Elkins, who examined results of the Canadian Election Studies in the 1960s and 1970s (Simeon and Elkins, 1974; Elkins and Simeon, 1980). The authors concluded that there are variations in efficacy and trust across Canada, producing four distinct citizen types: critic, supporter, deferential and disaffected. Respondents in the eastern provinces and French Canadians displayed much lower levels of political efficacy than their counterparts in British Columbia and Ontario. This pattern also holds true for political trust, although French Canadians appear more trusting that their Atlantic counterparts. The Atlantic provinces, which displayed low trust and efficacy, were deemed disaffected. Voters in Ontario and British Columbia were characterized as, respectively, critics and supporters, French Canadians as deferentials. The authors noted that each of the four categories would be present in any provincial population, but that the overall classification of the province flows from the existence of cultural boundaries that are meaningful to voters. In short, Canadian provinces possessed distinct political cultures as a result of distinct provincial institutions. Variations in demographic characteristics that might otherwise account for deviations in political attitudes are thus not solely responsible for these differences. Provincial differences remained even when community size, social class, education, age and sex are controlled for.

Elkins and Simeon subsequently updated their analysis to incorporate later data and to clarify their argument (Elkins and Simeon 1980). *Small Worlds* contains a broader range of attitudes on which to examine provincial political cultures and shows significant differences according to national identity, role of government, social policy preferences and spending and partisan identification. Throughout, the collected papers argue that the province presents an enduring boundary, although often acting in concert with socio-demographic factors such as class, employment and immigrant status. On some measures such as national identity, constitutional renewal, support for a multicultural Canada and patterns of public expenditure, provinces present diverging political attitudes and behaviours. On most areas of public policy, however, provinces appear to have converging preferences.

These findings are consistent with research on provincial political cultures in Canada (Nevitte, 1995; Wilson, 1974). Among such works there is a belief that provincial sub-cultures reflect very real variations in political practice. In his analysis of regional political cultures in Canada, for example, John Wilson made reference to past practices such as the absence of Hansard in British Columbia, the underdeveloped role for the opposition in Ontario, the absence of nominating conventions for the Liberal party in Newfoundland and differing approaches to patronage, some more enthusiastic than others (Wilson, 1974). Such variations, according to Wilson, were symptomatic of different stages of political development, which in turn could account for variations in political values. Researchers on political cleavages also notes that there are variations in attitudes and behaviour between women and men, French and

English speakers, among different religious groups and rural and urban voters (Burt, 1986; Everitt, 1998; Mendelsohn and Nadeau, 1997; Nevitte, 1996; O'Neill, 2001; Wearing and Wearing, 1991; Gidengil, 1989; 1990; Ornstein, 1986). Some of these characteristics cluster in different regions, compounding the potential existence of regional political preferences.

Regionalism and the existence of provincial political cultures has been an enduring element in attitude research since Simeon and Elkins first published their research. This analysis should be revised, however, for two main reasons. First, the original analysis draws on data that are almost forty years old. But, the questions on which the original work rests its conclusions have been replicated in many of the subsequent election studies. Thus, an investigation of more recent data would allow us to determine whether there are still significant variations in political attitudes. Updating the analysis does not allow much for its advancement but tests its continued applicability. As a result this would be more of a mechanical manipulation than a conceptual advancement of the work. The second reason for revisiting this work is the fit between theory and data. Simeon and Elkins argue that provincial political cultures exist first, because provincial political institutions create meaningful cultural boundaries around citizens, and second, because of the varied relationship between the federal government and voters across the country. Although the updated analysis in 1980 incorporated perceptions of different levels of government, thus far analyses of provincial political cultures have conflated the notions of provincial culture and regional reaction. With the exception of 1984, the Canadian Election Study has never asked respondents about their views of provincial politics, the supposed motor behind pan-Canadian variations. Thus, when survey respondents identify their perceptions of the federal government, they are responding to indicators that tap into the regionalized aspect of Canadian political culture rather than the existence of provincial sub-cultures. Responses for these individuals are then aggregated at the provincial level, forcing a provincial analysis on to regional data.

The following analysis revisits Simeon and Elkins' original data and then addresses the conceptual relationship between provincial sub-cultures and regional variant cultures. It examines the existence of regions within Canada by analyzing the social, demographic and economic characteristics of federal election districts. In his assessment of the renaissance of political culture William Reisinger claimed that future research must seek to explain how sub-cultures relate conceptually to the overall societal culture (Reisinger, 1995). Elkins and Simeon, in a methodological piece on political culture, also suggest that the "culture-bearing unit" must be identified (Elkins and Simeon, 1979). For both these works, sub-cultures require bounded communities, as would be the case with provincial political culture. In contrast, regional variations in political attitudes that do not conform to provincial boundaries reflect the different experiences that voters have with the federal government. There is a conceptual difference between asking individuals how they feel about politics during a federal election—an exercise that would heighten awareness of regional divisions—and arguing for the existence of provincial political cultures as created by provincial institutions. Simeon and Elkins argued, for example, that voters in Atlantic Canada possess low efficacy and low trust. It is worth determining if variations in attitudes can better be explained by province or by region. At present, asking about Ottawa and dividing by province does not allow us to determine whether both, one or neither is relevant. This article, then, determines whether regional clusters can substitute for provinces as the constituent units of political culture, without loss of explanatory power.

Data and Analysis

The analysis relies primarily on two datasets. The first dataset is the 2000 Canadian Election Survey (CES), which contains a rolling cross-section sample of respondents who completed two waves of interviews (before and after the election) and a self-completion questionnaire. The questions have a considerable amount of continuity from the first election study in 1965. Where applicable, data have been compared with earlier years that relied on similar coding. In most cases this facilitates a comparison between 1974, when 5-point Likert scales were used, rather than earlier years. The second dataset consists of Federal Election Profiles (FEP) for all federal constituencies, data for which are drawn from the 2001 census. The profiles offer counts for a variety of ethnic, linguistic, racial, economic and demographic measures. These data were recoded to represent percentages or rates rather than raw counts for each constituency. Further manipulation, explained later in this section, facilitated the sorting of constituencies into coherent clusters for analysis. Each constituency in the FEP dataset was then assigned to a cluster. To determine the relationship between a regional cluster and political attitudes, each respondent in the 2000 CES was assigned the cluster that corresponded to the federal constituency in which he/she resided. Differences in political attitudes could then be tracked according to province and to region. The use of both datasets allows for an analysis of the differential impact of province or region on the political attitudes of respondents.

Contemporary Data

Simeon and Elkins argued that significant differences among provincial respondents pointed to the existence of provincial political cultures. Central to this conclusion was an analysis of efficacy, trust and political involvement data from the 1965, 1968 and 1974 election studies. Table 1 compares the responses of provincial respondents for the efficacy measures in 1974 and 2000. Data from 1974 are used, as this year employed a Likert scale similar to the one currently used in the CES. Before this year, respondents were asked if they agreed or disagreed with a particular statement, rather than if they agreed, or agreed strongly, disagreed or disagreed strongly. Furthermore, Table 1 only contains responses for the efficacy questions, as trust variables in the earlier studies have not been replicated in recent versions of the CES. With this in mind, Table 1 reports the percentage of individuals who indicated that they agreed or agreed strongly with three measures of political efficacy. Architects of institutional reform argue that change is needed because voters are becoming increasingly frustrated with politicians, and possess declining confidence and satisfaction, efficacy and trust. As Table 1 shows, however, the widespread decrease in efficacy that politicians have feared has not materialized. Over the last thirty years the proportion of people who feel that they have no say in politics has decreased in Canada, as has the proportion of individuals who feel that politics is too complicated. The proportion of respondents who indicate that it is not worth voting remains unchanged in Canada. We know, of course, that one of the best predictors of efficacy, formal education, has increased in the last thirty years. While not the focus of this paper, changes such as these could account for improved efficacy. These are, of course, not the only measures of political dissatisfaction. In addition, the perception that voting is not a worthwhile activity, stable since 1974, cannot account for the decline in turnout from 1974 to the present. What we do know, however, is that by these limited measures the proportion of "low-efficacy" respondents in Canada has decreased over time. This in itself is interesting, but for our purposes the differences among provinces prove more revealing.

In 1974, provincial respondents offered widely varying responses. As Simeon and Elkins noted, far more Atlantic residents expressed low efficacy, while voters in British Columbia expressed more positive responses. In the following thirty years, however, there appear to have been dramatic changes within provinces and a levelling off among respondents. In 1974, Quebec francophones, Newfoundlanders and New Brunswickers respectively had the largest proportion of low-efficacy voters according to the three questions listed here. Today, almost thirty years later, Saskatchewan voters record the largest proportion expressing low efficacy on two of the three questions, while a large proportion of Newfoundlanders remain convinced that politics is too complicated for them. At the same time, while British Columbians once had the lowest proportion of low-efficacy respondents, this mantle has now passed to anglophone and francophone voters in Quebec, and residents of PEI. In fact, of francophone voters in Quebec, only 14 percent believe they have no say in politics. By contrast, the proportion of

TABLE 1   Efficacy Scores in Provinces over Time

	C	NF	PEI	NS	NB	QEng	QFr	O	MB	SK	AB	BC
Efficacy												
People like me have no say												
1974	53	67	65	44	51	51	70	45	66	58	51	37
2000	37	43	26	56	54	58	14	39	40	59	54	53
Politics too complicated												
1974	65	86	63	57	80	66	63	62	85	71	75	56
2000	52	63	46	53	55	41	58	46	55	57	53	48
So many voters, no point voting												
1974	14	18	20	20	27	18	22	10	19	10	14	6
2000	14	15	9	10	13	15	15	12	16	32	10	15

Source: CES 1974, CES 2000. Results are percent who agree or agree strongly with the statement. Complete question wording is included in the appendix.

Canadians who feel this way is 37 percent. Provinces with previously large proportions of respondents indicating minimal efficacy have seen a drop in their numbers. Efficacy appears to have improved in most of the Atlantic provinces. At the same time, provinces on the opposite end of the scale in 1974 also appear to have had a change in attitudinal patterns. Ontario, once home to a relatively small number of respondents expressing a lack of efficacy, has seen a small rise in the number of voters who feel there is little point in voting. Although the ranges in proportions appear similar across time, the patterns of change are interesting. Within the Atlantic provinces, some have seen a marked drop in the proportion of respondents with low efficacy, while others have seen a dramatic rise. If culture has an enduring influence on politics, and can explain the presence of critics, supporters, disaffecteds or deferentials in any province, and if Atlantic provinces possessed similar "deferential" cultures in 1974, how can we account for opposing trends within categories? An analysis of regional political cultures addresses this point.

Province or Region?

Students of political culture in the United Kingdom have long attempted to prove the existence of national political cultures. In part, the argument for devolution was based on the existence of different approaches to policy and government in Scotland and Wales. Quantitative research on the subject, however, has had very limited success in proving the existence of constituent cultures in the United Kingdom (Henderson, 2001; Miller, Timpson et al., 1996). In most cases, proof of difference is found only upon stretching political culture as a concept to include voting preferences for nationalist parties or national identity (Dickson, 1996; Brown, McCrone et al., 1998). More often, research on political culture in the United Kingdom indicates that the boundaries around the historic nations are less relevant than the social and demographic characteristics of various regions (Curtice, 1988; 1992; 1996). John Curtice argues that there is neither a distinct Scottish political culture, nor a Welsh or English political culture, but northern and southern variations of political attitudes fostered mainly by the different economic experiences of voters. For Curtice, region feeds nationalism, a fact not disputed in most literature on nationalism in Scotland (Brown, McCrone et al., 1998; Mitchell, 1996).

Simeon and Elkins acknowledged the impact of socio-economic characteristics and indicated that many of these characteristics were distributed unequally across the country. Pointing to the diversity of political attitudes within such provinces as Alberta and Saskatchewan, however, they warned that "it is dangerous to assume citizens of geographically proximate areas share the same attitudes" (Simeon and Elkins, 1974: 401). For them, not all Albertans think alike, nor do all Westerners. This view does not preclude the existence of regions that occur within and across jurisdictional boundaries, a topic of research much more developed in American political science.

In his analysis of American federalism, Daniel J. Elazar identified three main political cultures in America: an individualistic culture, a traditional culture and a moralistic culture (Elazar, 1972). For those in the individualistic type, politics and government operate as a marketplace, while for the moralistic type, the responsibility of government is to build a commonwealth in which all benefit. The traditionalistic view falls between these two poles and tends to advocate elitist or deferential approaches to politics. The different groups were created, Elazar argued, by patterns of early migration. The arrival of ethnic and religious blocks of voters, coupled with the pattern of Western migration, led to pockets of homogeneity in which pre-existing views of politics could influence American political life. Once cemented in institutions, these pre-existing approaches continually reinforce political attitudes. In this, Elazar's analysis fits well with fragment theories of Canadian political culture. The analysis is based on an intuitive understanding of the way American politics has developed. Subsequent research has sought to improve upon Elazar's model, subjecting it to a more rigorous statistical analysis (Clynch, 1972; Schlitz and Rainey, 1978; Savage, 1981; Sharkansky, 1969). One approach in particular is useful for our purposes.

In his 1993 article Joel Lieske sought to determine whether there was a more systematic way to identify regional political cultures in the United States. To accomplish this goal he created a database that contained aggregated data for counties in the United States. The racial, ethnic, religious and linguistic profiles of the counties were recorded alongside information on urban population, population mobility, presence of certain age cohorts, employment in various economic sectors, university education and income. The author then employed cluster analysis to identify the existence of coherent groups of counties and identified seven distinct clusters of counties in the United States. In an effort to determine whether his method provided a better explanation of variations in political attitudes in the US, the author assigned respondents in the national election study to each of the clusters based on their county of residence. He then ran a series of analyses of variance tables to determine whether the clusters demonstrated statistically significant differences in political attitudes. One of the advantages of Lieske's approach is that it does not identify the clusters based on responses to political attitudes, but rather it relies on what he refers to as the constituent units of culture, namely ethnicity, race, language, religion and social structure. As much of the literature on political culture argues, voter attitudes are proxy measures of culture. Individuals themselves do not possess political cultures (Simeon and Elkins, 1980), nor regional variants nor sub-cultures, but have attitudes and behaviours that allow us to examine what the dominant political culture might look like. Relying on the sources of political culture rather than its products allows for an investigation that is conceptually cleaner. This method has been employed in a Canadian context once before. In his 1990 article Robert MacDermid sought to identify different regional clusters within Ontario. His research points to seven distinct clusters within Ontario, which vary according to two axes: urban–rural and economic activity. This reflects the indicators selected by MacDermid, which include measures of income and employment, and single indicators for language, ethnicity, religion and education (MacDermid, 1990).

In an effort to determine whether there are regional variants of Canadian political culture, this article draws on a similar methodology. In particular, the analysis relies on a dataset of all federal constituencies and relevant demographic information from

Statistics Canada. The data draw on the profiles of federal election districts that contain information on ethnicity, race, income, education, mobility, population and employment. Rather than mimic exactly Lieske's categories, which are better suited to the American migration patterns and the particular racial profile of the United States, the following analysis employs a list of indicators that better reflect variation among Canadian constituencies. The cluster analysis relies on four main variables, with a number of constituent indicators.

Ethnicity/Race/Religion: % Québécois/Acadian, % British, % Scandinavian, % Protestant Europe, % Catholic Europe, % Asian, % Black/African, % Slavic, % Aboriginal origins, % Jewish

Language: % English mother tongue, % French mother tongue, % bilingual, % Native languages, % Asian, % Scandinavian, % Western European language, % Slavic, % sub-continent, % Gaelic

Immigration: % immigrants, % old immigrants, % new immigrants, % 3rd generation Canadians or older

Social structure: % over 65, % internal migrants, % non-movers, % common law, % university degree, % managerial, % professional, % natural resources, % women in labour force

These four variables are intended to capture the ethnic and linguistic migration patterns that were considered to have an impact on Canada's initial fragment cultures, in addition to social-demographic information that currently influences political attitude variations. Ethnicity has been coded so that it identifies those reporting Jewish ethnicity or an ethnic background of a Protestant or Catholic European country.[3] Federal election districts were then classified on the basis of common cultural characteristics, using cluster analysis. The number of clusters was set at nine, in the expectation that districts would be grouped according to the following categories: eastern Canada, Prairies, western provincial north, southwestern Ontario, northern Ontario, homogeneous Quebec, metropolitan Toronto, metropolitan Vancouver, metropolitan Montreal. Such an arrangement reflects the vision of Canada as a country of five regions, while recognizing the multicultural nature of its larger urban centres. Results of the cluster analysis support grouping the constituencies into nine relatively homogeneous clusters.[4] The characteristics of the clusters suggest the following descriptive labels based on their geographic location:

1. Cosmopolitan Quebec
2. Suburban Toronto and Vancouver
3. Urban Canada
4. Rural and mid-northern
5. Manufacturing belt
6. New France
7. British North America
8. Far north
9. Metropolitan Toronto

Some of these clusters exist entirely within a province while others cross provincial and territorial boundaries.[5] As expected, the analysis produced separate clusters for metropolitan Toronto and homogeneous Quebec (labelled here as New France). Atlantic Canada is not a coherent region, although many of the Atlantic constituencies appear in a cluster characterized by large proportions of respondents with British ancestry. This cluster has been labelled British North America as it contains areas to which United Empire Loyalists emigrated both in the Atlantic provinces and in Ontario. Other constituencies in Atlantic Canada are incorporated into the manufacturing belt cluster, which also contains constituencies in Ontario such as Sudbury and the "nickel belt." Metropolitan Vancouver did not receive its own cluster although much of metropolitan Montreal is contained within the cosmopolitan Quebec cluster. Instead, many of the Vancouver constituencies appear along with other urban centres in the urban cluster. This cluster contains urban constituencies, mostly from the richer "have" provinces, and unlike the others, it is not geographically concentrated in one region. Suburban Toronto and Vancouver include constituencies from the 905 area and Vancouver area constituencies such as Burnaby. There are two clusters for the north. The rural and mid-north cluster contains respondents from across the western portion of the provincial north, including Ontario, Saskatchewan, Manitoba, Alberta, British Columbia and the Yukon. The far north includes the NWT and Nunavut, in addition to two larger northern constituencies in the western provinces.

The typical vision of regional variations in Canadian political culture is that they operate on an east–west basis. The cluster analysis suggests that we must acknowledge the north–south dimension of Canadian politics, not only as it relates to the territorial north but to the provincial north as well (Coates and Morrison, 1992). This analysis also highlights the heterogeneous nature of western Canada, which is often lumped together as a distinct entity. At its most nuanced, the west often is treated as three distinct groups: British Columbia, Alberta and the prairie provinces of Manitoba and Saskatchewan. Here, however, the west contains elements of an urban cluster, which includes cities such as Edmonton and Winnipeg, and a rural cluster, which includes the elements of provinces across the west. In addition, these are distinguished from suburban Vancouver, which has more in common with suburban Toronto than with more proximate constituencies in rural British Columbia. The characteristics of each cluster reinforce this point.

The far north cluster contains a large proportion of native residents and the British North America cluster contains a larger proportion of English, Scottish, Irish and Welsh residents. Metropolitan Toronto has a high mean score for immigrants from "old Europe," while suburban Toronto and Vancouver contain more Asian and sub-continent residents. The rural and mid-northern constituencies have larger mean scores for Slavic residents, a fact that reflects the ethnic characteristics of early migrants to the prairies. The New France cluster contains far fewer constituencies of British stock. The size of each cluster ranges from four, for the far north cluster, to the sixty constituencies that comprise the New France cluster. To be useful, however, the division of constituencies into regions must be accompanied by an analysis of their impact on political attitudes.

In light of the comparison of efficacy indicators earlier, Table 2 contains the proportion of respondents who agreed or agreed strongly, sorted by regional cluster. The regional clusters possess varying efficacy responses that reflect, in many cases, the answers in relevant provinces. The New France cluster, for example, has a small proportion of respondents who feel they have no say. Interesting differences appear in clusters that are geographically close to each other. Suburban Toronto and Vancouver have a larger proportion of low-efficacy respondents than metropolitan Toronto. Rural and mid-northern constituencies have a larger proportion of low-efficacy respondents than urban constituencies in "have" provinces. The constituent attitudes of any political culture include more than measures of efficacy. The following analysis employs seven main variables. Attitudes to basic responses to efficacy questions are included alongside groups of questions probing perceptions on voting and views of political parties. Further explanations of these variables are contained within the appendix.

The analysis also includes an additive index of political activity, counting respondents who have performed any of five protest behaviours. Individuals who would consider acting in a similar manner were not included in the index counts. An additional index tracks confidence in public institutions such as the government and police. Last, the analysis contains two measures of political ideology, one old, one of more recent origin. Placement on a left–right spectrum is included, as is a test for post-materialism. In sum, these seven variables were used to compare the differences among respondents according to province of residence of regional cluster.

TABLE 2   Efficacy Scores in Clusters

	Clusters							
	Cosmo Q	Sub TO&V	Urban	Rural	Manuf	NFr	BNA	Met TO
	(1)	(2)	(3)	(4)	(5)	(6)	(7)	(9)
People like me have no say % agree, agree strongly	21.5	56.7	38.9	53.1	45.7	16.8	43.3	35.1
Politics too complicated % agree, agree strongly	51.3	51.7	45.6	54.7	60	58.3	49.6	39.8
So many voters, no point voting % agree, agree strongly	14.1	25.9	10.0	18.8	8.7	14.5	11.7	12.0
N	246	94	588	609	108	1055	709	222

Cluster 8 has been excluded because of insufficient respondents.

TABLE 3   Comparison of Province and Regional Clusters

	F	
	Province	**Regional cluster**
Efficacy	3.006**	2.048*
Voting	.657	.555
Parties	.594	.967
Political activity	1.627	2.249*
Confidence	1.844	1.140
Left–right	3.137**	3.957**
Post-materialism	.379	.538
Wilks' Lambda	.837	.856
	F = 1.648**	F = 1.845**

*p < .05, **p < .05

Table 3 summarizes the analysis of variance for province and regional cluster. There is a significant difference among provincial respondents according to measures of efficacy, which confirms the earlier findings of Simeon and Elkins, and significant differences according to left–right ideology. There is also a significant difference among the respondents when clustered by region. These differences are summarized in the ANOVA F scores, which examine the variation between groups, and the variation within groups. A significant F score indicates that there are clear divisions among the categories of the variables. Here, efficacy, left–right placement and political activity produce significant deviations in results among clustered respondents. Results of the multinomial logistic model further illustrate this point.

Tables 4 and 5 contain the predicted probabilities of membership in the province or regional cluster based on the seven political variables. The results demonstrate first that political attitudes are able to predict membership in regional clusters as well as they are able to predict province of residence. The pseudo-R^2s for both models are similar. We are hoping for a McFadden's score greater than .2, which does not occur in either model.[6] Second, the tables show that some variables produce statistically significant estimates of membership. The betas in multinomial logistic regression report the maximum probability of observing the values of the dependent variable that were observed, given the values of the independent variables. These predicted probabilities are recorded as the natural logs of the odds ratio. In other words, as efficacy increases by one unit the probability of correctly predicting residence in Quebec increases by a multiplicative factor of .62. Within the regional model, as left-wing beliefs increase by one unit a respondent is four times more likely to be classified as residing in cosmopolitan Quebec. The tables also indicate the percentage of cases in any grouping that were correctly predicted by the model. The proportion of cases correctly predicted for both models appears similar, at 37 percent for the provincial model and 30 percent for the regional model. The preceding analysis suggests that

TABLE 4   Predicted Probabilities of Provincial Membership

	Model	NF	PEI	NS	NB	Q	ON	MB	SK	AB
Efficacy		.255	-.510	-.764	-.252	-.478**	.032	-.162	-.228	-.787***
Voting		-.073	-.212	-.328	.314	.219	.002	.004	-.045	.092
Parties		.094	-.066	.300	.258	.298	.264	-.184	-.007	.368
Post-materialism		.599	1.551	.549	1.272	.029	.159	.506	.320	.600
Political activity		-.208	-.947	2.715	-1.075	.375	.041	-1.849	-1.920	-.096
Confidence		4.935*	5.126	5.399	4.316*	3.801***	1.101	5.286**	2.806	2.512
Left		.125	.679	-.974	-.102	1.004**	.083	.112	-.441	-1.420**
% correctly predicted	36.7%	0%	0%	0%	0%	20.9%	71.8%	0%	0%	7%
Cox and	.163									
Snell	.047									
McFadden's	104.82***									
chi-square	.163									

Predictions are based on the estimated coefficients of the multinomial logistic model.
Reference category is British Columbia.

*p < 0.1, **p < .05, ***p < .01

TABLE 5   Predicted Probabilities of Cluster Membership

	Model	Cosmo Q (1)	Sub TO & V (2)	Urban (3)	Rural (4)	Manuf (5)	NFr (6)	BNA (7)
Efficacy		.323	-.338	.040	-.312	-.305	-.583**	.093
Voting		.113	.179	-.088	.025	.015	.190	-.004
Parties		-.287	-.090	-.217	-.547**	-.899**	-.173	-.423*
Post-materialism		-.730	-.745	-.726	-.326	.499	-.739	-.383
Political activity		-1.357	-.065	.097	-.833	-.094	1.058	1.041
Confidence		-.630	-.828	-.133	2.433	6.417**	3.583**	1.249
Left		1.395*	-.763	-.695	-1.183**	-.884	.301	-.378
% correctly predicted	30%	0%	0%	29.3%	51.9%	0%	21.1%	19.4%
Cox and	.143							
Snell	.042							
McFadden's	90.73***							
chi-square								

Respondents from cluster 8 are excluded from the analysis because of small numbers.

Predictions are based on the estimated coefficients of the multinomial logistic model.

Reference category is cluster 9 (Metropolitan Toronto).

*p < 0.1, **p < .05, ***p < .01

further research should more fully explore the existence and influence of regions in generating variations of political attitudes and behaviour across Canada.

Existing research on political culture highlights the importance of regionalism in Canada, something that this article confirms. From earlier works exploring the relevance of migrant groups in New France and British North America, to more recent evidence on varying levels of efficacy across the country, such research emphasizes both the existence of east–west variations, and provincial political cultures. The first significant finding, then, is that regionalism in Canada is not an exclusively east–west phenomenon, nor does the role of provinces appear to be of unparalleled influence, as previously thought. By noting that regional clusters can equally account for variations in political attitudes and behaviour across Canada, this article clearly notes that regionalism in Canada does not conform to provincial boundaries. The existence of multiple cultures within the west, and the identification of two distinct northern clusters suggest that the west is much less homogeneous than once assumed, and that the long-ignored north is not only relevant, but diverse. The analysis notes also the existence of not one but three distinct urban clusters, something suggested in MacDermid's 1990 research on Ontario. This in itself suggests that the rural–urban dichotomy should in future distinguish among those living in large metropolitan centres, suburban areas, mid-sized urban towns and more rural areas.

Perhaps most significant, the research questions the importance of political institutions in the generation of assessments of their performance. Previously, regional political cultures in Canada have been seen as the products of institutions. Provincial legislatures and the policy they generate could account for much of the variation in attitudes to politics, the remainder of which was attributed to the different ways in which the Canadian Parliament and its legislation affected citizens in different portions of the country. If regional clusters perform as effectively as provincial boundaries in accounting for variations in political attitudes and behaviour, then there is reason to doubt, at the very least, the impact of provincial institutions. We should be cautious, though, in our assessments of provincial impact, if only because indicators directly probing efficacy and trust in provincial politics have long been excluded from the Canadian Election Study. Clearly, though, provincial boundaries are not the only way to account for variations in political culture across Canada. That these clusters exist within and across provincial boundaries points to the greater need for research into the interaction among socio-demographic variables, provincial boundaries and attitudes to the federal government.

Conclusion

This article performed two tasks. First, it examined variations in provincial attitudes to federal politics in light of recent data in the CES, and demonstrated that the number of low-efficacy respondents is falling and that inter-provincial differences appear stable over time. Second, it demonstrated the existence of regional clusters that could account for variations in attitudes to federal politics. Regionalism in Canada, usually seen as an east–west phenomenon, also contains an important north–south dimension.

In addition, indicators of political culture, including perceptions of parties, voting, efficacy, left–right beliefs and post-materialism, can predict membership in regional clusters as successfully as they can residence in provinces.

In its exploratory investigation of the current state of provincial political cultures in Canada, this paper sought to clarify whether provincial political institutions or regional clusters could better account for variations in federal political attitudes. Additional research would help to further clarify the relationship between province and region. Such research could examine the predictors of provincial political attitudes, re-examine the measures of political culture at the provincial level and determine the role of regional clusters in driving attitudes to provincial politics. The data explored here do not disprove the existence of significant provincial variations, but suggest that greater attention should be paid to the role of regions in the generation of political attitudes. It would appear that what we have been measuring thus far in political culture research is not the existence of provincial sub-cultures, but that of regional variations. The structure of any existing sub-cultures remains an under-explored area of research.

Appendix

Variables

Variable	Explanation	Coded
	Cluster Analysis for FEPs	
Ethnicity		
Québécois/Acadian	Québécois, Acadian, French	%
British	Scottish, English, Irish, Welsh, British	%
Scandinavian	Norwegian, Swedish, Finnish, Icelandic	%
Protestant Europe	German, Dutch, Danish	%
Catholic Europe	Italian, Portuguese, Spanish	%
Asian	Chinese, Filipino, Vietnamese, Korean, Japanese, South Asian	%
Black/African	Jamaican, African/black, Haitian, West Indian, Black, Guyanese, Trinidadian	%
Slavic	Ukrainian, Polish, Russian	%
Aboriginal origins	First Nations, Métis, Inuit	%
Jewish	Jewish	%
Language		%
English	English mother tongue	%
French	French mother tongue	%
Bilingual	Bilingual English + French	%
Native	Cree, Ojibway, Inuktitut, Montagnais, Micmac, Blackfoot, Dakota, South slave, Nishga'a, Chipewyan, Gwichin, Tlingit, Dogrib	%
Asian	Cantonese, Mandarin, Chinese, Tagalog, Vietnamese, Khmer, Malay, Thai, Malayalam	%
Scandinavian	Swedish, Norwegian, Icelandic, Finnish	%
Western European	Italian, German, Spanish, Portuguese, Dutch, Flemish	%
Slavic	Ukrainian, Polish, Russian	%
Sub-continent	Punjabi, Hindi, Gujarati, Urdu, Tamil, Bengali, Sinhalese	%
Gaelic	Gaelic languages	%
Immigration		%
Immigrants	Emigrated to Canada	%
Old immigrants	Arrived before 1961	%
New immigrants	Arrived in last 10 years	%
3rd generation	3rd generation Canadian	%

Continued

Continued

Variable	Explanation	Coded
Social structure		%
Over 65	Male and female population 65 years and older	%
Internal migrants	Intra-provincial and inter-provincial migrants in the last 5 years	%
Non-movers	Individuals residing in same census enumeration district	%
Common law	Individuals living in common-law relationship	%
University	Completed university degree	%
Women in labour force	Female participation in labour force	%
Manufacturing	Employed in manufacturing and construction sectors (1997 North American classification)	%
Natural resources	Employed in natural resources sector (1997 N Am classification)	%
Professional	Employed in professional job (1997 N Am classification)	%
Managerial	Employed in managerial job (1997 N Am classification)	%

Variable	Explanation	Coding
	CES	
Efficacy	Measured by an efficacy scale developed from factor analysis (Cronbach's Alpha .72). The scale is formed from the following seven questions: 1. Parties in Canada care what ordinary people think. 2. MPs soon lose touch with the people (changed direction). 3. Political parties do more to divide the country than to unite it (changed direction). 4. Elections are conducted fairly. 5. Satisfied with democracy. 6. System needs parties. 7. Political parties look after the best interests of everybody.	Continuous

Continued

Continued

Variable	Explanation	Coding
Voting	Measured by a voting scale developed from factor analysis (Cronbach's Alpha .62). The scale is formed from the following four questions: 1. It is important to vote. 2. It is the duty of every citizen to vote. 3. If I did not vote, I would feel guilty. 4. My vote hardly counts for anything (changed direction).	Continuous
Parties	Measured by a parties' scale developed from factor analysis (Cronbach's Alpha .72). The scale is formed from the following three questions: 1. Parties are good at finding solutions. 2. Parties present clear choices. 3. Parties express concerns of ordinary people.	Continuous
Confidence	Cumulative Index of 11 confidence items (Cronbach's Alpha .75).	Continuous, recoded 0–1
Political activity	Measured by an additive scale (Cronbach's Alpha .55) formed from the following five items (1 = have done): 1. Signing a petition 2. Joining in boycotts 3. Attending unlawful demonstrations 4. Joining unofficial strikes 5. Occupying buildings or factories	Continuous, recoded 0–1
Left	And finally, you personally. Would you say you are on the left, on the right, in the centre, or are you not sure? 1 = left, .5 = centre, 0 = right	
Post-materialism	Measured by the 3-point Inglehart scale (Inglehart 1990).	1 = post-materialist, .5 = mixed, 0 = materialist

Notes

1. See, for example, Trudeau, 1959; Macpherson, 1962.
2. Exceptions include Lipset, 1968.
3. A more explicit test of religion produced similar results. Income has not been included in large part because it does not provide an accurate measure of wealth or poverty. The variable cost of living in Canada could mean that someone earning $35,000 could have widely varying levels of relative wealth in, for example, Iqaluit, Toronto and Halifax.
4. The analysis was repeated by setting the number of clusters both higher and lower than nine. The nature of the analysis remained similar. When forced to select a smaller number of clusters, the urban, suburban and metropolitan clusters merged. When forced to select a smaller number of clusters, the far north cluster fractured to distinguish Nunavut from the rest of the territorial north.
5. A full list of the constituencies within each cluster may be obtained from the author.
6. A McFadden's R^2 below .2 would suggest that less than 20 percent of the variation of the dependent variable can be attributed to the variation in the independent variable.

References

Adams, M. 1998. *Sex in the Snow: Canadian Social Values at the End of the Millennium.* Toronto: Penguin.

Adams, M. 2003. *Fire and Ice: The United States, Canada and the Myth of Converging Values.* Toronto: Penguin.

Almond, G. and S. Verba. 1963. *The Civic Culture.* Princeton: Princeton University Press.

Beck, J.M. 1981. "An Atlantic Region Political Culture: A Chimera." In *Eastern and Western Perspectives,* eds. D.J. Bercusson and P.A. Buckner. Toronto: University of Toronto Press, pp. 147–168.

Blake, D. 1972. "The Measurement of Regionalism in Canadian Voting Patterns." *Canadian Journal of Political Science* 5(1): 55–81.

Brown, A. and J. Gray, eds. 1979. *Political Culture in Communist States.* 2nd ed. London: Macmillan.

Brown, A., D. McCrone and L. Paterson. 1998. *Politics and Society in Scotland.* 2nd ed. Basingstoke: Macmillan.

Burt, S. 1986. "Different Democracies? A Preliminary Examination of the Political Worlds of Canadian Men and Women." *Women & Politics* 6: 57–79.

Chilton, S. 1988. "Defining Political Culture." *Western Political Quarterly* 41(3): 419–445.

Clynch, E.J. 1972. "A Critique of Ira Sharkansky's 'The Utility of Elazar's Political Culture.'" *Polity* 5: 139–141.

Coates, K. and W. Morrison. 1992. *The Forgotten North.* Toronto: Lorimer.

Curtice, J. 1988. "One Nation?" In *British Social Attitudes: The Fifth Report,* eds. R. Jowell, S. Witherspoon and L. Brook. Aldershot: Gower.

Curtice, J. 1992. "The North–South Divide." In *British Social Attitudes Survey* the 9th report, eds. R. Jowell et al. Aldershot: Gower, pp. 71–99.

Curtice, J. 1996. "One Nation Again?" In *British Social Attitudes 13,* eds. R. Jowell et al. Aldershot: Dartmouth, pp. 1–18.

Dickson, M. 1996. "Scottish Political Culture: Is Scotland Different?" *Strathclyde Papers on Government and Politics,* no. 108.

Elazar, D. 1984. *American Federalism.* 3rd ed. New York: Harper & Row.

Elkins, D.J. and R.E.B. Simeon. 1979. "A Cause in Search of Its Effect, or What Does Political Culture Explain?" *Comparative Politics* 11: 127–145.

Elkins, D. and R. Simeon, eds. 1980. *Small Worlds: Provinces and Parties in Canadian Political Life.* Toronto: Methuen.

Everitt, J. 1998. "The Gender Gap in Canada: Now You See It, Now You Don't." *Canadian Review of Sociology and Anthropology* 35: 191–219.

Foster, C. 1982. "Political Culture and Regional Ethnic Minorities." *Journal of Politics* 44(2): 560–569.

Gidengil, E. 1989. "Class and Region in Canadian Voting: A Dependency Interpretation." *Canadian Journal of Political Science* 22: 563–587.

Gidengil, E. 1990. "Centres and Peripheries: The Political Culture of Dependency." *Canadian Review of Sociology and Anthropology* 27(1): 23–48.

Heath, A. and R. Topf. 1987. "Political Culture." In *British Social Attitudes: The 1987 Report,* eds. R. Jowell, S. Witherspoon and L. Brook. Aldershot: Gower, pp. 51–67.

Henderson, A. 2001. "Negotiated Identity, Contested Belonging and Political Inclusion: National Identity and Political Culture in Scotland and Quebec." Unpublished doctoral dissertation. University of Edinburgh, Edinburgh, Scotland.

Janda, K. and R. Gillies. 1983. "How Well Does 'Region' Explain Political Party Characteristics?" *Political Geography Quarterly* 2(3): 179–203.

Key, V.O., Jr. 1949. *Southern Politics in State and Nation.* New York: Knopf.

Lieske, J. 1993. "Regional Subcultures of the United States." *Journal of Politics* 55(4): 888–913.

Lipset, S.M. 1968. *Agrarian Socialism: the CCF in Saskatchewan.* Garden City: Doubleday Anchor.

Lipset, S.M. 1990. *Continental Divide: The Values and Institutions of the United States and Canada.* New York: Routledge.

MacDermid, R.H. 1990. "Regionalism in Ontario." In *Canadian Politics: An Introduction to the Discipline,* eds. Alain Gagnon and James Bickerton. Peterborough: Broadview, 360–390.

Macpherson, C.B. 1962. *Democracy in Alberta: Social Credit and the Party System.* Toronto: University of Toronto Press.

Mendelsohn, M. and R. Nadeau. 1997. "The Religious Cleavage and the Media in Canada." *Canadian Journal of Political Science* 30: 129–146.

Miller, W., A.M. Timpson and M. Lessnoff. 1996. *Political Culture in Contemporary Britain: People and Politicians, Principles and Practice.* Oxford: Clarendon.

Mitchell, J. 1996. *Strategies for Self-Government: The Campaigns for a Scottish Parliament.* Edinburgh: Polygon.

Nesbitt-Larking, P. 1998. "Canadian Political Culture: The Problem of Americanization." In *Crosscurrents,* eds. M. Charlton and P. Barker. Toronto: Nelson, pp. 21–38.

Nevitte, N. 1996. *The Decline of Deference.* Peterborough: Broadview Press.

Nevitte, N. 1995. "The Dynamics of Canadian Political Culture(s)." In *Introductory Readings in Canadian Government and Politics* 2nd ed., eds. Robert Krause and R.H. Wagenberg. Toronto: Copp Clark.

O'Neill, B. 2001. "A Simple Difference of Opinion? Religious Beliefs and Gender Gaps in Public Opinion in Canada." *Canadian Journal of Political Science* 34(2): 275–298.

Ornstein, M. 1986. "Regionalism and Canadian Political Ideology." In *Regionalism in Canada,* ed. Robert Brym. Richmond Hill: Irwin.

Peacock, M. 1998. "Socialism as Nationalism: Why the Alleged Americanization of Canadian Political Culture Is a Fraud" In *Crosscurrents,* eds. M. Charlton and P. Barker. Toronto: Nelson, pp. 39–54.

Putnam, R. 1993. *Making Democracy Work.* Princeton: Princeton University Press.

Pye, L.W. 1997. "The Elusive Concept of Culture and the Vivid Reality of Personality." *Political Psychology* 18(2): 241–254.

Reisinger, W.J. 1995. "The Renaissance of a Rubric: Political Culture as Concept and Theory." *International Journal of Public Opinion Research* 7(4): 328–352.

Savage, R.L. 1981. "Looking for Political Subcultures: A Critique of the Rummage-Sale Approach." *Western Political Quarterly* 34(2): 331–336.

Schlitz, T.D. and R.L. Rainey. 1978. "The Geographic Distribution of Elazar's Political Subcultures Among the Mass Population: A Research Note." *Western Political Quarterly* 31(3): 410–415.

Schudson, M. 1994. "Culture and the Integration of National Societies." *International Social Science Journal* 139: 63–83.

Sharkansky, I. 1969. "The Utility of Elazar's Political Culture: A Research Note." *Polity* 2: 66–83.

Simeon, R. and D. Elkins. 1974. "Regional Political Cultures in Canada." *Canadian Journal of Political Science* 7(3): 397–437.

Simeon, R. and D.J. Elkins. 1980. "Provincial Political Cultures in Canada." In *Small Worlds: Provinces and Parties in Canadian Political Life*, eds. D. Elkins and R. Simeon. Toronto: Methuen, pp. 31–76.

Simeon, R. and D. Blake. 1980. "Regional Preferences: Citizen's Views of Public Policy." In *Small Worlds: Provinces and Parties in Canadian Political Life*, eds. D. Elkins and R. Simeon. Toronto: Methuen, pp. 77–105.

Stewart, I. 1994. *Roasting Chestnuts: The Mythology of Maritime Political Culture*. Vancouver: UBC Press.

Street, J. 1994. "Review Article: Political Culture—from Civic Culture to Mass Culture." *British Journal of Political Science* 24: 95–114.

Weakliem, D.L. and R. Biggert. 1999. "Region and Political Opinion in the Contemporary United States." *Social Forces* 77(3): 863–886.

Wearing, P and J. Wearing. 1991. "Does Gender Make a Difference in Voting Behaviour?" In *The Ballot and Its Message: Voting in Canada*, ed. J. Wearing. Toronto: Copp Clark Pitman.

Welch, S. 1993. *The Concept of Political Culture*. New York: St. Martin's Press.

Weller, G.R. 1977. "Hinterland Politics: The Case of Northwestern Ontario." *Canadian Journal of Political Science* 10(4): 727–754.

Wilson, J. 1974. "The Canadian Political Cultures: Towards Redefinition of the Nature of the Canadian Political System." *Canadian Journal of Political Science* 7(3): 438–483.

Wilson, R. 1997. "American Political Culture in Comparative Perspective." *Political Psychology* 18(2): 483–502.

Wilson, R. 2000. "The Many Voices of Political Culture: Assessing Different Approaches." *World Politics* 52(2): 246–273.

Wiseman, N. 1996. "Provincial Political Cultures." In *Provinces*, ed. C. Dunn. Peterborough: Broadview.

Glossary

James Roy*

Apportionment

The process of distributing seats in Parliament between the various units of a federal state. In Canada, seats in the House of Commons are apportioned to the provinces and territories according to the fundamental principle of "representation by population." However, wide latitude has been given to regional representation in the apportionment formula, as seven provinces have more seats in the House of Commons than their populations warrant.

Ballot design

The structure of the ballot and the procedures governing how a voter completes a valid vote. Depending on the type of voting system, a ballot can be nominal, where the voter places an "X" next to his or her preferred candidate(s); or ordinal, where the voter ranks his or her preferred candidates in numerical order (first, second, third, and so on).

Brokerage party

A political party that accommodates or "brokers" many competing interests in order to present itself as a broadly inclusive "big tent" party. A brokerage party is therefore not oriented exclusively toward ideology, region, ethnicity, or other significant cleavages in the electorate. Canada has a long tradition (especially at the federal level) of brokerage parties being the major players on the political scene.

Candidate selection/nomination

The process by which a political party selects its candidate in an electoral district for election to the House of Commons or provincial legislature. Political parties have broad discretion in the methods they can use to nominate local candidates. To date, there has not been a concerted effort by any government to regulate the internal procedures of Canadian political parties—including nominating local candidates.

---

* Selected entries have been adapted from the glossary that appears in Dennis Pilon, *The Politics of Voting: Reforming Canada's Electoral System* (Toronto: Emond Montgomery, 2007).

Cleavage

A social issue or interest that may be mobilized into the political realm by actors in civil society, such as advocacy groups or political parties. Traditional cleavages that have been mobilized into Canadian politics include class, region, language, ethnic identity, and religion. Once mobilized, these new political cleavages may influence elections and political activity.

Coalition government

A Cabinet comprising members of two or more political parties. Coalition governments are usually formed when no single party holds a majority of seats in a Parliament or legislature. The parties in a coalition government often negotiate a formal agreement with respect to Cabinet positions and the broad legislative agenda of the coalition. Coalition governments have been very rare in Canada.

Competitive (or marginal) district

An electoral district that more than one political party has a reasonable chance of winning at any given election. In Canada, political party election campaigns are predominantly focused on competitive districts.

Constituency (*see* Riding/constituency/electoral district)

Constituency association

A constituency association, composed of the local members of a political party in each electoral district, is the basic functional unit of a party. The constituency association usually coordinates the local ground campaign during elections, and (subject to ratification by the party leader) nominates the party's candidate in the electoral district. Constituency associations once had a significant role in selecting the party leader, but as parties have moved toward a direct vote for all party members in leadership elections, their influence has diminished.

Contagion effect

The general idea that once one political party gains success by responding to an issue —say, bettering the legislative representation of women—other parties will be forced to respond or risk allowing the innovating party to be the only one to gain advantage. This effect is more dramatic in electoral systems where party competition is more open (for example, proportional ones).

Convention

In addition to being the name of the event at which party members typically elect a leader, "convention" also refers to an unwritten rule or tradition of the political system that, while not having the force of law, is followed by all the relevant political actors. For example, there is no law requiring a prime minister who has lost a confidence vote to resign or call an election. However, there is a well-recognized convention that a prime minister must take one of these courses of action should he or she lose a confidence vote.

Conversion (political)

A campaign strategy undertaken by a political party during election campaigns that focuses on convincing supporters of other political parties (usually *flexible partisans*) to "convert" and cast a ballot for their party instead. This strategy can be effective in convincing supporters of smaller parties to vote strategically for one major party in order to increase the possibility of defeating another major political party that they prefer even less. (*See also* Partisanship.)

Democratic deficit

A generic expression meant to draw attention to the substantive shortcomings of conventional Western democracies, particularly the lack of meaningful space for public participation in democratic decision making and the weak accountability between government and the governed. The term has become particularly popular for those addressing the declining levels of voter turnout.

Electoral boundary commission

An independent and impartial commission that proposes the names and boundaries of new electoral districts when the electoral map is redrawn. In Canada, the recommendations of electoral boundary commissions are usually adopted.

Electoral boundary readjustment

The process of redistributing electoral districts and readjusting their boundaries in order to conform to the principle of representation by population. In Canada, this process usually occurs every ten years, after the population is determined by a recent census.

Electoral district (*see* Riding/constituency/electoral district)

Electoral law

The field of law that regulates and administers the electoral process in Canada. It includes designing the electoral system, regulating financial donations to political parties, ballot design, and electoral boundary readjustment procedures.

Electoral system (*see* Voting system)

Equalization hypothesis

The theory that the Internet has placed minor and fringe political parties on an equal footing with the major parties because all parties have the same capacity to reach citizens online.

Framing

A tactic used by a political party (through its media strategy, advertising, policy proposals, speeches, et cetera) in order to narrow or "frame" a complex policy issue into a simple theme. Framing enables the party to contrast its position with that of other parties and attempt to increase its electoral success by garnering support from voters concerned about the issue. In journalistic terms, framing refers to the way in which media outlets choose to present their coverage of a news item. A frame is created by the context and information that readers or viewers are provided with, as the media attempt to make sense of events and present what are regarded as the most important issues. Media critics often focus on the framing of a story in an attempt to determine any sort of political or other bias in media coverage.

Franchise

Also known as *suffrage*, the franchise refers to those people (defined as "electors") with the right to vote in elections. While the franchise was at one time restricted to male landowners, for the past 40 years Canada has had universal adult franchise— every Canadian citizen over the age of 18 has the right to vote in an election.

Gerrymandering

Drawing the boundaries of electoral districts (often resulting in odd-shaped districts) in order to ensure victory for one political party over another. Because electoral boundary commissions are now responsible for drawing the electoral map, gerrymandering has become very rare in Canada.

Grandfather clause

In terms of political representation, the grandfather clause refers to an amendment to the Constitution of Canada that guarantees each province—regardless of its population—at least as many seats in the House of Commons as it had in 1985. This clause currently ensures that all provinces except Alberta, British Columbia, and Ontario have more seats in the House of Commons than their populations warrant.

Ground campaign

The local campaign in each electoral district during an election campaign. Being dependent almost exclusively on volunteers, the ground campaign predominantly consists of pamphleteering and canvassing door-to-door, while leaving television and other media strategies to the national party campaign office.

Intra-party coalition

An intra-party coalition occurs when the various wings of the party (each often reflecting a cleavage in the electorate as a whole) negotiate (almost always out of public view) the party's election platform and policies in order to "broker" the competing interests and views *within* the party. Intra-party coalitions are more common within brokerage parties and under plurality voting systems, whereas in proportional representation systems, coalitions often take place *between* parties.

Issue salience

The perceived importance of a particular issue (for example, health care) to the public. Election campaigns are often fought over salient issues. Political parties highlight as being salient those issues they believe will win them votes. Conversely, they downplay as unimportant those issues that may cost the party votes.

Majoritarian

Sometimes plurality and majority voting systems are referred to collectively as *majoritarian voting systems* because, it is believed, both tend to exaggerate the legislative support of the most popular parties, contributing to single-party majority governments.

Majority

Colloquially understood as "50% plus one." Majority also refers to majority voting systems, which include the alternative vote and the double ballot.

Majority government

In parliamentary systems, a majority government is one that commands a majority of seats in the lower house, and thus can be assured of passing its legislation. In majoritarian systems, such legislative majorities are typically held by a single party and are often premised on a minority of the popular vote. In proportional systems, by contrast, majority governments are typically composed of a coalition of different parties that also represent a majority of the popular vote.

Mandate

The view that a party that gains a legislative majority through an election has been authorized by voters to introduce the policies that it promoted during the election. This idea is controversial in any setting but comes under particular criticism in majoritarian systems because the party that wins a legislative majority typically represents just a minority of the voters. By contrast, there are cases in proportional systems where a coalition of parties makes a pre-election pact to govern together if elected and subsequently gains a majority of the votes between them.

Median voter

The voter who is located in the centre of the political spectrum and thus more likely to switch his or her support at election time between right and left. Voters who are solidly right or left are essentially "captive" to their respective political parties, who can only gain further advantage by expanding their appeal to the "median voter." This competitive bid to gain the allegiance of the uncommitted median voter ironically leads to less choice as both left and right parties converge on the centre of the political spectrum.

Microtargeting

Framing an issue and tailoring a campaign strategy by a political party to target a relatively small but important group of potential voters over the Internet, often through social networking sites. (*See also* Framing.)

Minority government

In parliamentary systems, a minority government is one that does not command a majority of votes in the legislature, and thus cannot be assured of passing its legislation. In majoritarian systems, minority governments tend to be unstable and short-lived as governing parties and/or opposition parties may precipitate an election when they perceive that a slight shift in popular support may allow them to secure a legislative majority government (though one still typically based on a minority of votes). In proportional representation systems, by contrast, minority governments tend to be much more stable and last for longer periods of time because it is much less likely that an election will produce an inflated result for the leading vote getter or turn minority popular support for one party into a legislative majority for that party.

Mixed-member proportional (MMP)

A hybrid form of proportional representation that combines single-member districts elected by plurality with a compensatory party list that is used to ensure that the overall election results are proportional for the parties. Voters have two votes, one for the local plurality contest and another for their party choice, with the latter totals forming the basis of the parties' claims for their proportional share of the total seats.

Mobilization hypothesis

The theory that the informational and interactive capabilities of the Internet have the potential to mobilize politically disengaged elements of society, especially youth.

Multi-member riding

An electoral district where more than one member will be elected to represent the area.

Partisanship

The degree of identification a person has with a particular political party. There are two broad categories of partisanship: durable and flexible partisans. *Durable partisans* usually identify with the same party on a long-term basis. *Flexible partisans* often shift their support based on an assessment of a party's past performance, evaluation of the party leader, and/or an evaluation of the party's policy proposals. Over the past three decades, a majority of Canadians have shifted from being durable to flexible partisans.

Party discipline

This tradition in parliamentary forms of government operates where the legislative members of a political party agree, or are required by their leaders, to vote together on issues to maximize their influence. Critics hold that party discipline is a negative feature of the political system because, they claim, it forces individual representatives to vote in certain ways, sometimes against the wishes of the voters in the locality they represent. But this claim ignores that nearly all successful political candidates agree to run for office as the representatives of a party, and as voters make their voting decision primarily on the basis of party label, their election is due more to party factors (like the party's policies on issues) than any local consensus on issues.

Party platform

The comprehensive policy proposals of a political party detailing (with varying degrees of specificity) its promises as to what actions it will take should the party be elected to form the next government.

Plurality

The voting formula where the candidate with the most votes in a pool of candidates is declared the winner, regardless of whether this represents a majority of all votes cast for all candidates.

Political culture

A comprehensive product of many factors, including the public's beliefs about politics and political institutions, shared perceptions of the legitimacy of the political system, the predominant political values of the society, inherited civic traditions, and well-recognized principles as to how society should be governed.

Political mobilization

A campaign strategy undertaken by political parties during election campaigns that focuses on mobilizing their own supporters (durable partisans) to vote.

Populist/populism

A popular description of anti-politician and anti-party sentiment as it translates into political activity.

Proportional representation (PR)

A generic term for any voting system that roughly matches the proportion of legislative representation achieved by different political parties with their proportion of the popular vote. Examples include party list-PR, mixed-member proportional (MMP), and single transferable vote (STV).

Public subsidies
Providing public funds to political parties and candidates in order to defray election expenses. In Canada, this includes providing tax exemptions for donations to political parties and candidates, reimbursing a portion of candidates' election expenses, and providing an annual subsidy to political parties based on the number of votes received in the most recent general election.

Regional party
A political party that has a legitimate chance of winning seats in only a specific region of the country. There are two types: an *exclusive regional party* (for example, the Bloc Québécois), which only runs candidates in one region; and *effectively regional parties* (for example, the Reform Party), which may run candidates on a national basis but only elects representatives from a single region.

Regional representation
The practice of maintaining a stable degree of representation in Parliament or a legislature for specific regions, regardless of population. Canada has historically gone to great lengths to modify the principle of representation by population in order to provide for stable regional representation, especially at the federal level.

Responsible government
In parliamentary forms of government, particularly those with British roots, the notion of responsible government refers to the necessity of a government to be sustained in the legislatures on votes of confidence. If a government loses such a vote, they must resign and be replaced or call an election.

Riding/constituency/electoral district
These terms are interchangeable and refer to the geographic space within which a member or a number of members will be elected to represent the voters in that area.

Safe seat/safe electoral district
An electoral district where only one political party has a reasonable chance of electing its candidate in any given election. Only in rare elections will a safe district elect an MP from a different political party. In Canada, political parties often ignore safe seats (held both by themselves and other parties) during election campaigns.

Single transferable vote (STV)
A form of proportional representation where voters mark their preferences (first, second, third, and so on) from among the range of candidates in a multi-member riding. Candidates who obtain the quota are declared elected. The ballot counting proceeds by stages, beginning with an initial count of the first choices marked on all the ballots. If in this first stage a candidate exceeds the quota, he or she is declared

elected and any surplus above the quota is distributed to other candidates on the basis of the second preferences marked. This process continues until no more candidates meet the quota. Then the candidate with the fewest first choices is eliminated and his or her ballots are redistributed on the basis of the second choices marked. This process continues until someone obtains the quota. These two aspects of the vote-counting process, distributing surpluses or eliminating low vote-getters, continues until all the available positions are filled.

Single-member district
A district that elects only one member to represent it in Parliament or a legislature.

Strategic voting
The practice of voting for the candidate considered the most likely to win (or the candidate more likely to defeat a candidate the voter least wants to win) rather than voting for the candidate that the voter most prefers. Critics feel that strategic voting incentives are particularly strong in plurality and majoritarian voting systems.

Suffrage (*see* Franchise)

Third party
Small parties that may receive a significant share of the popular vote and may be represented in Parliament or a legislative assembly but have little chance of forming a government. Plurality electoral systems often (but not always) generate a political system dominated by two major parties. Thus, there is usually insufficient public support to enable a third party to elect a substantial number of representatives. Canada is an exception (especially at the federal level) as it has third parties in almost all jurisdictions that are much stronger than traditional third parties in plurality electoral systems.

Third-party election spending
Spending undertaken during an election campaign by a person or organization that is not acting on behalf of a candidate or political party seeking election (for example, environmental, labour, or taxpayers' groups). In Canada, third-party election spending is by law restricted to a much lower amount than that permitted by political parties and candidates.

Threshold
The threshold of election refers to the minimum amount of support that a political party must gain to get their first seat. In purely proportional system with 100 seats, the threshold would be 1 percent of the votes cast. In some cases, explicit thresholds of exclusion exist to limit the election of political parties with low levels of support. In most proportional representation (PR) systems, the threshold is fixed (for example, in Germany, at 5 percent) but in majoritarian systems, the threshold shifts depending

on the number of competitive parties in a district. Majoritarian thresholds are generally much higher than those in PR systems.

Two-party system

A political system where two political parties dominate. The overwhelming majority of votes are cast for the two major parties and members of these two parties hold virtually all of the seats in Parliament or a legislature. Plurality electoral systems are likely to produce a two-party system, though there are exceptions (such as Canada). Conversely, most proportional representation electoral systems usually generate multiparty systems.

Voter parity

Drawing an electoral map in order to ensure that each electoral district has the same number of voters (voter parity) or the same population (population parity).

Voting formula

The rule that sets out how votes should be added up to determine the winner or winners in an election. The basic formulas include plurality, majority, and proportional.

Voting system/electoral system

These terms gain their meaning largely by conventional usage and are often used interchangeably to refer to many aspects of elections and electoral process. In this volume, *voting system* has generally been used to designate the rules that determine how votes are translated into representation in an election. By contrast, *electoral system* has been used to refer to the broader set of election rules, including such things as campaign finance, voter registration methods, et cetera, of which the voting system is only one part. See Chapter 3 for a full description.

Wasted vote

A colloquial term used to designate a validly cast ballot that nonetheless does not end up contributing to the election of a representative. The term is applied to majoritarian voting systems whose "all or nothing" decision rule for winning a seat typically means that a majority or a considerable minority of the votes are not cast for the winner. This is contrasted with proportional voting systems where only a marginal percentage of votes do not contribute to the election of a representative.

Index